Film Form and *The Film Sense*

film + Poetry
—p. 115, B-58

film + the other arts— p. 181, 193

John Allen

Film Form

ESSAYS IN FILM THEORY

AND

The Film Sense

BY SERGEI EISENSTEIN

edited and translated by Jay Leyda

Meridian Books

THE WORLD PUBLISHING COMPANY

CLEVELAND AND NEW YORK

Sergei Eisenstein

Sergei Eisenstein, born in Riga in 1898, was educated in the fields of engineering and architecture. Introduced to the visual arts while serving in the Red Army, he rapidly gained foremost renown in the Russian motion picture industry. Some of his early films which brought him world wide fame are *The Strike, Potemkin, Ten Days That Shook The World,* and *Old And New.* Installed as a faculty member of the State Cinema Technicum in 1928, he progressed to a professorship of Cinema Research at The All-Union State Cinema Institute, and in 1947 became Head of The Cinema Research Center under The Academy of Arts and Sciences of the U.S.S.R. Among his most important sound films are *Ivan The Terrible,* and *Alexander Nevsky,* for which he was awarded the Order of Lenin. Later, he was to receive the title of Doctor of Art and The Stalin Prize. He died in 1948.

A MERIDIAN BOOK
Published by The World Publishing Company
2231 West 110th Street, Cleveland, Ohio 44102
First Meridian printing August 1957
Seventh Printing May, 1967
FILM FORM copyright 1949 by Harcourt, Brace & Company; THE FILM SENSE copyright 1942 by Harcourt, Brace & Company.
Reprinted by arrangement with Harcourt, Brace & Company from two different volumes, FILM FORM, 1949, and the new revised edition, 1947, of THE FILM SENSE
Library of Congress Catalog Card Number: 57-10839
Printed in the United States of America.   7 BP567

EDITOR'S NOTE

FOR Eisenstein, teaching was as vital a function as creation. Film teaching and film making must have seemed to him parts of the same job, equally proper to his particular genius, so inseparable were their hopes: the most effective film would stimulate the most thought in its audience; the most effective teaching by one generation would stimulate the best creative work in the next generation's films.

The great amount of writing accomplished by Eisenstein during his short life bound together these two threads of his work. The film-teacher examined, analyzed and defended the film-maker's work; the film-teacher often exercised his theories in print before subjecting them to more strenuous trials. Before his death in 1948 Eisenstein planned a Russian edition of all his best theoretical writing, and drafted an introduction for it. Most of those principal essays are included in this American reprint of his *FILM FORM* and *THE FILM SENSE*, and it seems fitting for Eisenstein himself to introduce an essay collection that can be of such service to film students. The following passages are translated from his draft introduction (dated at Moscow-Kratovo, August 1946), first published in a 1956 Russian edition of his essays.

If there is any hint of his serious illness, or of his awareness that he might not be able to make another film, it is well concealed here. The dominant note is a hopeful one. In speaking of television and all technological change in film production, he says to film makers and film students, "We need fear nothing from their advance"—so long as we learn all that the past and present offer to the future.

J. L.

April, 1957

FILM FORM

Illustrations follow page 52

THE FILM SENSE

FOREWORD

FOREWORD

FILM, naturally, is the most international of arts.

Not only because the audiences of the world see films produced by all countries and points of view—

But because it is particularly the film medium, with its rich technical potentialities and its abundant creative invention, that provides an international meeting place for living ideas.

Yet the first half century of cinema history has witnessed remarkably little exploration of its infinite possibilities.

Please don't misunderstand me.

This is not merely a question of what has been done—what splendid achievements there have been! In content alone there has been a flood of new ideas and new ideals.

The question is—what *can* be done—within *this* medium. What can be created only with *film* means.

The problem of synthesizing the arts, organically fusing them in the film medium, awaits resolution.

Meanwhile fresh problems crowd upon us. No sooner have we mastered the element of color than new problems of volume and space stand before us, summoned by the stereoscopic film. And then, suddenly, the immediacy of television seems to threaten all that was on the verge of mastery, so carefully accumulated in our experience of silent and sound films.

Montage, for example, was no more (and no less) than a fixing of an artist's perception of events around him. Suddenly television pulls this whole process forward to the moment of perception—resulting in an exciting junction of two extremes.

The first link in a chain of evolving forms of performance is the human actor-performer, who transmits to the spectator a re-creation of his ideas and feelings. He can now reach out towards a higher form of theater future, for in television's future a director-magician will be ready, swift as a glance or a thought, to juggle numbers of lenses and camera positions in order to provide the actor with a never-to-be-repeated moment, to send his most perfected interpretation of an event to millions of looking and listening witnesses, in a flow of acting moments that are always both first *and* final.

If this sounds unlikely, why should it, in an age where radar has already heard the echoes of signals sent to the moon and beyond, where aircraft can be sent through the sound barrier to the blue dome's edge of atmosphere? . . .

The film has passed its fiftieth anniversary. Its huge and intricate possibilities are ready for the mastery by mankind, just as mankind as a whole must now master the beneficent aspects of a new atomic era of physics opened to it.

How little has been applied of the centuries' esthetic researches to master the means and potentialities of cinema! Yet we lack neither the capacity nor the impulse.

No—we are held back only by conservatism, inertia, and esthetic "escapes" away from these unprecedented problems that overtake each other as the technical development of cinema races ahead.

We need fear nothing from their advance.

Our task is to gather and sum up all the experiences of the past and the present, arming ourselves with this experience to meet new problems and to conquer them enthusiastically, remaining aware in so doing that *the genuine basis of esthetics and the most valuable material of a new technique is and will always be profound truth in theme and content* . . .

As Soviet film craftsmen we felt obliged, from the first days of our new enterprise, to conserve every smallest grain of our collective experience, so that each glimmer of thoughtful film creativity would be made the property of all film workers. We did this not only in films, but in essays and research, in general and in detail, to illuminate what we sought, what we found, and to what we aspired.

That is how my essays came into being. Seeing the pieces in this collection, written at various times, for various reasons, in various years, I am moved again by those same feelings: to contribute to the store of all film-makers in their mastery of the broad potentialities of the film. To these feelings I must add the joy of having worked in this wonderfully beautiful and infinitely absorbing medium.

Sergei Eisenstein

Film Form

INTRODUCTION

THE COMPILATION of this book of essays was one of its author's last tasks. Though too weak in his last two years of life to resume film work, Eisenstein was too strong to relax his theoretical activity. His fatal attack, on the night of February 10, 1948, interrupted him at work; when he was found the next morning, before him were his last words—an unfinished essay on color, its use in the unfinished *Ivan the Terrible*. It is precisely because he was so far from being finished, as film-maker or theoretician, that we feel his loss so deeply.

A great artist leaves his work behind him, but a contemplation of Eisenstein's completed work does little to ease the shock of his death, for all these films pointed to further work in which his heroic and tireless expansion of the film medium would push beyond all the limits that lesser artists have set around it. Each step forward by Eisenstein promised a hundred following unexpected steps, and death at the age of forty-nine leaves many steps untaken.

As a great teacher he left an even richer heritage: from his students and the large body of his theory we can expect further fruit, even beyond our generation. It was said of Bach, "Only he who knows much can teach much," and we can be eternally grateful that Eisenstein's immense knowledge was poured not only into six finished films but also, directly and indirectly, into an incalculable number of pupils.

A steady source for his imagination, as artist and as teacher, lay in his consciousness of the artist's real influence in society, an influence to be fully realized only within an equally powerful sense of responsibility to society. This dual pull determined his every decision: in esthetics, for example, it made

xvii

him impatient with every lean towards surface naturalism—
for he could see the unwillingness, the laziness, ignorance and
often opportunism behind such an evasion of the difficult but
central problem. The film artist's job was to learn his principles from a profound investigation of all arts and all levels
of life, to measure these principles against an unfaltering understanding of himself, and if he then did anything less than
create—with bold, living works that moved their audiences to
excitement and understanding—he was neither good artist nor
positive member of society. In film, with all its easy satis-
factions, there was more temptation to skirt this primary issue
than in any other art, but once Eisenstein chose cinema as
the supremely expressive medium, he undertook to wage upon
it, as upon a battlefield, a perpetual war against the evils of
dishonesty, satisfaction, superficiality. He fought with the
arrogance of an assured artist—he knew how much we all
needed him, whether we admitted it or not. His aim was a
poetry possible only to films, a realism heightened by *all* the
means in the film-artist's power. Though both he and the
surrealists would have denied his relation to the term, this
was sur-realism—but the dynamic aim and accomplishment of
Sergei Eisenstein need no category or label.

To challenge laziness and naturalism puts the challenger at
a disadvantage: it attaches "anti-natural" labels to the challenger's principles and practice, and forces him to prove, in
works, that they can be affective beyond those works whose
"simplicity" is essentially negative. The affective test was
passed by each of Eisenstein's films; the principles were stub-
bornly enunciated in writing that in sheer quantity outdoes
the public thinking of any film-maker. He admitted to being
neither a smooth nor a talented writer, and was dependent on
the energy of his ideas and the clarity of their expression; he
employed circumstantial as well as poetic proof—and he drew
on the world for his illustrations. His "right way," swerving
sharply from standard thinking, or rather, standard non-think-
ing about films, forced his theoretical writing to combine
polemic, rhetoric, self-defense, essay, gallery tour, analysis,

lecture, sermon, criminal investigation, chalk-talk—and to be as valid for the local, immediate problem, as for the general, lasting issue. A many-sided, never-ending education stocked his armory of illustration: criticized for distortion, he would point to the "purposeful distortion" employed by a Sharaku or a Flaubert; accused of "unlifelike theories" he would hold up precedents from the fields of philology and psychology; accusations of "leftism" and "modernism" brought out defenses by Milton, Pushkin, El Greco that not only solidified his argument, but gave it a fresh dimension, and stimulated the reader to investigate these neglected riches.

His first readers were always, as were his first audiences, his fellow film-makers and his students, furnishing, even in their maintenance of opposite views, a body of encouragement and stimulation that would be hard to equal outside that electric Moscow-Leningrad-Kiev circuit of film-enthusiasts. His foreign readers have been variously handicapped, by an unavoidable remoteness from this stimulating atmosphere and by a remoteness from the issues under discussion there, that motivated a great deal of Eisenstein's combative writing; but the greatest handicap for his readers (and professionally interested spectators) abroad was the distortion, by misuse, imitation, and misinterpretation, of his basic terms and concepts. To read, for example, about "montage" through the distorting haze of superficiality with which this term has been brought into our studios, has not aided an understanding of Eisenstein's theoretical writing. In recent years, however, general information on Eisenstein's theories has tended to escape these earlier prejudices and apings, and it seems that his films and writings alike will be now examined with more profit in this country than during his lifetime. It is hoped that this second volume of his writing to appear in English * will contribute to this profit and comprehension.

Of his hundreds of essays, this group was selected to show certain key-points in the development of his film theory and,

* *The Film Sense*, his first book, originally appeared in 1942; the revised edition in 1947.

in particular, of his analysis of the sound-film medium. Despite the existence of *Alexander Nevsky* and *Ivan the Terrible*, the study of Eisenstein's theories usually finds its illustrations in his "silent" films. This almost makes more poignant the revelation in these essays of his long planning and contemplation of sound as an *essential* element in his vision of the total film, and he was fully aware of the apparent strangeness that he "should resemble the last to arrive at the wedding." Yet the still restless couple—sight and sound—has lost its most hopeful conciliator and advisor in Eisenstein's death, for no sound-film program has achieved either the solidity of his "Statement" of 1928 and his "Achievement" of 1939 or the adventure of his plans for *An American Tragedy* (discussed in "A Course in Treatment"). The sure simplicity of audio-visual experiment in *Nevsky* and the grand experiment in heroic style of *Ivan the Terrible, Part I* have not yet been properly gauged for their instructional virtues, and the rich fund of discussion of the sound-film in these essays must be added to the sum of his completed films to gain a rounded view on his intellectually mature grasp of the film medium.

Some of these essays have been previously available, sometimes in inadequate English renderings; the relation of the present texts to these earlier translations is indicated at the end of the volume.

Generous assistance on all levels has been given this book by Esther and Harold Leonard, by Jane and Gordon Williams, by Sergei Bertensson, Richard Collins, Robert Payne, and other friends. John Winge made the new translation from Eisenstein's German manuscript (lent by the Museum of Modern Art Film Library) of "A Dialectic Approach to Film Form," and the frames chosen by Eisenstein for its illustration were prepared for reproduction here by Irving Lerner. I am particularly grateful to the Hon. Ivor Montagu whose long association with the personality and ideas of the author produced translations so conscientious and scrupulous that a minimum of adjustment has been necessary in adding them to this collection. The library staffs that contributed their talents so patiently were those of the University of California at Los Angeles, the Los Angeles Public Library, the Beverly Hills Public Library, Columbia University, the Museum of Modern Art, and the American-Russian Institute.

JAY LEYDA

FILM FORM

THROUGH THEATER TO CINEMA

IT IS interesting to retrace the different paths of today's cinema workers to their creative beginnings, which together compose the multi-colored background of the Soviet cinema. In the early 1920s we all came to the Soviet cinema as something not yet existent. We came upon no ready-built city; there were no squares, no streets laid out; not even little crooked lanes and blind alleys, such as we may find in the cinemetropolis of our day. We came like bedouins or gold-seekers to a place with unimaginably great possibilities, only a small section of which has even now been developed.

We pitched our tents and dragged into camp our experiences in varied fields. Private activities, accidental past professions, unguessed crafts, unsuspected eruditions—all were pooled and went into the building of something that had, as yet, no written traditions, no exact stylistic requirements, nor even formulated demands.

Without going too far into the theoretical debris of the specifics of cinema, I want here to discuss two of its features. These are features of other arts as well, but the film is particularly accountable to them. *Primo:* photo-fragments of nature are recorded; *secundo:* these fragments are combined in various ways. Thus, the shot (or frame), and thus, montage.

Photography is a system of reproduction to fix real events and elements of actuality. These reproductions, or photo-reflections, may be combined in various ways. Both as reflections and in the manner of their combination, they permit any degree of distortion—either technically unavoidable or deliberately calculated. The results fluctuate from exact naturalistic

3

combinations of visual, interrelated experiences to complete alterations, arrangements unforeseen by nature, and even to abstract formalism, with remnants of reality.

The apparent arbitrariness of matter, in its relation to the *status quo* of nature, is much less arbitrary than it seems. The final order is inevitably determined, consciously or unconsciously, by the social premises of the maker of the film-composition. His class-determined tendency is the basis of what seems to be an arbitrary cinematographic relation to the object placed, or found, before the camera.

We should like to find in this two-fold process (the fragment and its relationships) a hint as to the specifics of cinema, but we cannot deny that this process is to be found in other art mediums, whether close to cinema or not (and which art is not close to cinema?). Nevertheless, it is possible to insist that these features are specific to the film, because film-specifics lie not in the process itself but in the degree to which these features are intensified.

The musician uses a scale of sounds; the painter, a scale of tones; the writer, a row of sounds and words—and these are all taken to an equal degree from nature. But the immutable fragment of actual reality in these cases is narrower and more neutral in meaning, and therefore more flexible in combination, so that when they are put together they lose all visible signs of being combined, appearing as one organic unit. A chord, or even three successive notes, seems to be an organic unit. Why should the combination of three pieces of film in montage be considered as a three-fold collision, as impulses of three successive images?

A blue tone is mixed with a red tone, and the result is thought of as violet, and not as a "double exposure" of red and blue. The same unity of word fragments makes all sorts of expressive variations possible. How easily three shades of meaning can be distinguished in language—for example: "a window without light," "a dark window," and "an unlit window."

Now try to express these various nuances in the composition of the frame. Is it at all possible?

If it is, then what complicated context will be needed in order to string the film-pieces onto the film-thread so that the black shape on the wall will begin to show either as a "dark" or as an "unlit" window? How much wit and ingenuity will be expended in order to reach an effect that words achieve so simply?

The frame is much less independently workable than the word or the sound. Therefore the mutual work of frame and montage is really an enlargement in scale of a process microscopically inherent in all arts. However, in the film this process is raised to such a degree that it seems to acquire a new quality.

The shot, considered as material for the purpose of composition, is more resistant than granite. This resistance is specific to it. The shot's tendency toward complete factual immutability is rooted in its nature. This resistance has largely determined the richness and variety of montage forms and styles—for montage becomes the mightiest means for a really important creative remolding of nature.

Thus the cinema is able, more than any other art, to disclose the process that goes on microscopically in all other arts.

The minimum "distortable" fragment of nature is the shot; ingenuity in its combinations is montage.

Analysis of this problem received the closest attention during the second half-decade of Soviet cinema (1925-1930), an attention often carried to excess. Any infinitesimal alteration of a fact or event before the camera grew, beyond all lawful limit, into whole theories of documentalism. The lawful necessity of combining these fragments of reality grew into montage conceptions which presumed to supplant all other elements of film-expression.

Within normal limits these features enter, as elements, into any style of cinematography. But they are not opposed to nor can they replace other problems—for instance, the problem of *story*.

To return to the double process indicated at the beginning of these notes: if this process is characteristic of cinema, finding its fullest expression during the second stage of Soviet cinema, it will be rewarding to investigate the creative biographies of film-workers of that period, seeing how these features emerged, how they developed in pre-cinema work. All the roads of that period led towards one Rome. I shall try to describe the path that carried me to cinema principles.

Usually my film career is said to have begun with my production of Ostrovsky's play, *Enough Simplicity in Every Sage*, at the Proletcult Theatre (Moscow, March 1923). This is both true and untrue. It is not true if it is based solely on the fact that this production contained a short comic film made especially for it (not separate, but included in the montage plan of the spectacle). It is more nearly true if it is based on the character of the production, for even then the elements of the specifics mentioned above could be detected.

We have agreed that the first sign of a cinema tendency is one showing events with the least distortion, aiming at the factual reality of the fragments.

A search in this direction shows my film tendencies beginning three years earlier, in the production of *The Mexican* (from Jack London's story). Here, my participation brought into the theater "events" themselves—a purely cinematographic element, as distinguished from "reactions to events"—which is a purely theatrical element.

This is the plot: A Mexican revolutionary group needs money for its activities. A boy, a Mexican, offers to find the money. He trains for boxing, and contracts to let the champion beat him for a fraction of the prize. Instead he beats up the champion, winning the entire prize. Now that I am better acquainted with the specifics of the Mexican revolutionary struggle, not to mention the technique of boxing, I would not think of interpreting this material as we did in 1920, let alone using so unconvincing a plot.

The play's climax is the prize-fight. In accordance with the most hallowed Art Theatre traditions, this was to take place backstage (like the bull-fight in *Carmen*), while the actors on stage were to show excitement in the fight only they can see, as well as to portray the various emotions of the persons concerned in the outcome.

My first move (trespassing upon the director's job, since I was there in the official capacity of designer only) was to propose that the fight be brought into view. Moreover I suggested that the scene be staged in the center of the auditorium to re-create the same circumstances under which a real boxing match takes place. Thus we dared the concreteness of factual events. The fight was to be carefully planned in advance but was to be utterly realistic.

The playing of our young worker-actors in the fight scene differed radically from their acting elsewhere in the production. In every other scene, one emotion gave rise to a further emotion (they were working in the Stanislavsky system), which in turn was used as a means to affect the audience; but in the fight scene the audience was excited directly.

While the other scenes influenced the audience through intonation, gestures, and mimicry, our scene employed realistic, even textural means—real fighting, bodies crashing to the ring floor, panting, the shine of sweat on torsos, and finally, the unforgettable smacking of gloves against taut skin and strained muscles. Illusionary scenery gave way to a realistic ring (though not in the center of the hall, thanks to that plague of every theatrical enterprise, the fireman) and extras closed the circle around the ring.

Thus my realization that I had struck new ore, an actual-materialistic element in theater. In *The Sage*, this element appeared on a new and clearer level. The eccentricity of the production exposed this same line, through fantastic contrasts. The tendency developed not only from illusionary acting movement, but from the physical fact of acrobatics. A gesture expands into gymnastics, rage is expressed through a somersault, exaltation through a *salto-mortale*, lyricism on "the mast of death." The grotesque of this style permitted leaps from one type of expression to another, as well as unexpected inter-twinings of the two expressions. In a later production, *Listen, Moscow* (summer 1923), these two separate lines of "real doing" and "pictorial imagination" went through a synthesis expressed in a specific technique of acting.

These two principles appeared again in Tretiakov's *Gas Masks* (1923-24), with still sharper irreconcilability, broken so noticeably that had this been a film it would have remained, as we say, "on the shelf."

What was the matter? The conflict between material-practical and fictitious-descriptive principles was somehow patched up in the melodrama, but here they broke up and we failed completely. The cart dropped to pieces, and its driver dropped into the cinema.

This all happened because one day the director had the marvelous idea of producing this play about a gas factory—in a real gas factory.

As we realized later, the real interiors of the factory had nothing to do with our theatrical fiction. At the same time the plastic charm of reality in the factory became so strong that the element of acuality rose with fresh strength—took things into its own hands—and finally had to leave an art where it could not command.

Thereby bringing us to the brink of cinema.

But this is not the end of our adventures with theater work. Having come to the screen, this other tendency flourished, and became known as "typage." This "typage" is just as typical a feature of this cinema period as "montage." And be it known that I do not want to limit the concept of "typage" or "montage" to my own works.

I want to point out that "typage" must be understood as broader than merely a face without make-up, or a substitution of "naturally expressive" types for actors. In my opinion, "typage" included a specific approach to the events embraced by the content of the film. Here again was the method of least interference with the natural course and combinations of events. In concept, from beginning to end, *October* is pure "typage."

A typage tendency may be rooted in theater; growing out of the theater into film, it presents possibilities for excellent stylistic growth, in a broad sense—as an indicator of definite affinities to real life through the camera.*

And now let us examine the second feature of film-specifics, the principles of montage. How was this expressed and shaped in my work before joining the cinema?

In the midst of the flood of eccentricity in *The Sage*, including a short film comedy, we can find the first hints of a sharply expressed montage.

The action moves through an elaborate tissue of intrigue. Mamayev sends his nephew, Glumov, to his wife as guardian. Glumov takes liberties beyond his uncle's instructions and his aunt takes the courtship seriously. At the same time Glumov begins to negotiate for a marriage with Mamayev's niece, Turussina, but conceals these intentions from the aunt, Mamayeva. Courting the aunt, Glumov deceives the uncle; flattering the uncle, Glumov arranges with him the deception of the aunt.

Glumov, on a comic plane, echoes the situations, the overwhelming passions, the thunder of finance, that his French prototype, Balzac's Rastignac, experiences. Rastignac's type in Russia was still in the cradle. Money-making was still a sort of child's game between uncles and nephews, aunts and their gallants. It remains in the family, and remains trivial. Hence, the comedy. But the intrigue and entanglements are already present, playing on two fronts at the same time—with

---

* Eisenstein has said that one might define typage as a modern development of the *Commedia dell'arte*—with its seven stock figures multiplied into infinity. The relationship lies not in numbers, but in audience conditioning. Upon entrance of Pantalone or the Captain, his mask tells the audience immediately what to expect of this figure. Modern film typage is based on the need for presenting each new figure in our first glimpse of him so sharply and completely that further use of this figure may be as a known element. Thus new, immediate conventions are created. An amplification of this approach is given in the author's comments on Lavater, on page 127.—EDITOR.

both hands—with dual characters . . . and we showed all this
with an intertwined montage of two different scenes (of
Mamayev giving his instructions, and of Glumov putting them
into execution). The surprising intersections of the two dialogues sharpen the characters and the play, quicken the tempo,
and multiply the comic possibilities.

For the production of *The Sage* the stage was shaped like
a circus arena, edged with a red barrier, and three-quarters surrounded by the audience. The other quarter was hung with
a striped curtain, in front of which stood a small raised platform, several steps high. The scene with Mamayev (Shtraukh)
took place downstage while the Mamayeva (Yanukova) fragments occurred on the platform. Instead of changing scenes,
Glumov (Yezikanov) ran from one scene to the other and
back—taking a fragment of dialogue from one scene, inter-
rupting it with a fragment from the other scene—the dialogue
thus colliding, creating new meanings and sometimes word-
plays. Glumov's leaps acted as *caesurae* between the dialogue
fragments.

And the "cutting" increased in tempo. What was most
interesting was that the extreme sharpness of the eccentricity
was not torn from the context of this part of the play; it
never became comical just for comedy's sake, but stuck to its
theme, sharpened by its scenic embodiment.

Another distinct film feature at work here was the new
meaning acquired by common phrases in a new environment.

Everyone who has had in his hands a piece of film to be
edited knows by experience how neutral it remains, even
though a part of a planned sequence, until it is joined with
another piece, when it suddenly acquires and conveys a
sharper and quite different meaning than that planned for it
at the time of filming.

This was the foundation of that wise and wicked art of re-
editing the work of others, the most profound examples of
which can be found during the dawn of our cinematography,

when all the master film-editors—Esther Schub,* the Vassiliyev brothers, Benjamin Boitler, and Birrois—were engaged in reworking ingeniously the films imported after the revolution.

I cannot resist the pleasure of citing here one montage *tour de force* of this sort, executed by Boitler. One film bought from Germany was *Danton*, with Emil Jannings. As released on our screens, this scene was shown: Camille Desmoulins is condemned to the guillotine. Greatly agitated, Danton rushes to Robespierre, who turns aside and slowly wipes away a tear. The sub-title said, approximately, "In the name of freedom I had to sacrifice a friend. . . ." Fine.

But who could have guessed that in the German original, Danton, represented as an idler, a petticoat-chaser, a splendid chap and the only positive figure in the midst of evil characters, that this Danton ran to the evil Robespierre and . . . spat in his face? And that it was this spit that Robespierre wiped from his face with a handkerchief? And that the title indicated Robespierre's hatred of Danton, a hate that in the end of the film motivates the condemnation of Jannings-Danton to the guillotine?!

Two tiny cuts reversed the entire significance of this scene!

Where did my montage experiment in these scenes of *The Sage* come from?

There was already an "aroma" of montage in the new "left" cinema, particularly among the documentalists. Our replacement of Glumov's diary in Ostrovsky's text with a short "film-diary" was itself a parody on the first experiments with newsreels.

---

* Schub, long a familiar name to world-documentalists, is known abroad only by the film exhibited in America as *Cannons and Tractors*. The first time Eisenstein ever joined together two pieces of "real film" was while assisting Esther Schub in the re-editing of Lang's *Dr. Mabuse*. This was shortly after the production of *The Sage*. The Vassiliyevs' *Chapayev* establishes their place in cinema history.—EDITOR.

I think that first and foremost we must give the credit to the basic principles of the circus and the music-hall—for which I had had a passionate love since childhood. Under the influence of the French comedians, and of Chaplin (of whom we had only heard), and the first news of the fox-trot and jazz, this early love thrived.

The music-hall element was obviously needed at the time for the emergence of a "montage" form of thought. Harlequin's parti-colored costume grew and spread, first over the structure of the program, and finally into the method of the whole production.

But the background extended more deeply into tradition. Strangely enough, it was Flaubert who gave us one of the finest examples of cross-montage of dialogues, used with the same intention of expressive sharpening of idea. This is the scene in *Madame Bovary* where Emma and Rodolphe grow more intimate. Two lines of speech are interlaced: the speech of the orator in the square below, and the conversation of the future lovers:

Monsieur Derozerays got up, beginning another speech . . . praise of the Government took up less space in it; religion and agriculture more. He showed in it the relations of these two, and how they had always contributed to civilization. Rodolphe with Madame Bovary was talking dreams, presentiments, magnetism. Going back to the cradle of society, the orator painted those fierce times when men lived on acorns in the heart of woods. Then they had left off the skins of beasts, had put on cloth, tilled the soil, planted the vine. Was this a good, and in this discovery was there not more of injury than of gain? Monsieur Derozerays set himself this problem. From magnetism little by little Rodolphe had come to affinities, and while the president was citing Cincinnatus and his plough, Diocletian planting his cabbages, and the Emperors of China inaugurating the year by the sowing of seed, the young man was explaining to the young woman that these irresistible attractions find their cause in some previous state of experience.

"Thus we," he said, "why did we come to know one another? What chance willed it? It was because across the infinite, like two streams that flow but to unite, our special bents of mind had driven us towards each other."

And he seized her hand; she did not withdraw it.

"For good farming generally!" cried the president.

"Just now, for example, when I went to your house."

"To Monsieur Bizat of Quincampoix."

"Did I know I should accompany you?"

"Seventy francs."

"A hundred times I wished to go; and I followed you—I remained."

"Manures!"

"And I shall remain to-night, to-morrow, all other days, all my life!" [1]

And so on, with the "pieces" developing increasing tension.

As we can see, this is an interweaving of two lines, thematically identical, equally trivial. The matter is sublimated to a monumental triviality, whose climax is reached through a continuation of this cross-cutting and word-play, with the significance always dependent on the juxtaposition of the two lines.

Literature is full of such examples. This method is used with increasing popularity by Flaubert's artistic heirs.

Our pranks in regard to Ostrovsky remained on an "avant garde" level of an indubitable nakedness. But this seed of montage tendencies grew quickly and splendidly in *Patatra,* which remained a project through lack of an adequate hall and technical possibilities. The production was planned with "chase tempos," quick changes of action, scene intersections, and simultaneous playing of several scenes on a stage that surrounded an auditorium of revolving seats. Another even earlier project attempted to embrace the entire theater building in its composition. This was broken up during rehearsals and later produced by other hands as a purely theatrical conception. It was the Pletnëv play, *Precipice,* which Smishlayev and I worked on, following *The Mexican,* until we disagreed on principles and dissolved our partnership. (When I returned

[1] See Sources, pp. 268-272.

to Proletcult a year later, to do *The Sage*, it was as a director, although I continued to design my own productions.)

Precipice contains a scene where an inventor, thrilled by his new invention, runs, like Archimedes, about the city (or perhaps he was being chased by gangsters—I don't remember exactly). The task was to solve the dynamics of city streets, as well as to show the helplessness of an individual at the mercy of the "big city." (Our mistaken imaginings about Europe naturally led us to the false concept of "urbanism.")

An amusing combination occurred to me, not only to use running scenery—pieces of buildings and details (Meyerhold had not yet worked out, for his *Trust D. E.*, the neutral polished shields, *murs mobiles*, to unify several places of action)—but also, possibly under the demands of shifting scenery, to connect these moving decorations with people. The actors on roller skates carried not only themselves about the stage, but also their "piece of city." Our solution of the problem—the intersection of man and milieu—was undoubtedly influenced by the principles of the cubists. But the "urbanistic" paintings of Picasso were of less importance here than the need to express the dynamics of the city—glimpses of façades, hands, legs, pillars, heads, domes. All of this can be found in Gogol's work, but we did not notice that until Andrei Belyi enlightened us about the special cubism of Gogol.[2] I still remember the four legs of two bankers, supporting the façade of the stock-exchange, with two top-hats crowning the whole. There was also a policeman, sliced and quartered with traffic. Costumes blazing with perspectives of twirling lights, with only great rouged lips visible above. These all remained on paper—and now that even the paper has gone, we may become quite pathetically lyrical in our reminiscences.

These close-ups cut into views of a city become another link in our analysis, a film element that tried to fit itself into the stubborn stage. Here are also elements of double and multiple exposure—"superimposing" images of man onto images of buildings—all an attempt to interrelate man and his milieu in a single complicated display. (The fact that the film *Strike* was full of this sort of complexity proves the "infantile malady of leftism" existing in these first steps of cinema.)

Out of mechanical fusion, from plastic synthesis, the attempt evolves into thematic synthesis. In *Strike*, there is more than a transformation into the technique of the camera. The composition and structure of the film as a whole achieves the effect and sensation of uninterrupted unity between the collective and the milieu that creates the collective. And the organic unity of sailors, battleships, and sea that is shown in plastic and thematic cross-section in *Potemkin* is not by trickery or double-exposure or mechanical intersection, but by the general structure of the composition. But in the theater, the impossibility of the *mise-en-scène* unfolding throughout the auditorium, fusing stage and audience in a developing pattern, was the reason for the concentrated absorption of the *mise-en-scène* problems within the scenic action.

The almost geometrically conventional *mise-en-scène* of *The Sage* and its formal sequel, *Listen, Moscow*, becomes one of the basic elements of expression. The montage intersection eventually became too emphatically exact. The composition singled out groups, shifted the spectator's attention from one point to another, presented close-ups, a hand holding a letter, the play of eyebrows, a glance. The technique of genuine *mise-en-scène* composition was being mastered—and approaching its limits. It was already threatened with becoming the knight's move in chess, the shift of purely plastic contours in the already non-theatrical outlines of detailed drawings.

Sculptural details seen through the frame of the *cadre*, or shot, transitions from shot to shot, appeared to be the logical way out for the threatened hypertrophy of the *mise-en-scène*. Theoretically it established our dependence on *mise-en-scène* and montage. Pedagogically, it determined, for the future, the approaches to montage and cinema, arrived at through the mastering of theatrical construction and through the art of *mise-en-scène.** Thus was born the concept of *mise-en-cadre*. As the *mise-en-scène* is an interrelation of people in action, so the *mise-en-cadre* is the pictorial composition of mutually dependent *cadres* (shots) in a montage sequence.

In *Gas Masks* we see all the elements of film tendencies meeting. The turbines, the factory background, negated the last remnants of make-up and theatrical costumes, and all elements appeared as independently fused. Theater accessories in the midst of real factory plastics appeared ridiculous. The element of "play" was incompatible with the acrid smell of gas. The pitiful platform kept getting lost among the real platforms of labor activity. In short, the production was a failure. And we found ourselves in the cinema.

Our first film opus, *Strike* [1924-25], reflected, as in a mirror, in reverse, our production of *Gas Masks*. But the film floundered about in the flotsam of a rank theatricality that had become alien to it.

At the same time, the break with the theater in principle was so sharp that in my "revolt against the theater" I did away with a very vital element of theater—the story.

At that time this seemed natural. We brought collective and mass action onto the screen, in contrast to individualism and the "triangle" drama of the bourgeois cinema. Discarding the individualist conception of the bourgeois hero, our films of this period made an abrupt deviation—insisting on an understanding of the mass as hero.

No screen had ever before reflected an image of collective action. Now the conception of "collectivity" was to be pictured. But our enthusiasm produced a one-sided representation of the masses and the collective; one-sided because collectivism means the maximum development of the individual within the collective, a conception irreconcilably opposed to bourgeois individualism. Our first mass films missed this deeper meaning.

* As indicated in "A Course in Treatment," the first two years of Eisenstein's course for directors at the State Cinema Institute emphasize a thorough study of *theater* principles.—EDITOR.

Still, I am sure that for its period this deviation was not only natural but necessary. It was important that the screen be first penetrated by the general image, the collective united and propelled by one wish. "Individuality within the collective," the deeper meaning, demanded of cinema today, would have found entrance almost impossible if the way had not been cleared by the general concept.

In 1924 I wrote, with intense zeal: "Down with the story and the plot!" Today, the story, which then seemed to be almost "an attack of individualism" upon our revolutionary cinema, returns in a fresh form, to its proper place. In this turn towards the story lies the historical importance of the third half-decade of Soviet cinematography (1930-1935).

And here, as we begin our fourth five-year period of cinema, when abstract discussions of the epigones of the "story" film and the embryones of the "plotless" film are calming down, it is time to take an inventory of our credits and debits.

I consider that besides mastering the elements of filmic diction, the technique of the frame, and the theory of montage, we have another credit to list—the value of profound ties with the traditions and methodology of literature. Not in vain, during this period, was the new concept of film-language born, film-language not as the language of the film-critic, but as an expression of cinema thinking, when the cinema was called upon to embody the philosophy and ideology of the victorious proletariat.

Stretching out its hand to the new quality of literature—the dramatics of subject—the cinema cannot forget the tremendous experience of its earlier periods. But the way is not back to them, but forward to the synthesis of all the best that has been done by our silent cinematography, towards a synthesis of these with the demands of today, along the lines of story and Marxist-Leninist ideological analysis. The phase of monumental synthesis in the images of the people of the epoch of socialism—the phase of socialist realism.

[1934]

THE UNEXPECTED

Hark! the voice of a pheasant
Has swallowed the wide field
At a gulp.

YAMEI [1]

Givochini, the famous comedian of the
Malii Theatre, was once forced to substitute
at the last moment for the popular Moscow
basso, Lavrov, in an opera, *The Amorous
Bayaderka*. But Givochini had no singing
voice. His friends shook their heads sympa-
thetically. "How can you possibly sing the
role, Vasili Ignatyevich?" Givochini was not
disheartened. Said he, happily, *"Whatever
notes I can't take with my voice, I'll show
with my hands."* [2]

WE HAVE been visited by the Kabuki theater—a wonderful
manifestation of theatrical culture.*

Every critical voice gushes praise for its splendid craftsmanship. But there has been no appraisal of what constitutes
its wonder. Its "museum" elements, though indispensable in
estimating its value, cannot alone afford a satisfactory estimate of this phenomenon, of this wonder. A "wonder" must
promote cultural progress, feeding and stimulating the intellectual questions of our day. The Kabuki is dismissed in plati-
tudes: "How musical!" "What handling of objects!" "What
plasticity!" And we come to the conclusion that there is
nothing to be learned, that (as one of our most respected
critics has announced) there's nothing new here: Meyerhold

* In its European tour during 1928 a troupe of Kabuki actors, headed
by Ichikawa Sadanji, performed in Moscow and Leningrad; in the latter
city the magazine *Zhizn Iskusstva* devoted to this visit an issue (19 August 1928), to which Eisenstein contributed this essay.

has already plundered everything of use from the Japanese theater!

Behind the fulsome generalities, there are some real attitudes revealed. Kabuki is conventional! How can such conventions move Europeans! Its craftsmanship is merely the cold perfection of form! And the plays they perform are *feudal!*—What a nightmare!

More than any other obstacle, it is this conventionalism that prevents our thorough use of all that may be borrowed from the Kabuki.

But the conventionalism that we have learned "from books" proves in fact to be a conventionalism of extremely interesting relationships. The conventionalism of Kabuki is by no means the stylized and premeditated mannerism that we know in our own theater, artificially grafted on outside the technical requirements of the premise. In Kabuki this conventionalism is profoundly logical—as in any Oriental theater, for example, in the Chinese theater.

Among the characters of the Chinese theater is "the spirit of the oyster"! Look at the make-up of the performer of this rôle, with its series of concentric touching circles spreading from the right and left of his nose, graphically reproducing the halves of an oyster shell, and it becomes apparent that this is quite "justified." This is neither more nor less a convention than are the epaulettes of a general. From their narrowly utilitarian origin, once warding off blows of the battle-axe from the shoulder, to their being furnished with hierarchic little stars, the epaulettes are indistinguishable in principle from the blue frog inscribed on the forehead of the actor who is playing the frog's "spirit."

Another convention is taken directly from life. In the first scene of *Chushingura* (*The Forty-Seven Ronin*), Shocho, playing a married woman, appears without eyebrows and with blackened teeth. This conventionalism is no more unreal than the custom of Jewish women who shear their heads so that the ears remain exposed, nor of that among girls joining the Komsomol who wear red kerchiefs, as some sort of "form."

In distinction from European practice, where marriage has been made a guard against the risks of freer attachments, in ancient Japan (of the play's epoch) the married woman, once the need had passed, destroyed her attractiveness! She removed her eyebrows, and blackened (and sometimes extracted) her teeth.

Let us move on to the most important matter, to a conventionalism that is explained by the specific world-viewpoint of the Japanese. This appears with particular clarity during the direct *perception* of the performance, to a peculiar degree that no description has been able to convey to us.

And here we find something totally unexpected—a junction of the Kabuki theater with these extreme probings in the theater, where theater is transformed into cinema.* And where cinema takes that latest step in its development: the *sound* film.

The sharpest distinction between Kabuki and our theater is—if such an expression may be permitted—in a *monism of ensemble*.

We are familiar with the emotional ensemble of the Moscow Art Theatre—the ensemble of a unified collective "re-experience"; the parallelism of ensemble employed in opera (by orchestra, chorus, and soloists); when the settings also make their contribution to this parallelism, the theater is designated by that dirtied word "synthetic"; the "animal" ensemble finally has its revenge—that outmoded form where the whole stage clucks and barks and moos a naturalistic imitation of the life that is led by the "assisting" human beings.

The Japanese have shown us another, extremely interesting form of ensemble—*the monistic ensemble*. Sound—movement—space—voice here *do not accompany* (nor even parallel) each other, but function *as elements of equal significance*.

The first association that occurs to one in experiencing

* It is my conviction that cinema is *today's level* of theater. That theater in its older form has died and continues to exist only by inertia. [The author's commentary of eleven years later on this viewpoint can be found in "Achievement," p. 191.—EDITOR.]

Kabuki is *soccer*, the most collective, ensemble sport. Voice, clappers, mimic movement, the narrator's shouts, the folding screens—all are so many backs, half-backs, goal-keepers, forwards, passing to each other the dramatic ball and driving towards the goal of the dazed spectator.

It is impossible to speak of "accompaniments" in Kabuki—just as one would not say that, in walking or running, the right leg "accompanies" the left leg, or that both of them accompany the diaphragm!

Here a single monistic sensation of theatrical "provocation" takes place. The Japanese regards each theatrical element, not as an incommensurable unit among the various categories of affect (on the various sense-organs), but as a single unit of *theater*.

. . . the patter of Ostuzhev no more than the pink tights of the prima-donna, a roll on the kettledrums as much as Romeo's soliloquy, the cricket on the hearth no less than the cannon fired over the heads of the audience.[3]

Thus I wrote in 1923, placing a sign of equality between the elements of every category, establishing theoretically the basic *unity of theater*, which I then called "attractions."

The Japanese in his, of course, instinctive practice, makes a fully one hundred per cent appeal with his theater, just as I then had in mind. Directing himself to the various organs of sensation, he builds his summation to a grand *total* provocation of the human brain, without taking any notice *which* of these several paths he is following.*

In place of *accompaniment*, it is the naked method of *transfer* that flashes in the Kabuki theater. Transferring the basic affective aim from one material to another, from one category of "provocation" to another.

In experiencing Kabuki one involuntarily recalls an American novel about a man in whom are transposed the hearing

* Not even what is *eaten* in this theater is accidental! I had no opportunity to discover if it is ritual food eaten. Do they eat whatever happens to be there, or is there a definite menu? If the latter, we must also include in the ensemble the sense of taste!

and seeing nerves, so that he perceives light vibrations as sounds, and tremors of the air—as colors: he *hears light* and *sees sound*. This is also what happens in Kabuki! We actually "hear movement" and "see sound."

An example: Yuranosuke leaves the surrendered castle. And moves from the depth of the stage towards the extreme foreground. Suddenly the background screen with its gate painted in natural dimensions (close-up) is folded away. In its place is seen a second screen, with a tiny gate painted on it (long shot). This means that he has moved even further away. Yuranosuke continues on. Across the background is drawn a brown-green-black curtain, indicating: the castle is now hidden from his sight. More steps. Yuranosuke now moves out on to the "flowery way." This further removal is emphasized by . . . the *samisen,** that is—by sound!!

First removal—steps, i.e., a *spatial* removal by the actor.

Second removal—a flat *painting:* the change of backgrounds.

Third removal—an *intellectually*-explained indication: we understand that the curtain "effaces" something visible.

Fourth removal—*sound!*

Here is an example of pure cinematographic method from the last fragment of *Chushingura:*

After a short fight ("for several feet") we have a "break"— an empty stage, a landscape. Then more fighting. Exactly as if, in a film, we had cut in a piece of landscape to create a mood in a scene, here is cut in an empty nocturnal snow landscape

* ". . . samisen music depends almost completely on rhythm, rather than melody, to interpret emotion. Sound is inexhaustible, and by groupings of sounds in changing rhythms the samisen musicians gain the effects they desire. . . . Ripple-clang-bang; smoothness, roughness, villainy, tranquillity; falling snow, a flight of birds, wind in the tree-tops; skirmish and fray, the peace of moonlight, the sorrow of parting, the rapture of spring; the infirmity of age, the gladness of lovers—all these and much more the samisen expresses to those who are able to look beyond the curtain that shuts this musical world away from Western ears because of its baffling conventions of sound rather than melody." —KINCAID.[4]

(on an empty stage). And here after several feet, two of the "forty-seven faithful" observe a shed where the villain has hidden (of which the spectator is already aware). Just as in cinema, within such a sharpened dramatic moment, some brake has to be applied. In *Potemkin*, after the preparation for the command to "Fire!" on the sailors covered by the tarpaulin, there are several shots of "indifferent" parts of the battleship before the final command is given: the prow, the gun-muzzles, a life-preserver, etc. A brake is applied to the action, and the tension is screwed tighter.

The moment of the discovery of the hiding-place must be accentuated. To find the *right* solution for this moment, this accent must be shaped from the *same* rhythmic material—a return to the same nocturnal, empty, snowy landscape . . .

But now there are people on the stage! Nevertheless, the Japanese do find the right solution—and it is a *flute* that enters triumphantly! And you *see* the same snowy fields, the same echoing emptiness and night, that you *heard* a short while before, when you *looked* at the empty stage . . .

Occasionally (and usually at the moment when the nerves seem about to burst from tension) the Japanese double their effects. With their mastery of the equivalents of visual and aural images, they suddenly give *both*, "squaring" them, and brilliantly calculating the blow of their sensual billiard-cue on the spectator's cerebral target. I know no better way to describe that combination, of the moving hand of Ichikawa Ennosuke as he commits hara-kiri—*with* the sobbing sound off-stage, *graphically* corresponding with the movement of the knife.

There it is: "Whatever notes I can't take with my voice, I'll show with my hands!" But here it was taken by the voice *and* shown with the hands! And we stand benumbed before such a perfection of—montage.

We all know those three trick questions: What shape is a winding staircase? How would you describe "compactly"?

What is a "surging sea"? One can't formulate intellectually analyzed answers to these. Perhaps Baudouin de Courtenay * knows, but we are forced to answer with gestures. We show the difficult concept of "compactly" with a clenched fist, and so on.

And what is more, such a description is *fully satisfactory*. We also are slightly Kabuki! But not sufficiently!

In our "Statement" on the sound film † we wrote of a contrapuntal method of combining visual and aural images. To possess this method one must develop in oneself a new *sense: the capacity of reducing visual and aural perceptions to a "common denominator."*

This is possessed by Kabuki to perfection. And we, too—crossing in turn the successive Rubicons flowing between theater and cinema and between cinema and sound-cinema—must also possess this. We can learn the mastery of this required new sense from the Japanese. As distinctly as impressionism owes a debt to the Japanese print, and post-impressionism to Negro sculpture, so the sound film will be no less obliged to the Japanese.

And not to the Japanese theater, alone, for these fundamental features, in my opinion, profoundly penetrate all aspects of the Japanese world-view. Certainly in those incomplete fragments of Japanese culture accessible to me, this seems a penetration to their very base.

We need not look beyond Kabuki for examples of identical perceptions of naturalistic three-dimensionality and flat painting. "Alien?" But it is necessary for this pot to boil in its own way before we can witness the completely satisfactory resolution of a waterfall made of vertical lines, against which a silver-paper serpentine fish-dragon, fastened by a thread, swims desperately. Or, folding back the screen-walls of a strictly cubist tea-house "of the vale of fans," a hanging backdrop is disclosed, a "perspective" gallery racing obliquely down its

* A professor in comparative philology at the University of St. Petersburg.
† This "Statement" is printed in Appendix A.

center. Our theater design has never known such decorative cubism, nor such primitivism of painted perspective. Nor, moreover, such *simultaneity*—here, apparently, pervading everything.

Costume. In the Dance of the Snake Odato Goro enters, bound with a rope that is also expressed, through transfer, in the robe's pattern of a flat rope-design, and her sash, as well, is twisted into a three-dimensional rope—a *third* form.

Writing. The Japanese masters an apparently limitless quantity of hieroglyphs. Hieroglyphs developed from conventionalized features of objects, put together, express concepts, i.e., the picture of a concept—an ideogram. Alongside these exists a series of Europeanized phonetic alphabets: the Manyō kana, hiragana, and others. But the Japanese writes *all* letters, employing both forms at once! It is not considered remarkable to compose sentences of hieroglyph *pictures* concurrently with the *letters* of several absolutely opposed alphabets.

Poetry. The *tanka* is an almost untranslatable form of lyrical epigram of severe dimension: 5, 7, 5 syllables in the first strophe (*kami-no-ku*) and 7, 7 syllables in the second (*shimo-no-ku*).* This must be the most uncommon of all poetry, in both form and content. When written, it can be judged both pictorially and poetically. Its writing is valued no less as calligraphy than as a poem.

And content? One critic justly says of the Japanese lyric: "A Japanese poem should be sooner *seen* [i.e., *represented visually.*—S.E.] than *heard*." [6]

APPROACH OF WINTER

They leave for the East
A flying bridge of magpies
A stream across the sky . . .
The tedious nights
Will be trimmed with hoar-frost.

* "The measure of the classical stanza is known as the *shichigoto*, or seven-and-five movement, which all Japanese believe to echo the divine pulse-beat of the race."—BRYAN.[5]

Across a bridge of magpies in flight, it seems that Yakamochi (who died in 785) departs into the ether.

CROW IN THE SPRING MIST

The crow perched there
Is half-concealed
By the kimono of fog . . .
As is a silken songster
By the folds of the sash.

The anonymous author (ca. 1800) wishes to express that the crow is as incompletely visible through the morning mist as is the bird in the pattern of the silk robe, when the sash is wound around the robed figure.

Strictly limited in its number of syllables, calligraphically charming in description and in comparison, striking in an incongruity that is also wonderfully near (crow, half-hidden by the mist, and the patterned bird, half-hidden by the sash), the Japanese lyric evidences an interesting *"fusion"* of images, which appeals to the most varied senses. This original archaic "pantheism" is undoubtedly based on a *non-differentiation of perception—a well-known absence of the sensation of "perspective."* It could not be otherwise. Japanese history is too rich in historical experience, and the burden of feudalism, though overcome politically, still runs like a red thread through the *cultural* traditions of Japan. Differentiation, entering society with its transition to capitalism and bringing in its wake, as a consequence of economic differentiation, differentiated perceptions of the world,—is not yet apparent in many cultural areas of Japan. And the Japanese continue to think "feudally," i.e., undifferentiatedly.

This is found in children's art. This also happens to people cured of blindness where all the objects, far and near, of the world, do not exist in space, but crowd in upon them closely.

In addition to Kabuki, the Japanese also showed us a film, *Karakuri-musume*. But in this, non-differentiation, brought to such brilliant unexpectedness in Kabuki, is realized *negatively*.

Karakuri-musume is a melodramatic farce. Beginning in the manner of Monty Banks, it ends in incredible gloom, and for long intervals is criminally torn in both directions.

The attempt to tie these opposing elements together is generally the hardest of tasks.

Even such a master as Chaplin, whose fusion of these opposing elements in *The Kid* is unsurpassed, was unable in *The Gold Rush* to balance these elements. The material slid from plane to plane. But in *Karakuri-musume* there is a complete smash-up.

As ever the echo, the unexpected junction, is found only at polar extremes. The archaism of non-differentiated sense "provocations" of Kabuki on one side, and on the other—the acme of *montage thinking*.

Montage thinking—the height of differentiatedly sensing and resolving the "organic" world—is realized anew in a mathematic faultlessly performing instrument-machine.

Recalling the words of Kleist, so close to the Kabuki theater, which was born from marionettes:

. . . [grace] appears best in that human bodily structure which has no consciousness at all, or has an infinite consciousness—that is, in the mechanical puppet, or in the god.[7]

Extremes meet. . . .

Nothing is gained by whining about the soullessness of Kabuki or, still worse, by finding in Sadanji's acting a "confirmation of the Stanislavsky theory"! Or in looking for what "Meyerhold hasn't yet stolen"!

Let us rather—*hail the junction of Kabuki and the sound-film!*

[1928]

THE CINEMATOGRAPHIC PRINCIPLE
AND THE IDEOGRAM

IT IS a weird and wonderful feat to have written a pamphlet on something that in reality does not exist. There is, for example, no such thing as a cinema without cinematography. And yet the author of the pamphlet preceding this essay * has contrived to write a book about the *cinema* of a country that has no *cinematography*. About the cinema of a country that has, in its culture, an infinite number of cinematographic traits, strewn everywhere with the sole exception of—its cinema.

This essay is on the cinematographic traits of Japanese culture that lie outside the Japanese cinema, and is itself as apart from the preceding pamphlet as these traits are apart from the Japanese cinema.

Cinema is: so many corporations, such and such turnovers of capital, so and so many stars, such and such dramas.

Cinematography is, first and foremost, montage.

The Japanese cinema is excellently equipped with corporations, actors, and stories. But the Japanese cinema is completely unaware of montage. Nevertheless the principle of montage can be identified as the basic element of Japanese representational culture.

Writing—for their writing is primarily representational.

The hieroglyph.

The naturalistic image of an object, as portrayed by the skilful Chinese hand of Ts'ang Chieh 2650 years before our era,

---

* Eisenstein's essay was originally published as an "afterword" to N. Kaufman's pamphlet, *Japanese Cinema* (Moscow, 1929).

28

becomes slightly formalized and, with its 539 fellows, forms the first "contingent" of hieroglyphs. Scratched out with a stylus on a slip of bamboo, the portrait of an object maintained a resemblance to its original in every respect.

But then, by the end of the third century, the brush is invented. In the first century after the "joyous event" (A.D.)—paper. And, lastly, in the year 220—India ink.

A complete upheaval. A revolution in draughtsmanship. And, after having undergone in the course of history no fewer than fourteen different styles of handwriting, the hieroglyph crystallized in its present form. The means of production (brush and India ink) determined the form.

The fourteen reforms had their way. As a result:

In the fierily cavorting hieroglyph *ma* (a horse) it is already impossible to recognize the features of the dear little horse sagging pathetically in its hindquarters, in the writing style of Ts'ang Chieh, so well-known from ancient Chinese bronzes.

But let it rest in the Lord, this dear little horse, together with the other 607 remaining *hsiang cheng* symbols—the earliest extant category of hieroglyphs.

The real interest begins with the second category of hieroglyphs—the *huei-i*, i.e., "copulative."

The point is that the copulation (perhaps we had better say, the combination) of two hieroglyphs of the simplest series is to be regarded not as their sum, but as their product, i.e., as a value of another dimension, another degree; each, separately, corresponds to an *object*, to a fact, but their combination corresponds to a *concept*. From separate hieroglyphs has been fused—the ideogram. By the combination of two "depictables" is achieved the representation of something that is graphically undepictable.

For example: the picture for water and the picture of an eye signifies "to weep"; the picture of an ear near the drawing of a door = "to listen";

a dog + a mouth = "to bark";
a mouth + a child = "to scream";
a mouth + a bird = "to sing";
a knife + a heart = "sorrow," and so on.[1]

But this is—montage!

Yes. It is exactly what we do in the cinema, combining shots that are *depictive*, single in meaning, neutral in content—into *intellectual* contexts and series.

This is a means and method inevitable in any cinematographic exposition. And, in a condensed and purified form, the starting point for the "intellectual cinema."

For a cinema seeking a maximum laconism for the visual representation of abstract concepts.

And we hail the method of the long-lamented Ts'ang Chieh as a first step along these paths.

We have mentioned laconism. Laconism furnishes us a transition to another point. Japan possesses the most laconic form of poetry: the *haikai* (appearing at the beginning of the thirteenth century and known today as "haiku" or "hokku") and the even earlier *tanka* (mythologically assumed to have been created along with heaven and earth).

Both are little more than hieroglyphs transposed into phrases. So much so that half their quality is appraised by their calligraphy. The method of their resolution is completely analogous to the structure of the ideogram.

As the ideogram provides a means for the laconic imprinting of an abstract concept, the same method, when transposed into literary exposition, gives rise to an identical laconism of pointed imagery.

Applied to the collision of an austere combination of symbols this method results in a dry definition of abstract concepts. The same method, expanded into the luxury of a group of already formed verbal combinations, swells into a splendor of *imagist* effect.

The concept is a bare formula; its adornment (an expansion by additional material) transforms the formula into an image—a finished form.

Exactly, though in reverse, as a primitive thought process—imagist thinking, displaced to a definite degree, becomes transformed to conceptual thinking.

But let us turn to examples.

The *haiku* is a concentrated impressionist sketch:

> A lonely crow
> On leafless bough,
> One autumn eve.
>
> BASHŌ

> What a resplendent moon!
> It casts the shadow of pine boughs
> Upon the mats.
>
> KIKAKU

> An evening breeze blows.
> The water ripples
> Against the blue heron's legs.
>
> BUSON

> It is early dawn.
> The castle is surrounded
> By the cries of wild ducks.
>
> KYOROKU [2]

The earlier *tanka* is slightly longer (by two lines):

> O mountain pheasant
> long are the feathers trail'st thou
> on the wooded hill-side—
> as long the nights seem to me
> on lonely couch sleep seeking.

HITOMARO[?] [3]

From our point of view, these are montage phrases. Shot lists. The simple combination of two or three details of a material kind yields a perfectly finished representation of another kind—psychological.

And if the finely ground edges of the intellectual defined concepts formed by the combined ideograms are blurred in these poems, yet, in *emotional quality*, the concepts have blossomed forth immeasurably. We should observe that the emotion is directed towards the reader, for, as Yone Noguchi has said, "it is the readers who make the *haiku's* imperfection a perfection of art." [4]

It is uncertain in Japanese writing whether its predominating aspect is as a system of characters (denotative), or as an independent creation of graphics (depictive). In any case, born of the dual mating of the depictive by method, and the denotative by purpose, the ideogram continued both these lines (not consecutive historically but consecutive in principle in the minds of those developing the method).

Not only did the denotative line continue into literature, in the *tanka*, as we have shown, but exactly the same method (in its depictive aspect) operates also in the most perfect examples of Japanese pictorial art.

Sharaku—creator of the finest prints of the eighteenth century, and especially of an immortal gallery of actors' portraits. The Japanese Daumier. Despite this, almost unknown to us. The characteristic traits of his work have been analyzed only in our century. One of these critics, Julius Kurth, in discussing the question of the influence on Sharaku of sculpture, draws a parallel between his wood-cut portrait of the actor Nakayama Tomisaburō and an antique mask of the semi-religious Nō theater, the mask of a Rozo.

The faces of both the print and the mask wear an *identical expression. . . .* Features and masses are similarly arranged although the mask represents an old priest, and the print a young woman. This relationship is striking, yet these two works are otherwise totally dissimilar; this in itself is a demonstration of Sharaku's originality. While the carved mask was constructed according to fairly accurate anatomical proportions, the proportions of the portrait print are simply impossible. The space between the eyes comprises a width that makes mock of all good sense. The nose is almost twice as long in relation to the eyes as any normal nose would dare to be, and the chin stands in no sort of relation to the mouth; the brows, the mouth, and every feature—is hopelessly misrelated. *This observation may be made in all the large heads by Sharaku.* That the artist was unaware that all these proportions are false is, of course, out of the question. It was with a full awareness that he repudiated normalcy, and, while the drawing of the separate features depends on severely concentrated naturalism, their proportions have been subordinated to purely intellectual considerations. *He set up the essence of the psychic expression as the norm for the proportions of the single features.*[5]

Is not this process that of the ideogram, combining the independent "mouth" and the dissociated symbol of "child" to form the significance of "scream"?

Is this not exactly what we of the cinema do temporally, just as Sharaku in simultaneity, when we cause a monstrous disproportion of the parts of a normally flowing event, and suddenly dismember the event into "close-up of clutching hands," "medium shots of the struggle," and "extreme close-up of bulging eyes," in making a montage disintegration of the event in various planes? In making an eye twice as large as a man's full figure?! By combining these monstrous incongruities we newly collect the disintegrated event into one whole, but in *our* aspect. According to the treatment of our relation to the event.

The disproportionate depiction of an event is organically natural to us from the beginning. Professor Luriya, of the Psychological Institute in Moscow, has shown me a drawing by a child of "lighting a stove." Everything is represented in passably accurate relationship and with great care. Firewood. Stove. Chimney. But what are those zigzags in that huge central rectangle? They turn out to be—matches. Taking into account the crucial importance of these matches for the depicted process, the child provides a proper scale for them.*

The representation of objects in the actual (absolute) proportions proper to them is, of course, merely a tribute to

* It is possible to trace this particular tendency from its ancient, almost pre-historical source (". . . in all ideational art, objects are given size according to their importance, the king being twice as large as his subjects, or a tree half the size of a man when it merely informs us that the scene is out-of-doors. Something of this principle of size according to significance persisted in the Chinese tradition. The favorite disciple of Confucius looked like a little boy beside him and the most important figure in any group was usually the largest." 6) through the highest development of Chinese art, parent of Japanese graphic arts: ". . . natural scale always had to bow to pictorial scale . . . size according to distance never followed the laws of geometric perspective but the needs of the design. Foreground features might be diminished to avoid obstruction and overemphasis, and far distant objects, which were too minute to count pictorially, might be enlarged to act as a counterpoint to the middle distance or foreground." 7

orthodox formal logic. A subordination to an inviolable order of things.

Both in painting and sculpture there is a periodic and invariable return to periods of the establishment of absolutism. Displacing the expressiveness of archaic disproportion for regulated "stone tables" of officially decreed harmony.

Absolute realism is by no means the correct form of perception. It is simply the function of a certain form of social structure. Following a state monarchy, a state uniformity of thought is implanted. Ideological uniformity of a sort that can be developed pictorially in the ranks of colors and designs of the Guards regiments . . .

Thus we have seen how the principle of the hieroglyph— "denotation by depiction"—split in two: along the line of its purpose (the principle of "denotation"), into the principles of creating literary imagery; along the line of its method of realizing this purpose (the principle of "depiction"), into the striking methods of expressiveness used by Sharaku.*

And, just as the two outspreading wings of a hyperbola meet, as we say, at infinity (though no one has visited so distant a region!), so the principle of hieroglyphics, infinitely splitting into two parts (in accordance with the function of symbols), unexpectedly unites again from this dual estrangement, in yet a fourth sphere—in the theater.

Estranged for so long, they are once again—in the cradle period of the drama—present in a *parallel* form, in a curious dualism.

The *significance* (denotation) of the action is effected by the reciting of the *Jōruri* by a voice behind the stage—the *representation* (depiction) of the action is effected by silent marionettes on the stage. Along with a specific manner of movement this archaism migrated into the early Kabuki the-

* It has been left to James Joyce to develop in *literature* the depictive line of the Japanese hieroglyph. Every word of Kurth's analysis of Sharaku may be applied, neatly and easily, to Joyce.

ater, as well. To this day it is preserved, as a partial method,
in the classical repertory (where certain parts of the action
are narrated from behind the stage while the actor mimes).

But this is not the point. The most important fact is that into
the technique of acting itself the ideographic (montage)
method has been wedged in the most interesting ways.

However, before discussing this, let us be allowed the luxury
of a digression—on the matter of the shot, to settle the debated
question of its nature, once and for all.

A shot. A single piece of celluloid. A tiny rectangular frame
in which there is, organized in some way, a piece of an event.

"Cemented together, these shots form montage. When this
is done in an appropriate rhythm, *of course!*"

This, roughly, is what is taught by the old, old school of
film-making, that sang:

> "Screw by screw,
> Brick by brick . . ."

Kuleshov, for example, even writes with a brick:

If you have an idea-phrase, a particle of the story, a link in the
whole dramatic chain, then that idea is to be expressed and accumulated from shot-ciphers, just like bricks.[8]

"The shot is an element of montage. Montage is an assembly
of these elements." This is a most pernicious make-shift analysis.

Here the understanding of the process as a whole (connection, shot-montage) derives only from the external indications
of its flow (a piece cemented to another piece). Thus it would
be possible, for instance, to arrive at the well-known conclusion that street-cars exist in order to be laid across streets. An
entirely logical deduction, if one limits oneself to the external
indications of the functions they performed during the street-
fighting of February, 1917, here in Russia. But the materialist
conception of history interprets it otherwise.

The worst of it is that an approach of this kind does actually lie, like an insurmountable street-car, across the potenti-

alities of formal development. Such an approach overrules dialectical development, and dooms one to mere evolutionary "perfecting," in so far as it gives no bite into the dialectical substance of events.

In the long run, such evolutionizing leads either through refinement to decadence or, on the other hand, to a simple withering away due to stagnation of the blood.

Strange as it may seem, a melodious witness to both these distressing eventualities, simultaneously, is Kuleshov's latest film, *The Gay Canary* [1929].

The shot is by no means an *element* of montage.

The shot is a montage *cell*.

Just as cells in their division form a phenomenon of another order, the organism or embryo, so, on the other side of the dialectical leap from the shot, there is montage.

By what, then, is montage characterized and, consequently, its cell—the shot?

By collision. By the conflict of two pieces in opposition to each other. By conflict. By collision.

In front of me lies a crumpled yellowed sheet of paper. On it is a mysterious note:

"Linkage—P" and "Collision—E."

This is a substantial trace of a heated bout on the subject of montage between P (Pudovkin) and E (myself).

This has become a habit. At regular intervals he visits me late at night and behind closed doors we wrangle over matters of principle. A graduate of the Kuleshov school, he loudly defends an understanding of montage as a *linkage* of pieces. Into a chain. Again, "bricks." Bricks, arranged in series to *expound* an idea.

I confronted him with my viewpoint on montage as a *collision*. A view that from the collision of two given factors *arises* a concept.

From my point of view, linkage is merely a possible *special* case.

Recall what an infinite number of combinations is known in physics to be capable of arising from the impact (collision) of spheres. Depending on whether the spheres be resilient, non-resilient, or mingled. Amongst all these combinations there is one in which the impact is so weak that the collision is degraded to an even movement of both in the same direction.

This is the one combination which would correspond with Pudovkin's view.

Not long ago we had another talk. Today he agrees with my point of view. True, during the interval he took the opportunity to acquaint himself with the series of lectures I gave during that period at the State Cinema Institute. . . .

*   So, montage is conflict.

As the basis of every art is conflict (an "imagist" transformation of the dialectical principle). The shot appears as the *cell* of montage. Therefore it also must be considered from the viewpoint of *conflict*.

Conflict within the shot is potential montage, in the development of its intensity shattering the quadrilateral cage of the shot and exploding its conflict into montage impulses *between* the montage pieces. As, in a zigzag of mimicry, the *mise-en-scène* splashes out into a spatial zigzag with the *same* shattering. As the slogan, "All obstacles are vain before Russians," bursts out in the multitude of incident of *War and Peace*.

If montage is to be compared with something, then a phalanx of montage pieces, of shots, should be compared to the series of explosions of an internal combustion engine, driving forward its automobile or tractor: for, similarly, the dynamics of montage serve as impulses driving forward the total film.

Conflict within the frame. This can be very varied in character: it even can be a conflict in—the story. As in that "prehistoric" period in films (although there are plenty of instances

* dynamic tension a better word?

in the present, as well), when entire scenes would be photographed in a single, uncut shot. This, however, is outside the strict jurisdiction of the film-form.

These are the "cinematographic" conflicts within the frame:

Conflict of graphic directions.
(Lines—either static or dynamic)

Conflict of scales.

Conflict of volumes.

Conflict of masses.
(Volumes filled with various intensities of light)

Conflict of depths.

And the following conflicts, requiring only one further impulse of intensification before flying into antagonistic pairs of pieces:

Close shots and long shots.

Pieces of graphically varied directions. Pieces resolved in volume, with pieces resolved in area.

Pieces of darkness and pieces of lightness.

And, lastly, there are such unexpected conflicts as:

Conflicts between an object and its dimension—and conflicts between an event and its duration.

These may sound strange, but both are familiar to us. The first is accomplished by an optically distorted lens, and the second by stop-motion or slow-motion.

The compression of all cinematographic factors and properties within a single dialectical formula of conflict is no empty rhetorical diversion.

We are now seeking a unified system for methods of cinematographic expressiveness that shall hold good for all its elements. The assembly of these into series of common indications will solve the task as a whole.

Experience in the separate elements of the cinema cannot be absolutely measured.

Whereas we know a good deal about montage, in the theory of the shot we are still floundering about amidst the most academic attitudes, some vague tentatives, and the sort of harsh radicalism that sets one's teeth on edge.

To regard the frame as a particular, as it were, molecular case of montage makes possible the direct application of montage practice to the theory of the shot.

And similarly with the theory of lighting. To sense this as a collision between a stream of light and an obstacle, like the impact of a stream from a fire-hose striking a concrete object, or of the wind buffeting a human figure, must result in a usage of light entirely different in comprehension from that employed in playing with various combinations of "gauzes" and "spots."

Thus far we have one such significant principle of conflict: *the principle of optical counterpoint.*

And let us not now forget that soon we shall face another and less simple problem in counterpoint: *the conflict in the sound film of acoustics and optics.*

Let us return to one of the most fascinating of optical conflicts: the conflict between the frame of the shot and the object!

The camera position, as a materialization of the conflict between organizing logic of the director and the inert logic of the object, in collision, reflects the dialectic of the camera-angle.

In this matter we are still impressionistic and lacking in principle to a sickening degree. Nevertheless, a sharpness of principle can be had in the technique of this, too. The dry quadrilateral, plunging into the hazards of nature's diffuseness . . .

And once again we are in Japan! For the cinematographic method is used in teaching drawing in Japanese schools.

What is our method of teaching drawing? Take any piece of white paper with four corners to it. Then cram onto it, usually even without using the edges (mostly greasy from the long drudgery!), some bored caryatid, some conceited Corinthian capital, or a plaster Dante (not the magician performing at the Moscow Hermitage, but the other one—Alighieri, the comedy writer).

The Japanese approach this from a quite different direction:

Here's the branch of a cherry-tree.[9] And the pupil cuts out from this whole, with a square, and a circle, and a rectangle—compositional units:

He frames a shot!

These two ways of teaching drawing can characterize the two basic tendencies struggling within the cinema of today. One—the expiring method of artificial spatial organization of an event in front of the lens. From the "direction" of a sequence, to the erection of a Tower of Babel in front of the lens. The other—a "picking-out" by the camera: organization by means of the camera. Hewing out a piece of actuality with the ax of the lens.

However, at the present moment, when the center of attention is finally beginning, in the intellectual cinema, to be transferred from the materials of cinema, as such, to "deductions and conclusions," to "slogans" based on the material, both schools of thought are losing distinction in their differences and can quietly blend into a synthesis.

Several pages back we lost, like an overshoe in a street-car, the question of the theater. Let us turn back to the question of methods of montage in the Japanese theater, particularly in acting.

The first and most striking example, of course, is the purely cinematographic method of "acting without transitions." Along with mimic transitions carried to a limit of refinement, the Japanese actor uses an exactly contrary method as well. At a certain moment of his performance he halts; the black-shrouded *kurogo* obligingly conceals him from the spectators. And lo!—he is resurrected in a new make-up. And in a new wig. Now characterizing another stage (degree) of his emotional state.

Thus, for example, in the Kabuki play *Narukami*, the actor Sadanji must change from drunkenness to madness. This transition is solved by a mechanical cut. And a change in the arsenal of grease-paint colors on his face, emphasizing those streaks whose duty it is to fulfill the expression of a higher intensity than those used in his previous make-up.

This method is organic to the film. The forced introduction into the film, by European acting traditions, of pieces of "emotional transitions" is yet another influence forcing the cinema to mark time. Whereas the method of "cut" acting makes possible the construction of entirely new methods. Replacing one changing face with a whole scale of facial types of varying moods affords a far more acutely expressive result than does the changing surface, too receptive and devoid of organic resistance, of any single professional actor's face.

In our new film [*Old and New*] I have eliminated the intervals between the sharply contrasting polar stages of a face's expression. Thus is achieved a greater sharpness in the "play of doubts" around the new cream separator. Will the milk thicken or no? Trickery? Wealth? Here the psychological process of mingled faith and doubt is broken up into its two extreme states of joy (confidence) and gloom (disillusionment). Furthermore, this is sharply emphasized by light—illumination in no wise conforming to actual light conditions. This brings a distinct strengthening of the tension.

Another remarkable characteristic of the Kabuki theater is

the principle of "disintegrated" acting. Shocho, who played the leading female rôles in the Kabuki theater that visited Moscow, in depicting the dying daughter in *Yashaō* (*The Mask-Maker*), performed his rôle in pieces of acting completely detached from each other: Acting with only the right arm. Acting with one leg. Acting with the neck and head only. (The whole process of the death agony was disintegrated into solo performances of each member playing its own rôle: the rôle of the leg, the rôle of the arms, the rôle of the head.) A breaking-up into shots. With a gradual shortening of these separate, successive pieces of acting as the tragic end approached.

Freed from the yoke of primitive naturalism, the actor is enabled by this method to fully grip the spectator by "rhythms," making not only acceptable, but definitely attractive, a stage built on the most consecutive and detailed flesh and blood of naturalism.

Since we no longer distinguish in principle between questions of shot-content and montage, we may here cite a third example:

The Japanese theater makes use of a slow tempo to a degree unknown to our stage. The famous scene of hara-kiri in *Chushingura* is based on an unprecedented slowing down of all movement—beyond any point we have ever seen. Whereas, in the previous example, we observed a disintegration of the transitions between movements, here we see disintegration of the process of movement, viz., slow-motion. I have heard of only one example of a thorough application of this method, using the technical possibility of the film with a compositionally reasoned plan. It is usually employed with some purely pictorial aim, such as the "submarine kingdom" in *The Thief of Bagdad*, or to represent a dream, as in *Zvenigora*. Or, more often, it is used simply for formalist jackstraws and unmotivated camera mischief as in Vertov's *Man with the Movie-Camera*. The more commendable example appears to be in Jean Epstein's *La chute de la Maison Usher*—at least according to the press reports. In this film, normally acted emotions filmed with a speeded-up camera are said to give unusual emotional pressure by their unrealistic slowness on the screen. If it be borne in mind that the effect of an actor's performance on the audience is based on its identification by each spectator, it will be easy to relate both examples (the Kabuki play and the Epstein film) to an identical causal explanation. The intensity of perception increases as the didactic process of identification proceeds more easily along a disintegrated action.

Even instruction in handling a rifle can be hammered into the tightest motor-mentality among a group of raw recruits if the instructor uses a "break-down" method.

The most interesting link of the Japanese theater is, of course, its link with the sound film, which can and must learn its fundamentals from the Japanese—the reduction of visual and aural sensations to a common physiological denominator.*

So, it has been possible to establish (cursorily) the permeation of the most varied branches of Japanese culture by a pure cinematographic element—its basic nerve, montage.

And it is only the Japanese cinema that falls into the same error as the "leftward drifting" Kabuki. Instead of learning how to extract the principles and technique of their remarkable acting from the traditional feudal forms of their materials, the most progressive leaders of the Japanese theater throw their energies into an adaptation of the spongy shapelessness of our own "inner" naturalism. The results are tearful and saddening. In its cinema Japan similarly pursues imitations of the most revolting examples of American and European entries in the international commercial film race.

To understand and apply her cultural peculiarities to the cinema, this is the task of Japan! Colleagues of Japan, are you really going to leave this for us to do?

[1929]

* Discussed in the preceding essay.—EDITOR.

A DIALECTIC APPROACH TO FILM FORM

> In nature we never see anything isolated, but everything in connection with something else which is before it, beside it, under it, and over it.
>
> GOETHE [1]

> According to Marx and Engels the dialectic system is only the conscious reproduction of the dialectic course (substance) of the external events of the world.[2]

Thus:

The projection of the dialectic system of things
into the brain
into creating abstractly
into the process of thinking
yields: dialectic methods of thinking;
dialectic materialism—   PHILOSOPHY.

And also:

The projection of the same system of things
while creating concretely
while giving form
yields: ART.

The foundation for this philosophy is a *dynamic* concept of things:

Being—as a constant evolution from the interaction of two contradictory opposites.

Synthesis—arising from the opposition between thesis and antithesis.

45

A dynamic comprehension of things is also basic to the same degree, for a correct understanding of art and of all art-forms. In the realm of art this dialectic principle of dynamics is embodied in

CONFLICT

as the fundamental principle for the existence of every artwork and every art-form.

For art is always conflict:
(1) according to its social mission,
(2) according to its nature,
(3) according to its methodology.

According to its social mission *because:* It is art's task to make manifest the contradictions of Being. To form equitable views by stirring up contradictions within the spectator's mind, and to forge accurate intellectual concepts from the dynamic clash of opposing passions.

According to its nature *because:* Its nature is a conflict between natural existence and creative tendency. Between organic inertia and purposeful initiative. Hypertrophy of the purposive initiative—the principles of rational logic—ossifies art into mathematical technicalism. (A painted landscape becomes a topographical map, a painted Saint Sebastian becomes an anatomical chart.) Hypertrophy of organic naturalness— of organic logic—dilutes art into formlessness. (A Malevich becomes a Kaulbach, an Archipenko becomes a waxworks side-show.)

Because the limit of organic form (the passive principle of being) is *Nature*. The limit of rational form (the active principle of production) is *Industry*. At the intersection of Nature and Industry stands *Art*.

The logic of organic form *vs.* the logic of rational form yields, in collision,

the dialectic of the art-form.

The interaction of the two produces and determines Dynamism. (Not only in the sense of a space-time continuum, but also in the field of absolute thinking. I also regard the inception of new concepts and viewpoints in the conflict between customary conception and particular representation as dynamic—as a dynamization of the inertia of perception—as a dynamization of the "traditional view" into a new one.)

The quantity of interval determines the pressure of the tension. (See in music, for example, the concept of intervals. There can be cases where the distance of separation is so wide that it leads to a break—to a collapse of the homogeneous concept of art. For instance, the "inaudibility" of certain intervals.)

> *The spatial form of this dynamism is expression.*
> *The phases of its tension: rhythm.*

This is true for every art-form, and, indeed, for every kind of expression.

Similarly, human expression is a conflict between conditioned and unconditioned reflexes. (In this I cannot agree with Klages, who, *a*) does not consider human expression dynamically as a process, but statically as a result, and who, *b*) attributes everything in motion to the field of the "soul," and only the hindering element to "reason." [3] ["Reason" and "Soul" of the idealistic concept here correspond remotely with the ideas of conditioned and unconditioned reflexes.])

This is true in every field that can be understood as an art. For example, logical thought, considered as an art, shows the same dynamic mechanism:

. . . the intellectual lives of Plato or Dante or Spinoza or Newton were largely guided and sustained by their delight in the sheer beauty of the rhythmic relation between law and instance, species and individual, or cause and effect.[4]

This holds in other fields, as well, e.g., in speech, where all its sap, vitality, and dynamism arise from the irregularity of the part in relation to the laws of the system as a whole.

In contrast we can observe the sterility of expression in such artificial, totally regulated languages as Esperanto.

It is from this principle that the whole charm of poetry derives. Its rhythm arises as a conflict between the metric measure employed and the distribution of accents, over-riding this measure.

The concept of a formally static phenomenon as a dynamic function is dialectically imaged in the wise words of Goethe:

> *Die Baukunst ist eine ertarrte Musik.*
> (Architecture is frozen music.) [5]

Just as in the case of a homogeneous ideology (a monistic viewpoint), the whole, as well as the least detail, must be penetrated by a sole principle. So, ranged alongside the conflict of *social conditionality*, and the conflict of *existing nature*, the *methodology* of an art reveals this same principle of conflict. As the basic principle of the rhythm to be created and the inception of the art-form.

Art is always conflict, according to its methodology.

Here we shall consider the general problem of art in the specific example of its highest form—film.

Shot and montage are the basic elements of cinema.

Montage

has been established by the Soviet film as the nerve of cinema.

To determine the nature of montage is to solve the specific problem of cinema. The earliest conscious film-makers, and our first film theoreticians, regarded montage as a means of description by placing single shots one after the other like building-blocks. The movement within these building-block shots, and the consequent length of the component pieces, was then considered as rhythm.

A completely false concept!

This would mean the defining of a given object solely in relation to the nature of its external course. The mechanical process of splicing would be made a principle. We cannot describe such a relationship of lengths as rhythm. From this comes metric rather than rhythmic relationships, as opposed to one another as the mechanical-metric system of Mensendieck is to the organic-rhythmic school of Bode in matters of body exercise.

According to this definition, shared even by Pudovkin as a theoretician, montage is the means of *unrolling* an idea with the help of single shots: the "epic" principle.

In my opinion, however, montage is an idea that arises from the collision of independent shots—shots even opposite to one another: the "dramatic" principle.*

A sophism? Certainly not. For we are seeking a definition of the whole nature, the principal style and spirit of cinema from its technical (optical) basis.

We know that the phenomenon of movement in film resides in the fact that two motionless images of a moving body, following one another, blend into an appearance of motion by showing them sequentially at a required speed.

This popularized description of what happens as a *blending* has its share of responsibility for the popular miscomprehension of the nature of montage that we have quoted above.

Let us examine more exactly the course of the phenomenon we are discussing—how it really occurs—and draw our conclusion from this. Placed next to each other, two photographed immobile images result in the appearance of movement. Is this accurate? Pictorially—and phraseologically, yes.

But mechanically, it is not. For, in fact, each sequential element is perceived not *next* to the other, but on *top* of the other. For the idea (or sensation) of movement arises from the process of superimposing on the retained impression of the object's first position, a newly visible further position of the object. This is, by the way, the reason for the phenomenon of spatial depth, in the optical superimposition of two planes in stereoscopy. From the superimposition of two elements of the same dimension always arises a new, higher dimension. In the case of stereoscopy the superimposition of two nonidentical

* "Epic" and "dramatic" are used here in regard to methodology of form—not to *content* or *plot!*

two-dimensionalities results in stereoscopic three-dimensionality.

   In another field: a concrete word (a denotation) set beside
a concrete word yields an abstract concept—as in the Chinese
and Japanese languages,* where a material ideogram can indicate a transcendental (conceptual) result.

   The incongruence in contour of the first picture—already
impressed on the mind—with the subsequently perceived second picture engenders, in conflict, the feeling of motion. Degree of incongruence determines intensity of impression, and
determines that tension which becomes the real element of authentic rhythm.

   Here we have, temporally, what we see arising spatially on a
graphic or painted plane.

   What comprises the dynamic effect of a painting? The eye
follows the direction of an element in the painting. It retains
a visual impression, which then collides with the impression
derived from following the direction of a second element. The
conflict of these directions forms the dynamic effect in appre-
hending the whole.

   I. It may be purely linear: Fernand Léger, or Suprematism.

   II. It may be "anecdotal." The secret of the marvelous mobil-
ity of Daumier's and Lautrec's figures dwells in the fact that
the various anatomical parts of a body are represented in spatial circumstances (positions) that are temporally various, disjunctive. For example, in Toulouse-Lautrec's lithograph of
Miss Cissy Loftus, if one logically develops position A of the
foot, one builds a body in position A corresponding to it.
But the body is represented from knee up already in position
A + a. The cinematic effect of joined motionless pictures is
already established here! From hips to shoulders we can see
A + a + a. The figure comes alive and kicking!

   III. Between I and II lies primitive Italian futurism—such as
in Balla's "Man with Six Legs in Six Positions"—for II obtains

   * See discussion in preceding essay.

its effect by retaining natural unity and anatomical correctness, while I, on the other hand, does this with purely elementary elements. III, although destroying naturalness, has not yet pressed forward to abstraction.

IV. The conflict of directions may also be of an ideographic kind. It was in this way that we have gained the pregnant characterizations of a Sharaku, for example. The secret of his extremely perfected strength of expression lies in the anatomical and *spatial disproportion* of the parts—in comparison with which, our I might be termed *temporal disproportion.*

Generally termed "irregularity," this *spatial disproportion* has been a constant attraction and instrument for artists. In writing of Rodin's drawings, Camille Mauclair indicated one explanation for this search:

The greatest artists, Michelangelo, Rembrandt, Delacroix, all, at a certain moment of the upthrusting of their genius, threw aside, as it were, the ballast of exactitude as conceived by our simplifying reason and our ordinary eyes, in order to attain the fixation of ideas, the synthesis, the *pictorial handwriting* of their dreams.[6]

Two experimental artists of the nineteenth century—a painter and a poet—attempted esthetic formulations of this "irregularity." Renoir advanced this thesis:

Beauty of every description finds its charm in variety. Nature abhors both vacuum and regularity. For the same reason, no work of art can really be called such if it has not been created by an artist who believes in irregularity and rejects any set form. Regularity, order, desire for perfection (which is always a false perfection) destroy art. The only possibility of maintaining taste in art is to impress on artists and the public the importance of irregularity. Irregularity is the basis of all art.[7]

And Baudelaire wrote in his journal:

That which is not slightly distorted lacks sensible appeal; from which it follows that irregularity—that is to say, the unexpected, surprise and astonishment, are an essential part and characteristic of beauty.[8]

Upon closer examination of the particular beauty of irregularity as employed in painting, whether by Grünewald or by Renoir, it will be seen that it is a disproportion in the relation of a detail in one dimension to another detail in a different dimension.

The spatial development of the relative size of one detail in correspondence with another, and the consequent collision between the proportions designed by the artist for that purpose, result in a characterization—a definition of the represented matter.

Finally, color. Any shade of a color imparts to our vision a given rhythm of vibration. This is not said figuratively, but purely physiologically, for colors are distinguished from one another by their number of light vibrations.

The adjacent shade or tone of color is in another rate of vibration. The counterpoint (conflict) of the two—the retained rate of vibration against the newly perceived one—yields the dynamism of our apprehension of the interplay of color.

Hence, with only one step from visual vibrations to acoustic vibrations, we find ourselves in the field of music. From the domain of the spatial-pictorial—to the domain of the temporal-pictorial—where the same law rules. For counterpoint is to music not only a form of composition, but is altogether the basic factor for the possibility of tone perception and tone differentiation.

It may almost be said that in every case we have cited we have seen in operation the same *Principle of Comparison* that makes possible for us perception and definition in every field.

In the moving image (cinema) we have, so to speak, a synthesis of two counterpoints—the spatial counterpoint of graphic art, and the temporal counterpoint of music.

Within cinema, and characterizing it, occurs what may be described as:

visual counterpoint

In applying this concept to the film, we gain several leads to the problem of film grammar. As well as a *syntax* of film

1. GRAPHIC CONFLICT

2. CONFLICT OF PLANES

3. CONFLICT OF VOLUMES

4. SPATIAL CONFLICT

5.

STATIC ➤ CONFLICT ≡ DYNAMIC ◄ CAMERA

7.

6.

[from *October*]

[from *Potemkin*]

ARTIFICALLY PRODUCED IMAGES OF MOTION

a. Logical

8.

9.

ARTIFICIALLY PRODUCED IMAGES OF MOTION
b. Illogical

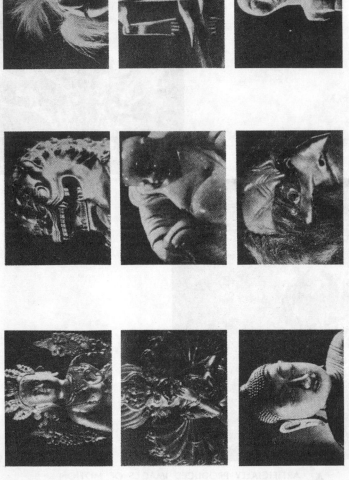

manifestations, in which visual counterpoint may determine a whole new system of forms of manifestation. (Experiments in this direction are illustrated in the preceding pages by fragments from my films.)

For all this, the *basic premise* is:

The shot is by no means an element of montage.
The shot is a montage cell (or molecule).

In this formulation the dualistic division of

Sub-title and shot
and
Shot and montage

leaps forward in analysis to a dialectic consideration as three different phases of one homogeneous task of expression, its homogeneous characteristics determining the homogeneity of their structural laws.

Inter-relation of the three phases:

Conflict within a thesis (an abstract idea)—*formulates* itself in the dialectics of the sub-title—*forms* itself spatially in the conflict within the shot—and *explodes* with increasing intensity in montage-conflict among the separate shots.

This is fully analogous to human, psychological expression. This is a conflict of motives, which can also be comprehended in three phases:

1. Purely verbal utterance. Without intonation—expression in speech.

2. Gesticulatory (mimic-intonational) expression. Projection of the conflict onto the whole expressive bodily system of man. Gesture of bodily movement and gesture of intonation.

3. Projection of the conflict into space. With an intensification of motives, the zigzag of mimic expression is propelled into the surrounding space following the same formula of distortion. A zigzag of expression arising from the spatial division caused by man moving in space. *Mise-en-scène.*

This gives us the basis for an entirely new understanding of the problem of film form.

We can list, as examples of types of conflicts within the form—characteristic for the conflict within the shot, as well as for the conflict between colliding shots, or, montage:

1. Graphic conflict (see Figure 1).
2. Conflict of planes (see Figure 2).
3. Conflict of volumes (see Figure 3).
4. Spatial conflict (see Figure 4).
5. Light conflict.
6. Tempo conflict, and so on.*

Nota bene: This list is of principal features, of *dominants*. It is naturally understood that they occur chiefly as complexes.

For a transition to montage, it will be sufficient to divide any example into two independent primary pieces, as in the case of graphic conflict, although all other cases can be similarly divided:

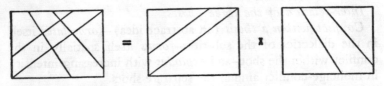

Some further examples:

7. Conflict between matter and viewpoint (achieved by spatial distortion through camera-angle) (see Figure 5).
8. Conflict between matter and its spatial nature (achieved by *optical distortion* by the lens).
9. Conflict between an event and its temporal nature (achieved by *slow-motion* and *stop-motion*)
  and finally
10. Conflict between the whole *optical* complex and a quite different sphere.

Thus does conflict between optical and acoustical experience produce:

sound-film,

* Further details on this film grammar of conflicts are given in the preceding essay, pp. 39-40.—EDITOR.

which is capable of being realized as

audio-visual counterpoint.

Formulation and investigation of the phenomenon of cinema as forms of conflict yield the first possibility of devising a homogeneous system of *visual dramaturgy* for all general and particular cases of the film problem.

Of devising a *dramaturgy of the visual film-form* as regulated and precise as the existing *dramaturgy of the film-story*.

From this viewpoint on the film medium, the following forms and potentialities of style may be summed up as a film syntax, or it may be more exact to describe the following as:

a tentative film-syntax.

We shall list here a number of potentialities of dialectical development to be derived from this proposition: The concept of the moving (time-consuming) image arises from the superimposition—or counterpoint—of two differing immobile images.

I. Each *moving fragment of montage.* Each photographed piece. Technical definition of the phenomenon of movement. *No composition as yet.* (A running man. A rifle fired. A splash of water.)

II. *An artificially produced image of motion.* The basic optical element is used for deliberate compositions:

A. *Logical*

Example 1 (from *October*): a montage rendition of a machine-gun being fired, by cross-cutting details of the firing.

Combination A: a brightly lit machine-gun. A different shot in a low key. Double burst: graphic burst + light burst. Close-up of machine-gunner.

Combination B (see Figure 6): Effect almost of double exposure achieved by *clatter* montage effect. Length of montage pieces—two frames each.

Example 2 (from *Potemkin*): an illustration of instantaneous action. Woman with pince-nez. Followed immediately—without transition—by the same woman with shattered pince-nez and bleeding eye: impression of a shot hitting the eye (see Figure 7).

B. *Illogical*

Example 3 (from *Potemkin*): the same device used for pictorial symbolism. In the thunder of the *Potemkin's* guns, a marble lion leaps up, in protest against the bloodshed on the Odessa steps (see Figure 8). Composed of three shots of three stationary marble lions at the Alupka Palace in the Crimea: a sleeping lion, an awakening lion, a rising lion. The effect is achieved by a correct calculation of the length of the second shot. Its superimposition on the first shot produces the first action. This establishes time to impress the second position on the mind. Superimposition of the third position on the second produces the second action: the lion finally rises.

Example 4 (from *October*): Example 1 showed how the firing was manufactured symbolically from elements outside the process of firing itself. In illustrating the monarchist *putsch* attempted by General Kornilov, it occurred to me that his militarist *tendency* could be shown in a montage that would employ religious details for its material. For Kornilov had revealed his intention in the guise of a peculiar "Crusade" of Moslems (!), his Caucasian "Wild Division," together with some Christians, against the Bolsheviki. So we intercut shots of a Baroque Christ (apparently exploding in the radiant beams of his halo) with shots of an egg-shaped mask of Uzume, Goddess of Mirth, completely self-contained. The temporal conflict between the closed egg-form and the graphic star-form produced the effect of an instantaneous *burst*—of a bomb, or shrapnel (see Figure 9).* (Figure 10, showing the opportunity for tendentious—or ideological—expressiveness of such materials, will be discussed below.)

Thus far the examples have shown *primitive-physiological*

---

* Examples of more primitive effects belong here also, such as simple cross-cutting of church spires, angled in mutual opposition.

cases—employing superimposition of optical motion *exclusively*.

III. *Emotional* combinations, not only with the visible elements of the shots, but chiefly with chains of psychological associations. *Association montage.* As a means for pointing up a situation emotionally.

In Example 1, we had two successive shots A and B, identical in subject. However, they were not identical in respect to the position of the subject within the frame:

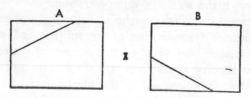

producing *dynamization in space*—an impression of spatial dynamics:

The degree of difference between the positions A and B determines the tension of the movement.

For a new case, let us suppose that the subjects of Shots A and B are not *identical*. Although the associations of the two shots are identical, that is, associatively identical.

This *dynamization of the subject*, not in the field of space but of psychology, i.e., *emotion*, thus produces:

emotional dynamization.

Example 1 (in *Strike*): the montage of the killing of the workers is actually a cross montage of this carnage with the butchering of a bull in an abattoir. Though the subjects are different, "butchering" is the associative link. This made for a powerful emotional intensification of the scene. As a matter of fact, homogeneity of gesture plays an important part in this case in achieving the effect—both the movement of the dynamic gesture within the frame, and the static gesture dividing the frame graphically.*

This is a principle subsequently used by Pudovkin in *The End of St. Petersburg*, in his powerful sequence intercutting shots of stock exchange and battlefield. His previous film, *Mother*, had a similar sequence: the ice-break on the river, paralleled with the workers' demonstration.

Such a means may decay pathologically if the essential viewpoint—emotional dynamization of the subject—is lost. As soon as the film-maker loses sight of this essence the means ossifies into lifeless literary symbolism and stylistic mannerism. Two examples of such hollow use of this means occur to me:

Example 2 (in *October*): the sugary chants of compromise by the Mensheviki at the Second Congress of Soviets— during the storming of the Winter Palace—are intercut with hands playing harps. This was a purely literary parallelism that by no means dynamized the subject matter. Similarly in Otzep's *Living Corpse*, church spires (in imitation of those in *October*) and lyrical landscapes are intercut with the courtroom speeches of the prosecutor and defense lawyer. This error was the same as in the "harp" sequence.

On the other hand, a majority of *purely dynamic* effects can produce positive results:

Example 3 (in *October*): the dramatic moment of the union of the Motorcycle Battalion with the Congress of Soviets was dynamized by shots of abstractly spinning bicycle wheels, in association with the entrance of the new delegates. In this way the large-scale emotional content of the event was transformed into actual dynamics.

This same principle—giving birth to concepts, to emotions, by juxtaposing two disparate events—led to:

IV. *Liberation of the whole action from the definition of time and space.* My first attempts at this were in *October*.

* The montage list of this sequence from *Strike* is given in Appendix 3 of *The Film Sense*.—EDITOR.

Example 1: a trench crowded with soldiers appears to be crushed by an enormous gun-base that comes down inexorably. As an anti-militarist symbol seen from the viewpoint of subject alone, the effect is achieved by an apparent bringing together of an independently existing trench and an overwhelming military product, just as physically independent.

Example 2: in the scene of Kornilov's *putsch*, which puts an end to Kerensky's Bonapartist dreams. Here one of Kornilov's tanks climbs up and crushes a plaster-of-Paris Napoleon standing on Kerensky's desk in the Winter Palace, a juxtaposition of purely symbolic significance.

This method has now been used by Dovzhenko in *Arsenal* to shape whole sequences, as well as by Esther Schub in her use of library footage in *The Russia of Nikolai II and Lev Tolstoy*.

I wish to offer another example of this method, to upset the traditional ways of handling plot—although it has not yet been put into practice.

In 1924-1925 I was mulling over the idea of a filmic portrait of *actual* man. At that time, there prevailed a tendency to show actual man in films only in *long* uncut dramatic scenes. It was believed that cutting (montage) would destroy the idea of actual man. Abram Room established something of a record in this respect when he used in *The Death Ship* uncut dramatic shots as long as 40 meters or 135 feet. I considered (and still do) such a concept to be utterly unfilmic.

Very well—what would be a linguistically accurate characterization of a man?

> His raven-black hair . . .
> The waves of his hair . . .
> His eyes radiating azure beams . . .
> His steely muscles . . .

Even in a less exaggerated description, any verbal account of a person is bound to find itself employing an assortment of waterfalls, lightning-rods, landscapes, birds, etc.

Now why should the cinema follow the forms of theater and painting rather than the methodology of language, which allows wholly new concepts of ideas to arise from the combination of two concrete denotations of two concrete objects? Language is much closer to film than painting is. For example, in painting the form arises from *abstract* elements of line and color, while in cinema the material *concreteness* of the image within the frame presents—as an element—the greatest difficulty in manipulation. So why not rather lean towards the system of language, which is forced to use the same mechanics in inventing words and word-complexes?

On the other hand, why is it that montage cannot be dispensed with in orthodox films?

The differentiation in montage-pieces lies in their lack of existence as single units. Each piece can evoke no more than a certain association. The accumulation of such associations can achieve the same effect as is provided for the spectator by purely physiological means in the plot of a realistically produced play.

For instance, murder on the stage has a purely physiological effect. Photographed in *one* montage-piece, it can function simply as *information*, as a sub-title. *Emotional* effect begins only with the reconstruction of the event in montage fragments, each of which will summon a certain association—the sum of which will be an all-embracing complex of emotional feeling. Traditionally:

1. A hand lifts a knife.
2. The eyes of the victim open suddenly.
3. His hands clutch the table.
4. The knife is jerked up.
5. The eyes blink involuntarily.
6. Blood gushes.
7. A mouth shrieks.
8. Something drips onto a shoe . . .

and similar film clichés. Nevertheless, in regard to the *action as a whole, each fragment-piece* is almost *abstract.* The more differentiated they are the more abstract they become, provoking no more than a certain association.

Quite logically the thought occurs: could not the same thing be accomplished more productively by not following the plot so slavishly, but by materializing the idea, the impression, of *Murder* through a free accumulation of associative matter? For the most important task is still to establish the idea of murder—the feeling of murder, as such. The plot is no more than a device without which one isn't yet capable of telling something to the spectator! In any case, effort in this direction would certainly produce the most interesting variety of forms.

Someone should try, at least! Since this thought occurred to me, I have not had time to make this experiment. And today I am more concerned with quite different problems. But, returning to the main line of our syntax, something there may bring us closer to these tasks.

While, with I, II, and III, tension was calculated for purely physiological effect—from the purely optical to the emotional, we must mention here also the case of the same conflict-tension serving the ends of new concepts—of new attitudes, that is, of purely intellectual aims.

Example 1 (in *October*): Kerensky's rise to power and dictatorship after the July uprising of 1917. A comic effect was gained by sub-titles indicating regular ascending ranks (*"Dictator"—"Generalissimo"—"Minister of Navy—and of Army"*—etc.) climbing higher and higher—cut into five or six shots of Kerensky, climbing the stairs of the Winter Palace, all with exactly the *same* pace. Here a conflict between the flummery of the ascending ranks and the "hero's" trotting up the same unchanging flight of stairs yields an intellectual result: Kerensky's essential nonentity is shown satirically. We have the counterpoint of a literally expressed conventional idea with the *pictured* action of a particular person who is unequal to his swiftly increasing duties. The incongruence of these two factors results in the spectator's purely *intellectual* decision at the expense of this particular person. Intellectual dynamization.

Example 2 (in *October*): Kornilov's march on Petrograd was under the banner of "In the Name of God and Country." Here we attempted to reveal the religious significance of this episode in a rationalistic way. A number of religious images, from a magnificent Baroque Christ to an Eskimo idol, were cut together. The conflict in this case was between the concept and the symbolization of God. While idea and image appear to accord completely in the first statue shown, the two elements move further from each other with each successive image (see Figure 10). Maintaining the denotation of "God," the images increasingly disagree with our concept of God, inevitably leading to individual conclusions about the true nature of all deities. In this case, too, a chain of images attempted to achieve a purely intellectual resolution, resulting from a conflict between a preconception and a *gradual discrediting of it in purposeful steps*.

Step by step, by a process of comparing each new image with the common denotation, power is accumulated behind a process that can be formally identified with that of logical deduction. The decision to release these ideas, as well as the method used, is already *intellectually* conceived.

The conventional *descriptive* form for film leads to the formal possibility of a kind of filmic reasoning. While the conventional film directs the *emotions*, this suggests an opportunity to encourage and direct the whole *thought process*, as well.

These two particular sequences of experiment were very much opposed by the majority of critics. Because they were understood as purely political. I would not attempt to deny that *this form is most suitable for the expression of ideologically pointed theses*, but it is a pity that the critics completely overlooked the purely filmic potentialities of this approach.

In these two experiments we have taken the first embryonic step towards a totally new form of film expression. Towards a purely intellectual film, freed from traditional limitations, achieving direct forms for ideas, systems, and concepts, without any need for transitions and paraphrases. We may yet have a

synthesis of art and science.

This would be the proper name for our new epoch in the field of art. This would be the final justification for Lenin's words, that "the cinema is the most important of all the arts."

Moscow, April 1929

THE FILMIC FOURTH DIMENSION

EXACTLY a year ago, on August 19, 1928, before the montage of *Old and New* had been begun, I wrote, in connection with the visit to Moscow of the Kabuki theater:

In the Kabuki . . . a single monistic sensation of theatrical "provocation" takes place. The Japanese regards each theatrical element, not as an incommensurable unit among the various categories of affect (on the various sense-organs), but as a single unit of *theatre*. . . . Directing himself to the various organs of sensation, he builds his summation [of individual "pieces"] to a grand *total* provocation of the human brain, without taking any notice *which* of these several paths he is following.

My characterization of the Kabuki theater proved prophetic. This method became the basis for the montage of *Old and New*.

Orthodox montage is montage *on the dominant*. I.e., the combination of shots according to their dominating indications. Montage according to tempo. Montage according to the chief tendency within the frame. Montage according to the length (continuance) of the shots, and so on. This is montage according to the foreground.

The dominating indications of two shots side by side produces one or another conflicting interrelation, resulting in one or another expressive effect (I am speaking here of a *purely montage* effect).

This circumstance embraces all intensity levels of montage juxtaposition—all *impulses*:

From a complete opposition of the dominants, i.e., a sharply contrasting construction, to a scarcely noticeable "modulation"

64

from shot to shot; *all* cases of conflict must therefore include cases of a complete *absence* of conflict.

As for the dominant itself, to regard it as something independent, absolute and invariably stable is out of the question. There are technical means of treating the shot so that its dominant may be made more or less specific, but in no case absolute.

The characteristics of the dominant are variable and profoundly relative. A revelation of its characteristics depends on that combination of shots which itself depends on the dominant!

A circle? An equation of two unknown quantities? A dog chasing its tail? No, this is simply an exact definition of a film law. A fact.

If we have even a *sequence* of montage pieces:

> A gray old man,
> A gray old woman,
> A white horse,
> A snow-covered roof,

we are still far from certain whether this sequence is working towards a dominating indication of "old age" or of "whiteness."

Such a sequence of shots might proceed for some time before we finally discover that guiding-shot which immediately "christens" the *whole* sequence in one "direction" or another. That is why it is advisable to place this identifying shot as near as possible to the beginning of the sequence (in an "orthodox" construction). Sometimes it even becomes necessary to do this with—a sub-title.

These considerations completely exclude a non-dialectic statement of the question concerning the *single-meaningness* of a frame within itself. The film-frame can never be an inflexible *letter of the alphabet*, but must always remain a multiple-meaning *ideogram*. And it can be read only in juxtaposition, just as an ideogram acquires its specific *significance, meaning,* and even *pronunciation* (occasionally in diametric opposition to one another) only when combined with a separately indicated reading or tiny meaning—an indicator for the exact reading—placed alongside the basic hieroglyph.

In distinction from orthodox montage according to *particular dominants*, *Old and New* was edited differently. In place of an "aristocracy" of individualistic dominants we brought a method of "democratic" equality of rights for all provocations, or stimuli, regarding them as a summary, as a complex.

The point is that the dominant (with all these recognized limitations on its relativity) appears to be, although the most powerful, far from the only stimulus of the shot. For example: the sex appeal of a beautiful American heroine-star is attended by many stimuli: of texture—from the material of her gown; of light—from the balanced and emphatic lighting of her figure; of racial-national (positive for an American audience: "a native American type," or negative: "colonizer-oppressor"— for a Negro or Chinese audience); of social-class, etc. (all brought together in an iron-bound unity of its reflex-physiological essence). In a word, the *central* stimulus (let it be, for instance, sexual as in our example) is attended always by a *whole complex* of secondary, or the physiological process of a highly nervous activity.

What takes place in acoustics, and particularly in the case of instrumental music, fully corresponds with this.

There, along with the vibration of a basic dominant tone, comes a whole series of similar vibrations, which are called *overtones* and *undertones*. Their impacts against each other, their impacts with the basic tone, and so on, envelop the basic tone in a whole host of secondary vibrations. If in acoustics these collateral vibrations become merely "disturbing" elements, these same vibrations in music—in composition, become one of the most significant means for affect by the experimental composers of our century, such as Debussy and Scriabin.

We find the same thing in optics, as well. All sorts of aberrations, distortions, and other defects, which can be remedied by systems of lenses, can also be taken into account compositionally, providing a whole series of definite compositional effects (employing lens-openings from 28 to 310).

In combinations which exploit *these collateral vibrations*—which is nothing less than *the filmed material itself*—we can achieve, completely analogous with music, *the visual overtonal complex of the shot.*

The montage of *Old and New* is constructed with this method. This montage is built, not on *particular* dominants, but takes as its guide the total stimulation through all stimuli. That is the original montage complex within the shot, arising from the collision and combination of the individual stimuli inherent in it.

These stimuli are heterogeneous as regards their "external natures," but their reflex-physiological essence binds them together in an iron unity. Physiological in so far as they are "psychic" in perception, this is merely the physiological process of a *higher nervous activity.*

In this way, behind the general indication of the shot, the physiological summary of its vibrations as a *whole*, as a complex unity of the manifestations of all its stimuli, is present. This is the peculiar *"feeling" of the shot*, produced by the shot as a whole.

This makes the shot as a montage-piece comparable to the separate scenes within the Kabuki method. The basic indication of the shot can be taken as the final summary of its effect on the cortex of the brain as a whole, irrespective of the paths by which the accumulated stimuli have been brought together. Thus the quality of the *totals* can be placed side by side in any conflicting combination, thereby revealing entirely new possibilities of montage solutions.

As we have seen, in the power of the very genetics of these methods, they must be attended by an extraordinary *physiological* quality. As in that music which builds its works on a two-fold use of overtones. Not the *classicism* of Beethoven, but the *physiological quality* of Debussy and Scriabin.

The extraordinary physiological quality in the affect of *Old and New* has been remarked by many of its spectators.

The explanation for this is that *Old and New* is *the first film edited on the principle of the visual overtone*. This method of montage can be interestingly verified.

If in the gleaming classical distances of the cinematography of the future, overtonal montage will certainly be used, simultaneously with montage according to the dominant indication, so as always at first—the new method will assert itself in a question sharpened in principle. Overtonal montage in its first steps has had to take a line in sharp *opposition* to the dominant.

There are many instances, it is true—and in *Old and New*, too—where "synthetic" combinations of tonal and overtonal montage may already be found. For example, in *Old and New*, the climax of the religious procession (to pray for relief from the drought), and the sequence of the grasshopper and the mowing-machine, are edited *visually* according to *sound* associations, with an express development which exists already in their spatial "similarity."

Of particular methodological interest, of course, are constructions that are wholly *a-dominant*. In these the dominant appears in the form of a purely *physiological formulation of the task*. For example, the montage of the beginning of the religious procession is according to "degrees of heat saturation" in the individual shots, or the beginning of the state-farm sequence is according to a line of "carnivorousness." Conditions outside cinematographic discipline provide the most unexpected physiological indications among materials that are logically (both formally and naturally) absolutely neutral in their relations to each other.

There are innumerable cases of montage joinings in this film that make open mockery of orthodox, scholastic montage according to the dominant. The easiest way to demonstrate this is to examine the film on the cutting table. Only then can one see clearly the perfectly "impossible" montage joinings in which *Old and New* abounds. This will also demonstrate the extreme simplicity of its metrics, of its "dimensions."

Entire large sections of certain sequences are made up of

pieces perfectly uniform in length or of absolutely primitively repeated short pieces. The whole intricate, rhythmic, and *sensual* nuance scheme of the combined pieces is conducted almost exclusively according to a line of work on the "psycho-physiological" vibrations of each piece.

It was on the cutting table that I detected the sharply defined scope of the particular montage of *Old and New*. This was when the film had to be condensed and shortened. The "creative ecstasy" attending the assembly and montage—the "creative ecstasy" of "hearing and feeling" the shots—all this was already in the past. Abbreviations and cuts require no inspiration, only technique and skill.

And there, examining the sequence of the religious procession on the table, I could not fit the combination of its pieces into any one of the orthodox categories, within which one can apply one's pure experience. On the table, deprived of motion, the reasons for their choice seem completely incomprehensible. The criteria for their assembly appear to be outside formally normal cinematographic criteria.

And here is observed one further curious parallel between the visual and the musical overtone: It cannot be traced in the static frame, just as it cannot be traced in the musical score. Both emerge as genuine values only in the dynamics of the musical or cinematographic *process*.

Overtonal conflicts, foreseen but unwritten in the score, cannot emerge without the dialectic process of the passage of the film through the projection apparatus, or that of the performance by a symphony orchestra.

The visual overtone is proved to be an actual piece, an actual element of —a fourth dimension!

In three-dimensional space, spatially inexpressible, and only emerging and existing in the fourth dimension (time added to the three dimensions).

The fourth dimension?! Einstein? Or mysticism? Or a joke?

It's time to stop being frightened of this new knowledge of a fourth dimension. Einstein himself assures us:

The non-mathematician is seized by a mysterious shuddering when he hears of "four-dimensional" things, by a feeling not unlike that awakened by thoughts of the occult. And yet there is no more common-place statement than that the world in which we live is a four-dimensional space-time continuum.[1]

Possessing such an excellent instrument of perception as the cinema—even on its primitive level—for the sensation of movement, we should soon learn a concrete orientation in this four-dimensional space-time continuum, and feel as much at home in it as in our own house-slippers. And we'll soon be posing the question of a fifth dimension!

Overtonal montage is revealed as a new category among the other montage processes known up till now. The *applied* significance of this method is immediately immense. And that is why this article appears in a number devoted to the sound film! *

In the article cited at the beginning, pointing to the "unexpected junction"—a similarity between the Kabuki theater and the sound film, I wrote on the contrapuntal method of combining the visual and aural images:

To possess this method one must develop in oneself a new sense: the capacity of reducing visual and aural perceptions to a "common denominator."

And yet we *cannot reduce aural* and *visual* perceptions to a common denominator. They are values of different dimensions. But the visual overtone and the sound overtone are values of a *singly measured* substance. Because, if the frame is a *visual perception*, and the tone is an aural perception, *visual as well as aural overtones are a totally physiological sensation*. And, consequently, they are *of one and the same kind*, outside the sound or aural categories that serve as guides, conductors to its achievement.

* This issue of the newspaper *Kino* for August 27, 1929, was chiefly devoted to the reports and speeches at the All-Union Conference on the Sound Film, held earlier in the month.

For the musical overtone (a throb) it is not strictly fitting to say: "I hear."

Nor for the visual overtone: "I see."

For both, a new uniform formula must enter our vocabulary: "I feel."

The theory and methodology of the overtone have been cultivated and made familiar by, among others, Debussy and Scriabin. *Old and New* introduces a concept of the *visual overtone*. And from the contrapuntal conflict between the visual and aural *overtones* will be born the composition of the Soviet sound film.

[1929]

METHODS OF MONTAGE

> In every art and every discovery, experience
> has always preceded precepts. In the course
> of time, a method has been assigned to the
> practice of the invention.
>
> GOLDONI [1]

IS THE method of overtonal montage unrelated to our previous experience, artificially grafted onto cinematography, or is it simply a quantitative accumulation of one attribute that makes a dialectic leap and begins to function as a new qualitative attribute?

In other words, is overtonal montage a dialectical stage of development within the development of the whole montage system of methods, standing in a successive relation to other forms of montage?

These are the formal categories of montage that we know:

1. *Metric Montage*

The fundamental criterion for this construction is the *absolute lengths* of the pieces. The pieces are joined together according to their lengths, in a formula-scheme corresponding to a measure of music. Realization is in the repetition of these "measures."

Tension is obtained by the effect of mechanical acceleration by shortening the pieces while preserving the original proportions of the formula. Primitive of the method: three-quarter-time, march-time, waltz-time ($\frac{3}{4}$, $\frac{2}{4}$, $\frac{1}{4}$, etc.), used by Kuleshov; degeneration of the method: metric montage using a measure of complicated irregularity ($\frac{16}{17}$, $\frac{22}{57}$, etc.).

Such a measure ceases to have a physiological effect, for it is contrary to the "law of simple numbers" (relationships).

Simple relationships, giving a clarity of impression, are for this reason necessary for maximum effectiveness. They are therefore found in healthy classics of every field: architecture; the color in a painting; a complex composition by Scriabin (always crystal clear in the relations between its parts); geometrical *mises-en-scène;* precise state planning, etc.

A similar example may be found in Vertov's *Eleventh Year,* where the metric beat is mathematically so complex that it is only "with a ruler" that one can discover the proportional law that governs it. Not by *impression* as perceived, but by *measurement.*

I do not mean to imply that the beat should be recognizable as part of the perceived impression. On the contrary. Though unrecognized, it is nevertheless indispensable for the "organization" of the sensual impression. Its clarity can bring into unison the "pulsing" of the film and the "pulsing" of the audience. Without such a unison (obtainable by many means) there can be no contact between the two.

Over-complexity of the metric beat produces a chaos of impressions, instead of a distinct emotional tension.

A third use of metric montage lies between its two extremes of simplicity and complexity: alternating two varying piece-lengths according to two kinds of content within the pieces. Examples: the sequence of the *lezginka* in *October* and the patriotic demonstration in *The End of St. Petersburg.* (The latter example can be considered as classic in the field of *purely metric* montage.)

In this type of metric montage the content within the frame of the piece is subordinated to the absolute length of the piece. Therefore, only the broadly dominant content-character of the piece is regarded; these would be "synonymous" shots.

2. *Rhythmic Montage*

Here, in determining the lengths of the pieces, the content within the frame is a factor possessing equal rights to consideration.

Abstract determination of the piece-lengths gives way to a flexible relationship of the *actual* lengths.

Here the actual length does not coincide with the mathematically determined length of the piece according to a metric formula. Here its practical length derives from the specifics of the piece, and from its planned length according to the structure of the sequence.

It is quite possible here to find cases of complete metric *identity* of the pieces and their rhythmic measures, obtained through a combination of the pieces according to their content.

Formal tension by acceleration is obtained here by shortening the pieces not only in accordance with the fundamental plan, but also by violating this plan. The most affective violation is by the introduction of material more intense in an easily distinguished tempo.

The "Odessa steps" sequence in *Potemkin* is a clear example of this. In this the rhythmic drum of the soldiers' feet as they descend the steps violates all *metrical* demands. Unsynchronized with the beat of the cutting, this drumming comes in *off-beat* each time, and the shot itself is entirely different in its solution with each of these appearances. The final pull of tension is supplied by the transfer from the rhythm of the descending feet to another rhythm—a new kind of downward movement—the next intensity level of the same activity—the baby-carriage rolling down the steps. The carriage functions as a directly progressing accelerator of the advancing feet. The stepping descent passes into a rolling descent.

Contrast this with the above example from *The End of St. Petersburg*, where intensity is gained by cutting *each and every piece* to its required minimum within the single metric measure.

Such metrical montage is perfectly suitable for similarly simple march-time solutions. But it is inadequate for more complex rhythmic needs.

When it is forcibly applied to such a problem, we find montage failure. This explains such an unsuccessful sequence as that of the religious mask dance in *Storm Over Asia*. Executed on the basis of a complex metrical beat, unadjusted to the specific content of the pieces, this neither reproduces the rhythm of the original ceremony nor organizes a cinematically affective rhythm.

In most cases of this sort, nothing more than perplexity is excited in the specialist, and nothing more than a confused impression is aroused in the lay spectator. (Although an artificial crutch of musical accompaniment may give some support to such a shaky sequence—as it did in the cited example—the basic weakness is still present.)

3. Tonal Montage

This term is employed for the first time. It expresses a stage beyond rhythmic montage.

In rhythmic montage it is movement within the frame that impels the montage movement from frame to frame. Such movements within the frame may be of objects in motion, or of the spectator's eye directed along the lines of some immobile object.

In tonal montage, movement is perceived in a wider sense. The concept of movement embraces *all affects* of the montage piece. Here montage is based on the characteristic *emotional sound* of the piece—of its dominant. The general *tone* of the piece.

I do not mean to say that the emotional sound of the piece is to be measured "impressionistically." The piece's characteristics in this respect can be measured with as much exactitude as in the most elementary case of "by the ruler" measurement in metrical montage. But the units of measurement differ. And the amounts to be measured are different.

For example, the degree of light vibration in a piece cannot only be gauged by a selenium light-element, but every gradation of this vibration is perceptible to the naked eye. If we give the comparative and emotional designation of "more gloomy" to a piece, we can also find for the piece a mathematical co-efficient for its degree of illumination. This is a case of "light tonality." Or, if the piece is described as having a "shrill sound," it is possible to find, behind this description, the many acutely angled elements within the frame, in comparison with other shape-elements. This is a case of "graphic tonality."

Working with combinations of varying degrees of soft-focus or varying degrees of "shrillness" would be a typical use of tonal montage.

As I have said, this would be based on the *dominant* emotional sound of the pieces. An example: the "fog sequence" in *Potemkin* (preceding the mass mourning over the body of Vakulinchuk). Here the montage was based exclusively on the emotional "sound" of the pieces—on rhythmic vibrations that do not affect spatial alterations. In this example it is interesting that, alongside the basic tonal dominant, a secondary, accessory *rhythmic* dominant is also operating. This links the tonal construction of the scene with the tradition of rhythmic montage, the furthest development of which is tonal montage. And, like rhythmic montage, this is also a special variation of metric montage.

This secondary dominant is expressed in barely perceptible changing movements: the agitation of the water; the slight rocking of the anchored vessels and buoys; the slowly ascending vapor; the sea-gulls settling gently onto the water.

Strictly speaking, these too are elements of a *tonal* order. These are movements that move according to tonal rather than to spatial-rhythmic characteristics. Here spatially immeasurable changes are combined according to their emotional sound. But the chief indicator for the assembly of the pieces was according to their basic element—optical light-vibrations (varying degrees of "haze" and "luminosity"). And the organization of these vibrations reveals a complete identity with a minor harmony in music. Moreover, this example furnishes a demonstration of consonance in combining movement as *change* and movement as *light-vibration*.

Increased tension in this level of montage, too, is produced by an intensification of the same "musical" dominant. An especially clear example of such intensification is furnished by the sequence of the delayed harvest in *Old and New*. The construction of this film as a whole, as in this particular sequence, adheres to a basic constructive process. Namely: a conflict between *story* and its *traditional form*.

Emotive structures applied to non-emotional material. The stimulus is transferred from its usual use as situation (for example, as eroticism is usually used in films) to structures paradoxical in tone. When "the pillar of industry" is finally discovered—it is a typewriter. The hero bull and heroine cow are happily wed. It is not the Holy Grail that inspires both doubt and ecstasy—but a cream-separator.*

Therefore, the thematic *minor* of the harvesting is resolved by the thematic *major* of the tempest, of the rain. Yes, and even the stacked harvest, itself—traditional major theme of fecundity basking in the sun—is a resolution of the minor theme, wetted as it is by the rain.

Here the increase of tension proceeds by internal reinforcement of a relentless dominant chord—by the growing feeling within the piece of "oppression before the storm."

As in the preceding example, the tonal dominant—movement as light-vibration—is accompanied by a secondary rhythmic dominant, i.e., movement as change.

Here it is expressed in the growing violence of the wind, embodied in a transfer from currents of air to torrents of rain —a definite analogy with the transfer from the downward steps to the downward rolling carriage.

In general structure the wind-rain element in relation to the dominant can be identified with the bond in the first example (the harbor mists) between its rhythmic rockings and its

---

* There was even a parallel with the ironic conclusion of *A Woman of Paris* in the original end planned for *Old and New*. This is, by the way, a film unique in the number of references (both in story and in style) to other films: the "pillar of industry" sequence playfully builds its satire on a similar but serious episode in Pudovkin's *End of St. Petersburg;* the tractor's final triumph is an inflated parody of a Wild West film chase, etc. Even Buster Keaton's *Three Ages* was consciously reflected in the original structure of *Old and New*.—EDITOR.

reticular afocality. Actually, the character of the inter-relation is quite different. In contrast with the consonance of the first example, we have here the reverse.

The gathering the skies into a black, threatening mass is contrasted with the intensifying dynamic force of the wind, and the solidification implied in the transition from currents of air to torrents of water is intensified by the dynamically blown petticoats and the scattering sheaves of the harvest.

Here a collision of tendencies—an intensification of the static and an intensification of the dynamic—gives us a clear example of dissonance in tonal montage construction.

From the viewpoint of emotional impression, the harvest sequence exemplifies the tragic (active) minor, in distinction from the lyrical (passive) minor of the harbor fog sequence.

It is interesting that in both examples the montage grows with the increasing change of its basic element—*color:* in the "harbor" from dark gray to misty white (life analogy—the dawn); in the "harvest" from light gray to leaden black (life analogy—the approach of crisis). I.e., along a line of light vibrations increasing in frequency in the one case, and diminishing in frequency in the other.

A construction in simple metrics has been elevated to a new category of movement—a category of higher significance.

This brings us to a category of montage that we may justly name:

4. *Overtonal Montage*

In my opinion, overtonal montage (as described in the preceding essay) is organically the furthest development along the line of tonal montage. As I have indicated, it is distinguishable from tonal montage by the collective calculation of all the piece's appeals.

This characteristic steps up the impression from a melodically emotional coloring to a directly physiological perception. This, too, represents a level related to the preceding levels.

These four categories are *methods* of montage. They become montage *constructions* proper when they enter into relations of conflict with each other—as in the examples cited.

Within a scheme of mutual relations, echoing and conflicting with one another, they move to a more and more strongly defined type of montage, each one organically growing from the other.

Thus the transition from metrics to rhythmics came about in the conflict between the length of the shot and the movement within the frame.

Tonal montage grows out of the conflict between the rhythmic and tonal principles of the piece.

And finally—overtonal montage, from the conflict between the principal tone of the piece (its dominant) and the overtone.

These considerations provide, in the first place, an interesting criterion for the appreciation of montage-construction from a "pictorial" point of view. Pictorialism is here contrasted with "cinematicism," esthetic pictorialism with physiological reality.

To argue about the pictorialism of the film-shot is naive. This is typical of persons possessing a decent esthetic culture that has never been logically applied to films. To this kind of thinking belong, for instance, the remarks on cinema coming from Kasimir Malevich.* The veriest novice in films would not think of analyzing the film-shot from an identical point of view with landscape painting.

The following may be observed as a criterion of the "pictorialism" of the montage-construction in the broadest sense: the conflict must be resolved *within* one or another category of montage, without allowing the conflict to be one of differing categories of montage.

Real cinematography begins only with the collision of various cinematic modifications of movement and vibration. For example, the "pictorial" conflict of figure and horizon (whether this is a conflict in statics or dynamics is unimportant). Or the alternation of differently lit pieces solely from

---

* The founder of the Suprematist school of painting had delivered some commonplaces about the "photographic" and naturalistic limitations of the cinema.—EDITOR.

the viewpoint of conflicting light-vibrations, or of a conflict between the form of an object and its illumination, etc.

We must also define what characterizes the affect of the various forms of montage on the psycho-physiological complex of the person on the perceiving end.

The first, metric category is characterized by a rude motive force. It is capable of impelling the spectator to reproduce the perceived action, outwardly. For example, the mowing contest in *Old and New* is cut in this way. The different pieces are "synonymous"—containing a single mowing movement from one side of the frame to the other; and I laughed when I saw the more impressionable members of the audience quietly rocking from side to side at an increasing rate of speed as the pieces were accelerated by shortening. The effect was the same as that of a percussion and brass band playing a simple march tune.

I have designated the second category as rhythmic. It might also be called primitive-emotive. Here the movement is more subtly calculated, for though emotion is also a result of movement, it is movement that is not merely primitive external change.

The third category—tonal—might also be called melodic-emotive. Here movement, already ceasing to be simple change in the second case, passes over distinctly into an emotive vibration of a still higher order.

The fourth category—a fresh flood of pure physiologism, as it were—echoes, in the highest degree of intensity, the first category, again acquiring a degree of intensification by direct motive force.

In music this is explained by the fact that, from the moment that overtones can be heard parallel with the basic sound, there also can be sensed vibrations, oscillations that cease to impress as tones, but rather as purely physical displacements of the perceived impression. This particularly refers to strongly pronounced timbre instruments with a great preponderance of the overtone principle. The sensation of physical displacement is sometimes also literally achieved: chimes, organ, very large Turkish drums, etc.

In some sequences *Old and New* succeeds in effecting junctions of the tonal and overtonal lines. Sometimes they even collide with the metric and rhythmic lines, as well. As in the various "tangles" of the religious procession: those who fall on their knees beneath the ikons, the candles that melt, the gasps of ecstasy, etc.

It is interesting to note that, in selecting the pieces for the montage of this sequence, we unconsciously furnished ourselves with proof of an essential equality between rhythm and tone, establishing this gradational unity much as I had previously established a gradational unity between the concepts of shot and montage.

Thus, tone is a level of rhythm.

For the benefit of those who are alarmed by such reductions to a common denominator, and the extension of the properties of one level into another for purposes of investigation and methodology, I recall Lenin's synopsis of the fundamental elements of Hegelian dialectics:

These elements may be presented in a more detailed way thus: . . .

10) an endless process of revealing *new* aspects, relationships, etc.

11) an endless process of deepening human perception of things, appearances, processes and so on, from appearance to essence and from the less profound to the more profound essence.

12) from co-existence to causality and from one form of connection and interdependence to another, deeper, more general.

13) recurrence, on the highest level, of known traits, attributes, etc. of the lowest, and

14) return, so to say, to the old (negation of the negation) . . .[2]

After this quotation, I wish to define the following category of montage—a still higher category:

5. Intellectual Montage

Intellectual montage is montage not of generally physiological overtonal sounds, but of sounds and overtones of an intellectual sort: i.e., conflict-juxtaposition of accompanying intellectual affects.

The gradational quality is here determined by the fact that there is no difference in principle between the motion of a man rocking under the influence of elementary metric montage (see above) and the intellectual process within it, for the intellectual process is the same agitation, but in the dominion of the higher nerve-centers.

And if, in the cited instance, under the influence of "jazz montage," one's hands and knees rhythmically tremble, in the second case such a trembling, under the influence of a different degree of intellectual appeal, occurs in identically the same way through the tissues of the higher nerve systems of the thought apparatus.

Though, judged as "phenomena" (appearances), they seem in fact different, yet from the point of view of "essence" (process), they are undoubtedly identical.

Applying the experience of work along lower lines to categories of a higher order, this affords the possibility of carrying the attack into the very heart of things and phenomena. Thus, the fifth category is the intellectual overtone.

An example of this can be found in the sequence of the "gods" in *October*, where all the conditions for their comparison are made dependent on an exclusively class-intellectual sound of each piece in its relation to God. I say class, for though the emotional principle is universally human, the intellectual principle is profoundly tinged by class. These pieces were assembled in accordance with a descending intellectual scale—pulling back the concept of God to its origins, forcing the spectator to perceive this "progress" intellectually.*

* A portion of this sequence (omitted from most of the American prints of *Ten Days That Shook the World*) is reproduced in the section of photographs between pages 52 and 53.

But this, of course, is not yet the intellectual cinema, which I have been announcing for some years! The intellectual cinema will be that which resolves the conflict-juxtaposition of the physiological and intellectual overtones. Building a completely new form of cinematography—the realization of revolution in the general history of culture; building a synthesis of science, art, and class militancy.

In my opinion, the question of the overtone is of vast significance for our film future. All the more attentively should we study its methodology and conduct investigation into it.

Moscow—London, Autumn 1929

A COURSE IN TREATMENT

> *Stephen.* (Looks behind.) So that gesture, not music, not odours, would be a universal language, the gift of tongues rendering visible not the lay sense but the first entelechy, the structural rhythm.
>
> JAMES JOYCE [1]

DISCUSSIONS ON "amusement" *vs.* "entertainment" irritate me. Having spent no small number of man-hours in the matter of the "enthusiasm" and "involvement" of the audience in a united and general impulse of absorption, the word "amusement" sounds opposed, alien and inimical to me. Whenever it is said that a film must "entertain," I hear a voice: "Help yourself."

When the worthy Ivan Ivanovich Pererepenko "treats you to snuff, he always first licks the lid of his snuff-box with his tongue, and then taps it with his finger, presenting it to you, and if you are an acquaintance, says: 'Shall I dare, my dear sir, to ask you to help yourself?' And if you aren't acquainted with him, he says: 'Shall I dare, my dear sir, although I have not the honor of knowing your rank, name and patronymic, to ask you to help yourself?'" But when Ivan Nikiforovich Dovgochkhun treats you to snuff, he "puts the snuff-box straight into your hand, and says only: 'Help yourself.'" [2]

I'm for Ivan Nikiforovich, with his direct "help yourself." The film's job is to make the audience "help itself," not to "entertain" it. To grip, not to amuse. To furnish the audience with cartridges, not to dissipate the energies that it brought into the theater. "Entertainment" is not really an entirely innocuous term: beneath it is a quite concrete, active process.

But amusement and entertainment must be understood pre-

84

cisely as only a quantitative empowering of the inner thematic material itself, and not in any sense as a qualitative power.

While we had films that "gripped," we did not speak of entertainment. We had no time to be bored. But then this gripping was lost somewhere. The skill of constructing films that gripped was lost. And we began to talk of entertainment.

It is impossible to realize this latter aim, without first mastering the former method.

The slogan in favor of entertainment was regarded by many as countenancing a certain retrogressive element and, in the worst sense, as a perversion of understanding in relation to the ideological premises of our films.

We must once more command a method, a directive guide to embody in stirring works of art. No one can help us in this. We must do it ourselves.

It is on the subject of how to do this,—at least how to get ready to do it, that I wish to speak.

To rehabilitate the ideological premise is not something to be introduced from without "at the pleasure of Repertkom," * but must be thought of as a basic, vivifying, powerful process, fertilizing nothing less than the most thrilling element in the creative work of film direction—the director's "treatment." That is the task of the present essay.

And there is a quite concrete occasion for this—namely, in connection with the formulation of pedagogical work in the third, or graduating, class of the directors' course in the State Cinema Institute where, according to the teaching program, the students must now walk out into creative mastery of directorial work.

The Talmudists of method—the academic high-Marxists— may berate me, but I wish to approach this theme and this teaching simply, as life—as work. For, actually, no one as yet knows concretely how to master this, whether screening oneself behind academic citations or not.

* The Repertory Committee is entrusted with the supervision of stage and film repertories.—EDITOR.

For some time, for years, I worried about those certain supernatural powers, transcending common sense and human reason, that seemed indispensable for the comprehension of the "mysteries" of creative film direction.

To dissect the music of creative film direction!

To dissect, but not as a corpse (in Salieri's manner *), the music of creative film direction—that was to be our work with the graduating students of the Institute.

We approach this problem simply, and not from a preconceived position of scholastic methods. And it won't be in the corpses of worn-out film works that we'll examine the processes of producing our own works. The anatomical theater and dissection slab are the least suitable trying grounds for the study of the theater. And the study of cinema must proceed inseparably with the study of theater.

To build cinematography, starting from "the idea of cinematography," and from abstract principles, is barbarous and stupid. Only by a critical comparison with the more basic early forms of the spectacle is it possible to master critically the specific methodology of the cinema.

Criticism must consist in comparing and contrasting a given fact, not with an idea, but with another fact; for this purpose it is only important that both facts, as far as possible, be carefully investigated, and that they both present, in relation to one another, different moments of development.[3]

We shall study this matter in the living creative process. And it will be done by us in this way, primarily.

We must build simultaneously a working process and a method. And we shall proceed not in the Plekhanov manner, from preconceived positions of "method in general" to the concrete particular case, but through given concrete work on particular materials we expect to arrive at a method of cinematographic creation for the director.

For this purpose we must bring out into the open the "inti-

* According to his opening soliloquy in Pushkin's *Mozart and Salieri*. —EDITOR.

* perhaps borne out by Bergman? On one way of proceeding?

mate" creative process of the director in all its phases and twistings, and stand it before the audience, "in full view."

Many surprises are in store for the youth who is filled with illusions.

In one connection may I, for a moment, list to the side of "entertainment"? Let us cite one of the greatest of all "entertainers"—Alexandre Dumas *père*, for whom his son, Dumas *fils*, apologized: "My father is a great baby of mine—born when I was quite a little child." [4]

Who has not been enchanted by the classic harmony in the labyrinthine structure of *The Count of Monte Cristo!* Who has not been struck by the deadly logic that weaves and interweaves the characters and events of the novel, as if these interrelationships had existed from its very conception. Who has finally not imagined that ecstatic moment when suddenly in the brain of that "fat black" Dumas there flashed the future architecture of the novel in all its details and subtleties, with the title, *Le Comte de Monte Cristo*, blazing across the façade. And this vision has its usual echo, "Oh, how could I ever achieve that!" And how pleasantly bracing it is to recognize by tasting that cooking, how such a remarkable composition was really brought together and given body. How the fabrication of this book came with savage diligence—not in a divine flash.

It is the work of a Negro, but toiling as hard as he would have under the whip of an overseer. Dumas was actually of Negro descent, and he was born in Haiti, as was Toussaint L'Ouverture, the hero of a film I want to make, *The Black Consul*.* The nickname of Dumas's grandfather—General Thomas Alexandre—was the "Black Devil." And Dumas himself was called "fat black" by his envious contemporaries and rivals. A certain humbly-named Jacquot, concealed behind the loftier sound of "Eugène de Mirecourt," published an attack entitled *Fabrique de Romans: Maison Alexandre Dumas et Cie*, in which he linked the origins and methods of Dumas:

* An unrealized wish. See "The Work of Eisenstein," in *The Film Sense.*—EDITOR.

Scratch M. Dumas' hide and you will find the savage. . . . He lunches on potatoes taken burning hot from the ashes of the hearth and devours them without removing the skins—a Negro! [As he needs 200,000 francs a year,] he hires intellectual deserters and translators at wages that degrade them to the condition of Negroes working under the lash of a mulatto! [5]

"Your father was black!" someone hurled in his face. "My grandfather was a monkey," he replied. He seems to have been more sensitive to the "factory" charge.

On one day only Dumas was truly grieved. Béranger, whom he really loved, wrote asking him to include an interesting exile "in the number of miners whom he employed to dig out the mineral which he transformed into sterling bullion"; and Dumas replied: "Dear old friend, My only miner is my left hand which holds the book open, while my right works twelve hours a day."

He was exaggerating. He had collaborators, "but as Napoleon had generals." [6]

It is difficult enough to find oneself working with such frenzy. But it is even more difficult to achieve anything adequate without this frenzy.

Miracles of composition—this is merely a question of persistence and the expenditure of time during the "training period" of one's autobiography.

From a viewpoint of productivity this period of romanticism is distinguished for the dizzying speed of its creative tempi: In eight days (from September 17 to September 26, 1829) Victor Hugo wrote 3,000 lines of *Hernani*, which stood the classic theater on its head, *Marion Delorme* in 23 days, *Le Roi s'Amuse* in 20 days, *Lucrèce Borgia* in 11 days, *Angelo* in 19 days, *Marie Tudor* in 19 days, *Ruy Blas* in 34 days. This is echoed quantitatively, as well. The literary heritage of Dumas *père* numbers 1,200 volumes.

The same opportunity of creating such works is equally accessible to all.

Let us examine *The Count of Monte Cristo* in particular. Lucas-Dubreton gives us the history of its composition:

In the course of a Mediterranean cruise, Dumas had passed near a little island, where he had not been able to land because "it was *en contumace*." It was the island of Monte-Cristo. The name struck him at the time. A few years later, in 1843, he arranged with an editor for the publication of a work to be called *Impressions de Voyage dans Paris*, but he needed a romantic plot. Then one day by good luck he read a story of twenty pages, *Le Diamant et la Vengeance*, which was laid in the period of the second Restoration and was included in Peuchet's volume, *La Police Devoilée*. It caught his fancy. Here was the subject of which he had dreamed: Monte-Cristo should discover his enemies hidden in Paris!

Then Maquet had the idea of telling the story of the love-affair of Monte-Cristo and the fair Mercedes and the treachery of Danglars; and the two friends started off on a new track—*Monte-Cristo*, from being travel impressions in the form of a romance turned into romance pure and simple. The Abbé Faria, a lunatic born at Goa whom Châteaubriand saw vainly trying to kill a canary by hypnotizing it, helped to increase the mystery; and the Château d'If began to appear on the horizon. . . .[7]

This is how things are really put together. And to re-experience this as it takes place, and to participate in it oneself, seems to me a most useful and productive process for a student.

The "method-ists" who preach otherwise and approve other "recipes" are simply wasting our precious time. But "chance" here is far less important than it might appear, and the "regularity" within the creative process is perceived and detected. There is method. But the whole villainy lies in this, that from preconceived methodological positions, nothing grows. And a tempestuous stream of creative energy, unregulated by method, yields even less.

Such analysis of the building of works of art, step by step, will clarify the most severe regularity, governing each support of the super-structure, with which they arise from basic social and ideological premises.

And the gold fever of money-making and self-enrichment of the Louis-Philippe epoch is no less a determining factor for the gilded legend of the fabulous wealth of the former sailor who becomes an omnipotent count, no less determining than Dumas's childhood memories of Scheherazade and the treasures of Ali Baba. And the very fact that a sailor could become a count, meant that "anyone" might.

In the general chase after gold and aristocratic titles, the sailor, Dantès who became the mythically rich Comte de Monte Cristo, served as a splendid "social ideal" for the bourgeoisie who were feverishly enriching themselves. It is not without reason that to this image is ascribed the features of an idealized self-portrait. For Dumas himself, along with the others, bathed in the turbid sea of suspicious gold accumulated through the dubious speculations of the reign of *le roi bourgeois*.

"A million? That's exactly the amount I ordinarily carry for pocket money!"

To an identical degree this remark was the unattainable ideal, both of the "fat black," then the literary sovereign of the newspaper, *feuilleton* and dramatic world of Paris, squandering words and money with equal recklessness, as well as of the vast hordes of greedy sharpers and rogues, overrunning the economic life of Paris.

However, to sense fully how sharply these social, economical and ideological premises determine every slightest twist of form, and how inseparably they are united in their processes, one must independently and conscientiously trace a continuous and complete creative cycle from start to finish.

Of course, what would be most interesting would be to catch another Goethe or Gogol, place him before an audience and set him to writing a third part of *Faust* or to create newly a second volume of *Dead Souls*. But we don't even have a live Alexandre Dumas at our disposal. So we of the Institute's third course transform ourselves into a collective director and film-builder.

The instructor is no more than *primus inter pares*—the first among equals. The collective (and later each member of it individually) works its way through all the difficulties and torments of creative work, through the whole process of creative formation, from the first faint, glimmering hint of the theme, down to a decision on whether the buttons on the leather jacket of the last extra player are suitable for filming purposes.

The instructor's task is only, by a well-timed dexterous shove, to push the collective in the direction of "normal" and "fruitful" difficulties, and to push it in the direction of the collective's correct and distinct presentation (to himself) of exactly those questions, the answers to which lead to *construction* and not to fruitless chatter "around" it.

That is how they teach you to fly in the circus. The trapeze is mercilessly held back, or the pupil finds a fist instead of a helping hand if his timing is false. No great harm if he falls once or twice outside the safety net onto the chairs around the arena. Next time—he won't make that mistake.

But no less carefully, at each stage of the unfolding creative process, must the indicated secondary material and the experience of the "inherited past," at the proper place, be thrust into the hands of the entangled or stuck "warriors." This is not enough, if at hand is not that exhausting synthetic giant of cinema who, at every turn, is more than the "inherited past" and the "living heir," forming in its own field a solid technique.

Within three years a systematic course in special subjects has replaced at the Institute a thin coating of sporadic lectures by all sorts of "prominent" film-workers. These people ran into the Institute as they would into a street-car, strange and unrelated to each other, just like street-car passengers, rushing to the exit as fast as possible, after blurting 45 minutes' worth of something unconnected and episodic. Then they were whirled out of the sight of their dazed proselytes, along the orbit of their private activities.

This "little episode" also had to be re-built in a fundamental way. Within the plan of the general course, specialists are invited in at the proper time, to deal with definite, concrete cases, at a definite stage of the general movement of the unfolding creative process. To deal with that particular question in which he is expert.

All this aims at a properly large project in which the collective or, later, the individual, is responsible to the very end. In getting rid of the "little episodes" in the instructional plan, we have also done away with the pitiable "little episodes" prepared by graduating students. These short "études" of the graduates, miscellaneous and miserable, but self-satisfying, even shorter in intelligence than they are in footage, must be dropped as being wholly inexpedient. After working on a graduate project on the scale, say, of a cathedral, the graduate architect usually finds himself building something accessible to everyone—a privy. But, after designing for graduation one tiny *pisoir*, it is risky to turn to, yes, to what you please! And yet, year after year, we have seen this happen to graduates from the Institute. This has to be fundamentally scrapped.

It is true that in practice a film is broken up into separate episodes. But these episodes all hang from the rod of a single ideological, compositional and stylistic whole.

The art of cinematography is not in selecting a fanciful framing, or in taking something from a surprising camera-angle.

The art is in every fragment of a film being an organic part of an organically conceived whole.

With such organically thought-out and photographed parts of one large significant and general conception, these must be segments of some whole, and by no means with stray, strolling études.

On these filmed segments, on the unfilmed but prepared episodes that are planned to precede or follow these, on the development of montage plans and lists according to the place of these parts in the whole—on such a base creative irresponsibility will be really liquidated among the students.

From beginning to end their work will be examined, simultaneously with responsible demonstrations as to how far they are capable of realizing in practice the firmly planned general concept; although at this stage it is not yet the student's own individual concept, but the collectively worked out concept, but this already teaches the hard lesson of self-discipline.

Self-discipline that will be even more needed at the moment when the concept will be individual and his own.

But before reaching this last stage, this last frontier, already bordering on production away from the school, the students run a long gantlet of living and dead "experts."

At a certain stage this will take the form of a long discussion of the type, image, and character of the characters in his project. The ashes of Balzac, Gogol, Dostoyevsky, and Ben Jonson will be stirred in such discussions. The question will arise as to the personification of such a type, image, or character. Here we'll depend on Kachalov's confession of his work on the rôle of the "Baron" in *The Lower Depths*, Batalov will talk with us, or Max Shtraukh will tell us of the mechanics of creating Rubinchik in Zarkhi's *Joy Street*.

Moving through the forests of story-construction, we'll pull apart with Aksënov the skeletons of the Elizabethans, we'll listen to Dumas *père* and Victor Shklovsky on the outlining of story structures, and on the methods of Weltmann's works. And then, having talked over dramatic situations with the late John Webster, Nathan Zarkhi and Volkenstein, we shall interest ourselves in how these situations are clothed in words.

Alexei Maximovich Gorky will probably not refuse to initiate us in the methods of writing the dialogue for *The Lower Depths* or *Yegor Bulichäv and Others*. Nikolai Erdmann will tell us how it is done in his plays. And Isaac Babel will speak of the specific texture of image and word and of the technique of the extreme laconism of literature's expressive means—Babel who, perhaps, knows in practice better than anyone else, that great secret, that "there is no iron that can enter the human heart with such stupefying effect as a period, placed at the right moment." [8] And he may speak of how, with this laconism, was created so inimitably his wonderful (and far from being sufficiently appreciated) play *Sunset*. This is perhaps the best example of fine dramatic dialogue in recent years.

All this will arise at the corresponding stages of the single progressing creative process of our collective director on his film.

The fusing of the separate stages along independent analytical excursions is not so very strange. Construction of theme and story can sometimes be completely independent of the development in words. Aren't both *Revizor* and *Dead Souls* brilliant examples of the development of stories "set" Gogol from outside? *

The question of a musical accompaniment for the sound medium. The question of material means. Analysis of a number of examples of our "heritage" in other areas as well, and each from the angle of that special need where it, and peculiarly it, can be doubly useful.

James Joyce and Emile Zola.

Honoré Daumier and Edgar Dégas.

Toulouse-Lautrec or Stendhal.

And lengthily and circumstantially will be analyzed by Marxist and Leninist specialists the question of the correct ideological formulation of the problem from the standpoint of approach to the theme and to a social understanding of this thing. In this way we expect to secure those, mobilized with experience and qualified by sustained guidance, who will be capable of creating films.

And the most serious and interesting part of this work—the central part of the director's creative work—is to train students in "treatment" and to work up with them the process of how this proceeds and is carried out.

We work essentially on such a low-experimental triviality of simplified perceived tasks, that we simply do not have occasion to observe works that are original, living, creative, that have an inter-related social treatment and conception, with developed form.

Our works are on such a level of simplification that one recalls the famous cartoon of the automatic sausage factory: from one side enter boxes with handles containing pigs, at the other side the same boxes come out, now containing sausages. Between the schematic scraped skeleton of *slogan* and the

* It was Pushkin who suggested the themes of both these works.—
EDITOR.

empty skin of outer *form* there are no layers of tangible, living flesh and muscle.

There are no organs, acting in relation to each other. And then people are surprised that the skin hangs so formlessly. And through its pitifully thin simplification juts the sharp bones of a mechanical perception of "social" thematics. Not enough flesh and muscle.

That is why Gorky's *Yegor Bulichëv and Others* was greeted with such unanimous joy. Even though the work has not answered a basic problem of ours: the men and women shown in it are not yet ours, and of today. We'll continue to wait for these from the mind of Alexei Maximovich.*

On the other hand, here is flesh. Here is muscle. And this flesh was made today, when all around us on stage and screen are not even the "men in boxes" that Chekhov wrote about, but simply boxes without men. Whereas, tightly packed as they are with vulgar citations, our works resemble the barbed wire of harsh truth, covered with muslin—and we are astonished that blood doesn't circulate through these barbs, and that the muslin doesn't beat an excited pulse.

From the sublime to the ridiculous is one step. From a sublimely premised idea, formulated in a slogan, to a living work of art—is several hundred steps. If we take but one step, we achieve only the ridiculous result of the accommodating trash of the present.

We must begin to learn how to do three-dimensional, rounded works, going from the two-dimensional flat patterns with a "direct wire" from the slogan to the story—without a transfer.

How an ideological concept works, making a serious approach towards a film, we can trace in my own work, although in somewhat unusual social circumstances. This was in Hollywood. In the world of Paramount Pictures, Inc. And the mat-

* *Yegor Bulichëv* was the first of a planned trilogy that was to reach the first post-revolutionary years.[9]

ter concerned the treatment and script of a work of exceptionally high quality.

Even though not beyond ideological defects, *An American Tragedy* by Theodore Dreiser is a work that has every chance of being numbered among the classics of its period and place. That this material contained the collision of two irreconcilable viewpoints—the "front office's" and ours—became clear from the moment of submitting the first rough draft of a script.

"Is Clyde Griffiths guilty or not guilty—in your treatment?" was the first question from the head of Paramount, B. P. Schulberg.

"Not guilty," was our answer.

"But then your script is a monstrous challenge to American society. . . ."

We explained that we consider the crime committed by Griffiths the sum total of those social relations, the influence of which he was subjected to at every stage of his unfolding biography and character, during the course of the film. For us this was, essentially, the whole interest of the work.

"We would prefer a simple, tight whodunit about a murder . . ."

". . . and about the love of a boy and girl," someone added, with a sigh.

The possibility of two such basically opposed treatments of the work's protagonist should not astonish you.

Dreiser's novel is as broad and shoreless as the Hudson; it is as immense as life itself, and allows almost any point of view on itself. Like every "neutral" fact of nature itself, his novel is ninety-nine per cent statement of facts and one per cent attitude towards them. This epic of cosmic veracity and objectivity had to be assembled in a tragedy—and this was unthinkable without a world-attitude of direction and point.

The studio heads were disturbed by the question of guilt or innocence from another point of view: guilty would mean—unattractive. How could we allow a hero to seem unattractive? What would the box-office say?

But if he weren't guilty . . .

Because of the difficulties around "this damned question" *An American Tragedy* lay inactive for five years after its purchase by Paramount. It was approached—but no more than approached—even by the patriarch of films, David Wark Griffith, and Lubitsch, and many others.

With their customary cautious prudence the "heads," in our case too, dodged a decision. They suggested that we complete the script "as you feel it," and then, "we'll see. . . ."

From what I have already said, it must be perfectly evident that in our case, as distinct from previous handlings, the matter of a difference of opinion was not based on a decision as to some particular situation, but was far deeper, touching the question of the social treatment—wholly and fundamentally.

It is now interesting to trace how in this way a taken aim begins to determine the modeling of the separate parts and how this particular aim, with its demands, impregnates all problems of determining situations, of psychological deepening, and of the "purely formal" aspect of the construction as a whole—and how it pushes one toward completely new, "purely formal" methods which, when generalized, can be assembled into a new theoretical realization of the guiding discipline of cinematography as such.

It would be difficult to set forth here the entire situation of the novel: one can't do in five lines what Dreiser required two bulky volumes to do. We shall touch upon only the outer central point of the outer story side of the tragedy—the murder itself, though the tragedy, of course, is not in this, but in that tragic course pursued by Clyde, whom the social structure drives to murder. And fundamental attention is drawn to this in our script.

Clyde Griffiths, having seduced a young factory girl employed in a department managed by him, cannot help her obtain an illegal abortion. He sees himself forced to marry her. Yet this would ruin all his visions of a career, as it would upset his marriage with a wealthy girl who is in love with him.

Clyde's dilemma: he must either relinquish forever a career and social success, or—get rid of the girl.

Clyde's adventures in his collisions with American realities have by this time already molded his psychology, so that after a long internal struggle (not with moral principles, but with his own neurasthenic lack of character), he decides on the latter course.

He elaborately thinks out and prepares her murder—a boat is to be upset, apparently accidentally. All the details are thought out with the over-elaboration of the inexperienced criminal, which subsequently entangles the dilettante in a fatal mesh of incontrovertible evidence.

He sets out with the girl in a boat. In the boat the conflict between pity and aversion for the girl, between his character-less vacillation and his greedy snatching at a brilliant material future, reaches a climax. Half-consciously, half-unconsciously, in a wild inner panic, the boat is overturned. The girl drowns.

Abandoning her, Clyde saves himself as he had planned beforehand, and falls into the very net that he had woven for his extrication.

The boat episode is effected in the way that similar incidents take place: it is neither fully defined nor completely perceived—it is an undifferentiated tangle. Dreiser presents the matter so impartially that the further development of events is left formally, not to the logical course of the story, but to the processes of law.

It was imperative for us to sharpen the *actual* and *formal* innocence of Clyde within the very act of perpetrating the crime.

Only thus could we make sufficiently precise the "monstrous challenge" to a society whose mechanism brings a rather characterless youth to such a predicament and then, invoking morality and justice, seats him in the electric chair.

The sanctity of the *formal* principle in the codes of honor, morality, justice, and religion—is primary and fundamental in America. On this is based the endless game of advocacy in the courts, and the elaborate games among lawyers and parliamentarians. The essence of what is being formally argued is an altogether subsidiary matter.

Therefore the conviction of Clyde, though essentially deserved by his rôle in this affair (which concerns no one), in spite of proof of his *formal* innocence, would be regarded in America as something "monstrous": a judicial murder.

It was therefore imperative to develop the boat scene with indisputable precision as to Clyde's *formal* innocence. Yet without whitewashing Clyde in any way, nor removing any particle of blame.

We chose this treatment: Clyde wants to commit the murder, but he *cannot*. At the moment that requires decisive action, he falters. Simply from weakness of will.

However, before this inner "defeat," he excites in the girl Roberta such a feeling of alarm that, when he leans toward her, already defeated inwardly and ready "to take everything back," she recoils from him in horror. The boat, off-balance, rocks. When, in trying to support her, he accidentally knocks his camera against her face, she finally loses her head and in her terror stumbles, falls, and the boat overturns.

For greater emphasis we show her rising to the surface again. We even show Clyde trying to swim to her. But the machinery of crime has been set in motion and continues to its end, even against Clyde's will: Roberta cries out weakly, tries to retreat from him in her horror, and, not being able to swim, drowns.

Being a good swimmer Clyde reaches the shore and, coming to his senses, continues to act in accordance with the fatal plan he had prepared for the crime—from which he had deviated only for a moment in the boat.

The psychological and tragic deepening of the situation in this form is indubitable. Tragedy is heightened to an almost Grecian level of "blind Moira—fate" that, once conjured into existence, will not relax her hold on the one who summoned her. Heightened to a tragic, racking "causality" that, once it claims its rights, drives on to a logical conclusion whatever has been brought to life through the pitiless course of its processes.

In this crushing of a human being by a "blind" cosmic principle, by the inertia of the progress of laws over which he has no control, we have one of the basic premises of antique tragedy. It mirrors the passive dependence of the man of that day on the forces of nature. It is analogous to what Engels, in connection with another period, wrote of Calvin:

His predestination doctrine was the religious expression of the fact that in the commercial world of competition success or failure does not depend upon a man's activity or cleverness, but upon circumstances uncontrollable by him. It is not of him that willeth or of him that runneth, but of the mercy of unknown superior economic powers. . . .[10]

An ascent to the atavism of primitive cosmic conceptions, seen through an accidental situation of our day, is always a means of racking a dramatic scene to the heights of tragedy. But our treatment was not limited by this. It was pregnant with meaningful sharpnesses along the whole further course of the action.

In Dreiser's book, "for the sake of preserving the honor of the family," Clyde's rich uncle supplies him with the "apparatus" of defense.

The defense lawyers have no essential doubt that a crime was committed. None the less, they invent a "change of heart" experienced by Clyde under the influence of his love and pity for Roberta. Simply invented on the spur of the moment, this is pretty good.

But this is made far more evil when there *really* was such a change. When this change comes from quite different motives. When there really was no crime. When the lawyers are convinced that there was a crime. And with a downright lie, so near the truth and at the same time so far from it, they endeavor in this slanderous way to whitewash and save the accused.

And it becomes still more dramatically evil when, in the adjacent moment, the "ideology" of your treatment disturbs the proportions and, in another place, the epic indifference of Dreiser's narrative.

Almost the whole of the second volume is filled with the

trial of Clyde for the murder of Roberta and with the hunting down of Clyde to a conviction, to the electric chair.

As part of the background of the trial it is indicated that the true aim of the trial and prosecution of Clyde, however, has no relation to him whatsoever. This aim is solely to create the necessary popularity among the farming population of the state (Roberta was a farmer's daughter) for the prosecuting District Attorney Mason, so that he may win the necessary support for his nomination as judge.

The defense take on a case which they know to be hopeless ("at best ten years in the penitentiary") on the same plane of political struggle. Belonging to the opposite political camp, their primary aim is to exert their utmost strength in defeating the ambitious prosecutor. For one side, as for the other, Clyde is merely a means to an end.

Already a toy in the hands of "blind" Moira, fate, "causality" à la greque, Clyde also becomes a toy in the hands of the far from blind machinery of bourgeois justice, machinery employed as an instrument of political intrigue.

Thus is tragically expanded and generalized the fortunes of the particular case of Clyde Griffiths into a genuinely "American tragedy in general"—a characteristic story of a young American at the beginning of the twentieth century.

The whole tangle of design within the trial itself was almost entirely eliminated in the script's construction, and was replaced by the pre-election bidding, visible through the manipulated solemnity of the courtroom, being used as nothing more than a drill-ground for a political campaign.

This fundamental treatment of the murder determines the tragic deepening and the strengthened ideological sharpness of yet another part of the film and another figure: the mother.

Clyde's mother runs a mission. Her religion is a purblind fanaticism. She is so convinced of her absurd dogma that her figure inspires one's involuntary respect and grows almost monumental; one detects the glow of a martyr's aureole.

Even in spite of the fact that she is the first embodiment of the guilt of American society in relation to Clyde: her teach-

ings and principles, her aim towards Heaven rather than training her son for work were the initial premises for the ensuing
tragedy.

Dreiser shows her fighting to the last for her son's innocence,
working as a trial-reporter for a newspaper in order to be near
her son, touring America (like the mothers and sisters of the
Scottsboro boys) with lectures, to collect enough money to
appeal the verdict in Clyde's case. She definitely acquires the
self-sacrificial grandeur of a heroine. In Dreiser's work this
grandeur radiates sympathy for her moral and religious doctrines.

In our treatment Clyde, in his death-cell, confesses to his
mother (rather than to the Reverend McMillan, as in the novel)
that, though he did not kill Roberta, he had planned to do so.

His mother, for whom the word is the deed, and the thought
of sin equivalent to its execution, is stunned by his confession.
In a way exactly opposite to the grandeur of the mother in
Gorky's novel, this mother also becomes her son's betrayer.
When she goes to the Governor with a petition for her son's
life, she is startled by his direct question: "Do you yourself
believe in your son's innocence?" At this moment that is to
decide the fate of her son—she is silent.

The Christian sophism of an ideal unity (of deed and
thought) and a material unity (*de facto*), a parody of dialectics, leads to the final tragic denouement.

The petition is disregarded, and the dogma and dogmatism
of its bearer are alike discredited. The mother's fatal moment
of silence cannot even be washed away by her tears when she
takes leave forever of the son whom she has, with her own
hands, delivered into the jaws of the Christian Baal. The more
poignant these last scenes become in sadness, the more bitterly
do they lash at the ideology that brought this sadness.

In my opinion our treatment succeeded in ripping some of
the masks—though not all—from the monumental figure of
the mother.

And Dreiser was the first to salute all that had been brought
to his work by our treatment.

In our treatment the tragedy within the framework of the novel was consummated far earlier than in these final scenes. This end—the cell—the electric chair—the brightly polished spittoon (which I saw myself at Sing-Sing) at his feet—all this is no more than an end to one particular embodiment of that tragedy which continues to be enacted every hour and every minute in the United States, far outside the covers of novels.

The choice of such a "dry" and "hackneyed" formula of social treatment affords more than a sharpening of situations and a deepening revelation of images and characters.

Such a treatment profoundly acts also upon purely formal methods. It was thanks particularly to this and out of this that was conclusively formulated the concept of the "inner monologue" in cinema, an idea that I had carried in my mind for six years previously. Before the advent of sound made possible its practical realization.

As we have seen, one needed an extraordinarily differentiated sharpness of exposition of what was taking place within Clyde before that moment of the boat's "accident," and we realized that to develop an outer presentation of this would not solve our problem.

The whole arsenal of knitted brows, rolling eyes, hard breathing, contorted postures, stony faces, or close-ups of convulsively working hands, was inadequate for the expression of those subtleties of the inner struggle in all its nuances.

The camera had to penetrate "inside" Clyde. Aurally and visually must be set down the feverish *race of thoughts,* intermittently with the outer actuality—the boat, the girl sitting opposite him, his own actions. The form of the "inner monologue" was born.

These montage sketches were wonderful.

Even literature is almost powerless in this domain. It is limited either to the primitive rhetoric used by Dreiser to describe Clyde's inner murmurings * or to the worse pseudo-

---

* A sample: "You might save her. But again you might not! For see how she strikes about. She is stunned. She herself is unable to save herself and by her erratic terror, if you draw near her now, may bring

classic tirades of O'Neill's heroes in *Strange Interlude* who tell
the audience, in "asides," what they are thinking, to supplement what they say to each other. In this the theater limps
more than does orthodox literary prose.

Only the film-element commands a means for an adequate
presentation of the whole course of thought through a disturbed mind.

Or, if literature can do it, it is only a literature that breaks
through the limits of its orthodox enclosure. Literature's most
brilliant achievement in this field has been the immortal "inner
monologues" of Leopold Bloom in *Ulysses*. When Joyce and
I met in Paris, he was intensely interested in my plans for the
inner film-monologue, with a far broader scope than is afforded
by literature.

Despite his almost total blindness, Joyce wished to see those
parts of *Potemkin* and *October* that, with the expressive means
of film culture, move along kindred lines.

The "inner monologue," as a literary method of abolishing
the distinction between subject and object in stating the hero's
re-experience in a crystallized form, is first observed by re-
search-workers in literary experiment as early as 1887, in the
work of Edouard Dujardin, pioneer on the "stream of consciousness," *Les lauriers sont coupés*.[12]

As theme, as world-perception, as "sensation," as description of an object, but not as method, one can find it, of course,
even earlier. "Slipping" from the objective into the subjective,
and back again, is a characteristic of the writings of the ro-
mantics—E. T. A. Hoffmann, Novalis, Gerard de Nerval.[13] But
as a method of literary style, rather than as an inter-lacing in
the story, or a form of literary description, we first find it
used by Dujardin, as a specific method of exposition, as a
specific method of construction; its absolute literary perfection
is achieved by Joyce and Larbaud, thirty-one years later.

about your own death also. But you desire to live! And her living will
make your life not worth while from now on. Rest but a moment—
a fraction of a minute! Wait—wait—ignore the pity of that appeal. And
then—then— But there! Behold. It is over. She is sinking now. You will
never, never see her alive any more—ever." [11]

It finds full expression, however, only in the cinema.

For only the sound-film is capable of reconstructing all phases and all specifics of the course of thought.

What wonderful sketches those montage lists were!

Like thought, they would sometimes proceed with visual images. With sound. Synchronized or non-synchronized. Then as sounds. Formless. Or with sound-images: with objectively representational sounds . . .

Then suddenly, definite intellectually formulated words—as "intellectual" and dispassionate as pronounced words. With a black screen, a rushing imageless visuality.

Then in passionate disconnected speech. Nothing but nouns. Or nothing but verbs. Then interjections. With zigzags of aimless shapes, whirling along with these in synchronization.

Then racing visual images over complete silence.

Then linked with polyphonic sounds. Then polyphonic images. Then both at once.

Then interpolated into the outer course of action, then interpolating elements of the outer action into the inner monologue.

As if presenting inside the characters the inner play, the conflict of doubts, the explosions of passion, the voice of reason, rapidly or in slow-motion, marking the differing rhythms of one and the other and, at the same time, contrasting with the almost complete absence of outer action: a feverish inner debate behind the stony mask of the face.

How fascinating it is to listen to one's own train of thought, particularly in an excited state, in order to catch yourself, looking at and listening to your mind. How you talk "to yourself," as distinct from "out of yourself." The syntax of inner speech as distinct from outer speech. The quivering inner words that correspond with the visual images. Contrasts with outer circumstances. How they work reciprocally. . . .

To listen and to study, in order to understand structural laws and assemble them into an inner monologue construction of the utmost tension of the struggle of tragic re-experience. How fascinating!

And what scope for creative invention and observation. And

how obvious it becomes that the material of the sound-film is not dialogue.

The true material of the sound-film is, of course, the monologue.

And how unexpectedly, in its practical embodiment of an unforeseen, particular, concrete case to be expressed, it calls across to the theoretically long foreseen "last word" on montage form in general. That the montage form, as structure, is a reconstruction of the laws of the thought process.

Here the particularity of treatment, fertilized by a new and not a former formal method, leaves its limits and generalizes in new theoretical scope and in principle the theory of montage form as a whole.

(However, this does not by any means imply that the *thought* process as a *montage form* must necessarily have the process of thought as its *subject!*)

The notes for this 180° advance in sound film culture—languished in a suitcase at the hotel and were eventually buried Pompeii-like, beneath a mass of books, and while they waited for realization . . .

An American Tragedy was given to Josef von Sternberg to film, and he directly, literally, discarded everything on which our treatment had been based, and restored everything that we had discarded.

As for an "inner monologue," it didn't occur to him. . . .

Sternberg confined his attention to the studio's wishes—and filmed a straight detective case.

The old gray lion Dreiser battled for our "distortion" of his work, and brought Paramount, who had filmed a formally and outwardly correct version of his story, into court.

Two years later O'Neill's *Strange Interlude* was "adapted" for the screen, and we were given double and triple explanatory voices around the silent face of the hero, giving additional tonnage to the playwright's cuneiform dramaturgy. A bloody mockery of what might be achieved with correct montage principles—in the inner monologue!

Work of a similar type. Solution by treatment of the work in hand. Estimation by treatment. But of greatest significance, a constructively artistic and formally fruitful rôle for this "boring," "obligatory," "imposed" ideology and ideological restraint.

Not a schematic realization but a living organism of production—this is the fundamental work facing the direction collective of the Third Course at the State Cinema Institute. And with all methods we shall seek the themes for this work in the many-sided thematic ocean all around us.

[1932]

FILM LANGUAGE

> Creation is a concept which we writers use all too freely, though we hardly possess the right to do so. Creation is a degree of tension reached in the work of the memory at which the speed of its working draws from the reserves of knowledge and impressions the most salient and characteristic facts, pictures, details, and renders them into the most precise, vivid and intelligible words. Our young literature cannot boast of possessing this quality. The stock of impressions, the sum of knowledge of our writers is not large, and there is no sign of any special anxiety to extend or enrich it.
>
> MAXIM GORKY [1]

GORKY'S SPEECH on the language of literature must be acknowledged—and considering the state of film language, we in films should feel called upon most of all to respond to it.

Film language, to a certain extent, is commonly associated with my works and my commentaries on them. And for this reason I shall take the initiative, by sniping at myself.

I do not propose to talk of the talking film—or, more exactly, of its talking portions. It speaks for itself. It even screams. And its quality, even before cinematically appraising it, contains so much poverty of a purely literary sort that its film claims may be put aside, for the moment.

In any case, it is not of this language I want to speak. (With my reputation as a literary stylist it would be laughable for me to do so.) I want to talk about the lack of culture in fundamentally cinematic diction that we may observe on the screen today.

In this matter of cinematic diction our cinema has accomplished a great deal for the world's film culture. And this accomplishment has been considerably deeper than mere fashion.

It is true that much that is specifically ours in the development of film expressiveness has been entrenched abroad no more deeply than as a passing fashion. Snippets of film, spliced together with nothing more reasonable than film cement, appear on the film-menu as "Russian cutting," "russischen Schnitt," very much in the way that restaurants use the term "Salade russe" for a certain dish of chopped and seasoned vegetables.

Fashion. Fashions pass—culture remains. Occasionally the culture behind the fashion is not noticed. Occasionally a cultural achievement is thrown out with the bath-water of fashion.

Negro sculpture, Polynesian masks, the Soviet manner of editing films have all been, for the West, merely exotica.

Of the extraction of general cultural values—of the mastery of principles—of the use of these accomplishments by the people who, in principle, move culture forward . . . but, of course, conversations on such themes are *so* passé.

What are fashions for? Tomorrow the magnates of mode—Patou, Worth, Mme. Lanvin, from their various yards, launch a new fashion. From somewhere in the Congo some "novelty" is brought—something carved from the ivory tusks of elephants by colonial slaves. Somewhere in the ravines of Mongolia a discovery is made—some patinized bronze sculptures created by the slaves of a long dead chieftain in a long dead epoch. All is well. It's all to the good. It all pays off.

The growth of culture? Who cares about that? It would seem that such relations to culture and to cultural achievements had long since been altered among us here by the October Revolution. One can't force one's way into museums on a free day. A worker with his wife and children stands in line to go through the Tretyakov Galley. One can't squeeze into the reading-rooms—too crowded. Readings, lectures—all overcrowded. Everywhere one finds attention, interest, thrift—an economical mastery of pre-revolutionary achievements.

Only in films is there a purely bourgeois absence of economy. Not only in budget. But thoughtlessness. And not only

in schedule. But a total illiteracy and neglect of all that which
in the Soviet period, with Soviet hands, on Soviet materials,
and by Soviet principles, has been brought into and created in
film culture.

Splendid: "We mastered the classics." (Splendid or not—
this is a quite different question, and a debatable one, at that!)
We are noting assets.

But this does not dismiss my question. Why must we therefore toss into oblivion all the expressive means and potentialities of cinematography, in which these classics have been
flashed on the screen?

"We have mastered actors from the theater." (Better than
classics.) Splendid!

There's another question, in Krylov's words: "Is auntie
holding on to the tail?" Even if this auntie is such a fine actress
as Tarasova! * Or is there a danger of film culture not profit-
ing, but being harmed by the excellence of her acting?

As for the shots—"rubbish." And the composition of the
shots—"you're just making trouble." And montage is obviously—"jumpy."

With the result, looking at the screen, that you feel a
sweetish sensation, as if your eye had been lifted by sugar-
tongs and oh-so-gently turned first to the right, then to the
left, and finally whirled in a full circle, in order to push it
back into a confused orbit. They say: "It's not our fault that
you have such eyes." "That's not important to the spectator."
"The spectator doesn't notice such things." "I don't hear the
spectator screaming." Quite true. Nor does the reader scream.
What is needed is not a scream, but a thundering shout. The
authoritative shout of Gorky, to make literature notice where
it is coming undone, how it is unraveling. The reader will not
die of "trouble-making." He doesn't see how "rubbish" can
bring him death. And he isn't pushed into his grave by a negli-
gence towards literary language.

* Alla Tarasova, of the Moscow Art Theatre, had appeared in a film
version of Ostrovsky's play *Thunderstorm* shortly before this essay
was written.—EDITOR.

Nevertheless it has been considered necessary to unite behind literature to defend the reader. In what way does the vision of the reader become worse when he enters a film-theater?

In what way is his ear worse when, united with his eye, it is present at some audio-visual catastrophe, pretending to be audio-visual counterpoint?

Characteristically, films have become known exclusively as "sound-films." Must this mean that what you see while you're listening does not deserve your attention? But this is apparently so.

At this point some viper must be hissing: "Aha! the old devil is going to gallop about montage again."

Yes, montage.

For many film-makers montage and leftist excesses of formalism—are synonymous. Yet montage is not this at all.

For those who are able, montage is the most powerful compositional means of telling a story. ✱

For those who do not know about composition, montage is a syntax for the correct construction of each particle of a film fragment.

And lastly, montage is simply an elementary rule of film-orthography for those who mistakenly put together pieces of a film as one would mix ready-made recipes for medicine, or to pickle cucumbers, or preserve plums, or ferment apples and cranberries together.

Not only montage . . . I should like to see the expressive activity of man's hand freed from these lesser portions of his toilette, away from these supporting aggregates.

One encounters in films individually fine shots, but under these circumstances the value of the shot and its independent pictorial quality contradict one another. Out of tune with the montage idea and composition, they become esthetic toys and aims in themselves. The better the shots, the closer the film comes to a disconnected assemblage of lovely phrases, a shop-window full of pretty but unrelated products, or an album of post-card views.

I do not stand, by any means, for the "hegemony" of mon-

✱ suppose one doesnt want to "tell a story" = ?

tage. The time has passed, when with the aims of pedagogy and training, it was necessary to perform tactical and polemical twists, in order to free montage broadly as an expressive means of cinema. But we must face the question of literacy in film-diction. And we must demand that the quality of montage, of film-syntax and film-speech not only never fall back behind the level of previous work, but that these go beyond and surpass their predecessors—this is why we should be deeply concerned in the struggle for a high quality of film culture.

It's easier for literature. In criticizing it, one can stand classics alongside it. Its heritage and achievement have undergone a great deal of investigation and study, down to the most delicate microscopic detail. The analysis of the compositional and imagery structure of Gogol's prose, made by the late Andrei Belyi, stands as a living reproach before any literary flippancy.[2]

And, by the way, Gogol has been brought also into films. Up till now burdened with formless film treatment, he has at last flashed with all the purity of montage form into the sound-film almost as if a Gogol text had been directly transposed into visual material.

Under the splendid visual poem of the Dnieper in the first reel of *Ivan* [1932], Dovzhenko, I believe, could successfully recite Gogol's description of the "wonderful Dnieper," from his *Terrible Revenge*.

The rhythm of the moving camera—floating by the shores. The cutting in of immobile expanses of water. In the alternation and shifting of these is the legerdemain and wizardry of Gogol's imagery and turns of speech. All this "neither stirs nor thunders." All this "you see and you do not know whether its immense breadth is moving or not . . . and it is enchanted, as if it had been poured glass," and so on. Here literature and cinema provide a model of the purest fusion and affinity. And this sequence also recalls—Rabelais. His poetic anticipation of the "imaging" of the theory of relationship is in his description of the isle "*en laquelle les chemins cheminent*":

. . . and he further informed us that Seleucus [a Roman mathe-matician of the first century] had been of the opinion that the earth really revolved around the poles, rather than the heavens, although the contrary seems to us to be the truth—just as, when we are on the river Loire, the trees along the bank appear to be moving, whereas it is not the trees at all, but ourselves upon the boat, who are in motion.[3] *

We paused on this example, for it seems like the swan-song for the purity of film language on our contemporary screen. For *Ivan*, as well. Its latter reels at no point ascend to the per-fection of this fragment.

I hear someone object, saying that the "wonderful Dnieper" is a poem. The core of the matter is not in this. Based on this it would have to be assumed that the structure of prose, that of Zola for example, must certainly display "naturalistic chaos."

And yet, in the progress of a study being made of his work, I chanced to see pages of *Germinal* broken up into the strophes of an epic poem—they could be recited with no less severity than Homeric hexameters.

These pages contained the episodes, leading up to the sinister scene when, during the uprising before the arrival of the gen-darmes, the women destroy the shop of the usurer and rapist Maigrat. When the infuriated women, under the leadership of La Brûlé and Mouquette, mutilate the corpse of the hated shopkeeper, who had slipped in his escape over the roof and broken his skull on the curbstone. When the bleeding "trophy" is hoisted on a stick and carried at the head of a procession . . .

"What is it they have at the end of that stick?" asked Cécile, who had grown bold enough to look out.

Lucie and Jeanne declared that it must be a rabbit-skin.

* The reader curious to see more of the *haiku* mentioned in a previous essay, will encounter another "anticipation" of Dovzhenko's poetic sequence:

> The sail hoisted,
> The willows on the shore
> Have run away.
>   JAKUSUI [4]

"No, no," murmured Madame Hennebeau, "they must have been pillaging a pork butcher's, it seems a remnant of a pig."

At this moment she shuddered and was silent. Madame Grégoire had nudged her with her knee. They both remained stupefied. The young ladies, who were very pale, asked no more questions, but with large eyes followed this red vision through the darkness.[5]

This scene, as well as the preceding scene, where this same crowd of women attempts to give a public flogging to Cécile, is a stylized transplanting, obviously, of an episode that struck Zola in the annals of the French Revolution.

The incident of Cécile's encounter with the women reproduces the well-known episode of the attack on Théroigne de Méricourt.

The second scene involuntarily forces a recollection of a less known and less popular episode recorded in the materials gathered by Mercier. When the crowd's hatred of the Princess de Lamballe, Marie Antoinette's closest intimate, burst at the gates of the prison of La Force, and the people's wrath obtained satisfaction from her, one of the participants *"lui coupa la partie virginale et s'en fit des moustaches."* [6]

A pointing finger, indicating the consciously used earlier source for these stylized adaptations, that could not possibly have been accidentally selected, is provided by the title itself, chosen from the calendar of this earlier epoch—*Germinal.* If this appeal for temperament and pathos to a previous pathetic epoch was made largely in the explicitly rhythmic clarity of form of his literary diction, this expanded treatment of little episodes is not amongst his most fortunate passages.

With an analogous image our film *October* also suffered in the sequence of the July uprising. For we had no intention to give, in the authentic incident of the murder of a Bolshevik worker by a brutalized bourgeois, any "note" of the Paris Commune's aftermath. Seen in context, the scene of the lady stabbing the worker with her parasol is completely apart in spirit from the general feeling of the pre-October days.

This is, by the way, an observation that may not be unhelpful. As literary heirs, we frequently make use of the cultural images and language of previous epochs. This naturally determines a large part of our works' color. And it is important to note failures in the use of such decided models.

To return anew to the question of purity of film form, I can easily counter the usual objection that the craft of film diction and film expressiveness is very young as yet, and has no models for a classic tradition. It is even said that I find too much fault with the models of film form at our disposal, and manage with literary analogies alone. Many even consider it dubious that this "half-art" (and you would be surprised to know how many, in and out of films, still refer to the cinema in this way) deserves such a broad frame of reference.

Forgive me. But this is the way things are.

And yet our film language, though lacking its classics, possessed a great severity of form and film diction. On a certain level our cinema has known such a severe responsibility for each shot, admitting it into a montage sequence with as much care as a line of poetry is admitted into a poem, or each musical atom is admitted into the movement of a fugue.

There are plenty of examples that may be brought in from the practice of our silent cinematography. Not having the time to analyze other specimens for this present purpose, I may be allowed to bring here a sample analysis from one of my own works. It is taken from material for the conclusion of my book *Direction* * (Part II—*Mise-en-cadre*) and concerns *Potemkin*. In order to show the compositional dependence between the plastic side of each of the shots, an example has been intentionally chosen not from a climax, but from an almost accidentally hit-upon place: fourteen successive pieces from the scene that precedes the fusillade on the Odessa steps. The scene where the "good people of Odessa" (so the sailors of the

* Left unfinished at the author's death, the completed sections of this definitive work may be prepared for publication by his literary executors. —EDITOR.

Potemkin addressed the population of Odessa) send yawls with provisions to the side of the mutinous battleship.

This sending of greetings is constructed on a distinct cross-cutting of two themes.

1. The yawls speeding towards the battleship.
2. The people of Odessa watching and waving.

At the end the two themes are merged. The composition is basically in two planes: depth and foreground. Alternately, the themes take a dominant position, advancing to the foreground, and thrusting each other by turns to the background.

The composition is built (1) on a plastic interaction of both these planes (within the frame) and (2) on a shifting of line and form in each of these planes from frame to frame (by montage). In the second case the compositional play is formed from the interaction of plastic impressions of the preceding shot in collision or interaction with the following shot. (Here the analysis is of the purely spatial and linear directions: the rhythmic and temporal relations will be discussed elsewhere.)

The movement of the composition takes the following course:

I. The yawls in movement. A smooth, even movement, parallel with the horizontals of the frame. The whole field of vision is filled with theme 1. There is a play of small vertical sails.

II. An intensified movement of the yawls of theme 1 (the entrance of theme 2 contributes to this). Theme 2 comes to the foreground with the severe rhythm of the vertical motionless columns. The vertical lines foreshadow the plastic distribution of the coming figures (in IV, V, etc.). Interplay of the horizontal wakes and the vertical lines of both sails and columns. The yawl theme is thrust back in depth. At the bottom of the frame appears the plastic theme of the arch.

III. The plastic theme of the arch expands into the entire frame. The play is effected by the shift in the frame's content—from vertical lines to the structure of the arch. The theme of verticals is maintained in the movement of the people—small figures moving away from the camera. The yawl theme is thrust completely into the background.

IV. The plastic theme of the arch finally moves into the foreground. The arc-formation is transposed to a contrary solution: the contours of a group are sketched, forming a circle (the parasol emphasizes the composition). This same transition in a contrary direction also takes place within a vertical construction: the backs of the small figures moving towards the depth are replaced by large standing figures, photographed frontally. The theme of the yawls in movement is maintained by reflection, in the expression of their eyes and in their movement in a horizontal direction.

V. In the foreground is a common compositional variant: an even number of persons is replaced by an uneven number. Two replaced by three. This "golden rule" in shifting the *mise-en-scène* is supported by a tradition that can be traced back to the principles of Chinese painting as well as to the practice of the *Commedia dell'arte*. (The directions of the glances also cross.) The arch motive is again bent, this time in a contrary curve. Repeating and supporting it is a new parallel arch-motif in the background: a balustrade—the yawl theme in movement. The eyes gaze across the whole width of the frame in a horizontal direction.

VI. Pieces I to V give a transition from the yawl theme to the watcher's theme, developed in five montage pieces. The interval from V to VI gives a sharp returning transition from the watchers to the yawls. Strictly following the content, the composition sharply transforms each of the elements in an opposite direction. The line of the balustrade is brought swiftly into the foreground, now as the line of the boat's gunwale. This is doubled by the adjacent line of the water's surface. The basic compositional elements are the same, but counterposed in treatment. V is static; VI is drawn by the dynamics of the boat in motion. The vertical division into "three" is maintained in both frames. The central element is texturally similar (the woman's blouse, and the canvas of the sail). The elements at the sides are in sharp contrast: the dark shapes of the men beside the woman, and the white spaces beside the central sail. The vertical distribution is also contrasted: three figures cut by the bottom horizontal are transformed into a vertical sail, cut by the upper horizontal of the frame. A new theme appears *in the background*—the side of the battleship, cut *at the top* (in preparation for piece VII).

VII. A sharply new thematic turn. A background theme— the battleship—is brought forward into the foreground (the thematic jump from V to VI serves somewhat as an anticipation of the jump from VI to VII). The viewpoint is turned 180°: shooting from the battleship towards the sea—reversing VI. This time the side of the battleship in the *foreground* is also cut—but by the *lower* horizontal of the frame. In the depth is the sail theme, developed in verticals. The verticals of the sailors. The static gun-barrel continues the line of the boat's movement in the preceding shot. The side of the battleship would seem to be an arch, bent into an almost straight line.

VIII. A repetition of IV with heightened intensity. The horizontal play of eyes is transformed into vertically waving hands. The vertical theme has moved from the depth into the foreground, repeating the thematic transfer to the watchers.

IX. Two faces, closer. Speaking generally, this is an unfortunate combination with the preceding shot. It would have been better to have brought between VIII and IX a shot of three faces, to have repeated V with a heightened intensity. This would have produced a 2:3:2 structure. Moreover, the repetition of the familiar groups of IV and V, ending with the new IX, would have sharpened the impression of the last shot. This error is somewhat remedied by the slight change in plane, coming closer to the figures.

X. The two faces change to a single, closer face. The arm is thrown very energetically up and out of the frame. A correct alternation of faces (if the suggested correction were made between VIII and IX)—2:3:2:1. A second pair of shots with a correct enlargement of the dimensions in relation to the first pair (a proper repetition with a qualitative variation). The line of odd numbers differs both in quantity and quality (differing in the dimensions of the faces and differing in their quantities, while retaining the common direction of the odd numbers).

XI. A new sharp thematic turn. A jump, repeating that of V-VI, with new intensity. The vertical *up-throw* of the arm in the preceding shot is echoed by the vertical *sail*. In this the vertical of this sail rushes past in a horizontal line. A repetition of the theme of VI in greater intensity. And a repetition of the composition of II with this difference, that the horizontal theme of the moving yawls and the verticals of the motionless columns are here molded into a single horizontal movement of the *vertical* sail. The composition repeats the *sequence's theme* of an identity between the yawls and the people on the shore (before moving on to the concluding theme of this reel, the fusion of the yawls and the battleship).

XII. The sail of XI is broken up into a multitude of vertical sails, scudding along horizontally (a repetition of piece I with increased intensity). The little sails move in a direction opposite to that of the large single sail.

XIII. Having been broken up into small sails, the large sail is newly re-assembled, but now not as a sail, but as the flag flying over the *Potemkin*. There is a new quality in this shot, for it is both static and mobile,—the mast being vertical and motionless, while the flag flutters in the wind. Formally, piece XIII repeats XI. But the change from sail to banner translates a principle of plastic unification to an ideological-thematic unification. This is no longer a vertical, a plastic union of separate elements of composition,—*this is a revolutionary banner, uniting battleship, yawls and shore.*

XIV. From here we have a natural return from the flag to the battleship. XIV repeats VII, with a lift in intensity. This shot introduces a new compositional group of *interrelationships between the yawls and the battleship*, distinguished from the first group, *yawls and shore*. The first group expressed the theme: "the yawls carry greetings and gifts from the shore to the battleship." This second group will express *the fraternization of yawls and battleship.*

The compositional dividing-point, and simultaneously the ideological uniter of both compositional groups, is the mast with the revolutionary banner.

Piece VII, repeated by the first piece of the second group, XIV, appears as a sort of foreshadowing of the second group and as an element linking the two groups together, as though the latter group had sent out a "patrol" into the territory of the first group. In the second group this rôle will be played by shots of waving figures, cut into scenes of the fraternization between yawls and battleship.

It should not be thought that the filming and montage of these pieces were done according to these calculations, drawn up *a priori*. Of course not. But the assembly and distribution of these pieces on the cutting table was already clearly dictated by the compositional demands of the film form. These demands dictated the selection of these particular pieces from all those available. These demands also established the regularity of the alternation of these pieces. Actually, these pieces, regarded only for their plot and story aspects, could be rearranged in any combination. But the compositional movement through them would hardly prove in that case quite so regular in construction.

One cannot therefore complain of the complexity of this analysis. In comparison with analyses of literary and musical forms my analysis is still quite descriptive and easy.

Setting aside for the present the question of rhythmic examination, in our analysis we have also analyzed the alternations of sound and word combinations.

An analysis of the very lenses employed in filming these shots, and their use along with camera-angles and lighting, all deriving from the demands of the style and the character of the film's content, would serve as an exact analogy to an analysis of the expressiveness of phrases and words and their phonetic indications in a literary work.

Of course the spectator, least of all, is able to verify with calipers the conformity to rule of the successive shot compositions within the montage. But in his perception of a fully realized montage composition the same elements are contributed that stylistically distinguish a page of cultured prose from the pages of "Count Amori," Verbitzkaya or Breshko-Breshkovsky.*

At present Soviet cinematography is historically correct in entering the campaign for the story. Along this path are still many difficulties, many risks of falsely understanding the principles of story-telling. Of these the most terrible is the neglect of those possibilities given us now and again to liberate from the old traditions of the story:

The possibility of principally and newly re-examining the foundations and problems of the film-story.

And to go ahead in a cinematographically progressive movement, not "back to the story," but "to the story ahead of us." There is not yet clear artistic orientation on these ways, although separate positive influences are already becoming visible.

In one way or another we approach the moment when we shall master clearly the realized principles of Soviet story films, and we must meet that moment with all the weapons of faultless purity and culture of film language and speech.

Our great masters of literature from Pushkin and Gogol to Mayakovsky and Gorky are valued by us not only as story-telling masters. We value in them the culture of masters of speech and word.

It is time with all sharpness to pose the problem of the culture of film-language. It is important that all the film-workers speak out in this cause. And before all else, in the language of the montage and shots of their own films.

[1934]

* Approximate English and American equivalents for these popular Russian writers of the early twentieth century: Elinor Glyn, Dorothy Dix, Rupert Hughes.—EDITOR.

FILM FORM: NEW PROBLEMS

EVEN THAT old veteran Heraclitus observed that no man can bathe twice in the same river. Similarly no esthetic can flourish on one and the same set of principles at two different stages in its development. Especially when the particular esthetic concerned happens to relate to the most mobile of the arts, and when the division between the epochs is the succession of two Five Year periods in the mightiest and most notable job of construction in the world—the job of building the first Socialist state and society in history. From which it is obvious that our subject is here the esthetic of film, and in particular the esthetic of film in the Soviet land.

During the last few years a great upheaval has taken place in the Soviet cinema. This upheaval is, first and foremost, ideological and thematic. The peak of achievement in the blossoming of the silent cinema was attained under the broadly expansive slogan of mass, the "mass-hero" and methods of cinematographic portrayal directly derivative therefrom, rejecting narrowly dramaturgical conceptions in favor of epos and lyrism, with "type" and episodic protagonists in place of individual heroes and the consequently inevitable principle of montage as the guiding principle of film expressiveness. But during the last few years—the first years, that is, of the Soviet sound-cinema—the guiding principles have changed.

From the former all-pervading mass imagery of movement and experiences of the masses, there begin at this stage to stand out individual hero-characters. Their appearance is accompanied by a structural change in those works where they appear. The former epical quality and its characteristic giant scale begin to contract into constructions closer to dramaturgy in the narrow sense of the word, to a dramaturgy, in fact, of

122

more traditional stamp and much closer to the foreign cinema than those films that once declared war to the death against its very principles and methods. The best films of the most recent period (*Chapayev*, for example) have none the less succeeded in partially preserving the epical quality of the first period of Soviet cinema development, with larger and happier results. But the majority of films have almost completely lost that luggage, comprised of principle and form, which determined in its day the specific and characteristic quality of face of the Soviet cinema, a quality not divorced from the newness and unusualness it bore as reflection of the unusual and never-heretofore-existing land of the Soviets, its strivings, aims, ideals and struggles.

To many it seems that the progressive development of the Soviet cinema has stopped. They speak of retrogression. This is, of course, wrong. And one important circumstance is underestimated by the fervent partisans of the old silent Soviet cinema, who now gaze bewilderedly as there appears Soviet film after film which in so many respects is formally similar to the foreign cinema. If in many cases there must indeed be observed the dulling of that formal brilliance to which the foreign friends of our films had become accustomed, this is the consequence of the fact that our cinematography, in its present stage, is entirely absorbed in another sphere of investigation and deepening. A measure of suspension in the further development of the forms and means of film expressiveness has appeared as an inevitable consequence of the diversion of investigation into another direction, a diversion recently and still obtaining: into the direction of deepening and broadening the thematic and ideological formulation of questions and problems within the content of the film. It is not accidental that precisely at this period, for the first time in our cinematography, there begin to appear the first finished images of personalities, not just of any personalities, but of the finest personalities: the leading figures of leading Communists and Bolsheviks. Just as from the revolutionary movement of the masses emerged the sole revolutionary party, that of the Bolsheviks, which heads the unconscious elements of revolution and leads them towards conscious revolutionary aims, so the film images of the leading men of our times begin during the present period to crystallize out of the general-revolutionary mass-quality of the earlier type of film. And the clarity of the Communist slogan rings more definitely, replacing the general-revolutionary slogan.

The Soviet cinema is now passing through a new phase—a phase of yet more distinct Bolshevization, a phase of yet more pointed ideological and essential militant sharpness. A phase historically logical, natural and rich in fertilizing possibilities for the cinema, as most notable of arts.

This new tendency is no surprise, but a logical stage of growth, rooted in the very core of the preceding stage. Thus one who is perhaps the most devoted partisan of the mass-epical style in cinema, one whose name has always been linked to the "mass"-cinema—the author of these lines—is subject to precisely this same process in his penultimate film—*Old and New*, where Marfa Lapkina appears already as an exceptional individual protagonist of the action.

The task, however, is to make this new stage sufficiently synthetic. To ensure that in its march towards new conquests of ideological depths, it not only does not lose the perfection of the achievements already attained, but advances them ever forward toward new and as yet unrealized qualities and means of expression. To raise form once more to the level of ideological content.

Being engaged at the moment on the practical solution of these problems in the new film *Bezhin Meadow*, only just begun, I should like to set out here a series of cursory observations on the question of the problem of form in general.

The problem of form, equally with the problem of content at the present stage, is undergoing a period of most serious deepening of principle. The lines which follow must serve to show the direction in which this problem is moving and the extent to which the new trend of thought in this sphere is closely linked in evolution to the extreme discoveries on this path made during the peak period of our silent cinema.

Let us start at the last points reached by the theoretical researches of the stage of Soviet cinema above referred to (1924-1929).

It is clear and undoubted that the *ne plus ultra* of those paths was the theory of the "intellectual cinema."

This theory set before it the task of "restoring emotional fullness to the intellectual process." This theory engrossed itself as follows, in transmuting to screen form the abstract concept, the course and halt of concepts and ideas—without intermediary. Without recourse to story, or invented plot, in fact directly—by means of the image-composed elements as filmed. This theory was a broad, perhaps even a too broad, generalization of a series of possibilities of expression placed at our disposal by the methods of montage and its combinations. The theory of intellectual cinema represented, as it were, a limit, the *reductio ad paradox* of that hypertrophy of the montage concept with which film esthetics were permeated during the emergence of Soviet silent cinematography as a whole and my own work in particular.

Recalling the "establishment of the abstracted concept" as a framework for the possible products of the intellectual cinema, as the basic foundation of its film canvasses; and acknowledging that the movement forward of the Soviet cinema is now following other aims, namely, the demonstration of such conceptual postulates by agency of concrete actions and living persons as we have noted above, let us see what can and must be the further fate of the ideas expressed at that time.

Is it then necessary to jettison all the colossal theoretical and creative material, in the turmoil of which was born the conception of the intellectual cinema? Has it proved only a curious and exciting paradox, a *fata morgana* of unrealized compositional possibilities? Or has its paradoxicality proved to lie not in its essence, but in the sphere of its application, so that now, after examining some of its principles, it may emerge that, in new guise, with new usage and new application, the postulates then expressed have played and may still continue to play a highly positive part in the theoretical grasping and understanding and mastering of the mysteries of the cinema?

The reader, doubtless, has already guessed that this is precisely how we incline to consider the situation, and all that follows will serve to demonstrate, perhaps only in broad outline, exactly what we understand by it, and use now as a working basis, and which, as a working hypothesis in questions of the culture of film form and composition, is fortified more and more into a complete logical conception of everyday practice.

I should like to begin with the following consideration:

It is exceedingly curious that certain theories and points of view which in a given historical epoch represent an expression of scientific knowledge, in a succeeding epoch decline as science, but continue to exist as possible and admissible not in the line of science but in the line of art and imagery.

If we take mythology, we find that at a given stage mythology is nothing else than a complex of current knowledge about phenomena, chiefly related in imagery and poetic language. All these mythological figures, which at the best we now regard as the materials of allegory, at some stage represented an image-compilation of knowledge of the cosmos. Later, science moved on from imagery narratives to concepts, and the store of former personified-mythological nature-symbols continued to survive as a series of pictorial images, a series of literary, lyrical and other metaphors. At last they become exhausted even in this capacity and vanish into the archives. Consider even contemporary poetry, and compare it with the poetry of the eighteenth century.

Another example: take such a postulate as the a-priority of the idea, spoken of by Hegel in relation to the creation of the world. At a certain stage this was the summit of philosophical knowledge. Later, the summit was overthrown. Marx turns this postulate head over heels in the question of the understanding of real actuality. However, if we consider our works of art, we do in fact have a condition that almost looks like the Hegelian formula, because the idea-satiation of the author, his subjection to prejudice by the idea, must determine actually the whole course of the art-work, and if every element of the art-work does not represent an embodiment of the initial idea, we shall never have as result an art-work realized to its utmost fullness. It is of course understood that the artist's idea itself is in no way spontaneous or self-engendered, but is a socially reflected mirror-image, a reflection of social reality. But from the moment of formation within him of the viewpoint and idea, that idea appears as determining all the actual and material structure of his creation, the whole "world" of his creation.

Suppose we take another field, Lavater's "Physiognomy." This in its day was regarded as an objective scientific system. But physiognomy is now no science. Lavater was already laughed at by Hegel, though Goethe, for example, still collaborated with Lavater, if anonymously. (To Goethe must be assigned the authorship of, for example, a physiognomical study devoted to the head of Brutus.) We do not attribute to physiognomy any objective scientific value whatsoever, but the moment we require, in course of the all-sided representation of character denoting some type, the external characterization of a countenance, we immediately start using faces in exactly the same way as Lavater did. We do so because in such a case it is important to us to create first and foremost an impression, the subjective impression of an observer, not the objective co-ordination of sign and essence actually composing character. In other words, the viewpoint that Lavater thought scientific is being "exhausted" by us in the arts, where it is needed in the line of imagery.

What is the purpose of examining all this? Analogous situations occur sometimes among the methods of the arts, and sometimes it occurs that the characteristics which represent logic in the matter of construction of form are mistaken for elements of content. Logic of this kind is, as a method, as a principle of construction, fully permissible, but it becomes a nightmare if this same method, this logic of construction, is regarded simultaneously as an exhaustive content.

You will perceive already whither the matter is tending, but I wish to cite one more example, from literature. The question relates now to one of the most popular of all literary genres—the detective story.

What the detective story represents, of which social formations and tendencies it is the expression, this we all know. On this subject Gorky recently spoke sufficiently at the Congress of Writers. But of interest is the origin of some of the characteristics of the genre, the sources from which derives the material that has gone towards creation of the ideal vessel of the detective story form in embodying certain aspects of bourgeois ideology.

It appears that the detective novel counts among its forerunners, aiding it to reach full bloom at the beginning of the nineteenth century, James Fenimore Cooper—the novelist of the North American Indians. From the ideological point of view, this type of novel, exalting the deeds of the colonizers, follows entirely the same current as the detective novel in serving as one of the most pointed forms of expression of private-property ideology. To this testified Balzac, Hugo, Eugène Sue, who produced a good deal in this literary-composition model from which later was elaborated the regular detective novel.

Recounting in their letters and diaries the inspirational images which guided them in their story constructions of flight and chase (*Les Miserables, Vautrin, Le Juif errant*), they all write that the prototype that attracted them was the dark forest background of James Fenimore Cooper, and that they had wished to transplant this dark forest and the action within it from the virgin backwoods of America to the labyrinth of the alleys and byways of Paris. The accumulation of clues derives from the methods of the "Pathfinders" whom Cooper portrayed in his works.

Thus the image "dark forest" and the technique of the "pathfinder" from Cooper's works serve the great novelists such as Balzac and Hugo as a sort of initial metaphor for their intrigue of detection and adventure constructions within the maze of Paris. They contribute also to formalizing as a genre those ideological tendencies which lay at the base of the detective novel. Thus is created a whole independent type of story construction. But, parallel with this use of the "heritage" of Cooper, we see yet another sort: the type of literal transplantation. Then we have indeed nonsense and nightmare. Paul Féval has written a novel in which redskins do their stuff in Paris and a scene occurs where three Indians scalp a victim in a cab!

I cite this example in order to return once more to the intellectual cinema. The specific quality of the intellectual cinema was proclaimed to be the content of the film. The trend of thoughts and the movement of thoughts were represented as the exhaustive basis of everything that transpired in the film, i.e., a substitute for the story. Along this line—exhaustive replacement of content—it does not justify itself. And in sequel perhaps to the realization of this, the intellectual cinema has speedily grown a new conception of a theoretical kind: the intellectual cinema has acquired a little successor in the theory of the "inner monologue."

The theory of the inner monologue warmed to some extent the ascetic abstraction of the flow of concepts, by transposing the problem into the more story-ish line of portraying the hero's emotions. During the discussions on the subject of the inner monologue, there was made none the less a tiny reservation, to the effect that this inner monologue could be used to construct things and not only for picturing an inner monologue.* Just a tiny hook hanging there in parentheses, but on it hung the crux of the whole affair. These parentheses must be opened immediately. And herein lies the principal matter with which I wish to deal.

* See "A Course in Treatment," page 106.

Which is—the syntax of inner speech as opposed to that of uttered speech. Inner speech, the flow and sequence of thinking unformulated into the logical constructions in which uttered, formulated thoughts are expressed, has a special structure of its own. This structure is based on a quite distinct series of laws. What is remarkable therein, and why I am discussing it, is that the laws of construction of inner speech turn out to be precisely those *laws which lie at the foundation of the whole variety of laws governing the construction of the form and composition of art-works*. And there is not one formal method that does not prove the spit and image of one or another law governing the construction of inner speech, as distinct from the logic of uttered speech. It could not be otherwise.

We know that at the basis of the creation of form lie sensual and imagist thought processes.* Inner speech is precisely at the stage of image-sensual structure, not yet having attained that logical formulation with which speech clothes itself before stepping out into the open. It is noteworthy that, just as logic obeys a whole series of laws in its constructions, so, equally, this inner speech, this sensual thinking, is subject to no less clear-cut laws and structural peculiarities. These are known and, in the light of the considerations here set out, represent an inexhaustible storehouse, as it were, of laws for the construction of form, the study and analysis of which have immense importance in the task of mastering the "mysteries" of the technique of form.

For the first time we are placed in possession of a firm storehouse of postulates, bearing on what happens to the initial thesis of the theme when it is translated into a chain of sensory images. The field for study in this direction is colossal. The

---

* This thesis is not offered as either new or original. Hegel and Plekhanov gave equal attention to sensual thought processes. What appears to be new here is a constructive distinction of the laws of this sensual thinking, for these classics do not particularize on this aspect, while no operative application of this thesis can be made to artistic practice and craft training without this distinction. The following development of these considerations, materials, and analyses, has set itself this particular operative aim of practical use.

point is that the forms of sensual, pre-logical thinking, which
are preserved in the shape of inner speech among the peoples
who have reached an adequate level of social and cultural
development, at the same time also represent in mankind at the
dawn of cultural development norms of conduct in general,
i.e., the laws according to which flow the processes of sensual
thought are equivalent for them to a "habit logic" of the future. In accordance with these laws they construct norms of
behavior, ceremonials, customs, speech, expressions, etc., and,
if we turn to the immeasurable treasury of folklore, of out-
lived and still living norms and forms of behavior preserved
by societies still at the dawn of their development, we find
that, what for them has been or still is a norm of behavior
and custom-wisdom, turns out to be at the same time precisely
what we employ as "artistic methods" and "technique of
embodiment" in our art-works. I have no space to discuss in
detail the question of the early forms of thought process. I
have no opportunity here to picture for you its basic specific
characteristics, which are a reflection of the exact form of the
early social organization of the communal structures. This is no
time to pursue the manner in which, from these general postulates, are worked out the separate characteristic marks and
forms of the construction of representations. I will limit myself
to quoting two or three instances exemplifying this principle,
that one or other given moment in the practice of form-creation is at the same time a moment of custom-practice from the
stage of development at which representations are still constructed in accordance with the laws of sensual thinking. I
emphasize here, however, that such construction is not of
course in any sense exclusive. On the contrary, from the very
earliest period there obtains simultaneously a flow of practical
and logical experiences, deriving from practical labor processes; a flow that gradually increases on the basis of them, discarding these earlier forms of thinking and embracing gradually all the spheres not only of labor, but also of other intellectual activities, abandoning the earlier forms to the sphere
of sensual manifestations.

Consider, for example, that most popular of artistic methods, the so-called *pars pro toto*. The power of its effectiveness is known to everyone. The pince-nez of the surgeon in *Potemkin* are firmly embedded in the memory of anyone who saw the film. The method consisted in substituting the whole (the surgeon) by a part (the pince-nez), which played his rôle, and, it so happened, played it much more sensual-intensively than it could have been played even by the re-appearance of the surgeon. It so happens that this method is the most typical example of a thinking form from the arsenal of early thought processes. At that stage we were still without the unity of the whole and the part as we now understand it. At that stage of non-differentiated thinking the part *is* at one and the same time also the whole. There is no unity of part and whole, but instead obtains an objective identity in representation of whole and part. It is immaterial whether it be part or whole—it plays invariably the rôle of aggregate and whole. This takes place not only in the simplest practical fields and actions, but immediately appears as soon as you emerge from the limits of the simplest "objective" practice. Thus, for example, if you receive an ornament made of a bear's tooth, it signifies that the whole bear has been given to you, or, what in these conditions signifies the same thing,* the strength of the bear as a whole. In the conditions of modern practice such a proceeding would be absurd. No one, having received a button off a suit, would imagine himself to be dressed in the complete suit. But as soon even as we move over into the sphere in which sensual and image constructions play the decisive rôle, into the sphere of artistic constructions, the same *pars pro toto* begins immediately to play a tremendous part for us as well. The pince-nez, taking the place of a whole surgeon, not only completely fills his rôle and place, but does so with a huge sensual-emotional increase in the intensity of the impression, to an extent considerably greater than could have been obtained by the re-appearance of the surgeon-character himself.

* A differentiated concept of "strength" outside the concrete specific bearer of that strength equally does not exist at this stage.

As you perceive, for the purposes of a sensual artistic impression, we have used, as a compositional method, one of those laws of early thinking which, at appropriate stages, appear as the norms and practice of everyday behavior. We made use of a construction of a sensual thinking type, and as a result, instead of a "logico-informative" effect, we receive from the construction actually an emotional sensual effect. We do not register the fact that the surgeon has drowned, we emotionally react to the fact through a definite compositional presentation of this fact.

It is important to note here that what we have analyzed in respect to the use of the close-up, in our example of the surgeon's pince-nez, is not a method characteristic solely of the cinema alone and specific to it. It equally has a methodological place and is employed in, for example, literature. *"Pars pro toto"* in the field of literary forms is what is known to us under the term synecdoche.

Let us indeed recall the definition of the two kinds of synecdoche. The first kind: this kind consists in that one receives *a presentation of the part instead of the whole.* This in turn has a series of sorts:

1. Singular instead of plural. ("The Son of Albion reaching for freedom" instead of "The sons of, etc.")

2. Collective instead of composition of the clan. ("Mexico enslaved by Spain" instead of "The Mexicans enslaved.")

3. Part instead of whole. ("Under the master's eye.")

4. Definite instead of indefinite. ("A hundred times we've said . . .")

5. Species instead of genus.

The second series of synecdoches consists in *the whole instead of the part.* But, as you perceive, both series and all their several subdivisions are subject to one and the same basic condition. Which condition is: the identity of the part and the whole and hence the "equivalence," the equal significance in replacing one by the other.

No less striking examples of the same occur in paintings

and drawings, where two color spots and a flowing curve give a complete sensual replacement of the whole object.

What is of interest here is not this list itself, but the fact that is confirmed by the list. Namely, that we are dealing here not with specific methods, peculiar to this or that art-medium, but first and foremost with a specific course and condition of embodied thinking—with sensual thinking, for which a given structure is a law. In this special, synecdochic, use of the "close-up," in the color-spot and curve, we have but particular instances of the operation of this law of *pars pro toto*, characteristic of sensual thinking, dependent upon whatever art-medium in which it happens to be functioning for its purpose of embodiment of the basic creative scheme.

Another example. We are well aware that every embodiment must be in strict artistic accord with the story situation being embodied. We know that this concerns costume, setting, accompanying music, light, color. We know that this accord concerns not only the demands made by naturalistic conviction, but also, and perhaps to a greater degree, the demands of sustaining the emotional expression. If a dramatist's scene "sounds" a certain key, then all elements of its embodiment must sound the same key. There is an unsurpassed classical example of this in *King Lear*, whose inner tempest echoes the tempest on the moor, raging round him on the stage. We can also find examples of a reverse construction—for purposes of contrast: say that a maximum raging of passion is to be resolved by an intentional static and immobile quality. Here, too, all elements of the embodiment would be realized with just as strict a sustaining and accord with the theme, though in this case with opposite indications, as well.

Such a demand also spreads over into the shot and the montage, whose means must likewise compositionally echo and respond to the basic compositional key for the treatment of the entire work and of each scene in it.*

---

* The considerable skill achieved in this field by our silent cinema fell perceptibly from the moment of transition to sound-film—for evidence, see most of our sound-films.

It appears that this element, sufficiently recognized and universal in art, can be found on a certain level of development in similar inevitable and obligatory modes of behavior in life. Here is an example from Polynesian practice—a practice that is preserved in customs today with little change. When any Polynesian woman is in confinement, there is a peremptory rule that all gates in the settlement must be opened, all doors thrown open, that everyone (including men, as well) is to remove any sashes, aprons, headbands, that all tied knots are to be untied, and so forth; that is, all circumstances, all concomitant details, must be arranged in a character exactly corresponding to the basic theme of what is occurring: everything must be opened, untied, to give maximum ease to the appearance in the world of the new child!

Let us now turn to another medium. Let us take a case where the material of the form-creation turns out to be the artist himself. This also confirms the truth of our thesis. Even more: in this instance the structure of the finished composition not only reproduces, as it were, a reprint of the structure of the laws along which flow sensual thought-processes. In this instance the circumstance itself, here united with the object-subject of creation, as a whole duplicates a picture of the psychic state and representation corresponding to the early forms of thought. Let us look once more at two examples. All investigators and travelers are invariably somewhat astonished at one characteristic of early forms of thought quite incomprehensible to a human being accustomed to think in the categories of current logic. It is the characteristic involving the conception that a human being, while being himself and conscious of himself as such, yet simultaneously considers himself to be also some other person or thing, and, further, to be so, just as definitely and just as concretely, materially. In the specialized literature on this subject there is the particularly popular example of one of the Indian tribes of Northern Brazil.

The Indians of this tribe—the Bororo—maintain that, while human beings, they are none the less at the same time also a special kind of red parakeet common in Brazil. Note that by this they do not in any way mean that they will become these birds after death, or that their ancestors were such in the remote past. Not at all. They directly maintain that they are in reality these actual birds. It is not here a matter of identity of names or relationship; they mean a complete simultaneous identity of both.

However strange and unusual this may sound to us, it is nevertheless possible to quote from artistic practice quantities of instances which would sound almost word for word like the Bororo idea concerning simultaneous double existence of two completely different and separate and, none the less, real images. It is enough only to touch on the question of the self-feeling of the actor during his creation or performance of a rôle. Here, immediately, arises the problem of "I" and "him." Where "I" is the individuality of the performer, and "he" the individuality of the performed image of the rôle. This problem of the simultaneity of "I" and "not I" in the creation and performance of a rôle is one of the central "mysteries" of acting creation. The solution of it wavers between complete subordination of "him" to "I"—and "he" (complete trans-substantiation). While the contemporary attitude to this problem in its formulation approaches the clear enough dialectic formula of the "unity of inter-penetrating opposites," the "I" of the actor and the "he" of the image, the leading opposite being the image, nevertheless in concrete self-feeling the matter is by a long way not always so clear and definite for the actor. In one way or another, "I" and "he," "their" inter-relationship, "their" connections, "their" interactions inevitably figure at every stage in the working out of the rôle. Let us quote at least one example from the most recent and popular opinions on the subject.

The actress Serafima Birman (an advocate of the second extreme) offers this:

> I read of a professor who celebrated neither his children's birth-days nor their name-days. He made an anniversary of the day

— "nothing-but-paint" + simultaneously a "living image of a person."

on which a child ceased to speak of himself in the third person: "Lyalya wants go walk," and said: "I want go walk." The same kind of anniversary for the actor is that day and even minute of that day on which he ceases to speak of the image as "he," and says "I." Where indeed this new "I" is not the personal "I" of the actor or actress but the "I" of his or her image. . . .[1]

No less revealing are descriptions in the memoirs of a whole series of actors of their behavior at the moment of putting on make-up or their costume, which they accompany by a complete "magic" operation of "transformation" with whisperings, such as "I am already not me," "I am already so-and-so," "See, I'm beginning to be him," and so on.

In one way or another, more or less controlled, simultaneous actuality in the playing of the rôle is bound to be present in the creative process of even, albeit, the most inveterate supporter of complete "trans-substantiation." There are, in fact, too few cases known in the history of the theater of an actor leaning on the "fourth [non-existent] wall!"

It is characteristic that a similarly fluctuating dual apprehension of stage action as both a reality of theater and a reality of representation exists also with the spectator. Here too, correct apprehension is a united duality, on the one hand preventing the spectator from killing the villain, in that he remembers the latter is not a reality, while on the other giving him the occasion for laughter or tears, in that he forgets that he is witnessing a representation, a play-acting.

Let us note another example. In his *Völkerpsychologie* Wilhelm Wundt quotes certain early speech constructions. (We are not concerned here with Wundt's own views, but only with a properly authenticated documentary specimen cited by him.) The meaning:

"The Bushman was at first received kindly by the white man in order that he might be brought to herd his sheep; then the white man maltreated the Bushman; the latter ran away, whereupon the white man took another Bushman, who suffered the same experience."

* the sense – impression (paint, actor, sound, light) so overwhelmed by the imaged-reality (spirit, meaning effect, etc)

This simple concept (describing a situation simple and casual in colonial manners) is approximately expressed in the language of the Bushman in this way:

"Bushman-there-go, here-run-to-white man, white man-give-to-bacco, Bushman-go-smoke, go-fill-tobacco-pouch, white man-give-meat-Bushman, Bushman-go-eat-meat, stand-up-go-home, go happily, go-sit-down, herd-sheep-white man, white man-go-strike Bushman, Bushman-cry-loud-pain, Bushman-go-run-away-white man, white man-run-after-Bushman, Bushman-then-another, this one-herd-sheep, Bushman-all-gone." [2]

We are astonished by this long series of descriptive single images, almost an asyntactic series. But suppose we take it into our heads to portray in action on the stage or screen those two lines of the situation implicit in the initial concept, we shall see to our surprise that we have begun to construct something very close to that which has been given as an example of Bushman construction. And this something, just as asyntactic, but supplied only with . . . a sequence of numbers, turns out to be something familiar to every one of us—a shooting script, an instrument to transpose a fact, abstracted into a concept, back into a chain of concrete single actions, which also happens to be the process of translating stage directions into action. "Ran away [from him]"—in Bushman language this appears as an orthodox editing description for two shots: "Bushman-go-run-away-white man," and "white man-run-after-Bushman"—the embryo for the montage of an American "chase sequence."

The abstract "received kindly" is expressed by most valuable concrete items, by means of which the representation of a kindly reception takes shape: a lighting of pipes, a filled tobacco pouch, cooked meat, etc. Again we have an example to show how, the moment we have to pass from informative to realistic expressiveness, we inevitably pass over to structural laws corresponding to sensual thinking, which plays the dominant rôle in representations characteristic of early development.

In this connection there is another illuminating example. It is known that still at this stage of development there are not yet generalizations and generalized "spinal" concepts. Lévy-Bruhl shows a factual instance of this in the Klamath language.[3] Their language contains no concept of "walking"; instead they employ an infinite series of terms for each particular form of walking. Rapid walking. Waddling. Tired walking. Stealthy walking, and so on. Each type of walking, no matter how delicate its nuances, is given its own term. This may seem strange to us—but only until we are called upon to open the parenthetical direction, "He approaches . . . ," in any play, and reveal it as a chain of approaching steps by one actor to another. The most splendidly conscious comprehension of the term "walking" fails one utterly. And if in the actor (and the director) this comprehension of "walking" does not at once flash "backwards" to a whole accumulation of possible and known particular cases of possible approaches, from which he can choose the most appropriate variant for his situation . . . then his performance can be expected to be a most sad and even tragic fiasco! *

How clear this is, even in details, can be seen by comparing different versions of a writer's manuscripts. Between the earlier drafts and the final version "the polish of style" in many works, particularly of poetry, very often takes the form of what seem insignificant transpositions of words, but this transposition is conditioned by exactly the same kind of laws. Indeed very often it is found that all that is involved in such transpositions is the mere shifting of a verb and noun. A business-like and prosaic statement, "An old woman lived there and then . . ." in its poetic variant inevitably runs, "There was an old woman who lived in a shoe." Preceding the introduction of the old

---

* The differences of both examples here will be that details of walking and selected movements, however refined they may be, in a genuine master would always be, at the same time, also a "conductor" of the generalized content which he produces in a particularized embodiment. Especially if his task is to transform the simple "approach" to an intricate reconstruction of an interplay of psychological states. Without this neither type nor realism is possible.

woman there appears a verbal form of an indefinite kind. And yet, thereby, the phrase at once assumes no longer the conversational character of everyday life, but one connected in some way with poetic-compositional representation.

This kind of effect has been pointed out by Herbert Spencer.[4] He recognizes such a transposition as more artistic. However, he gives no explanation of it. At best, he refers only to the "economy of the mental energies and sensibilities" of the second type of construction, which in itself most certainly requires a better explanation.

Meanwhile the secret lies hidden precisely in that fact which we persist in pointing to. The cause of it resides, once again, in the fact that this transposition corresponds to a thought process of earlier times. A characterization of this process may be found in Engels:

When we consider and reflect upon nature at large, or the history of mankind, or our own intellectual activity, at first we see the picture of an endless entanglement of relations and reactions, permutations and combinations, in which nothing remains what, where, and as it was, but everything moves, changes, comes into being and passes away. We see, therefore, at first the picture as a whole, with its individual parts still more or less kept in the background; we observe the movements, transitions, connections, rather than the things that move, combine, and are connected.[5]

It follows that a word-order in which the term describing movement or action (the verb) precedes the person or thing moving or acting (the noun) corresponds more nearly to that form of construction that is more primal. This is true moreover outside the limits of our own language—Russian—as of course it should be inasmuch as it is linked, primarily, with the specific structure of thinking. In German *Die Gänse flogen* (the geese flew) sounds dry and informative, whereas even merely such a turn of speech as *Es flogen die Gänse* already contains an element of verse or balladry.

The indications of Engels and the characteristics of the phenomena just described, as phenomena of approach and re-

turn to forms characteristic for earlier levels, can be well illustrated with cases in which we ourselves are faced by graphic
and attested pictures of psychic regression. For example, such
phenomena of regression can be observed in certain brain
operations. In the Moscow Neuro-Surgical Clinic, specializing
in brain surgery, I have had the opportunity of witnessing the
most interesting case of this sort. One of the patients, immediately after the operation, in proportion to his psychic regression, showed his verbal definition of an object going gradually
and clearly through the phases outlined above: in this instance
objects previously *named* were then identified by the *specific
verbs indicating an act performed with the aid of the object.*

In the course of my exposition I have repeatedly had occasion to make use of the phrase "early forms of thought-process" and to illustrate my reflections by representational images
current with peoples still at the dawn of culture. It has already
become a traditional practice with us to be on our guard in
all instances involving these fields of investigation. And not
without reason: These fields are thoroughly contaminated by
every kind of representative of "race theory," or even less
concealed apologists for the colonial politics of imperialism.
It would not be bad, therefore, to emphasize sharply that the
considerations here expressed follow a sharply different line.

Usually the construction of so-called early thought-processes
is treated as a form of thinking fixed in itself once and for
all, characteristic of the so-called "primitive" peoples, racially
inseparable from them and not susceptible to any modification
whatsoever. In this guise it serves as scientific apologia for
the methods of enslavement to which such peoples are subjected by white colonizers, inasmuch as, by inference, such
peoples are "after all hopeless" for culture and cultural reci-
procity.

In many ways even the celebrated Lévy-Bruhl is not exempt
from this conception, although he does not pursue such an
aim consciously. Along this line we quite justly attack him,
since we know that forms of thinking are a reflection in consciousness of the social formations through which, at the given

historical moment, this or that community collectively is passing. But in many ways, also, the opponents of Lévy-Bruhl fall into the opposite extreme, trying carefully to avoid the specificity of this independent individuality of early thought-forms. Among these, for instance, is Olivier Leroy, who, on the basis of analyzing-out a high degree of logic in the productive and technical inventiveness of the so-called "primitive" peoples, completely denies any difference between their system of thought-process and the postulates of our generally accepted logic. This is just as incorrect, and conceals beneath it an equal measure of denial of the dependence of a given system of thought from the specifics of the production relations and social premises from which it derives.

The basic error, in addition to this, is rooted in both camps in that they appreciate insufficiently the quality of gradation subsisting between the apparently incompatible systems of thought process, and completely disregard the qualitative nature of the transition from one to the other. Insufficient regard for this very circumstance frequently scares even us whenever discussion centers round the question of early thought-processes. This is the more strange in that in the Engels work cited there are actually three whole pages comprising an exhaustive examination of all the three stages of construction of thinking through which mankind passes in development. From the early diffuse-complex, part of the remarks about which we quoted above, through the formal-logical stage that negates it. And, at last, to the dialectical, absorbing "in photographic degree" the two preceding. Such a dynamic perception of phenomena does not of course exist for the positivistic approach of Lévy-Bruhl.

But of principal interest in all this matter is the fact that not only does the process of development itself not proceed in a straight line (just like any development process), but that it marches by continual shifts backwards and forwards, independently of whether it be progressively (the movement of backward peoples towards the higher achievements of culture under a socialist regime), or retrogressively (the regress of spiritual super-structures under the heel of national-socialism).

This continual sliding from level to level, forwards and backwards, now to the higher forms of an intellectual order, now to the earlier forms of sensual thinking, occurs also at each point once reached and temporarily stable as a phase in development. Not only the content of thinking, but even its construction itself, are deeply qualitatively different for the human being of any given, socially determined type of thinking, according to whatever state he may be in. The margin between the types is mobile and it suffices a not even extraordinarily sharp affective impulse to cause an extremely, it may be, logically deliberate person suddenly to react in obedience to the never dormant inner armory of sensual thinking and the norms of behavior deriving thence.

When a girl to whom you have been unfaithful, tears your photo into fragments "in anger," thus destroying the "wicked betrayer," for a moment she re-enacts the magical operation of destroying a man by the destruction of his image (based on the early identification of image and object).* By her momentary regression the girl returns herself, in a temporary aberration, to that stage of development in which such an action appeared fully normal and productive of real consequences. Relatively not so very long ago, on the verge of an epoch that already knew minds such as Leonardo and Galileo, so brilliant a politician as Catherine de' Medici, aided by her court magician, wished ill to her foes by sticking pins into their miniature wax images.

In addition to this we know also not just momentary, but (temporarily!) irrevocable manifestations of precisely this same psychological retrogression, when a whole social system is in regress. Then the phenomenon is termed reaction, and the most brilliant light on the question is thrown by the flames

* Even to the present day Mexicans in some of the remoter regions of the country, in times of drought, drag out from their temples the statue of the particular Catholic saint that has taken the place of the former god responsible for rains and, on the edge of the fields, whip him for his non-activity, imagining that thereby they cause pain to him whom the statue portrays.

of the national-fascist *auto-da-fé* of books and portraits of un-
wanted authors in the squares of Berlin!

One way or another, the study of this or that thinking construction locked within itself is profoundly incorrect. The
quality of sliding from one type of thinking to another, from
category to category, and more—the simultaneous co-presence
in varying proportions of the different types and stages and the
taking into account of this circumstance, are equally as important, explanatory and revealing in this as in any other
sphere:

> An exact representation of the universe, of its evolution, of the
> development of mankind, and of the reflection of this evolution
> in the minds of men, can therefore only be obtained by the
> methods of dialectics, with its constant regard to the innumerable
> actions and reactions of life and death, of progressive or retrogres-
> sive changes.[6]

The latter in our case has direct relation to those transitions
in the forms of sensual thinking which appear sporadically in
states of aberrations or similar conditions, and the images
constantly present in the elements of form and composition
based on the laws of sensual thinking, as we have tried to
demonstrate and illustrate above.

After examining the immense material of similar phenomena,
I naturally found myself confronted with a question which
may excite the reader, too. This is, that art is nothing else but
an artificial retrogression in the field of psychology towards
the forms of earlier thought-processes, i.e., a phenomenon
identical with any given form of drug, alcohol, shamanism,
religion, etc.! The answer to this is simple and extremely interesting.

The dialectic of works of art is built upon a most curious
"dual-unity." The affectiveness of a work of art is built upon
the fact that there takes place in it a dual process: an impetuous progressive rise along the lines of the highest explicit steps
of consciousness and a simultaneous penetration by means of
the structure of the form into the layers of profoundest sensual

thinking. The polar separation of these two lines of flow creates that remarkable tension of unity of form and content characteristic of true art-works. Apart from this there are no true art-works.

In this remarkable fact and attribute concerning a work of art lies its infinite distinction in principle from all adjacent, similar, analogous, and "reminiscent" areas, where phenomena attached to "early forms of thought" also have a place. In an inseparable unity of these elements—of sensual thinking with an explicitly conscious striving and soaring—art is unique and inimitable in those fields where a comparative deciphering is depended upon for correlative analysis. That is why, with this basic thesis in mind, we need not be afraid of an analytical deciphering of the most basic laws of sensual thinking, by firmly keeping in mind the necessity for unity and harmony in both elements, which produce a fully worthy work only in this unity.

By allowing one or the other element to predominate the art-work remains unfulfilled. A drive towards the thematic-logical side renders the work dry, logical, didactic. But over-stress on the side of the sensual forms of thinking with insufficient account taken of thematic-logical tendency—this is equally fatal for the work: the work becomes condemned to sensual chaos, elementalness, raving. Only in the "dually united" interpenetration of these tendencies resides the true tension-laden unity of form and content. Herein resides the root principle difference between the highest artistic creative activity of man and, in contradistinction therefrom, all other fields wherein also occur sensual thinking or its earlier forms (infantilism, schizophrenia, religious ecstasy, hypnosis, etc.).

And if we are now on the verge of considerable successes in the field of comprehension of the universe in the first line (to which the latest film productions bear witness), then, from the viewpoint of the technique of our craftsmanship, it stands necessary for us in every way to delve more deeply now also into the questions of the second component. These, however fleeting, notes that I have been able to set forth here serve this task. Work here is not only not finished, it has barely begun. But work here is in the extremest degree indispensable for us. The study of the corpus of material on these questions is highly important to us.

By study and absorption of this material we shall learn a very great deal about the system of laws of formal constructions and the inner laws of composition. And along the line of knowledge in the field of the system of laws of formal constructions, cinematography and indeed the arts generally are still very poor. Even at the moment we are merely probing in these fields a few bases of the systems of laws, the derivative roots of which lie in the nature itself of sensual thinking.

In comparison with music or literature, we find little, but by analyzing along this line a whole series of problems and phenomena, we shall store up in the field of form a great corpus of exact knowledge, without which we shall never attain that general ideal of simplicity which we all have in mind. To attain this ideal and to realize this line, it is very important to guard ourselves against another line which might also begin to crop up: the line of simplificationism. This tendency is to some extent already present in the cinema, which a few already wish to expound in this way, that things should be shot "straight" and, in the last resort, it does not matter how. This is terrible, for we all know that the crux is not in shooting ornately and prettily (photography becomes ornate and pretty-pretty when the author knows neither what he wants to take nor how he must take what he wants).

The essence is in shooting expressively. We must travel toward *the ultimate-expressive and ultimate-affective form and use the limit of simple and economic form that expresses what we need.* These questions, however, can successfully be approached only by means of very serious analytical work and by means of very serious knowledge of the inward nature of artistic form. Hence we must proceed not by the path of mechanical simplification of the task, but by the path of planned analytical ascertaining of the secret of the very nature of affective form.

I have sought here to show the direction in which I am now working on these problems, and I think this is the right road of investigation. If we now look back at the intellectual cinema, we shall see that the intellectual cinema did one service, in spite of its self-*reductio ad absurdum* when it laid claim to exhaustive style and exhaustive content.

This theory fell into the error of letting us have not a unity of form and content, but a coincidental identity of them, because in unity it is complicated to follow exactly how an affective embodiment for ideas is built. But when these things become "telescoped" into "one," *then was discovered the march of inner thinking as the basic law of construction of form and composition.* Now we can use the laws thus discovered already not along the line of "intellectual constructions," but along the line of completely manifold constructions, both from story and image viewpoints, since we already know some "secrets," and fundamental laws of construction of form and affective structure generally.

From what I have elucidated along the lines of the past and along the lines on which I am now working, one more qualitative difference appears:

It is this, that when in our various "schools" we proclaimed the paramount importance of montage, or of the intellectual cinema, or of documentalism or some such other fighting program, it bore primarily the character of a tendency. What I am now trying briefly to expound about what I am now working on has an entirely different character. It bears a character not specifically tendentious (as futurism, expressionism or any other "program")—but delves into the question of the nature of things and here questions are already not concerned with the line of some given stylization, but with the line of search for a general method and mode for the problem of form, equally essential and fit for any genre of construction within our embracing style of *socialist realism*. Questions of tendentious interests begin to spread over into a deepened interest in the whole culture itself of the medium in which we work, i.e., the tendentious line here takes a turn towards the research-academic line. I have experienced this not merely creatively, but also biographically: at the moment at which I began to interest myself in these basic problems of the culture of form and the culture of cinema, I found myself in life not in film production, but engaged in creation of an academy of cinematography, the road to which has been laid down by my three years' work in the All-Union State Cinema Institute, in Moscow, and which is only now developing. Moreover, it is of interest that the phenomenon noted above is not at all isolated, this quality is not at all exclusively characteristic of our cinematography. We can perceive a whole series of theoretical and tendentious routes ceasing to exist as original "currents," and beginning by way of transmutation and gradual change to be included in questions of methodology and science.

It is possible to point to such an example in the teaching of Marr, and the fact that his teaching, which was formerly a "japhetic" tendency in the science of languages, has now been revised from the viewpoint of Marxism and entered practice no longer as a tendency but as a generalized method in the study of languages and thinking. It is not by chance that on almost all fronts around us there are now being born academies; it is not by chance that disputes in the line of architecture are no longer a matter of rival tendencies (Le Corbusier or Zheltovski); discussion proceeds no longer about this question, but controversy is about a synthesis of "the three arts," the deepening of research, the nature itself of the phenomenon of architecture.

I think that in our cinematography something very similar is now occurring. For, at the present stage, we craftsmen have no differences of principle and disputes about a whole series of program postulates such as we had in the past. There are, of course, individual shades of opinion within the comprehensive conception of the single style: Socialist Realism.

And this is in no way a sign of moribundity, as might appear to some—"unless they fight, they're stiffs"—quite the contrary. Precisely here, and precisely in this, I find the greatest and most interesting sign of the times.

I think that now, with the approach of the sixteenth year of our cinematography, we are entering a special period. These signs, to be traced today also in the parallel arts as well as being found in the cinema, are harbingers of the news that Soviet cinematography, after many periods of divergence of opinion and argument, is entering into its classical period, because the characteristics of its interests, the particular approach to its series of problems, this thirst for synthesis, this postulation of and demand for complete harmony of all the elements from the subject matter to composition within the frame, this demand for fullness of quality and all the features on which our cinematography has set its heart—these are the signs of highest flowering of an art.

I consider that we are now on the threshold of the most remarkable period of classicism in our cinematography, the best period in the highest sense of the word. Not to participate creatively in such a period is no longer possible. And if for the last three years I have been completely engrossed in scientific-investigatory and pedagogical work (a side of which is very briefly related above), then now I undertake simultaneously once again to embark upon production,* in order to strive for a classicism that will contain some part of the huge endowment left us.

[1935]

* In the spring of 1935 Eisenstein did return to active production, with *Bezhin Meadow* from a scenario by Alexander Rzheshevsky. The film was left unfinished in 1937; see *The Film Sense*, appendices 1 (page 226) and 8 (page 274).

THE STRUCTURE OF THE FILM

This is an Art
Which does mend Nature: change it rather, but
The Art itselfe, is Nature.

SHAKESPEARE, *The Winter's Tale*

All is in man—all is for man.

GORKY [1]

LET US say that grief is to be represented on the screen.
There is no such thing as grief "in general." Grief is concrete;
it is always attached to something; it has conveyors, when
your film's characters grieve; it has consumers, when your
portrayal of grief makes the spectators sorrow, too.

This latter result is not always obligatory for your portrayal of grief: the grief of an enemy, after his defeat, arouses
joy in the spectator, who identifies his feelings with those of
the conqueror on the screen.

Such considerations are obvious enough, yet beneath them
lies one of the most difficult problems in constructing works
of art, touching the most exciting part of our work: *the problem of portraying an attitude toward the thing portrayed.*

One of the most active means of portraying this attitude is
in composition. Though this attitude can never be shown by
composition alone. Nor is it the sole task of composition.

I wish to take up in this essay this particular question: how
far the embodiment of this attitude can be achieved within
narrowly compositional means. We have long since realized
that an attitude to a portrayed fact can be embodied in the
way the fact is presented. Even such a master of "attitude" as
Franz Kafka recognized physical viewpoint as critical:

The diversity of ideas which one can have, say, of an apple: the
apple as it appears to the child who must stretch his neck so as

150

barely to see it on the table, and the apple as it appears to the master of the house who picks it up and lordily hands it to his guest.[2]

At once the question arises: with what methods and means must the filmically portrayed fact be handled so that it simultaneously shows not only *what* the fact is, and the character's attitude towards it, but also *how* the author relates to it, and how the author wishes the spectator to receive, sense, and react to the portrayed fact.

Let us look at this from the viewpoint of composition alone, and there examine an instance where this task, of embodying the author's relation to a thing, is served primarily by composition, here understood as a law for the construction of a portrayal. This is extremely important for us, for though little enough has been written on the rôle of composition in cinema, the features of composition that we speak of here have been left unmentioned in film literature.

The object of imagery and the law of structure, by which it is represented, can coincide. This would be the simplest of cases, and the compositional problem in such an aspect more or less takes care of itself. This is the simplest type of structure: "sorrowful sorrow," "joyful joy," "a marching march," etc. In other words: the hero sorrows, and in unison with him sorrows nature, and lighting, sometimes the composition of the shot, and (more rarely) the rhythm of the montage—but most often of all, we just add sad music to it. The same thing happens when we handle "joyful joy," and other similar simplicities.

Even in these simplest cases it is perfectly evident what nourishes composition and from where it derives its experience and material: *composition takes the structural elements of the portrayed phenomena* and from these composes its *canon for building the containing work.*

In doing this composition actually takes such elements, first of all, from the structure of the *emotional behavior of man,* joined with the *experienced content* of this or that portrayed phenomenon.

It is for this reason that real composition is invariably *pro-foundly human*—be it the "leaping" rhythmic structure of gay episodes, the "drawn-out monotonal" montage of a sad scene, or the "joyful sparkling" tone of a shot.

Diderot deduced the theory that compositional *principles* in vocal, and later in instrumental, music derived from the basic intonations of living emotional speech (as well as from sound phenomena perceived by our ancestors in surrounding nature).

And Bach—master of the most intricate compositional forms —maintained a similarly *human approach* to the fundamentals of composition as a direct pedagogical premise. In describing Bach's teaching methods, Forkel writes:

He considered his voices as if they were persons who conversed together like a select company. If there were three, each could sometimes be silent and listen to the others till it again had something to the purpose to say.[3]

It is exactly thus, on a base of interplaying human emotions, on a base of human experience, that the cinema must also build its structural approaches and its most difficult compositional constructions.

Take, for example, one of the most successful scenes in *Alexander Nevsky*—the attack by the German wedge on the Russian army-at the beginning of the Battle on the Ice.

This episode passes through all the shades of an experience of increasing terror, where approaching danger makes the heart contract and the breathing irregular. The structure of this "leaping wedge" in *Alexander Nevsky* is, with variations, exactly modeled on the inner process of such an experience. This dictated all the rhythms of the sequence—cumulative, disjunctive, the speeding up and slowing down of the movement. The boiling pulsing of an excited heart dictated the rhythm of the leaping hoofs: pictorially—the *leap* of the galloping knights; compositionally—the *beat* to the bursting point of an excited heart.

To produce the success of this sequence, both the pictorial

and compositional structures are fused in the welded unity of a terrifying image—the beginning of a battle that is to be a fight to the finish.

And the event, as it is unfolded on the screen according to a timetable of the running of this or that passion, thrown back from the screen, involves the emotions of the spectator according to the same timetable, arousing in him the same tangle of passions which originally designed the compositional scheme of the work.

This is the secret of the genuinely emotional affect of real composition. Employing for source *the structure of human emotion, it unmistakably appeals to emotion,* unmistakably arouses the complex of those feelings that gave birth to the composition.

In all the media of art—and in film art most of all, no matter how neglected by this medium—it is by such means, primarily, that is achieved what Lev Tolstoy said of music:

Music carries me immediately and directly into that mental condition in which the man was who composed it.[4]

That—from the simplest to the most complicated cases—is *one* of the possible *types* of construction to be considered.

But there is also another case, when, instead of a resolution of the "joyful joy" type, the author is forced to find the compositional vessel for, say, the theme of "life-affirming death."

What would happen here?

Apparently, the law of constructing works of art in such a case cannot be nourished *exclusively* by elements issuing directly from the natural and habitual emotions, conditions, and sensations of man, attendant on such a phenomenon.

Yet the law of composition remains unchanged in such a case.

Such schemes of composition will have to be sought not so much among the emotions attached to the portrayed thing, but primarily among the emotions attached to the author's *relationship to the thing portrayed.*

Strictly speaking, this also is a factor in the above example of the "wedge" in *Alexander Nevsky*, only with this peculiarity, that there the emotion of the portrayed thing *coincides* with the emotion of the author's relationship to the portrayed thing.

But such a case is rather rare and is by no means obligatory for all cases. In such cases there commonly arises a quite curious and often unexpected picture of a transferred phenomenon, constructed in a way unusual in "normal" circumstances. Literature abounds in such examples of all degrees, often touching the primary elements of compositional development, such as an imagist structure, resolved possibly through a system of similes.

The pages of literature offer us models of completely unexpected compositional structures, in which are presented phenomena that "in themselves" are quite ordinary. These structures are not in the least determined, nourished, or brought into being by formalist excesses or extravagant researches.*

The examples I have in mind come from realistic classics—and they are classical because with these means the examples embody with maximum clarity a maximum clear *judgment* of a phenomenon, a maximum clear *relation* to the phenomenon.

How often in literature do we encounter descriptions of "adultery"! No matter how varied the situations, circumstances, and imagist comparisons in which this has been portrayed—there is hardly a more impressive picture than the one where "the sinful embrace of the lovers" is imagistically compared with—murder.

She felt so guilty, so much to blame, that it only remained for her to humble herself and ask to be forgiven; but she had no one in the world now except him, so that even her prayer for forgiveness was addressed to him. Looking at him, she felt her humiliation physically, and could say nothing more. He felt what a murderer must feel when looking at the body he has deprived of life. The body he had deprived of life was their love, the first period of their love. There was something frightful and revolting in the recollection of what had been paid for with this terrible

* Two phrases commonly employed by Eisenstein's critics.—EDITOR.

price of shame. The shame she felt at her spiritual nakedness communicated itself to him. But in spite of the murderer's horror of the body of his victim, that body must be cut in pieces and hidden away, and he must make use of what he has obtained by the murder.

Then, as the murderer desperately throws himself on the body, as though with passion, and drags it and hacks it, so Vronsky covered her face and shoulders with kisses.

She held his hand and did not move. Yes! These kisses were what had been bought by that shame! "Yes, and this hand, which will always be mine, is the hand of my accomplice." [5]

In this passage from *Anna Karenina* the imagist structure of its simile throughout the whole magnificently ferocious scene is resolved from the most profound relation of its author to the phenomenon, rather than from the feelings and emotions of its participants (as is this same theme, for example, in infinite variations, solved by Zola throughout the *Rougon-Macquart* cycle).

On *Anna Karenina* Tolstoy placed an epigraph from the Epistle to the Romans: *"Vengeance is mine; I will repay, saith the Lord."* In a letter to Veresayev (23 May 1907) Mikhail Sukhotin quoted what Tolstoy meant by this epigraph, which had moved Veresayev:

. . . I must repeat, that I chose this epigraph to express the idea that whatever is evil, whatever man does, brings bitter consequences, not from people, but from God and from what Anna Karenina experiences herself.[6]

It is in the second part of the novel, from which our passage is taken, that Tolstoy assumes the particular task of demonstrating "whatever is evil, whatever man does."

The temperament of the writer forces him to feel in the forms of the highest level of evil—in crime. The temperament of the moralist forces him to appraise this evil on the highest level of crime against a person—murder. And finally, the temperament of the artist forces this estimate of the behavior of his character to be presented with the help of all expressive means available to him.

Crime—murder—is established as *the basic expressive relation of the author* to the phenomenon, and is simultaneously established as *the determinant of all basic elements for the compositional treatment of the scene*.

It dictates the images and the similes:

He felt what a murderer must feel when looking at the body he has deprived of life. The body he had deprived of life was their love. . . .

as well as the images of the characters' behavior, prescribing the fulfillment of actions, peculiar to love, in forms peculiar to murder:

. . . as the murderer desperately throws himself on the body, as though with passion, and drags it and hacks it, so Vronsky covered her face and shoulders with kisses.

These absolutely exact "directives," defining the shading of behavior, were chosen from thousands of possibilities for the reason that they correspond identically with the relation of the author himself to the phenomenon.

The idea of evil, compositionally expressed through the image of crime—murder—as resolved in the cited scene, can be encountered elsewhere in Tolstoy's art. For him, this is a beloved image.

This is his compositional-imagist structure, not only for "adultery," but also for the "swinish connexion" within the bonds of marriage.

We again find this theme in *The Kreutzer Sonata*. Two fragments from Pozdnyshev's narrative show it clearly. The second of these (regarding the children) expands the frame of reference, providing a renewed unexpectedness of outer compositional construction, issuing as a whole, however, from Tolstoy's inner relation to the theme:

"I wondered what embittered us against one another, yet it was perfectly simple: that animosity was nothing but the protest of our human nature against the animal nature that overpowered it.

"I was surprised at our enmity to one another; yet it could not have been otherwise. That hatred was nothing but the mutual hatred of accomplices in a crime—both for the incitement to the crime and for the part taken in it. What was it but a crime, when she, poor thing, became pregnant in the first month, and our *swinish* connexion continued? You think I am straying from my subject? Not at all! I am telling you *how* I killed my wife. They asked me at the trial with what, and how, I killed her. Fools! They thought I killed her with a knife, on the 5th of October. It was not then I killed her, but much earlier. Just as they are all now killing, all, all. . . ." [7]

"So the presence of children not only failed to improve our life, but poisoned it. Besides, the children were a new cause of dissension. As soon as we had children they became the means and the object of our discord, and more often the older they grew. They were not only the object of discord, but the weapons of our strife. We used our children, as it were, to fight one another with. Each of us had a favorite weapon among them for our strife. I used to fight her chiefly through Vasya, the eldest boy, and she me through Lisa. . . . They, poor things, suffered terribly from this, but we, with our incessant warfare, had no time to think of that. . . ." [8]

As we can see, no matter what example we take, the method of composition remains the same. In all cases, its basic determinant remains primarily *the relation of the author*. In all cases, it is the *deed* of man and the *structure* of human deeds that prefigures the composition.

The decisive factors of the compositional structure are taken by the author from the basis of his relation to phenomena. This dictates structure and characteristics, through which the portrayal itself is unfolded. Losing none of its reality, the portrayal emerges from this, immeasurably enriched in both intellectual and emotional qualities.

Another example may be offered here. Its interest lies in the delineation of two characters by an imagery that is customary and even routine, perfectly natural in both structure and characteristics, but the structural means is consciously produced by . . . *an exchange of structures!*

These personages are a German officer and a French prostitute.

The imagist structure of a "noble officer" is employed for the prostitute. In the same way the most repellent elements in the imagist structure of a prostitute serve as skeletal outline for the German officer.

This ingenious "contra-dance" idea was Maupassant's—used in "Mademoiselle Fifi."

The image of the Frenchwoman is woven from all the traits of nobility, linked with a middle-class attitude towards army officers. Consistent with this method, the *substance* of the German officer is revealed in its prostitute nature. From this "nature" Maupassant seized only one trait—its destructiveness of the "moral principles" of bourgeois society. Further interest for us is lent to this aspect in that Maupassant took this over from a similar scheme that in a finished form was well-known and fresh in the public's memory—perhaps so that his readers could not possibly miss his point! The portrait structure of his German officer is cut from a pattern designed by Zola.

The Baron Wilhelm von Eyrick, nicknamed "Mademoiselle Fifi," is, of course, "Nana."

Not the whole figure of Nana, but Nana in that part of the novel where Zola raises this image to immense destructive powers that are directed against well-ordered families, symbolically climaxed by Nana's destructive caprice in smashing the family heirlooms brought to her by her admirers. The generalized presentation of the courtesan's destructive powers for family and society is further "materialized" by the particular breaking of the bonbonnière of Dresden china and her "general massacre" of the heap of other valuable gifts that serve as a symbol of the "high society" which is mockingly broken by Nana's caprices.

The structure of the officer's behavior is absolutely identical with the structure of Nana's behavior in this scene. Even within the surface similarity of the names of "Nana" and "Fifi" there is a further clue to this identity: the Baron's nickname was given him for his habit of expressing his contempt for everyone and everything around him—"*fi, fi, donc!*"

And in the story as a whole we have a fine model of the compositional re-channeling of a customary naturalistic imagery into a structural framework suitable to the author's requirements.

We have examined cases that are quite descriptive, palpable, and easily apparent. The very same principles, however, lie in the deepest elements of compositional structure, in those strata that can be uncovered only by the scalpel of the most pedantic and probing analysis.

And everywhere we see as basic the same *humanity* and *human psychology, nourishing and shaping the most intricate compositional elements of form exactly as it feeds and defines the content of the work.*

I wish to illustrate this with two complex and seemingly abstract examples, in regard to the composition of *Potemkin*. These will serve as examples of structure and composition in the broadest sense of the terms, corroborating what has been said above.

When *Potemkin* is discussed two of its features are commonly remarked: The organic construction of its composition as a whole. And the pathos * of the film. Sacrificing grace to precision, we can refer to these two qualities as:

ORGANIC-NESS and PATHOS

Taking these two most noticed features of *Potemkin*, let us attempt to uncover the means by which they were achieved, primarily in the field of composition. We shall observe the first feature in the composition as a whole. For the second, we shall take the episode of the Odessa steps, where the pathos of the film achieves its greatest dramatic tension.

We are here concerned with how the organic-ness and pathos of the theme are resolved by specifically compositional

* This is a much abused term, used here in its original sense.

means. In the same way we could take apart these qualities to see how they are resolved by other factors; we could examine the contribution to organic-ness and pathos made by the actors' performances, by the treatment of the story, by the light and color scale of the photography, by the mass-scenes, by the natural backgrounds, etc.

That is, we take up this matter from one narrow, particular question of structure, and by no means pretend to a thorough analysis of all the film's aspects.

However, in an organic work of art, elements that nourish the work as a whole pervade all the features composing this work. A unified canon pierces not only the whole and each of its parts, but also each area that is called to participate in the work of composition. One and the same principle will feed any area, advancing in each its own qualitative signs of distinction. And only in such a case may one speak of the organic-ness of a work, for an organism is here understood as defined by Engels in *Dialectics of Nature:* "... *the organism is certainly a higher unity* ..."

These considerations bring us at once to our first matter—to the question of the "organic" structure of *Potemkin*.

We shall attempt to approach this question, proceeding from the premise established at the opening of this essay. The organic-ness of a work, as well as the sensation of organic-ness that is received from the work, must rise in that case where the law of building the work answers *the law of structure in natural organic phenomena.*

It must be quite evident that we are speaking here of the sensation of compositional organic-ness in the whole. This can break down the resistance even of that spectator whose class allegiance is in sharp opposition to the direction taken by the subject and the theme of the work, i.e., those spectators for whom neither theme nor subject is "organic." This partially explains the reception given *Potemkin* outside the Soviet Union.

Let us be more precise: What do we mean by the organic-ness of building the work? I should say that we have two kinds of organic-ness.

The first is characteristic of any work that possesses whole-ness and inner laws. In this case organic-ness can be defined by the fact that the work as a whole is governed by a certain law of structure and that all its parts are subordinated to this canon. The German estheticians would label this: organic-ness of a general order. It is apparent that in our instance of this principle we have a pattern of the principle on which natural phenomena are built and about which Lenin said:

The particular does not exist outside that relationship which leads to the general. The general exists only in the particular, through the particular. . . .[9]

But the *law* itself by which these natural phenomena are constructed, as yet in this first case by no means certainly coincides with that canon on which one or another work of art is constructed.

The second kind of organic-ness of a work is present to-gether with not only the very *principle of organic-ness*, but also the *canon itself*, according to which natural phenomena are built. This may be termed organic-ness of a *particular* or *exceptional kind*. And it is this that is of especial interest for us.

We have before us a case where a work of art—*an art-ificial work*—is built on those same laws by which *non*-artistic phe-nomena—the "organic" phenomena of nature—are constructed.

There is in this case, not only a truthful realistic subject, but also, in its forms of compositional embodiment, a truthful and full reflection of a canon peculiar to actuality.

Evidently, whatever may be the kind of organic-ness in it, the work has a completely individual affect on its perceivers, not only because it is raised to the level of natural phenomena, but also because the laws of its construction are simultaneously the laws governing those who perceive the work, inasmuch as this audience is also part of organic nature. Each spectator feels himself organically related, fused, united with a work of such a type, just as he senses himself united and fused with organic nature around him.

To a greater or lesser degree each of us inevitably experiences this sensation, and the secret lies in the fact that in this case *we and the work* are governed *by one and the same canon.* We can observe nature operating within this canon in both the examples chosen, though they would appear to touch two different and independent questions. These do, however, meet each other finally.

The first example is devoted to an analysis of this canon in static conditions; the second analyzes the dynamic operation of this canon.

Our first example will raise questions of parts and *proportions* in the structure of the work. Our second—the *movement* of the structure of the work.

This means that the solution of the first question of the organic structure of *Potemkin* must begin with the deciphering of that which is subordinate to the first structural condition—*organic-ness of a general kind.*

Potemkin looks like a chronicle (or newsreel) of an event, but it functions as a drama.

The secret of this lies in the fact that the chronicle pace of the event is fitted to a severely tragic composition. And furthermore, to tragic composition in its most canonic form—the five-act tragedy. Events, regarded almost as naked facts, are broken into five tragic acts, the facts being selected and arranged in sequence so that they answer the demands set by classical tragedy: a third act quite distinct from the second, a fifth distinct from the first, and so on.

The utility in the choice of a five-act structure in particular for this tragedy was, of course, by no means accidental, but was the result of prolonged natural selection—but we need not go into this history here. Enough that for the basis of our drama we took a structure that had been particularly tested by the centuries. This was further emphasized by the individual titling of each "act." * Here, in condensation, are the contents of the five acts:

Part I—"*Men and Maggots.*" Exposition of the action. Milieu of the battleship. Maggoty meat. Discontent ferments among the sailors.

Part II—"*Drama on the Quarterdeck.*" "All hands on deck!" Refusal of the wormy soup. Scene with the tarpaulin. "Brothers!" Refusal to fire. Mutiny. Revenge on the officers.

Part III—"*Appeal from the Dead.*" Mist. The body of Vakulinchuk is brought into Odessa port. Mourning over the body. Indignation. Demonstration. Raising the red flag.

Part IV—"*The Odessa Steps.*" Fraternization of shore and battleship. Yawls with provisions. Shooting on the Odessa steps. The battleship fires on the "generals' staff."

Part V—"*Meeting the Squadron.*" Night of expectation. Meeting the squadron. Engines. "Brothers!" The squadron refuses to fire. The battleship passes victoriously through the squadron.

In the action of its episodes each part of the drama is totally unlike the others, but piercing and, as it were, cementing them, there is a repeat.

In "Drama on the Quarterdeck," a tiny group of rebelling sailors (a small particle of the battleship) cries "Brothers!" as they face the guns of the firing squad. And the guns are lowered. The whole organism of the battleship joins them.

In "Meeting the Squadron," the whole rebellious battleship (a small particle of the fleet) throws the same cry of "Brothers!" towards the guns of the flagship, pointed towards the *Potemkin.* And the guns are lowered: the whole organism of the fleet has joined them.

From a tiny cellular organism of the battleship to the organism of the entire battleship; from a tiny cellular organism

* When *Potemkin* was exhibited outside the Soviet Union, these part-titles were invariably removed by the various adaptors; the only foreign prints of *Potemkin* restored to its original form are those circulated by the Museum of Modern Art Film Library.—EDITOR.

of the fleet to the organism of the whole fleet—thus flies
through the theme the revolutionary feeling of brotherhood.
And this is repeated in the structure of the work containing
this theme—brotherhood and revolution.

Over the heads of the battleship's commanders, over the
heads of the admirals of the tzar's fleet, and finally over the
heads of the foreign censors, rushes the whole film with its
fraternal "Hurrah!" just as within the film the feeling of
brotherhood flies from the rebellious battleship over the sea
to the shore. The organic-ness of the film, born in the cell
within the film, not only moves and expands throughout the
film as a whole, but appears far beyond its physical limits—
in the public and historical fate of the same film.

Thematically and emotionally this would, perhaps, be sufficient in speaking of organic-ness, but let us be formally more
severe.

Look intently into the structure of the work.

In its five acts, tied with the general thematic line of revolutionary brotherhood, there is otherwise little that is similar
externally. But in one respect they are absolutely *alike:* each
part is distinctly broken into two almost equal halves. This can
be seen with particular clarity from the second act on:

II. Scene with the tarpaulin   → mutiny
III. Mourning for Vakulinchuk → angry demonstration
IV. Lyrical fraternization   → shooting
V. Anxiously awaiting the fleet → triumph

Moreover, at the "transition" point of each part, the halt
has its own peculiar kind of *caesura.*

In one part (III), this is a few shots of clenched fists, through
which the theme of mourning the dead leaps into the theme of
fury.

In another part (IV), this is a sub-title—*"SUDDENLY"*—
cutting off the scene of fraternization, and projecting it into
the scene of the shooting.

The motionless muzzles of the rifles (in Part II). The gap-
ing mouths of the guns (in Part V). And the cry of "Brothers,"

upsetting the awful pause of waiting, in an explosion of brotherly feeling—in both moments.

And it should be further noted that the transition within each part is not merely a transition to a merely *different* mood, to a merely *different* rhythm, to a merely *different* event, but each time the transition is to a sharply opposite quality. Not merely contrasting, but *opposite*, for each time it *images exactly that theme from the opposite point of view*, along with the theme that *inevitably grows from it*.

The explosion of mutiny after the breaking point of oppression has been reached, under the pointed rifles (Part II).

Or the explosion of wrath, organically breaking from the theme of mass mourning for the murdered (Part III).

The shooting on the steps as an organic "deduction" of the reaction to the fraternal embrace between the *Potemkin's* rebels and the people of Odessa (Part IV), and so on.

The unity of such a canon, recurring in *each act* of the drama, is already self-evident.

But when we look at the work as a whole, we shall see that such is the whole structure of *Potemkin*.

Actually, near the middle, the film as a whole is cut by the dead halt of a *caesura;* the stormy action of the beginning is completely halted in order to take a fresh start for the second half of the film. This similar *caesura*, within the film as a whole, is made by the episode of the dead Vakulinchuk and the harbor mists.

For the entire film this episode is a halt before the same sort of transfer that occurs in those moments cited above within the separate parts. And with this moment the theme, breaking the ring forged by the sides of one rebellious battleship, bursts into the embrace of a whole city which is topographically *opposed to the ship*, but is in feeling fused into a unity with it; a unity that is, however, broken away from it by the soldiers' boots descending the steps at that moment when the theme once more returns to the drama at sea.

We see how organic is the progressive development of the theme, and at the same time we also see how the structure of

hence the graphic opposition of circles + lines? Horizontals, verticals! etc...

Potemkin, as a whole, flows from this movement of the theme, which operates *for the whole* exactly as it does *for its fractional members.*

We need not seek in nature for what appears to be pathos *per se.* We shall confine ourselves to an analysis in a work of pathos from the viewpoint of its receiver or, more exactly, in regard to the theatrical media, from the viewpoint of its affect on the spectator. Moving from these basic features of affect we shall attempt to define those basic features of construction which a composition of pathos must possess. And then we can verify these features with the particular example that concerns us. Nor will I deny myself the satisfaction of concluding with a few general considerations.

For our purpose let us first sketch in a few words the affect of pathos. We'll deliberately do this with the most trivial and banal symptoms possible. Out of this the most prominent and characteristic features will bring themselves to our attention.

For the most primitive illustration let us take a simple description of the superficial signs of external behavior in a spectator gripped by pathos.

But these signs are so symptomatic that they at once bring us to the core of the question. Pathos shows its affect—when the spectator is compelled to jump from his seat. When he is compelled to collapse where he stands. When he is compelled to applaud, to cry out. When his eyes are compelled to shine with delight, before gushing tears of delight. . . . In brief— when the spectator is forced "to go out of himself."

To use a prettier term, we might say that the affect of a work of pathos consists in whatever "sends" the spectator into ecstasy. Actually there is nothing to be added to such a formulation, for the symptoms above say exactly this: *ex-stasis*— literally, "standing out of oneself," which is to say, "going out of himself," or "departing from his ordinary condition."

All our symptoms follow this formula to the letter. Seated—

he stands. Standing—he collapses. Motionless—he moves. Silent—he cries out. Dull—he shines. Dry—he is moistened by tears. In each instance occurs a "departure from a condition," a "going out of himself."

But this is not all: "to go out of oneself" is not to go into *nothing*. To go out of oneself inevitably implies a transition to something else, to something different in quality, to something opposite to what was (immobility—into movement; silence—into noise; etc.).

Even in such a superficial description of ecstatic affect, produced by a structure of pathos, it is self-evident what basic indications structure must possess in a composition of pathos. By all its indications such a structure must maintain the condition of "going out of oneself" and incessant transition to differing qualities.

To leave oneself, to remove oneself from one's customary equilibrium and condition, and to pass over into a new condition—all this of course penetrates the affective conditions of every art that is capable of gripping a perceiver. And the media of art tend to group themselves according to their capability in achieving this affect. Ranged in this way, the possession of this general quality shows its fundamental vitality to the highest degree. Apparently, structures of pathos are the culminating points along this single road.

And, apparently, all other varieties of composition in artistic works may be examined, and they will be found to be *diminished* derivatives of *maximum instances* (producing "departures from oneself" to a maximum degree), employing a *pathetic type of structure*.

No one should be alarmed by the fact that in speaking of pathos, I have not yet once touched the question of theme and content. We are not discussing here pathetic content in general, but rather of the meaning of pathos as realized in composition. The same fact may enter a work of art in any aspect of treatment: from the cold protocol form of a précis to a hymn of genuine pathos. And it is these particular artistic means, lifting the "recording" of an event to the heights of pathos, that interest us here.

Unquestionably this primarily depends on the author's relation to the content. But composition in this meaning, as we comprehend it here, *is also a construction which, in the first place, serves to embody the author's relation to the content*, at the same time compelling the spectator to relate himself to the content in the same way.

In this essay we are therefore less interested in the question of the "nature" of pathos in one or another phenomenon; this is always socially relative. We shall also not pause on the character of the author's pathetic *relation* to this or to that phenomenon, just as obviously socially relative. We are interested (by the *a priori* presence of both) in the narrowly posed problem of how this "relation" to "natural phenomena" is realized by composition within the conditions of a pathetic structure.

And so, in following that thesis, already once justified in the question of organic-ness, we can affirm that, in wishing to gain a maximum "departure from oneself" in the spectator, we are obliged in the work to suggest to him a corresponding "guide." Following this guide he will enter into the desired condition.

The simplest "prototype" of such imitative behavior will be, of course, that of a person ecstatically following, on the screen, a personage gripped by pathos, a personage who in one way or another, "goes out of himself."

Here structure will coincide with imagery. And the object of the imagery—the *behavior* of such a man—will *itself* flow according to the conditions of "ecstatic" structure. This may even be shown in speech indications. The *unorganized* customary flow of speech, made pathetic, immediately invents the pattern of clearly behavioristic *rhythm;* prose that is also *prosaic* in its forms, begins to scintillate at once with forms and turns of speech that are *poetic* in nature (unexpected metaphors, the appearance of expressive images, etc.). There is no indication of speech or other human manifestation that would not show, at such a moment, this transfer *from one quality into a new quality*.

On this ladder the first rung is a line of compositional possibilities. A case will become more complicated and more affective when this basic condition does not stop with man, but goes itself "beyond the limits" of man, radiating out into the surroundings and environment of a personage, that is, when his very surroundings also are presented in, say, his condition of "frenzy." Shakespeare has given us a classical example of this in the "frenzy" of Lear, a frenzy that goes beyond the boundaries of the personage, into the "frenzy" of nature itself—into a tempest.

For the same resolutions of material in any customary means, examples may be found in the richest abundance among the naturalists of the Zola school and, in the first place, in Zola himself. In Zola the very description of the surroundings, fusing its details with the separate phases of an event in each scene, is always selected and presented in a *realistic* and *physical* way, but always as required *by the structure* of the condition.* This holds true for any of his compositional structures, but is particularly graphic in those cases where Zola raises to pathos an event that is by no means obliged to be pathetic.

Not in the rhythm of prose, nor in a system of images and similes, nor in the scenic structure—nor in any purely compositional elements of episodes does a structural canon seem absolutely necessary to Zola for his scenes; he is almost solely guided by his formula in portraying phenomena and the portrayed people act according to the author's laws.

This is so typical for Zola's manner that it would be possible to take this as a specific process characteristic of the methods

---

* Though Zola prided himself on his "scientific documentation," he was a master in selecting and arranging raw material for his own undeniably artistic purposes. Even in his "documentary" notes for *L'Assommoir* one sees the compositional imagination at work in the naked "lists" describing, for example, his central tenement, or the opening violence in the washing-house, or the bitterly fantastic details of Coupeau's alcoholic death.[10] The works of Frank Norris reveal similar environmental compositions.

used by the naturalists of this school. In this way _primary_
value is given to *an arrangement of phenomena, which themselves flow ecstatically*, in themselves "going out of themselves," for it is at exactly such moments of their existence that
they are seized for description.

And this method is also accompanied by a second, already
rudimentary compositional method: the representation of
phenomena as distributed in such a way *among themselves,
that each of them in relation to each other seems a transition
from one intensity to another, from one "dimension" to another.*

And it is only in the third and last place that this school
rarely employs conditions pointing towards such purely compositional elements as movements within the changing rhythms
of prose, within the nature of the language, or general structure in the movement of episodes and links between episodes.

This part of work falls historically to the share of the school
that replaced that of "naturalism," the school which in its
enthusiasm for this side of the matter often achieves this to
the detriment of a good "Rubens-esque" materiality of imagery, so characteristic for Zola.

With this in mind let us return to the principal object of
our inspection—to the "Odessa steps." Look how this event
there is presented and arranged.

In the first place, noticing the *frenzied condition of the
people and masses that are portrayed*, let us go on to find
what we are looking for in structural and compositional indications.

Let us concentrate on the line of *movement*.

There is, before all else, a chaotic *close-up* rush of figures.
And then, as chaotic a rush of figures in *long-shot*.

Then the *chaos* of movement changes to a design: the
rhythmic descending feet of the soldiers.

Tempo increases. Rhythm accelerates.

In this acceleration of *downward* rushing movement there
is a suddenly upsetting opposite movement—*upward:* the
break-neck movement of the *mass* downward leaps over into a

slowly solemn movement upward of the mother's *lone* figure, carrying her dead son.

Mass. Break-neck speed. Downward.

And then suddenly: A lone figure. Slow solemnity. Upward.

But—this is only for an instant. Once more we experience a returning leap to the downward movement.

Rhythm accelerates. Tempo increases.

Suddenly the tempo of the *running crowd* leaps over into the next category of speed—into a *rolling baby-carriage*. It propels the idea of rushing downward into the next dimension—*from rolling, as understood "figuratively," into the physical fact of rolling*. This is not merely a change in levels of *tempo*. This is furthermore as well a *leap in display method* from the figurative to the physical, taking place within the representation of rolling.

Close-ups leap over into long-shots.

Chaotic movement (of a mass)—into *rhythmic* movement (of the soldiers).

One aspect of moving speed (rushing people)—into the next stage of the same theme of moving speed (rolling baby-carriage).

Movement *downward*—into movement *upward*.

Many volleys of *many* rifles—into *one* shot from *one* of the battleship's guns.

Stride by stride—a leap from dimension to dimension. A leap from quality to quality. So that in the final accounting, rather than in a separate episode (the baby-carriage), *the whole method of exposing* the entire event likewise accomplishes its leap: a *narrative* type of exposition is replaced (in the montage rousing of the stone lion) and transferred to the concentrated structure of *imagery*. Visually rhythmic prose leaps over into visually poetic speech.

In a compositional structure identical with human behavior in the grip of pathos, as remarked above, the sequence of the Odessa steps is carried along with such transfers to opposites: chaos is replaced by rhythm, prose—by poetic treatment, etc. Down each step gallops the action, propelled downward by an *ascending* leap from quality to quality, to deeper intensity, to broader dimension.

And we see the theme of pathos, rushed down the steps by the pathos of the shooting, piercing as well to the depths of the basic structure, which gives a plastic and rhythmic accompaniment to the event.*

Is this episode on the steps unique? Does it fall away from, in this feature, from the general type of construction? Not in the least. In it these features, characteristic for the method, are only a pointed culmination, as pointed as the episode itself, which is a culmination in the tragic quality of the film as a whole.

I have mentioned the *caesurae* in the action, "leaping over" or "transferring" to a new quality that was, in each case, the *maximum of all availables*, and was, each time, a leap *into opposition*. All determining compositional elements encountered anywhere appear in such a way, showing us a fundamental ecstatic formula: the leap "out of oneself" invariably becomes a leap to a new quality, and most often of all achieves the diapason of a leap into opposition.

Here is another organic secret: a leaping imagist movement from quality to quality is *not a mere formula of growth*, but is more, *a formula of development*—a development that involves us in its canon, not only as *a single "vegetative" unit, subordinate to the evolutionary laws of nature*, but makes us, instead, *a collective and social unit, consciously participating in its development*. For we know that this very leap, in the interpretation of social phenomena, is present in those revolutions to which social development and the movement of society are directed.

For the third time the organic-ness of *Potemkin* appears before us, *for that leap which characterizes the structure of each compositional link and the composition of the film as a whole, is an infusion into the compositional structure of the most de-*

---

* I have pointed out previously that this analysis is of solely compositional "main-lines." The fabric of *Potemkin* holds up, however, just as well under more microscopic examination, as in the analysis of fourteen shots, on pages 115-120.

termining element of the content's very theme—the revolution-
ary explosion, as one of the leaps which function as inseparable
bonds of the conducting consciousness of social development.

But:

A leap. A transition from quantity to quality. A transition to opposition.

All these are elements of a dialectical movement of development, elements which enter into the comprehension of materialist dialectics. And from this—for the structure of the work we are analyzing as well as for the structure of any construction of pathos—we can say that a pathetic structure is one that compels us, echoing its movement, *to re-live the moments of culmination and substantiation* that are in the canon of all dialectical processes.

We understand a *moment* of culmination to mean those points in a process, those *instants* in which water becomes a new substance—steam, or ice—water, or pig-iron—steel. Here we see the same going out of oneself, moving from one condition, and passing from quality to quality, *ecstasis*. And if we could register psychologically the perceptions of water, steam, ice, and steel at these critical *moments*—moments of *culmination* in the leap, this would tell us something of pathos, of ecstasy!

Born from the pathos of the theme, the compositional structure echoes that basic and unique canon, by which is achieved the organic, social, or any other process given substance by the universe and through participation in this canon (the reflection of which is our consciousness, and its area of application—all our existence) cannot but fill us to the highest point with emotional sensation—pathos.

A question remains—How is the artist to achieve practically these formulae of composition? By a druggist's prescription? By some slide-rule? By specimens of penmanship? With a skeleton key?

These compositional formulae are to be found in any fully pathetic work. But they are not to be achieved by any single *a priori* compositional computation. Skill alone, craftsmanship alone, mastery alone, is not enough.

To achieve the heights of genuine organic-ness, of genuine pathos, in its highest form, all this is absolutely necessary, but this alone is too little.

Only when the work becomes organic, only when it can enter the conditions of a higher organic-ness—into the field of pathos as we understand it, when the theme and content and idea of the work become an organically continuous unity with the ideas, the feelings, with the very breath of the author.

Only when organic-ness itself takes on the strictest forms of constructing a work, only when the artistry of a master's perceptions reach the last gleam of formal perfection.

Then and then only will occur a genuine organic-ness of a work, which enters the circle of natural and social phenomena as a fellow member with equal rights, as an independent phenomenon.

1 January 1939

Post Scriptum:

This may be the most appropriate place for an answer to a question in regard to the connection between the eccentricism that was characteristic of my theater work, and the pathos that distinguishes my film work. This is an apparent paradox that was pointed out, many years ago, by Victor Shklovsky:

> For the creation of his heroic style Eisenstein had to come to it through the montage of eccentric attractions.[11]

Let us go back to those tendencies in the field of expressiveness that led to eccentricism in my theater work of 1920-23.

I dreamed then of a theater "of such emotional saturation that the wrath of a man would be expressed in a backward somersault from a trapeze."

And this dream was connected with the dramatic or, more exactly, the melodramatic—the *serious*—theater!

Of course, this was not without the intertwining of the most varied influences, but in this initial formula there was already the inference of two basic theses, altogether individual and characteristic for my future program of activity as well as for the methods of its execution.

The first was *a maximum degree of passion as a point of departure*. And, second—*a breaking of the customary dimension as a method of its embodiment*.

From this point of view, our program doesn't sound so "crazy."

In those first days, however, these theses were used not as *principles*, but were carried out *directly* and *literally*. And therefore they found their way, not into drama, but were made familiar through the buffonade, eccentricism, and the montage of attractions.

This dream was realized in its purest form in the circus treatment given Ostrovsky's *Enough Simplicity in Every Sage*. In one scene Maxim Shtraukh, playing Mamayev, and growing angry with his nephew for a caricature he had made of him, threw himself at him head first, breaking through the paper of the portrait in a flying somersault beyond the frame.

This moment can be thought of as symbolic of the whole production both in form and in execution: intensity of action everywhere "flew" beyond the limits of the accepted norm of representation, forcing the action with an unusual degree of tension to jump beyond the limits of the accepted measure and the accepted dimension.

In another part of the play we needed a "tense" scene. Glumov's diary is stolen by Golutvin and handed over to Mamayeva.

"Tension" was taken beyond the frame of a tense performance of the dialogue: we introduced a *new measure* of tension into the scene—a tight-rope. Golutvin, balancing and running along it, spoke his lines. The tension of such an "act on wire" extends the *conventional* tension of acting and transfers it into a new level of *real* physical tension.

Throughout the production there was a continuity of theatrical playing, but at the slightest "rise in temperature," this theatrical "play" leaped over into circus "work": a running jump from quality to quality.

A gesture turns into gymnastics, rage is expressed through a somersault, exaltation through a salto-mortale, lyricism on "the mast of death." The grotesque of this style permitted leaps from one type of expression to another. . . . *

The method worked in comedy, for the leap—a *dynamic* characteristic in a successive process—always proceeds from inside a *static* condition—of a forced external observance of *simultaneity* (i.e., of the same dimension).

The "new quality" was treated as if it were the old—the "preceding" quality. This is in itself one of the means of achieving comic effects. How amusing it is, for example, when the latest stage of conveyance is forced to be dependent on the conveyance of an earlier epoch—when an automobile is harnessed to . . . oxen (as in *Little Red Devils*) or to mules (as in *Le dernier milliardaire*).

It is important that the author himself, in this case, while accomplishing the leap from theater to cinema, also accomplished an inner leap in understanding the method: in practice he understood that the method of the leap, comical under conditions of static appearance, works pathetically under conditions of a dynamic process. But this is something to be discussed in more detail on another occasion.

It is sufficient in the present essay to say that the connection between my eccentric theater work and my pathetic cinema work is more sequential and organic than one might have supposed at first glance!

A NOTE:

Sometimes it seems strange that in matters of practice in the sound-film, that I should resemble the last to arrive at the wedding! Youngest of our directors at the time of its inaugura-

* See "Through Theater to Cinema," above, page 7.

tion, and last to take part in its work. But on closer examination this is not quite so.

My first work in the sound-film was . . . in 1926. And in connection with (again!) *Potemkin*.

Potemkin—at least in its foreign circulation—had a special score written for it. The composer was Edmund Meisel, who wrote music for other silent films, both before and after his work on *Potemkin*. But there was nothing particularly extraordinary in this fact—for the history of silent films is sprinkled with such special scores. Music had even been used within the *filming* of certain films—for example, Ludwig Berger had filmed *Ein Walzertraum* to the music of Strauss.

Less usual, perhaps, was the way the *Potemkin* score was composed. It was written very much as we work today on a sound-track. Or rather, as we *should always work*, with creative friendship and friendly creative collaboration between composer and director.

With Meisel this took place in spite of the short time for composition that he was given, and the brevity of my visit to Berlin in 1926 for this purpose. He agreed at once to forego the purely illustrative function common to musical accompaniments at that time (and not only at that time!) and stress certain "effects," particularly in the "music of machines" in the last reel.

This was my only categorical demand: not only to reject customary melodiousness for this sequence of "Meeting the Squadron," relying entirely on a rhythmic beating of percussion, but also to give substance to this demand by establishing in the music as well as in the film at the decisive place a "throwing over" into a "new quality" in the *sound structure*.

So it was *Potemkin* at this point that stylistically broke away from the limits of the "silent film with musical illustrations" into a new sphere—into *sound-film*, where true models of this art-form live in a unity of fused musical and visual images,*

---

* As we see, our "Statement," appearing two years later [see page 257], posing in this way the question of the audio-visual image, was based on a few proved experiments.

composing the work with a united audio-visual image. It is exactly owing to these elements, *anticipating the potentialities of an inner substance for composition in the sound-film,* that the sequence of "Meeting the Squadron" (which along with the "Odessa steps" had such "crushing" effect abroad) deserves a leading place in the anthology of cinema.

It is especially interesting for me that the general construction of *Potemkin* (a leap into a new quality) maintained in the music everything that pierced the pathetic construction—the condition of a qualitative leap which we have seen in *Potemkin* was inseparable from the organism of the theme.

Here the "silent" *Potemkin* teaches the sound-film a lesson, emphasizing again and again the position that for an organic work a single law of construction must penetrate it decisively in all its "significances," and in order to be not "off-stage," but stand as an organic part of the film, the music must also be governed, not only by the same images and themes, but as well by the same basic laws and principles of construction that govern the work as a whole.

To a considerable degree I was able to accomplish this in the sound-film proper—in my first sound-film, *Alexander Nevsky.* It was possible to accomplish this, thanks to the collaboration with such a wonderful and brilliant artist as Sergei Prokofiev.[12]

ACHIEVEMENT

NEW INTELLECTUAL content, new forms for the embodiment of this content, new methods of theoretical comprehension—these are what startled foreign audiences of the Soviet cinema.

Though not always complete in their thematic solutions, nor perfected in their formal embodiment, and far from conclusive in theoretical knowledge and comprehension (all of which was critically perceived by ourselves), our films came as a revelation in the capitalist countries.

What an unexpected intellectual shock came to America and Europe with the appearance of films in which social problems were suddenly presented with all the dots on all the "i's"—to audiences that had heretofore seen only the rarest and vaguest hints of even an undotted "i" on their screens.

But that in itself was not enough. In this first formally imperfect period, our films, though novel in theme, aroused little more than curiosity.

I recall a half-ironical, half-fastidious appraisal (in, I believe, *Filmkurier*) at the time *Palace and Fortress*, one of our first exported films, was shown in Berlin:

This eye-scratching imperfection of harsh lighting, plus the crudeness of the whole treatment, does have a certain appeal and even piquancy for our jaded vision. . . .

And how deeply the emotions of the foreign spectator were scratched when, after *Potemkin*, our films charged down on him!

Born of new intellectual demands, and of the desire to live up to these demands and to be adequate to them, the formal singularities of our films astonished these audiences no less than had their themes and ideas.

Often preceding official, diplomatic recognition of our country, our films successfully forced their way across frontiers, despite the obstacles of censorship, and with their art enlisted friends even among those who could not immediately realize the scope of our ideals.

So it was our cinema—youngest in years, but the most vigorous, vital and rich in emotion and depth of idea—that very soon took the lead of its older sister arts on the other side of the barriers around us.

And its influence abroad was immense.

If in our beginnings we were more than a little indebted to American film-makers, it may also be said that this debt has been repaid with interest.

When I arrived in New York in 1930 I was literally swamped with clippings referring to Milestone's film version of *All Quiet on the Western Front*, which had just appeared. There was not one review that did not mention our influence on the making of this film!

If Raisman had happened to arrive simultaneously with the appearance of King Vidor's *Our Daily Bread*, he would doubtless have seen similar references to *The Soil Is Thirsty*.

Sternberg's *Shanghai Express* was called to life by Ilya Trauberg's *China Express*, and the obligation of *Wild Boys of the Road* to *Road to Life* is generally admitted.

The German film industry considered *Unser Emden* a direct reply to *Potemkin*, while it may be said that *Viva Villa* reflected the influence of all Soviet film-makers, including *October*—not to mention our unfinished Mexican film, *Que Viva Mexico!* Mamoulian's first film, *Applause*, was completely enslaved by "symbolism of objects," so typical of our films of the 1920's.

This influence of the Soviet cinema is many-sided—with countless indirect instances for each of the cited direct examples. It is sometimes revealed in attempts to deal with broader themes than the eternal triangle—or in a bolder portrayal of reality, a characteristic of our films' search for fidelity—or in the mere wish to make use of those formal methods that are the fruit of our cinema's new intellectual content.

As for a theoretical comprehension of the cinema, there are still few individual efforts in this field outside our country, for only here is there any intensive or systematic attempt by film-makers themselves to work on research and analysis of this most amazing of the arts.

As a genuinely major *art* the cinema is unique in that it is, in the full sense of the term, a child of socialism. The other arts have centuries of tradition behind them. The *years* covered by the *entire* history of cinematography are fewer than the *centuries* in which the other arts have developed.

Yet what is most essential is that *cinema as an art* in general, and, further, as an art not only equal to, but in many respects superior to, its fellow-arts, began to be spoken of seriously only with the beginning of Socialist cinematography.

Though it was a matter of years before the full realization of our cinema, that some of the greatest minds pointed in our country to the cinema as the most important of the arts and the one of greatest mass-potency, it required the appearance of a brilliant constellation of Soviet films before people across the frontier began to speak of the cinema as an art deserving as serious attention as is ordinarily given the theater, literature, or painting.

It was only then that the cinema rose above the level of the music-hall, the amusement park, the zoo, and the chamber of horrors, to take its place within the family of great arts.

The cinema would seem to be the highest stage of embodiment for the potentialities and aspirations of each of the arts.

Moreover, the cinema is that genuine and ultimate synthesis of all artistic manifestations that fell to pieces after the peak of Greek culture, which Diderot sought vainly in opera, Wagner in music-drama, Scriabin in his color-concerti, and so on and on.

For sculpture—cinema is a chain of changing plastic forms, bursting, at long last, ages of immobility.

For painting—cinema is not only a solution for the problem of movement in pictorial images, but is also the achievement

of a new and unprecedented form of graphic art, an art that
is a free stream of changing, transforming, commingling forms,
pictures, and compositions, hitherto possible only in music.

Music has always possessed this possibility, but with the
advent of cinema, the melodious and rhythmic flow of music
acquired new potentialities of imagery—visual, palpable, concrete (true, our practice of the new art knows as yet but few
cases of any complete fusion of aural and visual images).

For literature—cinema is an expansion of the strict diction
achieved by poetry and prose into a new realm where the desired image is directly materialized in audio-visual perceptions.

And finally, it is only in cinema that are fused into a real
unity all those separate elements of the spectacle once inseparable in the dawn of culture, and which the theater for centuries has vainly striven to amalgamate anew.

Here is real unity:

Of mass and individual, in which the mass is genuine, and
not a handful of participants in a "crowd scene," hurrying
around back-stage in order to reappear from the opposite
wings to give a "bigger" impression.

Here is a unity of man and space. How many inventive
minds have striven unsuccessfully to solve this problem on the
stage! Gordon Craig, Adolphe Appia, and how many others!
And how easily this problem is solved in cinema.

The screen need not adapt itself to the abstractions of Craig
in order to make man and his environment commensurate.
Not satisfied with the mere reality of the setting, the screen
compels reality itself to participate in the action. "Our woods
and hills will dance"—this is no longer merely an amusing line
from a Krylov fable, but the orchestral part played by the
landscape, which plays as much of a part in the film as does
everything else. In a single cinematographic act, the film fuses
people and a single individual, town and country. It fuses them
with dizzying change and transfer. With an all-embracing
compass of whole countries or of any single character. With
its ability to follow watchfully not only the clouds gathering
in the hills, but also the swelling of a tear from beneath an
eyelash.

The diapason of the dramatist's creative potentialities widens beyond all limits. And the keyboard of the sound mixer, who long ago ceased to be a mere composer, stretches for miles to the right and to the left, embracing not only all the sounds of nature, but also any that the author may invent.

We sometimes forget that we have in our hands—a genuine miracle, a miracle of technical and artistic potentialities, only a fraction of which we have as yet learned to utilize.

We who have learned that there are neither limits nor insurmountable barriers to creative activity shall do well to recall this.

Again and again and again will all the advantages of the cinema flash out if we can picture the arts arranged according to the degree in which they are adapted to their chief task—the reflection of reality and the master of this reality—man.

How narrow is the diapason of sculpture which in most cases is obliged to tear man from his inseparable environment and society in order to hint—by his features and posture—at his inner world which is a mirror of the world around him. A diapason bereft of word, color, movement, the changing phases of drama, the progressive unfolding of events.

How frustrated have been those efforts by composers—Richard Strauss, in particular—to burden music with the task of conveying specific images.

How bound is literature, capable of penetrating into the most subtle coils of a man's consciousness, as well as into the movement of events and epochs, with speculative methods and melodic-rhythmic means, but can only hint at that amplitude of the senses, called for by every line and every page.

How imperfect and limited, too, is the theater in this respect! Only by external *"physical action" and behavior* is it able to convey to the spectator the inner content, the inner movement of consciousness and feelings, the inner world in which live the characters and the author himself. But this is not the material of representation alone.

Rejecting incidentals as well as the "imitative limitations" of the arts as defined by Lessing, and basing ourselves on the most important factors, we might describe the method of each of the arts:

The method of sculpture—patterned on the human body's structure.

The method of painting—patterned on the positions of bodies and their relations with nature.

The method of literature—patterned on the interrelations of reality and man.

The method of theater—patterned on the behavior and activity of people roused by outer and inner motives.

The method of music—patterned on the laws of the inner harmonies of emotionally apprehended phenomena.

In one way or another, all of these—from the most external and lapidary, but more material and less ephemeral, to the most subtle and plastic, but less concrete and tragically ephemeral—with all the means at their disposal, strain towards a single aim.

And that is, through their structures and methods—to reconstruct, to reflect reality, and above all the consciousness and feelings of man. None of the "previous" arts has been able to achieve this purpose to the full.

For the ceiling of one is—the body of man.

The ceiling of another—his acts and behavior.

The ceiling of a third—is the elusive emotional harmony that attends these.

The full embrace of the whole inner world of man, of a whole reproduction of the outer world, cannot be achieved by any one of them.

When any of these arts strives to accomplish this end, by venturing outside its own frame, the very base that holds the art together is inevitably broken.

The most heroic attempt to achieve this in literature was made by James Joyce in *Ulysses* and in *Finnegans Wake*.

Here was reached the limit in reconstructing the reflection and refraction of reality in the consciousness and feelings of man.

Joyce's originality is expressed in his attempt to solve this task with a special dual-level method of writing: unfolding the display of events simultaneously with the particular manner in which these events pass through the consciousness and feelings, the associations and emotions of one of his chief characters. Here literature, as nowhere else, achieves an almost physiological palpability. To the whole arsenal of literary methods of influence has been added a compositional structure that I would call "ultra-lyrical." For while the lyric, equally with the imagery, reconstructs the most intimate passage of the inner logic of feeling, Joyce patterns it on the physiological organization of the emotions, as well as on the embryology of the formation of thought.

The effect at times is astounding, but the price paid is the entire dissolution of the very foundation of literary diction, the entire decomposition of literary method itself; for the lay reader the text has been turned into abracadabra.

In this Joyce shared the sad fate of all the so-called "left" tendencies in art that reached full flower with the entry of capitalism into its imperialist stage.

And if we examine these "leftist" arts from the viewpoint of the tendency as described, we find an extremely curious explanation of this phenomenon.

On the one hand, there is a firm belief in the permanency of the existing order, and hence—a conviction of the limitations of man.

On the other hand, the arts feel a need to step beyond their limitations.

This frequently produces an explosion, but an explosion directed not outwards, towards the widening of the art's frame, which is only to be achieved by extending its content in an anti-imperialist and revolutionary direction, but inwards, towards *means*, not towards *content*. The explosion is not creative and progressive, but destructive.

The arts themselves can escape the fetters of bourgeois limitations only in a revolutionary ideology and in revolutionary themes.

As for their expressive means, escape here lies in a transition to a more perfected stage of all their potentialities—to cinema.

For only the cinema can take, as the esthetic basis of its

dramaturgy, not only the statics of the human body and the dynamics of its action and behavior, but an infinitely broader diapason, reflecting the manifold movement and changing feelings and thoughts of man. This is not merely material for the depiction of man's action and behavior on the screen, but is also the compositional framework over which is distributed a conscious and sensed reflection of the world and reality.

How easily the cinema is able to spread out in an equal graphic of sound and sight the richness of actuality and the richness of its controlling forces, compelling the theme more and more to be born through the process of cinematographic narrative, written from a position of emotion indivisible from the feeling and thinking man.

This is not a task for the theater. This is a level above the "ceiling" of its possibilities. And when it wishes to leap over the limits of these possibilities it also, no less than literature, has to pay the price of its life-like and realistic qualities. It has to retire into the immateriality of a Maeterlinck, as we have seen in his works, and whose *"program"* dreamed for the theater found this ideal as elusive as his own blue-bird!

What debris of anti-realism does the theater inevitably land in the moment it sets itself "synthetic" aims! We need only point to two illustrations of this truth: the *Théâtre d'Art* and the *Théâtre des Arts*—both opening in Paris, in 1890 and 1910 respectively.

The maxim of the first of these theaters, founded by the symbolist poet Paul Fort, was: *La parole crée le décor comme le reste.*[1]

In practice, this led to the productions such as of Pierre Quillard's *La Fille aux mains coupées* (1891). This play,

. . . in the form of a dialogue poem, was staged in this way: a narrator, standing at the side of the proscenium, read the prose passages indicating scene-changes and plot-exposition, while on the stage, veiled by a gauze curtain, the actors moved and declaimed the verses against the background of a golden panel representing primitive ikon-like figures of angels in prayer, painted by Paul Séruzier. This stylized scenery was . . . to serve as a means for "disclosing the lyricism imprisoned in the verses."[2]

The critic Pierre Véber wrote:

Preference is given the lyrical word. The theater seems to van-ish, to make way for dialogue declamation, itself a sort of poetic scenery.

Pierre Quillard demanded that "the scenery be a purely ornamental figment, serving to supplement the illusion by analogies, in color and line, with the drama." [3]

Seeking new methods of "inductive contagion" of the specta-tors, Paul Fort's theater sought to give the substance of practice to the theory of correspondences between the different senses, a popular idea among the poets and theoreticians of symbol-ism. . . .[4]

These new directions in the theater, by no means repre-hensible in themselves, led to the most absurd and superficial excesses.

[Paul Fort] presented Le Cantique des Cantiques by J.-Napoléon Roinard "in eight mystical emblems and three paraphrases," with an accompaniment of music and of perfumes "composed in a tonal-ity corresponding to the various verses." For the author, inspired by Rimbaud's Voyelles, by René Ghil's theory of instrumentation and by the Livre d'orchestration des Parfums by Chardin Hardan-court, sought to establish a harmony of musical tone, of poem and of setting, and of the odors of perfumes.[5]

I believe that it was an imperfection of correspondence found among the other elements that led to this absurdity.

The program of the latter theater (founded by the wealthy dilettante, Jacques Rouché) contained many items of a similar nature, such as, "the designers Dethomas, Drésa, and Piot ex-celled in the invention of conventionalized scenery, attempt-ing to compose 'a symphony of colors supplementing the symphony of sounds.' " [6]

All such attempts at synthesis inevitably wreck themselves and lead only to anti-realism.

Yet when these same aims are set for cinema, they not only do not lead it away from realism, but actually increase the power of its realistic affect.

The unexpected "informing" narrator, for example, who is patterned after the narrator in the Kabuki theater, was perfectly and organically interwoven in the form of sub-titles into the texture of the film even in its silent period.

Today the sub-title still unobtrusively narrates "prose passages indicating scene-changes and plot-exposition," while leaving the lyrical experience of the characters to the pictorial element of the film.

Even in the silent film we made attempts to move further in this direction by weaving the sub-titles into the very thick of the action, dramatizing them with montage and varying proportions within the frame. Recall the titles within the opening sequence of *Old and New*, which were brought directly into the emotional rhythm and the atmosphere of the film.

100

not 10,

not 20,

but precisely

one hundred

billion   and so on.[7]

In the sound-film the sub-title, maintaining its place among the expressive means (try to remove the titles from *Minin and Pozharsky* * and see what is left!), and its counterpart, the actual voice of the narrator (a "convention" nearly identical with that of the theaters we have been describing), are successfully employed. The latter means is a voice whose dramatically weaving potentialities have scarcely been touched by the cinema.

The late Pirandello used to dream aloud of what could be done with this voice, when we met in Berlin in 1929.

How close is such a voice, intervening in the action from outside the action, to Pirandello's whole concept! Its employment for ironical purposes was quite successfully demonstrated by René Clair in *Le dernier milliardaire*, and even more cleverly by Kuleshov in his O. Henry film, *The Great Consoler*.

In Soviet films the only dramatic and even tragic design has been given this voice by Esther Schub and the author of her commentary, Vsevold Vishnevsky, in *Spain*, though its effect was obscured by insufficiently considered composition of the narration and by poor recording. However, the original for this and many other similar uses in the documentary film can be found in Ernest Hemingway's text, written and spoken for Ivens's *The Spanish Earth*.

The "mystery" of the gauze stretched across the stage of the *Théâtre d'Art* apparently lies in a desire to "unify" the diversity of the materially real environment of painted scenery, three-dimensional people, and real textures (such as gilded surfaces).

This is the most difficult of problems for the theater (a solution for it has been sought in hundreds of variations, almost always leading to some degree of meaninglessness), but the cinema is able to solve the problem with the greatest of ease, operating as it does with photographically captured images equally as real in appearance as the objects themselves. In the

* Written by Victor Shklovsky and directed by Pudovkin, this is the least known of Pudovkin's films in the United States, receiving here in 1940 only a limited circulation without superimposed English titles. —EDITOR.

mysteries of fanciful, active, and not merely naturalistically passive sound-recording, lies the similar secret potentiality of harmonizing sounds, which in their direct, life-like substance, may not be capable of combination and orchestration.

Lastly, the cinema achieves its greatest success in a field from which the theater has had to retire, defeated. This is not only in that "symphony of colors supplementing the symphony of sounds," where the cinema has enjoyed an especially happy victory.*

No, this is in a victory within reach of the cinema alone.

This is a genuine and complete "disclosure of the lyricism imprisoned in the verses,"—that lyricism which inevitably possesses the author of a film in its particularly emotional passages.

We have remarked the frustrating results of this attempt in both the "left" theater and in "left" literature.

The solution of this problem has been left entirely to the cinema.

Only here can real events, preserving all the richness of material and sensual fullness, be *simultaneously*—

epic, in the revelation of their content,

dramatic, in the treatment of their subject, and

lyrical to that degree of perfection from which is echoed the most delicate nuance of the author's experience of the theme—possible only in such an exquisite model of form as the system of audio-visual images of the cinema.

When a film-work or any part of one achieves this triple dramatic synthesis, its impressive power is particularly great.

The three sequences which I consider most successful in my own work have this character: they are epic, dramatic, and at the same time, most lyrical, if lyricism is understood as those nuances of multiple individual experience which determine the resulting forms.

These sequences are the "Odessa steps" and "meeting the

---

* I do not mean only in the use of processes, such as Technicolor, Agfacolor, etc., but in the sensitive use of the rich range from black to white, within the sound film.

squadron" in *Potemkin*, and the "attack of the knights" in *Alexander Nevsky*. I have written in detail * of the first and third of these sequences, saying of the steps sequence that in its compositional progress "it behaves like a human being in a state of ecstasy," and that the advancing gallop of the knights is "in subject—the beat of hoofs; in structure—the beat of an excited heart. . . ."

The same may be said of the *Potemkin's* meeting with the fleet, where the pounding machinery was meant to embody the excited collective heart of the battleship, while the rhythm and cadences of this beating were meant to reproduce the lyrical experience of the author as he imagined himself in the position of the rebellious ship.

Cinema solves such problems with the utmost ease.

But the point is not the ease with which it does so, nor that it can do so at all. What matters is the concreteness, materiality, and absolute compatibility of all these achievements with the demands of realism, that categorical condition for vital, worthy, and fruitful art—for Socialist art.

Thus, in respect to all these features the cinema is a step ahead of all related fields, while remaining a contemporary of theater, painting, sculpture, and music. There was a time when, with youthful presumption, I considered that it was time for all the other arts to retire, now that an art had appeared more advanced than any of them in their own potentialities and functions. Fifteen years ago, when I was just "contemplating" film work, I called theater and cinema "the two skulls of Alexander the Great." [8] Recalling the anecdote of the museum show-booth, among whose displays were the skull of Alexander at the age of twenty-five and, alongside it, his skull at the age of forty, I held that the existence of the theater alongside the cinema was equally absurd, for the cinema was actually the grown-up age of the theater. . . .

Of course, this was rather a fact from my own biography, for it was I that was growing up, out of the theater into cin-

* In the preceding essay.

ema. It cannot be denied that the theater has staunchly with-stood my attacks, and is still consorting peaceably with its more advanced form, which is cinema.

Perhaps this advance is not quite obvious to somebody? Is there any need to pile instance on instance to prove this self-evident fact over and over again?

Let us confine the case at this time to one theatrical ele-ment, to the most theatrical element in the theater—the actor. Has not the cinema made demands on the actor that surpass in refinement all that he needs for survival on the stage?

Look at the film work of even the best actors, especially in their first steps in this medium. Isn't it true that what seemed the height of truth and emotional fidelity on the stage howls from the screen as the most extraordinary overacting and epi-leptic grimaces?

How much effort had to be made by even the finest masters of the stage before they were able to rebuild a craft developed in the wide frame of the theater—in the "narrow gate" of the screen! How much more exquisite and subtle their acting be-comes from scene to scene, and even from film to film! Under the very eyes of the spectator "theatricality" is transformed into genuine vitality on the screen. How astonishing and illu-minating in this respect was the development of the late Boris Shchukin not only from rôle to rôle, but from film to film, playing the same rôle! Watch him in *Lenin in October*, and then in *Lenin in 1918!*

Self-control exerted to the millimeter of movement. A de-gree of fidelity of feeling that permits no refuge in theatrical conventions abolished by cinema. Super-concentration and in-stantaneous assumption of rôle, both incomparably more dif-ficult in films than in the theater where the actor does not have to burn under the lights of the studio or create his rôle in the midst of a city street, or in the ocean surf, or in the cockpit of a supposedly looping plane—or to first play death and then two months later, to play the cold that led to it!

As we can see, the indices are the same, but the demands have grown enormously, and a retrospective enrichment of previous stages of development, proceeding alongside, is obvious and undeniable.

And conversely.

To discriminate and, having discriminated, to develop one or another element of cinema is possible only through a thorough study of the basic phenomena of cinema. And the origin of each of these elements lies in other arts.

No one, without learning all the secrets of *mise-en-scène* completely, can learn montage.

An actor who has not mastered the entire arsenal of theater craft can never fully develop his screen potentialities.

Only after mastering the whole culture of the graphic arts can a cameraman realize the compositional basis of the shot.

And only on a foundation of the entire experience of dramaturgy, epos, and lyricism, can a writer create a finished work in that unprecedented literary phenomenon—film-writing, which includes in itself just such a synthesis of literary forms as the cinema as a whole comprises a synthesis of all forms of art.

The inexhaustible potential of all art, having achieved its highest level of development in the form of cinema, is offered not only to masters, artists, craftsmen. Just as priceless is what this furthest development of art as a whole offers to those who meditate on the general laws of artistic creation—and to those who endeavor theoretically to grasp the phenomena of art generally as a social phenomenon with its original and inimitable methods of reflecting the world and actuality.

For this purpose our cinema is an inexhaustible quarry for the definition of general laws and conditions of art as one of the most characteristic reflections of man's spiritual activity.

Having at our disposal so perfect a stage of development of all the arts, fused into one—in cinematography, we may already make infinite deductions from it as to the entire system and method of art, exhaustive for all arts, yet peculiar and individual for each of them.

For here—in cinema—for the first time we have achieved *a genuinely synthetic art—an art of organic synthesis in its very*

essence, not a "concert" of co-existent, contiguous, "linked,"
but actually independent arts.

At last we have had placed in our hands a means of learning
the fundamental laws of art—laws which hitherto we could
snatch at only piecemeal, here a bit from the experience of
painting, there a bit from theater practice, somewhere else
from musical theory. So, the *method of cinema, when fully*
comprehended, will enable us to reveal an understanding of the
method of art in general.

We indeed have something to be proud of on this twentieth
anniversary of our cinema. Within our country. And beyond
its borders. Within the art of cinema itself—and far beyond its
borders, throughout the whole system of art.

Yes, we have something to be proud of—and to work
towards.

[1939]

DICKENS, GRIFFITH,
AND THE FILM TODAY

> People talked as if there had been no dramatic or descriptive music before Wagner; no impressionist painting before Whistler; whilst as to myself, I was finding that the surest way to produce an effect of daring innovation and originality was to revive the ancient attraction of long rhetorical speeches; to stick closely to the methods of Molière; and to lift characters bodily out of the pages of Charles Dickens.
>
> GEORGE BERNARD SHAW [1]

"THE KETTLE began it. . . ."

Thus Dickens opens his *Cricket on the Hearth*.

"The kettle began it. . . ."

What could be further from films! Trains, cowboys, chases . . . And *The Cricket on the Hearth?* "The kettle began it!" But, strange as it may seem, movies also were boiling in that kettle. From here, from Dickens, from the Victorian novel, stem the first shoots of American film esthetic, forever linked with the name of David Wark Griffith.

Although at first glance this may not seem surprising, it does appear incompatible with our traditional concepts of cinematography, in particular with those associated in our minds with the American cinema. Factually, however, this relationship is organic, and the "genetic" line of descent is quite consistent.

Let us first look at that land where, although not perhaps its birthplace, the cinema certainly found the soil in which to grow to unprecedented and unimagined dimensions.

We know from whence the cinema appeared first as a world-wide phenomenon. We know the inseparable link between the cinema and the industrial development of America. We know how production, art and literature reflect the capitalist breadth and construction of the United States of America. And we also know that American capitalism finds its sharpest and most expressive reflection in the American cinema.

But what possible identity is there between this Moloch of modern industry, with its dizzy tempo of cities and subways, its roar of competition, its hurricane of stock market transactions on the one hand, and . . . the peaceful, patriarchal Victorian London of Dickens's novels on the other?

Let's begin with this "dizzy tempo," this "hurricane," and this "roar." These are terms used to describe the United States by persons who know that country solely through books—books limited in quantity, and not too carefully selected.

Visitors to New York City soon recover from their astonishment at this sea of lights (which is actually immense), this maelstrom of the stock market (actually its like is not to be found anywhere), and all this roar (almost enough to deafen one).

As far as the speed of the traffic is concerned, one can't be overwhelmed by this in the streets of the metropolis for the simple reason that speed can't exist there. This puzzling contradiction lies in the fact that the high-powered automobiles are so jammed together that they can't move much faster than snails creeping from block to block, halting at every crossing not only for pedestrian crowds but for the counter-creeping of the cross-traffic.

As you make your merely minute progress amidst a tightly packed glacier of other humans, sitting in similarly high-powered and imperceptibly moving machines, you have plenty of time to ponder the duality behind the dynamic face of America, and the profound interdependence of this duality in everybody and everything American. As your 90-horsepower motor pulls you jerkily from block to block along the steep-cliffed streets, your eyes wander over the smooth surfaces of the skyscrapers. Notions lazily crawl through your brain: "Why don't they seem high?" "Why should they, with all that height, still seem cozy, domestic, small-town?"

You suddenly realize what "trick" the skyscrapers play on you: although they have many floors, each floor is quite low. Immediately the soaring skyscraper appears to be built of a number of small-town buildings, piled on top of each other. One merely needs to go beyond the city-limits or, in a few cities, merely beyond the center of the city, in order to see the same buildings, piled, not by the dozens, and fifties, and hundreds, on top of each other, but laid out in endless rows of one- and two-storied stores and cottages along Main Streets, or along half-rural side-streets.

Here (between the "speed traps") you can fly along as fast as you wish; here the streets are almost empty, traffic is light—the exact opposite of the metropolitan congestion that you just left—no trace of that frantic activity choked in the stone vises of the city.

You often come across regiments of skyscrapers that have moved deep into the countryside, twisting their dense nets of railroads around them; but at the same rate small-town agrarian America appears to have overflowed into all but the very centers of the cities; now and then one turns a skyscraper corner, only to run head on into some home of colonial architecture, apparently whisked from some distant savannah of Louisiana or Alabama to this very heart of the business city.

But there where this provincial wave has swept in more than a cottage here or a church there (gnawing off a corner of that monumental modern Babylon, "Radio City"), or a cemetery, unexpectedly left behind in the very center of the financial district, or the hanging wash of the Italian district, flapping just around the corner, off Wall Street—this good old provincialism has turned inward to apartments, nestling in clusters around fireplaces, furnished with soft grandfather-chairs and the lace doilies that shroud the wonders of modern technique: refrigerators, washing-machines, radios.

And in the editorial columns of popular newspapers, in the aphorisms of broadcast sermon and transcribed advertisement, there is a firmly entrenched attitude that is usually defined as "way down East"—an attitude that may be found beneath many a waistcoat or bowler where one would ordinarily expect to find a heart or a brain. Mostly one is amazed by the abundance of small-town and patriarchal elements in American life and manners, morals and philosophy, the ideological horizon and rules of behavior in the middle strata of American culture.

In order to understand Griffith, one must visualize an America made up of more than visions of speeding automobiles, streamlined trains, racing ticker tape, inexorable conveyor-belts. One is obliged to comprehend this second side of America as well—America, the traditional, the patriarchal, the provincial. And then you will be considerably less astonished by this link between Griffith and Dickens.

The threads of both these Americas are interwoven in the style and personality of Griffith—as in the most fantastic of his own parallel montage sequences.

What is most curious is that Dickens appears to have guided *both* lines of Griffith's style, reflecting both faces of America: Small-Town America, and Super-Dynamic America.

This can be detected at once in the "intimate" Griffith of contemporary or past American life, where Griffith is profound, in those films about which Griffith told me, that "they were made for myself and were invariably rejected by the exhibitors."

But we are a little astonished when we see that the construction of the "official," sumptuous Griffith, the Griffith of tempestuous tempi, of dizzying action, of breathtaking chases—has also been guided by the same Dickens! But we shall see how true this is.

First the "intimate" Griffith, and the "intimate" Dickens.

The kettle began it. . . .

As soon as we recognize this kettle as a typical close-up, we exclaim: "Why didn't we notice it before! Of course this is the purest Griffith. How often we've seen such a close-up at the beginning of an episode, a sequence, or a whole film by him!" (By the way, we shouldn't overlook the fact that one of Griffith's earliest films was based on *The Cricket on the Hearth!* *)

Certainly, this kettle is a typical Griffith-esque close-up. A close-up saturated, we now become aware, with typically Dickens-esque "atmosphere," with which Griffith, with equal mastery, can envelop the severe face of life in *Way Down East,* and the icy cold moral face of his characters, who push the guilty Anna (Lillian Gish) onto the shifting surface of a swirling ice-break.

Isn't this the same implacable atmosphere of cold that is given by Dickens, for example, in *Dombey and Son?* The image of Mr. Dombey is revealed through cold and prudery. And the print of cold lies on everyone and everything—everywhere. And "atmosphere"—always and everywhere—is one of the most expressive means of revealing the inner world and ethical countenance of the characters themselves.

We can recognize this particular method of Dickens in Griffith's inimitable bit-characters who seem to have run straight from life onto the screen. I can't recall who speaks with whom in one of the street scenes of the modern story of *Intolerance.* But I shall never forget the mask of the passer-by with nose pointed forward between spectacles and straggly beard, walking with hands behind his back as if he were manacled. As he passes he interrupts the most pathetic moment in the conversation of the suffering boy and girl. I can remember next to nothing of the couple, but this passer-by, who is visible in the shot only for a flashing glimpse, stands alive before me now—and I haven't seen the film for twenty years!

Occasionally these unforgettable figures actually walked into Griffith's films almost directly from the street: a bit-player, developed in Griffith's hands to stardom; the passer-by who may never again have been filmed; and that mathematics

* Released on May 27, 1909, with Herbert Pryor, Linda Arvidson Griffith, Violet Mersereau, Owen Moore, this film followed the dramatic adaptation of the *Cricket* made by Albert Smith with Dickens's approval.

teacher who was invited to play a terrifying butcher in *America*—the late Louis Wolheim—who ended the film career thus begun with his incomparable performance as "Kat" in *All Quiet on the Western Front*.

These striking figures of sympathetic old men are also quite in the Dickens tradition; and these noble and slightly one-dimensional figures of sorrow and fragile maidens; and these rural gossips and sundry odd characters. They are especially convincing in Dickens when he uses them briefly, in episodes.

The only other thing to be noticed about [Pecksniff] is that here, as almost everywhere else in the novels, the best figures are at their best when they have least to do. Dickens's characters are perfect as long as he can keep them out of his stories. Bumble is divine until a dark and practical secret is entrusted to him. . . . Micawber is noble when he is doing nothing; but he is quite unconvincing when he is spying on Uriah Heep. . . . Similarly, while Pecksniff is the best thing in the story, the story is the worst thing in Pecksniff. . . .[2]

Free of this limitation, and with the same believability; Griffith's characters grow from episodic figures into those fascinating and finished images of living people, in which his screen is so rich.

Instead of going into detail about this, let us rather return to that more obvious fact—the growth of that second side of Griffith's creative craftsmanship—as a magician of tempo and montage; a side for which it is rather surprising to find the same Victorian source.

When Griffith proposed to his employers the novelty of a parallel "cut-back" for his first version of *Enoch Arden* (*After Many Years*, 1908), this is the discussion that took place, as recorded by Linda Arvidson Griffith in her reminiscences of Biograph days:

When Mr. Griffith suggested a scene showing Annie Lee waiting for her husband's return to be followed by a scene of Enoch cast away on a desert island, it was altogether too distracting. "How can you tell a story jumping about like that? The people won't know what it's about."

"Well," said Mr. Griffith, "doesn't Dickens write that way?"
"Yes, but that's Dickens; that's novel writing; that's different."
"Oh, not so much, these are picture stories; not so different." [3]

But, to speak quite frankly, all astonishment on this subject and the apparent unexpectedness of such statements can be ascribed only to our—ignorance of Dickens.

All of us read him in childhood, gulped him down greedily, without realizing that much of his irresistibility lay not only in his capture of detail in the childhoods of his heroes, but also in that spontaneous, childlike skill for story-telling, equally typical for Dickens and for the American cinema, which so surely and delicately plays upon the infantile traits in its audience. We were even less concerned with the technique of Dickens's composition: for us this was non-existent—but captivated by the effects of this technique, we feverishly followed his characters from page to page, watching his characters now being rubbed from view at the most critical moment, then seeing them return afresh between the separate links of the parallel secondary plot.

As children, we paid no attention to the mechanics of this. As adults, we rarely re-read his novels. And becoming filmworkers, we never found time to glance beneath the covers of these novels in order to figure out what exactly had captivated us in these novels and with what means these incredibly many-paged volumes had chained our attention so irresistibly.

Apparently Griffith was more perceptive . . .

But before disclosing what the steady gaze of the American film-maker may have caught sight of on Dickens's pages, I wish to recall what David Wark Griffith himself represented to us, the young Soviet film-makers of the 'twenties.

To say it simply and without equivocation: a revelation.

Try to remember our early days, in those first years of the October socialist revolution. The fires *At the Hearthsides* of our native film-producers had burnt out, the *Nava's Charms* *

* *Nava's Charms* (by Sologub) and *At the Hearthside*, two pre-Revolutionary Russian films, as is also *Forget the Hearth*. The names that follow are of the male and female film stars of this period.—EDITOR.

of their productions had lost their power over us and, whispering through pale lips, "Forget the hearth," Khudoleyev and Runich, Polonsky and Maximov had departed to oblivion; Vera Kholodnaya to the grave; Mozhukhin and Lisenko to expatriation.

The young Soviet cinema was gathering the experience of revolutionary reality, of first experiments (Vertov), of first systematic ventures (Kuleshov), in preparation for that unprecedented explosion in the second half of the 'twenties, when it was to become an independent, mature, original art, immediately gaining world recognition.

In those early days a tangle of the widest variety of films was projected on our screens. From out of this weird hash of old Russian films and new ones that attempted to maintain "traditions," and new films that could not yet be called Soviet, and foreign films that had been imported promiscuously, or brought down off dusty shelves—two main streams began to emerge.

On the one side there was the cinema of our neighbor, postwar Germany. Mysticism, decadence, dismal fantasy followed in the wake of the unsuccessful revolution of 1923, and the screen was quick to reflect this mood. *Nosferatu the Vampire*, *The Street*, the mysterious *Warning Shadows*, the mystic criminal *Dr. Mabuse the Gambler*,* reaching out towards us from our screens, achieved the limits of horror, showing us a future as an unrelieved night crowded with sinister shadows and crimes. . . .

The chaos of multiple exposures, of over-fluid dissolves, of split screens, was more characteristic of the later 'twenties (as in *Looping the Loop* or *Secrets of a Soul* †), but earlier German films contained more than a hint of this tendency. In the

---

* *Nosferatu* (1922), directed by F. W. Murnau; *Die Strasse* (1923), directed by Karl Grune; *Schatten* (1923), directed by Arthur Robison; *Dr. Mabuse, der Spieler* (1922), directed by Fritz Lang.

† *Looping the Loop* (1928), directed by Arthur Robison; *Geheimnisse einer Seele* (1926), directed by G. W. Pabst.

over-use of these devices was also reflected the confusion and chaos of post-war Germany.

All these tendencies of mood and method had been fore-shadowed in one of the earliest and most famous of these films, *The Cabinet of Dr. Caligari* (1920), this barbaric carnival of the destruction of the healthy human infancy of our art, this common grave for normal cinema origins, this combination of silent hysteria, particolored canvases, daubed flats, painted faces, and the unnatural broken gestures and actions of monstrous chimaeras.

Expressionism left barely a trace on our cinema. This painted, hypnotic "St. Sebastian of Cinema" was too alien to the young, robust spirit and body of the rising class.

It is interesting that during those years inadequacies in the field of film technique played a positive rôle. They helped to restrain from a false step those whose enthusiasm might have pulled them in this dubious direction. Neither the dimensions of our studios, nor our lighting equipment, nor the materials available to us for make-up, costumes, or setting, gave us the possibility to heap onto the screen similar phantasmagoria. But it was chiefly another thing that held us back: our spirit urged us towards life—amidst the people, into the surging actuality of a regenerating country. Expressionism passed into the formative history of our cinema as a powerful factor—of repulsion.

There was the rôle of another film-factor that appeared, dashing along in such films as *The Gray Shadow, The House of Hate, The Mark of Zorro.** There was in these films a world, stirring and incomprehensible, but neither repulsive nor alien. On the contrary—it was captivating and attractive, in its own way engaging the attention of young and future film-makers, exactly as the young and future engineers of the time were attracted by the specimens of engineering techniques unknown

---

* *The House of Hate* (1918), a serial directed by George Seitz, with Pearl White; *The Mark of Zorro* (1921), directed by Fred Niblo, with Douglas Fairbanks. The American film released in Russia as *The Gray Shadow* has not been identified.—EDITOR.

to us, sent from that same unknown, distant land across the ocean.

What enthralled us was not only these films, it was also their possibilities. Just as it was the possibilities in a tractor to make collective cultivation of the fields a reality, it was the boundless temperament and tempo of these amazing (and amazingly useless!) works from an unknown country that led us to muse on the possibilities of a profound, intelligent, class-directed use of this wonderful tool.

The most thrilling figure against this background was Griffith, for it was in his works that the cinema made itself felt as more than an entertainment or pastime. The brilliant new methods of the American cinema were united in him with a profound emotion of story, with human acting, with laughter and tears, and all this was done with an astonishing ability to preserve all that gleam of a filmically dynamic holiday, which had been captured in *The Gray Shadow* and *The Mark of Zorro* and *The House of Hate*. That the cinema could be incomparably greater, and that this was to be the basic task of the budding Soviet cinema—these were sketched for us in Griffith's creative work, and found ever new confirmation in his films.

Our heightened curiosity of those years in *construction and method* swiftly discerned wherein lay the most powerful affective factors in this great American's films. This was in a hitherto unfamiliar province, bearing a name that was familiar to us, not in the field of art, but in that of engineering and electrical apparatus, first touching art in its most advanced section—in cinematography. This province, this method, this principle of building and construction was *montage*.

This was the montage whose foundations had been laid by American film-culture, but whose full, completed, conscious use and world recognition was established by our films. Montage, the rise of which will be forever linked with the name of Griffith. Montage, which played a most vital rôle in the creative work of Griffith and brought him his most glorious successes.

Griffith arrived at it through the method of parallel action. And, essentially, it was on this that he came to a standstill. But we mustn't run ahead. Let us examine the question of how montage came to Griffith or—how Griffith came to montage.

Griffith arrived at montage through the method of parallel action, and he was led to the idea of parallel action by— Dickens!

To this fact Griffith himself has testified, according to A. B. Walkley, in *The Times* of London, for April 26, 1922, on the occasion of a visit by the director to London. Writes Mr. Walkley:

He [Griffith] is a pioneer, by his own admission, rather than an inventor. That is to say, he has opened up new paths in Film Land, under the guidance of ideas supplied to him from outside. His best ideas, it appears, have come to him from Dickens, who has always been his favorite author. . . . Dickens inspired Mr. Griffith with an idea, and his employers (mere "business" men) were horrified at it; but, says Mr. Griffith, "I went home, re-read one of Dickens's novels, and came back next day to tell them they could either make use of my idea or dismiss me."

Mr. Griffith found the idea to which he clung thus heroically in Dickens. That was as luck would have it, for he might have found the same idea almost anywhere. Newton deduced the law of gravitation from the fall of an apple; but a pear or a plum would have done just as well. The idea is merely that of a "break" in the narrative, a shifting of the story from one group of characters to another group. People who write the long and crowded novels that Dickens did, especially when they are published in parts, find this practice a convenience. You will meet with it in Thackeray, George Eliot, Trollope, Meredith, Hardy, and, I suppose, every other Victorian novelist. . . . Mr. Griffith might have found the same practice not only in Dumas *père*, who cared precious little about form, but also in great artists like Tolstoy, Turgeniev, and Balzac. But, as a matter of fact, it was not in any of these others, but in Dickens that he found it; and it is significant of the predominant influence of Dickens that he should be quoted as an authority for a device which is really common to fiction at large.

Even a superficial acquaintance with the work of the great English novelist is enough to persuade one that Dickens may have given and did give to cinematography far more guidance than that which led to the montage of parallel action alone.

Dickens's nearness to the characteristics of cinema in method, style, and especially in viewpoint and exposition, is indeed amazing. And it may be that in the nature of exactly these characteristics, in their community both for Dickens and for cinema, there lies a portion of the secret of that mass success which they both, apart from themes and plots, brought and still bring to the particular quality of such exposition and such writing.

What were the novels of Dickens for his contemporaries, for his readers? There is one answer: they bore the same relation to them that the film bears to the same strata in our time. They compelled the reader to live with the same passions. They appealed to the same good and sentimental elements as does the film (at least on the surface); they alike shudder before vice,* they alike mill the extraordinary, the unusual, the fantastic, from boring, prosaic and everyday existence. And they clothe this common and prosaic existence in their special vision.

Illumined by this light, refracted from the land of fiction back to life, this commonness took on a romantic air, and bored people were grateful to the author for giving them the countenances of potentially romantic figures.

This partially accounts for the close attachment to the novels of Dickens and, similarly, to films. It was from this that the universal success of his novels derived. In an essay on Dickens, Stefan Zweig opens with this description of his popularity:

* As late as April 17, 1944, Griffith still considered this the chief social function of film-making. An interviewer from the Los Angeles *Times* asked him, "What is a good picture?" Griffith replied, "One that makes the public forget its troubles. Also, a good picture tends to make folks think a little, without letting them suspect that they are being inspired to think. In one respect, nearly all pictures are good in that they show the triumph of good over evil." This is what Osbert Sitwell, in reference to Dickens, called the "Virtue *v.* Vice Cup-Tie Final."

The love Dickens's contemporaries lavished upon the creator of Pickwick is not to be assessed by accounts given in books and biographies. Love lives and breathes only in the spoken word. To get an adequate idea of the intensity of this love, one must catch (as I once caught) an Englishman old enough to have youthful memories of the days when Dickens was still alive. Preferably it should be someone who finds it hard even now to speak of him as Charles Dickens, choosing, rather, to use the affectionate nickname of "Boz." The emotion, tinged with melancholy, which these old reminiscences call up, gives us of a younger generation some ink-ling of the enthusiasm that inspired the hearts of thousands when the monthly instalments in their blue covers (great rarities, now) arrived at English homes. At such times, my old Dickensian told me, people would walk a long way to meet the postman when a fresh number was due, so impatient were they to read what Boz had to tell. . . . How could they be expected to wait patiently until the letter-carrier, lumbering along on an old nag, would arrive with the solution of these burning problems? When the appointed hour came round, old and young would sally forth, walking two miles and more to the post office merely to have the issue sooner. On the way home they would start reading, those who had not the luck of holding the book looking over the shoul-der of the more fortunate mortal; others would set about reading aloud as they walked; only persons with a genius for self-sacrifice would defer a purely personal gratification, and would scurry back to share the treasure with wife and child.

In every village, in every town, in the whole of the British Isles, and far beyond, away in the remotest parts of the earth where the English-speaking nations had gone to settle and colonize, Charles Dickens was loved. People loved him from the first mo-ment when (through the medium of print) they made his ac-quaintance until his dying day. . . .[4]

Dickens's tours as a reader gave final proof of public affec-tion for him, both at home and abroad. By nine o'clock on the morning that tickets for his lecture course were placed on sale in New York, there were two lines of buyers, each more than three-quarters of a mile in length:

The tickets for the course were all sold before noon. Members of families relieved each other in the queues; waiters flew across the streets and squares from the neighboring restaurant, to serve parties who were taking their breakfast in the open December air; while excited men offered five and ten dollars for the mere permission to exchange places with other persons standing nearer the head of the line! [5] *

Isn't this atmosphere similar to that of Chaplin's tour through Europe, or the triumphant visit to Moscow of "Doug" and "Mary," or the excited anticipation around the première of *Grand Hotel* in New York, when an airplane service assisted ticket buyers on the West Coast? The immense popular success of Dickens's novels in his own time can be equaled in extent only by that whirlwind success which is now enjoyed by this or that sensational film success.

Perhaps the secret lies in Dickens's (as well as cinema's) creation of an extraordinary plasticity. The observation in the novels is extraordinary—as is their optical quality. The characters of Dickens are rounded with means as plastic and slightly exaggerated as are the screen heroes of today. The screen's heroes are engraved on the senses of the spectator with clearly visible traits, its villains are remembered by certain facial expressions, and all are saturated in the peculiar, slightly unnatural radiant gleam thrown over them by the screen.

It is absolutely thus that Dickens draws his characters—this is the faultlessly plastically grasped and pitilessly sharply

* Dickens himself witnessed a modern by-product of popular success— speculators: "At Brooklyn I am going to read in Mr. Ward Beecher's chapel: the only building there available for the purpose. You must understand that Brooklyn is a kind of sleeping-place for New York, and is supposed to be a great place in the money way. We let the seats pew by pew! the pulpit is taken down for my screen and gas! and I appear out of the vestry in canonical form! . . . The sale of tickets there was an amazing scene. The noble army of speculators have now furnished (this is literally true, and I am quite serious) each man with a straw mattress, a little bag of bread and meat, two blankets, and a bottle of whisky. . . . It being severely cold at Brooklyn, they made an immense bonfire in the street—a narrow street of wooden houses—which the police turned out to extinguish. A general fight then took place; from which the people furthest off in the line rushed bleeding when they saw any chance of ousting others nearer the door, put their mattresses in the spots so gained, and held on by the iron rails. . . ."[6]

sketched gallery of immortal Pickwicks, Dombeys, Fagins, Tackletons, and others.

Just because it never occurred to his biographers to connect Dickens with the cinema, they provide us with unusually objective evidence, directly linking the importance of Dickens's observation with our medium.

[John] Forster speaks of Dickens's recollections of his childhood sufferings, and notes, as he could hardly fail to note, Dickens's amazingly detailed memory. He does not note, as he should, how this super-acuteness of physical vision contributed a basic element to Dickens's artistic method. For with that acuteness of physical vision, and that unerring recollection of every detail in the thing seen, went an abnormally complete grasp of the thing in the totality of its natural connections. . . .

And if ever a man had the gift of the eye—and not merely of the eye but of the ear, and of the nose—and the faculty of remembering with microscopic accuracy of detail everything ever seen, or heard, or tasted, smelled, or felt, that man was Charles Dickens. . . . The whole picture arises before us in sight, sound, touch, taste, and pervading odour, just exactly as in real life, and with a vividness that becomes positively uncanny.

To readers less sensitive than Dickens, this very vividness with which he visualizes plain things in plain everyday life appears to be "exaggeration." It is no such thing. The truth is that Dickens always sees instantly, and in every last, least, tiny detail, *all* that there is to be seen; while lesser mortals see only a part, and sometimes a trifling part at that.[7]

Zweig continues the case:

He cuts through the fog surrounding the years of childhood like a clipper driving through the waves. In *David Copperfield*, that masked autobiography, we are given reminiscences of a two-year-old child concerning his mother with her pretty hair and youthful shape, and Peggotty with no shape at all; memories which are like silhouettes standing out from the blank of his infancy. There are never any blurred contours where Dickens is concerned; he does not give us hazy visions, but portraits whose every detail is sharply defined. . . . As he himself once said, it is the little things that give meaning to life. He is, therefore, perpetually on the watch for tokens, be they never so slight; a spot of grease on a dress, an awkward gesture caused by shyness, a strand of reddish hair peeping from beneath a wig if its wearer happens to lose his temper. He captures all the nuances of a handshake, knows what the pressure of each finger signifies; detects the shades of meaning in a smile.

Before he took the career of a writer, he was parliamentary reporter for a newspaper. In this capacity he became proficient in the art of summary, in compressing long-winded discussions; as shorthand writer he conveyed a word by a stroke, a whole sentence by a few curves and dashes. So in later days as an author he invented a kind of shorthand to reality, consisting of little signs instead of lengthy descriptions, an essence of observation distilled from the innumerable happenings of life. He has an uncannily sharp eye for the detection of these insignificant externals; he never overlooks anything; his memory and his keenness of perception are like a good camera lens which, in the hundredth part of a second, fixes the least expression, the slightest gesture, and yields a perfectly precise negative. Nothing escapes his notice. In addition, this perspicacious observation is enhanced by a marvellous power of refraction which, instead of presenting an object as merely reflected in its ordinary proportions from the surface of a mirror, gives us an image clothed in an excess of characteristics. For he invariably underlines the personal attributes of his characters. . . .

This extraordinary optical faculty amounted to genius in Dickens. . . . His psychology began with the visible; he gained his insight into character by observation of the exterior—the most delicate and fine minutiae of the outward semblance, it is true, those utmost tenuosities which only the eyes that are rendered acute by a superlative imagination can perceive. Like the English philosophers, he does not begin with assumptions and suppositions, but with characteristics. . . . Through traits, he discloses types: Creakle had no voice, but spoke in a whisper; the exertion cost him, or the consciousness of talking in that feeble way, made his angry face much more angry, and his thick veins much thicker. Even as we read the description, the sense of terror the boys felt at the approach of this fiery blusterer becomes manifest in us as well. Uriah Heep's hands are damp and cold; we experience a loathing for the creature at the very outset, as though we were faced by a snake. Small things? Externals? Yes, but they invariably are such as to recoil upon the soul.[8]

The visual images of Dickens are inseparable from aural images. The English philosopher and critic, George Henry Lewes,[9] though puzzled as to its significance, recorded that "Dickens once declared to me that every word said by his characters was distinctly *heard* by him. . . ."

We can see for ourselves that his descriptions offer not only absolute *accuracy of detail*, but also an absolutely *accurate drawing of the behavior* and actions of his characters. And this is just as true for the most trifling details of behavior—even gesture, as it is for the basic generalized characteristics of the image. Isn't this piece of description of Mr. Dombey's behavior actually an exhaustive regisseur-actor directive?

He had already laid his hand upon the bell-rope to convey his usual summons to Richards, when his eye fell upon a writing-desk, belonging to his deceased wife, which had been taken, among other things, from a cabinet in her chamber. It was not the first time that his eye had lighted on it. He carried the key in his pocket; and he brought it to his table and opened it now—having previously locked the room door—with a well-accustomed hand.[10]

Here the last phrase arrests one's attention: there is a certain awkwardness in its description. However, this "inserted" phrase: *having previously locked the room door*, "fitted in" as if recollected by the author in the middle of a later phrase, instead of being placed where it apparently should have been, in the consecutive order of the description, that is, before the words, *and he brought it to his table*, is found exactly at this spot for quite *un*fortuitous reasons.

In this deliberate "montage" displacement of the time-continuity of the description there is a brilliantly caught rendering of the *transient thievery* of the action, slipped between the preliminary action and the act of reading another's letter, carried out with that absolute "correctness" of gentlemanly dignity which Mr. Dombey knows how to give to any behavior or action of his.

This very (montage) arrangement of the phrasing gives an exact direction to the "performer," so that in defining this decorous and confident opening of the writing-desk, he must "play" the closing and locking of the door with a hint of an entirely different shade of conduct. And it would be this "shading" in which would also be played the unfolding of the letter; but in this part of the "performance" Dickens makes this shading more precise, not only with a significant arrangement of the words, but also with an exact description of characteristics.

From beneath a heap of torn and cancelled scraps of paper, he took one letter that remained entire. Involuntarily holding his breath as he opened this document, and 'bating in the stealthy action something of his arrogant demeanour, he sat down, resting his head upon one hand, and read it through.

The reading itself is done with a shading of absolutely gentlemanly cold decorum:

He read it slowly and attentively, and with a nice particularity to every syllable. Otherwise than as his great deliberation seemed unnatural, and perhaps the result of an effort equally great, he allowed no sign of emotion to escape him. When he had read it through, he folded and refolded it slowly several times, and tore it carefully into fragments. Checking his hand in the act of throwing these away, he put them in his pocket, as if unwilling to trust them even to the chances of being reunited and deciphered; and instead of ringing, as usual, for little Paul, he sat solitary all the evening in his cheerless room.

This scene does not appear in the final version of the novel, for with the aim of increasing the tension of the action, Dickens cut out this passage on Forster's advice; in his biography of Dickens Forster preserved this passage to show with what mercilessness Dickens sometimes "cut" writing that had cost him great labor. This mercilessness once more emphasizes that sharp clarity of representation towards which Dickens strove by all means, endeavoring with purely cinematic laconism to say what he considered necessary. (This, by the way, did not in the least prevent his novels from achieving enormous breadth.)

I don't believe I am wrong in lingering on this example, for one need only alter two or three of the character names and change Dickens's name to the name of the hero of my essay, in order to impute literally almost everything told here to the account of Griffith.

From that steely, observing glance, which I remember from my meeting with him, to the capture *en passant* of key details or tokens—indications of character, Griffith has all this in as much a Dickens-esque sharpness and clarity as Dickens, on his part, had cinematic "optical quality," "frame composition," "close-up," and the alteration of emphasis by special lenses.

Analogies and resemblances cannot be pursued too far—they lose conviction and charm. They begin to take on the air of machination or card-tricks. I should be very sorry to lose the conviction of the affinity between Dickens and Griffith, allowing this abundance of common traits to slide into a game of anecdotal semblance of tokens.

All the more that such a gleaning from Dickens goes beyond the limits of interest in Griffith's individual cinematic craftsmanship and widens into a concern with film-craftsmanship in general. This is why I dig more and more deeply into the film-indications of Dickens, revealing them through Griffith—for the use of future film-exponents. So I must be excused, in leafing through Dickens, for having found in him even—a "dissolve." How else could this passage be defined—the opening of the last chapter of *A Tale of Two Cities:*

Along the Paris streets, the death-carts rumble, hollow and harsh. Six tumbrils carry the day's wine to La Guillotine. . . .

Six tumbrils roll along the streets. Change these back again to what they were, thou powerful enchanter, Time, and they shall be seen to be the carriages of absolute monarchs, the equipages of feudal nobles, the toilettes of flaring Jezebels, the churches that are not my Father's house but dens of thieves, the huts of millions of starving peasants!

How many such "cinematic" surprises must be hiding in Dickens's pages!

However, let us turn to the basic montage structure, whose rudiment in Dickens's work was developed into the elements of film composition in Griffith's work. Lifting a corner of the veil over these riches, these hitherto unused experiences, let us look into *Oliver Twist*. Open it at the twenty-first chapter. Let's read its beginning:

Chapter XXI *

1. It was a cheerless morning when they got into the street; blowing and raining hard; and the clouds looking dull and stormy.

The night had been very wet: for large pools of water had collected in the road: and the kennels were overflowing.

There was a faint glimmering of the coming day in the sky; but it rather aggravated than relieved the gloom of the scene: the sombre light only serving to pale that which the street lamps afforded, without shedding any warmer or brighter tints upon the wet housetops, and dreary streets.

There appeared to be nobody stirring in that quarter of the town; for the windows of the houses were all closely shut; and the streets through which they passed, were noiseless and empty.

2. By the time they had turned into the Bethnal Green Road, the day had fairly begun to break. Many of the lamps were already extinguished;

a few country waggons were slowly toiling on, towards London;

and now and then, a stage-coach, covered with mud, rattled briskly by:

the driver bestowing, as he passed, an admonitory lash upon the heavy waggoner who, by keeping on the wrong side of the road, had endangered his arriving at the office, a quarter of a minute after his time.

The public-houses, with gas-lights burning inside, were already open.

By degrees, other shops began to be unclosed; and a few scattered people were met with.

* For demonstration purposes I have broken this beginning of the chapter into smaller pieces than did its author; the numbering is, of course, also mine.

Then, came straggling groups of labourers going to their work;
then, men and women with fish-baskets on their heads:
donkey-carts laden with vegetables;
chaise-carts filled with live-stock or whole carcasses of meat;
milk-women with pails;
and an unbroken concourse of people, trudging out with various
supplies to the eastern suburbs of the town.

3. As they approached the City, the noise and traffic gradually
increased;
and when they threaded the streets between Shoreditch and
Smithfield, it had swelled into a roar of sound and bustle.
It was as light as it was likely to be, till night came on again; and
the busy morning of half the London population had begun. . . .

4. It was market-morning.
The ground was covered, nearly ankle-deep, with filth and mire;
and a thick steam, perpetually rising from the reeking bodies of
the cattle,
and mingling with the fog,
which seemed to rest upon the chimney-tops, hung heavily
above. . . .
Countrymen,
butchers,
drovers,
hawkers,
boys,
thieves,
idlers,
and vagabonds of every low grade,
were mingled together in a dense mass;

5. the whistling of drovers,
the barking of dogs,
the bellowing and plunging of oxen,
the bleating of sheep,
the grunting and squeaking of pigs;
the cries of hawkers,
the shouts, oaths and quarrelling on all sides;
the ringing of bells
and roar of voices, that issued from every public-house;

the crowding, pushing, driving, beating,
whooping and yelling;
the hideous and discordant din that resounded from every corner of the market;
and the unwashed, unshaven, squalid, and dirty figures constantly running to and fro, and bursting in and out of the throng;
rendered it a stunning and bewildering scene, which quite con-
founded the senses.

How often have we encountered just such a structure in the
work of Griffith? This austere accumulation and quickening
tempo, this gradual play of light: from burning street-lamps,
to their being extinguished; from night, to dawn; from dawn,
to the full radiance of day (*It was as light as it was likely to be,
till night came on again*); this calculated transition from purely
visual elements to an interweaving of them with aural elements:
at first as an indefinite rumble, coming from afar at the second
stage of increasing light, so that the rumble may grow into a
roar, transferring us to a purely aural structure, now concrete
and objective (section 5 of our break-down); with such scenes,
picked up *en passant,* and intercut into the whole—like the
driver, hastening towards his office; and, finally, these magnificently typical details, the reeking bodies of the cattle, from
which the steam rises and mingles with the over-all cloud of
morning fog, or the close-up of the legs in the almost ankle-
deep filth and mire, all this gives the fullest cinematic sensation
of the panorama of a market.

Surprised by these examples from Dickens, we must not forget one more circumstance, related to the creative work of
Dickens in general.

Thinking of this as taking place in "cozy" old England, we
are liable to forget that the works of Dickens, considered not
only against a background of English literature, but against a
background of world literature of that epoch, as well, were
produced as the works of a city artist. He was the first to
bring factories, machines, and railways into literature.

But indication of this "urbanism" in Dickens may be found
not only in his thematic material, but also in that head-spinning

tempo of changing impressions with which Dickens sketches
the city in the form of a dynamic (montage) picture; and this
montage of its rhythms conveys the sensation of the limits of
speed at that time (1838), the sensation of a rushing—stage-
coach!

As they dashed by the quickly-changing and ever-varying objects, it was curious to observe in what a strange procession they
passed before the eye. Emporiums of splendid dresses, the materials
brought from every quarter of the world; tempting stores of everything to stimulate and pamper the sated appetite and give new
relish to the oft-repeated feast; vessels of burnished gold and silver,
wrought into every exquisite form of vase, and dish, and goblet;
guns, swords, pistols, and patent engines of destruction; screws and
irons for the crooked, clothes for the newly-born, drugs for the
sick, coffins for the dead, church-yards for the buried—all these
jumbled each with the other and flocking side by side, seemed
to flit by in motley dance. . . .[11]

Isn't this an anticipation of a "symphony of a big city"? *
But here is another, directly opposite aspect of a city, out-
distancing Hollywood's picture of the City by eighty years.

It contained several large streets all very like one another, inhab-
ited by people equally like one another, who all went in and out
at the same hours, with the same sound upon the same pavements,
to do the same work, and to whom every day was the same as
yesterday and tomorrow, and every year the counterpart of the
last and the next.[12]

Is this Dickens's Coketown of 1853, or King Vidor's *The
Crowd* of 1928?

If in the above-cited examples we have encountered prototypes of characteristics for Griffith's *montage exposition*, then
it would pay us to read further in *Oliver Twist*, where we can
find another montage method typical for Griffith—the method
of a *montage progression of parallel scenes, intercut into each
other.*

* A reference to the Ruttmann-Freund film, *Berlin: Die Sinfonie der
Grosstadt* (1927).

For this let us turn to that group of scenes in which is set forth the familiar episode of how Mr. Brownlow, to show faith in Oliver in spite of his pick-pocket reputation, sends him to return books to the book-seller, and of how Oliver again falls into the clutches of the thief Sikes, his sweetheart Nancy, and old Fagin.

These scenes are unrolled absolutely à la Griffith: both in their inner emotional line, as well as in the unusual sculptural relief and delineation of the characters; in the uncommon full-bloodedness of the dramatic as well as the humorous traits in them; finally, also in the typical Griffith-esque montage of parallel interlocking of all the links of the separate episodes. Let us give particular attention to this last peculiarity, just as unexpected, one would think, in Dickens, as it is characteristic for Griffith!

Chapter XIV

COMPRISING FURTHER PARTICULARS OF OLIVER'S STAY AT MR. BROWN-
LOW'S, WITH THE REMARKABLE PREDICTION WHICH ONE MR. GRIM-
WIG UTTERED CONCERNING HIM, WHEN HE WENT OUT ON AN
ERRAND.

. . . "Dear me, I am very sorry for that," exclaimed Mr. Brown-low; "I particularly wished those books to be returned tonight."

"Send Oliver with them," said Mr. Grimwig, with an ironical smile; "he will be sure to deliver them safely, you know."

"Yes; do let me take them, if you please, Sir," said Oliver. "I'll run all the way, Sir."

The old gentleman was just going to say that Oliver should not go out on any account; when a most malicious cough from Mr. Grimwig determined him that he should; and that, by his prompt discharge of the commission, he should prove to him the injustice of his suspicions: on this head at least: at once.

[Oliver is prepared for the errand to the bookstall-keeper.]

"I won't be ten minutes, Sir," replied Oliver, eagerly.

[Mrs. Bedwin, Mr. Brownlow's housekeeper, gives Oliver the directions, and sends him off.]

"Bless his sweet face!" said the old lady, looking after him. "I can't bear, somehow, to let him go out of my sight."

At this moment, Oliver looked gaily round, and nodded before

he turned the corner. The old lady smilingly returned his salutation, and, closing the door, went back to her own room.

"Let me see; he'll be back in twenty minutes, at the longest,"
said Mr. Brownlow, pulling out his watch, and placing it on the
table. "It will be dark by that time."

"Oh! you really expect him to come back, do you?" inquired
Mr. Grimwig.

"Don't you?" asked Mr. Brownlow, smiling.

The spirit of contradiction was strong in Mr. Grimwig's breast,
at the moment; and it was rendered stronger by his friend's confident smile.

"No," he said, smiting the table with his fist, "I do not. The boy
has a new suit of clothes on his back; a set of valuable books under
his arm; and a five-pound note in his pocket. He'll join his old
friends the thieves, and laugh at you. If ever that boy returns to
this house, Sir, I'll eat my head."

With these words he drew his chair closer to the table; and there
the two friends sat, in silent expectation, with the watch between
them.

This is followed by a short "interruption" in the form of a
digression:

It is worthy of remark, as illustrating the importance we attach
to our own judgments, and the pride with which we put forth our
most rash and hasty conclusions, that, although Mr. Grimwig was
not by any means a bad-hearted man, and though he would have
been unfeignedly sorry to see his respected friend duped and deceived, he really did most earnestly and strongly hope, at that
moment, that Oliver Twist might not come back.

And again a return to the two old gentlemen:

It grew so dark, that the figures on the dial-plate were scarcely
discernible; but there the two old gentlemen continued to sit, in
silence: with the watch between them.

Twilight shows that only a little time has passed, but the
close-up of the watch, *already twice* shown lying between the
old gentlemen, says that a great deal of time has passed already.
But just then, as in the game of "will he come? won't he
come?", involving not only the two old men, but also the

kind-hearted reader, the worst fears and vague forebodings of the old housekeeper are justified by the cut to the new scene—Chapter XV. This begins with a short scene in the public-house, with the bandit Sikes and his dog, old Fagin and Miss Nancy, who has been obliged to discover the whereabouts of Oliver.

"You are on the scent, are you, Nancy?" inquired Sikes, proffering the glass.

"Yes, I am, Bill," replied the young lady, disposing of its contents; "and tired enough of it I am, too. . . ."

Then, one of the best scenes in the whole novel—at least one that since childhood has been perfectly preserved, along with the evil figure of Fagin—the scene in which Oliver, marching along with the books, is suddenly

startled by a young woman screaming out very loud, "Oh, my dear brother!" And he had hardly looked up, to see what the matter was, when he was stopped by having a pair of arms thrown tight round his neck.

With this cunning maneuver Nancy, with the sympathies of the whole street, takes the desperately pulling Oliver, as her "prodigal brother," back into the bosom of Fagin's gang of thieves. This fifteenth chapter closes on the now familiar montage phrase:

The gas-lamps were lighted; Mrs. Bedwin was waiting anxiously at the open door; the servant had run up the street twenty times to see if there were any traces of Oliver; and still the two old gentlemen sat, perseveringly, in the dark parlour: with the watch between them.

In Chapter XVI Oliver, once again in the clutches of the gang, is subjected to mockery. Nancy rescues him from a beating:

"I won't stand by and see it done, Fagin," cried the girl. "You've got the boy, and what more would you have? Let him be—let him be, or I shall put that mark on some of you, that will bring me to the gallows before my time."

By the way, it is characteristic for both Dickens and Griffith to have these sudden flashes of goodness in "morally degraded" characters and, though these sentimental images verge on hokum, they are so faultlessly done that they work on the most skeptical readers and spectators!

At the end of this chapter, Oliver, sick and weary, falls "sound asleep." Here the physical time unity is interrupted—an evening and night, crowded with events; but the montage unity of the episode is not interrupted, tying Oliver to Mr. Brownlow on one side, and to Fagin's gang on the other.

Following, in Chapter XVIII, is the arrival of the parish beadle, Mr. Bumble, in response to an inquiry about the lost boy, and the appearance of Bumble at Mr. Brownlow's, again in Grimwig's company. The content and reason for their conversation is revealed by the very title of the chapter: OLIVER'S DESTINY CONTINUING UNPROPITIOUS, BRINGS A GREAT MAN TO LONDON TO INJURE HIS REPUTATION . . .

"I fear it is all too true," said the old gentleman sorrowfully, after looking over the papers. "This is not much for your intelligence; but I would gladly have given you treble the money, if it had been favourable to the boy."

It is not at all improbable that if Mr. Bumble had been possessed of this information at an earlier period of the interview, he might have imparted a very different coloring to his little history. It was too late to do it now, however; so he shook his head gravely; and, pocketing the five guineas, withdrew. . . .

"Mrs. Bedwin," said Mr. Brownlow, when the housekeeper appeared; "that boy, Oliver, is an impostor."

"It can't be, Sir. It cannot be," said the old lady energetically. . . . "I never will believe it, Sir. . . . Never!"

"You old women never believe anything but quack-doctors, and lying story-books," growled Mr. Grimwig. "I knew it all along. . . ."

"He was a dear, grateful, gentle child, Sir," retorted Mrs. Bedwin, indignantly. "I know what children are, Sir; and have done these forty years; and people who can't say the same, shouldn't say anything about them. That's my opinion!"

This was a hard hit at Mr. Grimwig, who was a bachelor. As

it extorted nothing from that gentleman but a smile, the old lady tossed her head, and smoothed down her apron preparatory to another speech, when she was stopped by Mr. Brownlow.

"Silence!" said the old gentleman, feigning an anger he was far from feeling. "Never let me hear the boy's name again. I rang to tell you that. Never. Never, on any pretence, mind! You may leave the room, Mrs. Bedwin. Remember! I am in earnest."

And the entire intricate montage complex of this episode is concluded with the sentence:

There were sad hearts in Mr. Brownlow's that night.

It was not by accident that I have allowed myself such full extracts, in regard not only to the composition of the scenes, but also to the delineation of the characters, for in their very modeling, in their characteristics, in their behavior, there is much typical of Griffith's manner. This equally concerns also his "Dickens-esque" distressed, defenseless creatures (recalling Lillian Gish and Richard Barthelmess in *Broken Blossoms* or the Gish sisters in *Orphans of the Storm*), and is no less typical for his characters like the two old gentlemen and Mrs. Bedwin; and finally, it is entirely characteristic of him to have such figures as are in the gang of "the merry old Jew" Fagin.

In regard to the immediate task of our example of Dickens's montage progression of the story composition, we can present the results of it in the following table:

1. *The old gentlemen.*
2. Departure of Oliver.
3. *The old gentlemen and the watch. It is still light.*
4. Digression on the character of Mr. Grimwig.
5. *The old gentlemen and the watch. Gathering twilight.*
6. Fagin, Sikes and Nancy in the public-house.
7. Scene on the street.
8. *The old gentlemen and the watch. The gas-lamps have been lit.*
9. Oliver is dragged back to Fagin.
10. Digression at the beginning of Chapter XVII.

11. The journey of Mr. Bumble.
12. *The old gentlemen* and Mr. Brownlow's command to forget Oliver forever.

As we can see, we have before us a typical and, for Griffith, a model of parallel montage of two story lines, where one (the waiting gentlemen) emotionally heightens the tension and drama of the other (the capture of Oliver). It is in "rescuers" rushing along to save the "suffering heroine" that Griffith has, with the aid of parallel montage, earned his most glorious laurels!

Most curious of all is that in the *very center* of our breakdown of the episode, is wedged another "interruption"—a whole digression at the beginning of Chapter XVII, on which we have been purposely silent. What is remarkable about this digression? It is Dickens's own "treatise" on the principles of this montage construction of the story which he carries out so fascinatingly, and which passed into the style of Griffith. Here it is:

It is the custom on the stage, in all good murderous melodramas, to present the tragic and the comic scenes, in as regular alternation, as the layers of red and white in a side of streaky well-cured bacon. The hero sinks upon his straw bed, weighed down by fetters and misfortunes; and, in the next scene, his faithful but unconscious squire regales the audience with a comic song. We behold, with throbbing bosoms, the heroine in the grasp of a proud and ruthless baron: her virtue and her life alike in danger; drawing forth her dagger to preserve the one at the cost of the other; and just as our expectations are wrought up to the highest pitch, a whistle is heard: and we are straightway transported to the great hall of the castle: where a grey-headed seneschal sings a funny chorus with a funnier body of vassals, who are free of all sorts of places from church vaults to palaces, and roam about in company, carolling perpetually.

Such changes appear absurd; but they are not so unnatural as they would seem at first sight. The transitions in real life from well-spread boards to death-beds, and from mourning-weeds to holiday garments, are not a whit less startling; only, there, we are

busy actors, instead of passive lookers-on; which makes a vast difference. The actors in the mimic life of the theatre, are blind to
violent transitions and abrupt impulses of passion of feeling, which,
presented before the eyes of mere spectators, are at once condemned as outrageous and preposterous.

As sudden shiftings of the scene, and rapid changes of time and
place, are not only sanctioned in books by long usage, but are by
many considered as the great art of authorship: an author's skill
in his craft being, by such critics, chiefly estimated with relation
to the dilemmas in which he leaves his characters at the end of
every chapter: this brief introduction to the present one may perhaps be deemed unnecessary. . . .

There is another interesting thing in this treatise: in his own
words, Dickens (a life-long amateur actor) defines his direct
relation to the theater melodrama. This is as if Dickens had
placed himself in the position of a connecting link between the
future, unforeseen art of the cinema, and the not so distant
(for Dickens) past—the traditions of "good murderous melodramas."

This "treatise," of course, could not have escaped the eye
of the patriarch of the American film, and very often his structure seems to follow the wise advice, handed down to the
great film-maker of the twentieth century by the great novelist
of the nineteenth. And Griffith, hiding nothing, has more
than once acknowledged his debt to Dickens's memory.

We have already seen that the first screen exploitation of
such a structure was by Griffith in *After Many Years*, an exploitation for which he held Dickens responsible. This film is
further memorable for being the first in which the close-up
was *intelligently* used and, chiefly, *utilized.**

Lewis Jacobs has described Griffith's approach to the close-
up, three months earlier, in *For Love of Gold*, an adaptation
of Jack London's *Just Meat:*

* Close shots of heads and objects were not so rare in the pre-Griffith
film as is generally assumed; close shots can be found used solely for
novelty or trick purposes by such inventive pioneers as Méliès and the
English "Brighton School" (as pointed out by Georges Sadoul).

The climax of the story was the scene in which the two thieves begin to distrust each other. Its effectiveness depended upon the audience's awareness of what was going on in the minds of both thieves. The only known way to indicate a player's thoughts was by double-exposure "dream balloons." This convention had grown out of two misconceptions: first, that the camera must always be fixed at a viewpoint corresponding to that of a spectator in a theatre (the position now known as the long shot); the other, that a scene had to be played in its entirety before another was begun. . . .

Griffith decided now upon a revolutionary step. He moved the camera closer to the actor, in what is now known as the full shot (a larger view of the actor), so that the audience could observe the actor's pantomime more closely. No one before had thought of changing the position of the camera in the middle of a scene. . . .

The next logical step was to bring the camera still closer to the actor in what is now called the close-up. . . .

Not since Porter's *The Great Train Robbery,* some five years before, had a close-up been seen in American films. Used then only as a stunt (the outlaw was shown firing at the audience), the close-up became in *Enoch Arden* [*After Many Years*] the natural dramatic complement of the long shot and full shot. Going further than he had ventured before, in a scene showing Annie Lee brooding and waiting for her husband's return Griffith daringly used a large close-up of her face.

Everyone in the Biograph studio was shocked. "Show only the head of a person? What will people say? It's against all rules of movie making!" . . .

But Griffith had no time for argument. He had another surprise, even more radical, to offer. Immediately following the close-up of Annie, he inserted a picture of the object of her thoughts— her husband, cast away on a desert isle. This cutting from one scene to another, without finishing either, brought a torrent of criticism down upon the experimenter.[13]

And we have read how Griffith defended his experiment by calling on Dickens as a witness.

If these were only the first intimations of that which was to bring glory to Griffith, we can find a full fruition of his new method in a film made only a year after he began to direct films—*The Lonely Villa*. This is told in Iris Barry's monograph on Griffith:

By June, 1909, Griffith was already gaining control of his material and moved to further creative activity: he carried Porter's initial method * to a new stage of development in *The Lonely Villa*, in which he employed cross-cutting to heighten suspense throughout the parallel scenes where the burglars are breaking in upon the mother and children while the father is rushing home to the rescue. Here he had hit upon a new way of handling a tried device—the last-minute rescue—which was to serve him well for the rest of his career. By March, 1911, Griffith further developed this disjunctive method of narration in *The Lonedale Operator*, which achieves a much greater degree of breathless excitement and suspense in the scenes where the railwayman-hero is racing his train back to the rescue of the heroine attacked by hold-up men in the depot.[15]

Melodrama, having attained on American soil by the end of the nineteenth century its most complete and exuberant ripeness, at this peak must certainly have had a great influence on Griffith, whose first art was the theater, and its methods must have been stored away in Griffith's reserve fund with no little quantity of wonderful and characteristic features.

What was this period of American melodrama, immediately preceding the appearance of Griffith? Its most interesting aspect is the close scenic entwining of *both* sides that are characteristic for the future creation of Griffith; of those *two sides*, typical for Dickens's writing and style, about which we spoke at the beginning of this essay.

This may be illustrated by the theatrical history of the original *Way Down East*. Some of this history has been preserved for us in the reminiscences of William A. Brady. These

---

* Miss Barry had previously pointed out that "Edwin S. Porter in *The Great Train Robbery* had taken a vital step by introducing parallel action through a rough form of cross-cutting. . . ."[14]

are particularly interesting as records of the emergence and popularizing of that theatrical genre known as the "homespun" melodrama of locale. Certain features of this tradition have been preserved to our own day. The successes of such keenly modern works as Erskine Caldwell's *Tobacco Road* and John Steinbeck's *The Grapes of Wrath* (in their original and film versions) contain ingredients common to this popular genre. These two works complete a circle of rural poesy, dedicated to the American countryside.

Brady's reminiscences are an interesting record of the scenic embodiment of these melodramas on the stages of that era. For purely as staging, this scenic embodiment in many cases literally anticipates not only the themes, subjects and their interpretations, but even those staging methods and effects, which always seem to us so "purely cinematic," without precedent and . . . begotten by the screen! *

A variety actor named Denman Thompson in the late 'seventies was performing a sketch on the variety circuits called *Joshua Whitcomb*. . . . It happened that James M. Hill, a retail clothier from Chicago, saw *Joshua Whitcomb*, met Thompson, and persuaded him to write a four-act drama around Old Josh.[16]

Out of this idea came the melodrama, *The Old Homestead*, financed by Hill. The new genre caught on slowly, but skillful advertising did its work—recalling sentimental dreams and memories of the good old, and alas! deserted hearth-side; of life in good old rural America, and the piece played for twenty-five years, making a fortune for Mr. Hill.

Another success from the same formula was *The County Fair* by Neil Burgess:

* For this reason immediately after the facts on the circumstances and arrangement that brought success to the play of *Way Down East* in the 'nineties, I shall offer a description, in no less bold relief, of the scenic effects in the melodrama *The Ninety and Nine*, a success in the New York theater of 1902.

He introduced in the play, for the first time on any stage, a horse race on tread-mills. He patented the device and collected royalties the world over when it was used in other productions. *Ben Hur* used it for twenty years. . . .

The novelty and attraction of this thematic material cast in scenic devices of this sort quickly made it popular everywhere and "homespun dramas sprung up on every side. . . ."

Another long-lived earthy melodrama was *In Old Kentucky,* which with its Pickaninny Band made a couple of millions in ten years for its owner, Jacob Litt. . . . Augustus Thomas tried his hand writing a trio of rurals—*Alabama, Arizona,* and *In Missouri.*

An energetic all-round entrepreneur like Brady was sure to be drawn towards this new money-making dramatic form:

All through the 'nineties, I was a very busy person in and around Broadway. I tackled anything in the entertainment line— melodramas on Broadway or the Bowery, prize fights, bicycle races—long or short, six days, twenty-four hours, or sprints—league baseball. . . . Broadsword fights, cake-walks, tugs of war, wrestling matches—on the level and made to order. Masquerade balls for all nations at Madison Square Garden. Matching James J. Corbett against John L. Sullivan and winning the world's heavyweight championship. This put me on the top of the world, and so I had to have a Broadway theatre.

Brady leased the Manhattan Theatre with "a young fellow named Florenz Ziegfeld, Jr." and went looking for something to put into it.

A booking agent of mine named Harry Doel Parker brought me a script called *Annie Laurie* [by his wife, Lottie Blair Parker]. I read it, and saw a chance to build it up into one of those rural things that were cleaning up everywhere. . . . I told him that the play had the makings, and we finally agreed on an outright purchase price of ten thousand dollars, he giving me the right to call in a play doctor. I gave the job to Joseph R. Grismer, who rechristened the play *Way Down East.* . . .*

* Elsewhere, William A. Brady has given more detail on Grismer's contribution: "During the trial-and-error period at one time or another we had used every small town in the United States as dog for *Way*

. . . We booked it at our Broadway theater, where it ran seven months, never knowing a profitable week. The critics tore it to pieces. . . . During its Broadway run we used every trick known to the barnstormer to pull them in, but to no avail. . . . We depended on "snow"—sloughing New York and its suburbs with "Pass 2's."

One night a well-known minister dropped in and he wrote us a nice letter of appreciation. That gave us a cue. We sent out ten thousand "minister tickets" and asked them all for tributes and got them. They all said it was a masterpiece—made long speeches from the stage to that effect—and followed it up with sermons from their pulpits. I hired the big electric sign on the triangle building at Broadway and Twenty-third Street (the first big one in New York). It cost us a thousand dollars a month. How it did make the Rialto talk! In one of our weekly press notices, which *The Sun* printed, it stated that *Way Down East* was better than *The Old Homestead*. That gave us a slogan which lasted twenty years. . . .

The manager of the Academy of Music, the home of *The Old Homestead*, was asked to put *Way Down East* into his theater.

He was willing, but insisted that the show and its production was too small for his huge stage. Grismer and I put our heads together and decided on a huge production, introducing horses, cattle, sheep, all varieties of farm conveyances, a monster sleigh drawn by four horses for a sleigh-ride, an electric snowstorm, a double quartette singing at every opportunity the songs that mother loved —forming, all in all, a veritable farm circus. It went over with a bang, and stayed in New York a full season, showing profits exceeding one hundred thousand dollars. After that, it was easy

Down East, and no two of them ever saw the same version. . . . Grismer lived, slept and ate it. He certainly earned that credit-line which always ran in the program: 'Elaborated by Joseph R. Grismer.' Why, the mechanical snowstorm used in the third act, which had no small part in making the play a memorable success, was specially invented by him for the production and then patented. One of his inspirations was laying hands on a vaudeville actor named Harry Seamon, who had a small-time hick act, breaking his routine into three parts and running him into *Way Down East*." [17]

going. I launched a half-dozen touring companies. They all cleaned up.

The show was a repeater and it took twenty-one years to wear it out. The big cities never seemed to grow tired of it. . . .

The silent movie rights of *Way Down East* were purchased by D. W. Griffith for one hundred and seventy thousand dollars, twenty-five years after its first stage production.

In the fall of 1902, exactly a year before the production of *The Great Train Robbery*, a moralistic melodrama entitled *The Ninety and Nine* (the title derives from a familiar hymn by Sankey) opened at the same Academy of Music. Under a striking photo of the climactic scene in the production, *The Theatre Magazine* printed this explanatory caption:

A hamlet is encircled by a raging prairie fire and three thousand people are threatened. At the station, thirty miles away, scores of excited people wait as the telegraph ticks the story of peril. A special is ready to go to the rescue. The engineer is absent and the craven young millionaire refuses to take the risk to make the dash. The hero springs forward to take his place. Darkness, a moment of suspense, and then the curtain rises again upon an exciting scene. The big stage is literally covered with fire. Flames lick the trunks of the trees. Telegraph poles blaze and the wires snap in the fierce heat. Sharp tongues of fire creep through the grass and sweep on, blazing fiercely. In the midst of it all is the massive locomotive, full sized and such as draw the modern express trains, almost hidden from view in the steam or smoke. Its big drive wheels spin on the track, and it rocks and sways as if driven at topmost speed. In the cab is the engineer, smoke-grimed and scarred, while the fireman dashes pails of water on him to protect him from the flying embers.*

Further comment seems superfluous: here too is the tension of parallel action, of the race, the chase—the necessity to get

---

* In his accompanying review, Arthur Hornblow gives us some idea of how this effect was achieved: "This scene, which is the 'sensation' of the production, is one of the most realistic effects of machinery ever seen on any stage. . . . Tissue paper streamers, blown by concealed electric fans, on which brilliant red and yellow lights play, represent the flames, while the motion of the on-rushing locomotive is simulated by revolving the forest background in an inverse direction."

there in time, to break through the flaming barrier; here too is the moral preachment, capable of inflaming a thousand ministers; here too, answering the "modern" interests of the audience, is HOME in all its "exotic fullness"; here too are the irresistible tunes, connected with memories of childhood and "dear old mother." In short, here is laid out the whole arsenal with which Griffith later will conquer, just as irresistibly.

But if you should like to move the discussion from general attitudes of montage over to its more *narrowly specific* features, Griffith might have found still other "montage ancestors" for himself—and on his own grounds, too.

I must regretfully put aside Walt Whitman's huge montage conception. It must be stated that Griffith did not continue the Whitman *montage tradition* (in spite of the Whitman lines on "out of the cradle endlessly rocking," which served Griffith unsuccessfully as a refrain shot for his *Intolerance;* but of that later).

It is here that I wish, in connection with montage, to refer to one of the gayest and wittiest of Mark Twain's contemporaries—writing under the *nom de plume* of John Phoenix. This example of montage is dated October 1, 1853 (!), and is taken from his parody on a current novelty—illustrated newspapers.

The parody newspaper is entitled "Phoenix's Pictorial and Second Story Front Room Companion," and was first published in the San Diego *Herald.*[18] Among its several items, ingeniously illustrated with the miscellaneous "boiler-plate" found in any small-town newspaper print-shop of the time, there is one item of particular interest for us:

Fearful accident on the Princeton Rail Road!
Terrible loss of life!!

"By all the rules of the art" of montage, John Phoenix "conjures up the image." The montage method is obvious: the play of *juxtaposed detail*-shots, which in themselves are immutable and even unrelated, but from which is created the desired *image of the whole*. And particularly fascinating here is the "close-up" of the false teeth, placed next to a "long-shot" of the overturned railway coach, but both given in *equal size*, that is, exactly as if they were being shown on "a full screen"!

Curious also is the figure of the author himself, hiding beneath the pseudonym of Phoenix the honored name of Lieutenant George Horatio Derby, of the United States Army Engineers, wounded at Serro Gordo in 1846, a conscientious surveyor, reporter and engineer till his death in 1861. Such was one of the first American ancestors of the wonder-working method of montage! He was one of the first important American humorists of a new type, who belongs as well to the indubitable forerunners of that "violent" humor, which has achieved its wildest flourish in films, for example, in the work of the Marx Brothers.*

I don't know how my readers feel about this, but for me personally it is always pleasing to recognize again and again the fact that our cinema is not altogether without parents and without pedigree, without a past, without the traditions and rich cultural heritage of the past epochs. It is only very thoughtless and presumptuous people who can erect laws and an esthetic for cinema, proceeding from premises of some incredible virgin-birth of this art!

Let Dickens and the whole ancestral array, going back as far as the Greeks and Shakespeare, be superfluous reminders that both Griffith and our cinema prove our origins to be not

---

* Sufficient evidence of this lies in the anecdote by John Phoenix in which Tushmaker's new tooth-pulling machine "drew the old lady's skeleton completely and entirely from her body, leaving her a mass of quivering jelly in her chair! Tushmaker took her home in a pillowcase. She lived seven years after that, and they called her the 'India-Rubber Woman.' She had suffered terribly with the rheumatism, but after this occurrence, never had a pain in her bones. The dentist kept them in a glass case. . . ." [19]

solely as of Edison and his fellow inventors, but as based on an enormous cultured past; each part of this past in its own moment of world history has moved forward the great art of cinematography. Let this past be a reproach to those thoughtless people who have displayed arrogance in reference to literature, which has contributed so much to this apparently unprecedented art and is, in the first and most important place: the art of viewing—not only the *eye*, but *viewing*—both meanings being embraced in this term.

This esthetic growth from the *cinematographic eye* to the *image of an embodied viewpoint on phenomena* was one of the most serious processes of development of our Soviet cinema in particular; our cinema also played a tremendous rôle in the history of the development of world cinema as a whole, and it was no small rôle that was played by a basic understanding of the principles of film-montage, which became so characteristic for the Soviet school of film-making.

None the less enormous was the rôle of Griffith also in the evolution of the system of Soviet montage: a rôle as enormous as the rôle of Dickens in forming the methods of Griffith. Dickens in this respect played an enormous rôle in heightening the tradition and cultural heritage of preceding epochs; just as on an even higher level we can see the enormous rôle of those social premises, which inevitably in those pivotal moments of history ever anew push elements of the montage method into the center of attention for creative work.

The rôle of Griffith is enormous, but our cinema is neither a poor relative nor an insolvent debtor of his. It was natural that the spirit and content of our country itself, in themes and subjects, would stride far ahead of Griffith's ideals as well as their reflection in artistic images.

In social attitudes Griffith was always a liberal, never departing far from the slightly sentimental humanism of the good old gentlemen and sweet old ladies of Victorian England, just as Dickens loved to picture them. His tender-hearted film morals go no higher than a level of Christian accusation of human injustice and nowhere in his films is there sounded a protest against social injustice.

In his best films he is a preacher of pacifism and compromise with fate (*Isn't Life Wonderful?*) or of love of mankind "in general" (*Broken Blossoms*). Here in his reproaches and condemnations Griffith is sometimes able to ascend to magnificent pathos (in, for example, *Way Down East*).

In the more thematically dubious of his works—this takes the form of an apology for the Dry Law (in *The Struggle*) or for the metaphysical philosophy of the eternal origins of Good and Evil (in *Intolerance*). Metaphysics permeates the film which he based on Marie Corelli's *Sorrows of Satan*. Finally, among the most repellent elements in his films (and there are such) we see Griffith as an open apologist for racism, erecting a celluloid monument to the Ku Klux Klan, and joining their attack on Negroes in *The Birth of a Nation*.*

Nevertheless, nothing can take from Griffith the wreath of one of the genuine masters of the American cinema.

But montage thinking is inseparable from the general content of thinking as a whole. The structure that is reflected in the concept of Griffith montage is the structure of bourgeois society. And he actually resembles Dickens's "side of streaky, well-cured bacon"; in actuality (and this is no joke), he is woven of irreconcilably alternating layers of "white" and "red"—rich and poor. (This is the eternal theme of Dickens's novels, nor does he move beyond these divisions. His mature work, *Little Dorrit*, is so divided into two books: "Poverty" and "Riches.") And this society, perceived *only as a contrast between the haves and the have-nots*, is reflected in the consciousness of Griffith no deeper than the image of an intricate race between two parallel lines.

Griffith primarily is the greatest master of the most graphic form in this field—a master of *parallel montage*. Above all else,

* In all instances the craftsmanship of Griffith remains almost unaltered in these films, springing as it does from profound sincerity and a full conviction in the rightness of their themes, but before all else I am noting the themes themselves and their ideological aims.

Griffith is a great master of montage constructions that have been created in a direct-lined quickening and *increase of tempo* (chiefly in the direction of the higher forms of parallel montage).

The school of Griffith before all else is a school of *tempo*. However, he did not have the strength to compete with the young Soviet school of montage in the field of expression and of relentlessly affective *rhythm*, the task of which goes far beyond the narrow confines of tempo tasks.

It was exactly this feature of *devastating rhythm* as distinguished from effects of *tempo* that was noted at the appearance of our first Soviet films in America. After recognizing the themes and ideas of our works it was this feature of our cinema that the American press of 1926-27 remarked.

But true rhythm presupposes above all organic *unity*.

Neither a successive mechanical alternation of cross-cuts, nor an interweaving of antagonistic themes, but above all a unity, which in the play of inner contradictions, through a shift of the play in the direction of tracing its organic pulse—that is what lies at the base of rhythm. This is not an outer unity of story, bringing with it also the classical image of the chase-scene, but that inner unity, which can be realized in montage as an entirely different system of construction, in which so-called parallel montage can figure as one of the highest or particularly personal variants.

And, naturally, the montage concept of Griffith, as a primarily parallel montage, appears to be a copy of his dualistic picture of the world, running in two parallel lines of poor and rich towards some hypothetical "reconciliation" where . . . the parallel lines would cross, that is, in that infinity, just as inaccessible as that "reconciliation."

Thus it was to be expected that our concept of montage had to be born from an entirely different "image" of an understanding of phenomena, which was opened to us by a world-view both monistic and dialectic.

For us the microcosm of montage had to be understood as a unity, which in the inner stress of contradictions is halved, in order to be re-assembled in a new unity on a new plane, qualitatively higher, its imagery newly perceived.

I attempted to give theoretical expression to this *general tendency* of our understanding of montage, and advanced this in 1929, thinking least of all at that time to what degree our method of montage both generically and in principle was in opposition to the montage of Griffith.

This was stated in the form of a definition of the *stages* of relationship between the shot and montage. Of the thematic unity of content in a film, of the "shot," of the "frame," I wrote:

> The shot is by no means an *element* of montage.
> The shot is a montage *cell*.
> Just as cells in their division form a phenomenon of another order, the organism or embryo, so, on the other side of the dialectical leap from the shot, there is montage.

Montage is the expansion of intra-shot conflict (or, contradiction) at first in the conflict of two shots standing side by side:

> Conflict within the shot is potential montage, in the development of its intensity shattering the quadrilateral cage of the shot and exploding its conflict into montage impulses *between* the montage pieces.

Then—the threading of the conflict through a whole system of planes, by means of which ". . . we newly collect the disintegrated event into one whole, but in *our* aspect. According to the treatment of our relation to the event." *

Thus is broken up a *montage unit*—the cage—into a multiple chain, which *is anew gathered into a new unity—in the montage phrase, embodying the concept of an image of the phenomenon.*

It is interesting to watch such a process moving also through the history of language in relation to the word (the "shot")

---

* See "The Cinematographic Principle and the Ideogram," pages 34-38.

and the sentence (the "montage phrase"), and to see just such a primitive stage of "word-sentences" later "foliating" into the sentence, made up of separately independent words.

V. A. Bogoroditzky writes that ". . . in the very beginning mankind expressed his ideas in single words, which were also primitive forms of the sentence." [20] The question is presented in more detail by Academician Ivan Meshchaninov:

> Word and sentence appear as the product of history and are far from being identified with the whole lengthy epoch of gutturals. They are antedated by an unfoliated state, till this day undetected within the materials of incorporated languages.*
>
> Broken up into their component parts, word-sentences show a unity between the original words and their combination into the syntactic complex of the sentence. This gains a diversity of possibilities in expressive word-combinations. . . .
>
> The embryos of syntax, previously laid down, were in a latent form of incorporated word-sentences, then, later during its decomposition, projected outward. The sentence appeared to have been broken down to its chief elements, that is, the sentence is created as such with its laws of syntax. . . .[21]

We have previously stated the particularity of *our* attitude towards montage. However, the distinction between the American and our montage concepts gains maximum sharpness and clarity if we glance at such a difference in principle of the understanding of another innovation, introduced by Griffith into cinematography and, in the same way, receiving at our hands an entirely different understanding.

We refer to the *close-up*, or as we speak of it, the "large scale."

This distinction in principle begins with an essence that exists in the term itself.

We say: an object or face is photographed in "large scale," i.e., *large*.

---

* This is a term for those modern languages, preserving this character up to the present day, for example, the languages of the Chukchi, the Yukagirs and the Gilyaks. A full account for those of us especially interested in these languages may be found in Professor Meshchaninov's work.

The American says: *near,* or "close-up." *

We are speaking of the *qualitative* side of the phenomenon, linked with its meaning (just as we speak of a *large* talent, that is, of one which stands out, by its significance, from the general line, or of *large* print [bold-face] to emphasize that which is particularly essential or significant).

Among Americans the term is attached to *viewpoint.*

Among us—to *the value of what is seen.*

We shall see below what a profound distinction in principle is here, after we have understood the system which, both in method and in application, uses the "large scale" in our cinema in a way distinguished from the use of the "close-up" by the American cinema.

In this comparison immediately the first thing to appear clearly relating to the principal function of the close-up in our cinema is—not only and not so much to *show* or to *present,* as to *signify,* to *give meaning,* to *designate.*

In our own way we very quickly realized the very nature of the "close-up" after this had been hardly noticed in its sole capacity as a means of showing, in American cinema practice.

The first factor that attracted us in the method of the close-up was the discovery of its particularly astonishing feature: to create *a new quality of the whole from a juxtaposition of the separate parts.*

Where the isolated close-up in the tradition of the Dickens kettle was often a determining or "key" detail in the work of Griffith, where the alternation of close-ups of faces was an anticipation of the future synchronized dialogue (it may be apropos here to mention that Griffith, in his sound film, did not freshen a single method then in use)—there we advanced the idea of a *principally new qualitative fusion,* flowing out of the process of *juxtaposition.*

---

* Griffith himself, in his famous announcement in *The New York Dramatic Mirror* of December 3, 1913, employed both designations: "The large or close-up figures. . . ." But it is characteristic that in habitual American film usage it should be the latter term, "close-up," that has been retained.

For example, in almost my first spoken and written declarations of the 'twenties, I designated the cinema as above all else an "art of juxtaposition."

If Gilbert Seldes is to be believed, Griffith himself came to the point of seeing "that by dovetailing the ride of the rescuers and the terror of the besieged in a scene, he was multiplying the emotional effect enormously; the whole was infinitely greater than the sum of its parts," [22] but this was also insufficient for us.

For us this *quantitative accumulation* even in such "multiplying" situations was not enough: we sought for and found in juxtapositions more than that—*a qualitative leap*.

The leap proved beyond the *limits of the possibilities* of the stage—a leap beyond the *limits of situation:* a leap into the field of montage *image,* montage *understanding,* montage as a means before all else of revealing the *ideological conception.*

By the way, in another of Seldes's books there appears his lengthy condemnation of the American films of the 'twenties, losing their spontaneity in pretensions towards "artiness" and "theatricality."

It is written in the form of "An Open Letter to the Movie Magnates." It begins with the juicy salutation: "Ignorant and Unhappy People," and contains in its conclusion such remarkable lines as these:

. . . and then the new film will arrive without your assistance. For when you and your capitalizations and your publicity go down together, the field will be left free for others. . . . Presently it will be within the reach of artists. With players instead of actors and actresses, with fresh ideas (among which the idea of making a lot of money may be absent) these artists will give back to the screen the thing you have debauched—imagination. They will create with the camera, and not record . . . it is possible and desirable to create great epics of American industry and let the machine operate as a character in the play—just as the land of the West itself, as the corn must play its part. The grandiose conceptions of Frank Norris are not beyond the reach of the camera. There are painters willing to work in the medium of the camera and architects and photographers. And novelists, too, I fancy, would find much of interest in the scenario as a new way of expression. There is no end to what we can accomplish. . . . For the movie is the imagination of mankind in action. . . .[23]

Seldes expected this bright film future to be brought by some unknown persons who were to reduce the cost of films, by some unknown "artists," and by epics, dedicated to American industry or 'American corn. But his prophetic words justified themselves in an entirely different direction: they proved to be a prediction that in these very years (the book appeared in 1924) on the other side of the globe were being prepared the first Soviet films, which were destined to fulfill all his prophecies.

For only a new social structure, which has forever freed art from narrowly commercial tasks, can give full realization to the dreams of advanced and penetrating Americans!

In technique also, montage took on a completely new meaning at this time

To the parallelism and alternating close-ups of America we offer the contrast of uniting these in fusion; the MONTAGE TROPE.

In the theory of literature a *trope* is defined thus: "a figure of speech which consists in the use of a word or phrase in a sense other than that which is proper to it," [24] for example, a *sharp* wit (normally, a *sharp* sword).

Griffith's cinema does not know this type of montage construction. His close-ups create atmosphere, outline traits of the characters, alternate in dialogues of the leading characters, and close-ups of the chaser and the chased speed up the tempo of the chase. But Griffith at all times remains on a level of *representation and objectivity* and nowhere does he try through the *juxtaposition* of shots to shape *import and image*.

However, within the practice of Griffith there was such an attempt, an attempt of huge dimensions—*Intolerance*.

Terry Ramsaye, a historian of the American film, has definitively called it "a giant metaphor." No less definitively has he called it also "a magnificent failure." For if *Intolerance*—in its modern story—stands unsurpassed by Griffith himself, a brilliant model of his method of montage, then at the same time, along the line of a desire to get away from the *limits of story* towards *the region of generalization* and metaphorical allegory, the picture is overcome completely by failure. In explaining the failure of *Intolerance* Ramsaye claims:

Allusion, simile and metaphor can succeed in the printed and spoken word as an aid to the dim pictorial quality of the word expression. The motion picture has no use for them because it itself is the event. It is too specific and final to accept such aids. The only place that these verbal devices have on the screen is in support of the sub-title or legends. . . .[25]

But Terry Ramsaye is not correct in denying to cinematography *all possibility in general of imagistic story-telling*, in not permitting the assimilation of simile and metaphor to move, in its best instances, beyond the text of the sub-titles!

The reason for this failure was of quite another nature; particularly, in Griffith's misunderstanding, that the region of metaphorical and imagist writing appears in the sphere of *montage juxtaposition*, not of *representational montage pieces*.

Out of this came his unsuccessful use of the repeated refrain shot: Lillian Gish rocking a cradle. Griffith had been inspired to translate these lines of Walt Whitman,

. . . endlessly rocks the cradle, Uniter of Here and Hereafter.*

not in the structure, nor in *the harmonic recurrence of montage expressiveness*, but in *an isolated picture*, with the result that the cradle could not possibly be *abstracted into an image of eternally reborn epochs* and remained inevitably simply a *life-like cradle*, calling forth derision, surprise or vexation in the spectator.

We know of a nearly analogous blunder in our films, as well: the "naked woman" in Dovzhenko's *Earth*. Here is another

* This is Griffith's editing of two Whitman phrases, actually twenty lines apart: "Out of the cradle endlessly rocking . . ." ". . . uniter of here and hereafter."

example of a lack of awareness that for *imagist* and *extra-life-like* (or *sur*realist) "manipulation" of film-shots there must be an abstraction of the lifelike representation.

Such an abstraction of the lifelike may in certain instances be given by the *close-up*.

A healthy, handsome woman's body may, actually, be heightened to *an image of a life-affirming beginning,* which is what Dovzhenko had to have, to clash with his montage of the funeral in *Earth.*

A skillfully leading montage creation with *close-ups,* taken in the "Rubens manner," isolated from naturalism and abstracted in the necessary direction, could well have been lifted to such a "sensually palpable" image.

But the whole structure of *Earth* was doomed to failure, because in place of such montage material the director cut into the funeral *long shots* of the interior of the peasant hut, and the naked woman flinging herself about there. And the spectator could not possibly separate out of this concrete, lifelike woman that generalized sensation of blazing fertility, of sensual life-affirmation, which the director wished to convey of all nature, as a pantheistic contrast to the theme of death and the funeral!

This was prevented by the ovens, pots, towels, benches, tablecloths—all those details of everyday life, from which the woman's body could easily have been freed by *the framing of the shot,*—so that *representational* naturalism would not interfere with the embodiment of the *conveyed metaphorical* task.

But to return to Griffith—

If he made a blunder because of non-montage thinking in the treatment of a recurring "wave of time" through an unconvincing plastic idea of a rocking cradle, then at the opposite pole—in the gathering together of all four motifs of the film along the same principle of his montage, he made another blunder.

This weaving of four epochs was magnificently conceived.*

* It was Porter (again) who earlier explored, in film, this parallel thematic linking of unconnected stories. In *The Kleptomaniac* (1905), "The story told of two women, one poor and the other rich, who are

Griffith stated:

. . . the stories will begin like four currents looked at from a hilltop. At first the four currents will flow apart, slowly and quietly. But as they flow, they grow nearer and nearer together, and faster and faster, until in the end, in the last act, they mingle in one mighty river of expressed emotion.[26]

But the effect didn't come off. For again it turned out to be a combination of *four different stories*, rather than *a fusion of four phenomena* in *a single imagist generalization*.

Griffith announced his film as "a drama of comparisons." And that is what *Intolerance* remains—a drama of comparisons, rather than *a unified, powerful, generalized image.*

Here is the same defect again: an inability to abstract a phenomenon, without which it cannot expand beyond the *narrowly representational*. For this reason we could not resolve any "*supra*-representational," "conveying" (metaphorical) tasks.

Only by dividing "hot" from a *thermometer reading* may one speak of "a sense of heat."

Only by abstracting "deep" from *meters and fathoms* may one speak of "a sense of depth."

Only by disengaging "falling" from *the formula of the accelerated speed of a falling body* ($mv^2/2$) may one speak of "a sensation of falling!"

However, the failure of *Intolerance* to achieve a true "mingling" lies also in another circumstance: the four episodes chosen by Griffith are actually un-collatable. The *formal failure* of their mingling in *a single image* of Intolerance is only *a reflection of a thematic and ideological error.*

Is it possible that a tiny general feature—a general and superficially metaphysical and vague viewpoint towards Intolerance

caught shoplifting and are arrested. The rich one is freed; the poor one is jailed. The story's effectiveness depended on the paralleling of the causes of the actions and fates of the two women." (Jacobs) Griffith's most ambitious pre-*Intolerance* trial of this multiple story form seems to have been made in *Home, Sweet Home* (1914).

(with a capital *I!*)—can really unite in the spectator's consciousness such obvious historically uncollated phenomena as the religious fanaticism of St. Bartholomew's Eve with labor's struggle in a highly developed capitalist state! And the bloody pages of the struggle for hegemony over Asia with the complicated process of conflict between the colonial Hebrew people and enslaving Mother Rome?

Here we find a key to the reason why the problem of abstraction is not once stumbled upon by Griffith's montage method. The secret of this is not professional-technical, but ideological-intellectual.

It is not that representation cannot be raised with correct presentation and treatment to the structure of metaphor, simile, image. Nor is it that Griffith here altered his method, or his professional craftsmanship. But that he made no attempt at a genuinely thoughtful abstraction of phenomena—at an *extraction of generalized conclusions* on historical phenomena from a wide variety of historical data; that is the core of the fault.

In history and economics it was necessary for the gigantic work of Marx and the continuers of his teaching to aid us in understanding *the laws of the process* that stand behind miscellaneous *separate data*. Then science could succeed in abstracting *a generalization from the chaos of separate traits* characteristic for the phenomena.

In the practice of American film studios there is a splendid professional term—"limitations." Such a director is "limited" to musical comedies. The "limits" of a certain actress are within fashionable rôles. Beyond these "limitations" (quite sensible in most cases) this or that talent cannot be thrust. Risking departure from these "limitations" sometimes results in unexpected brilliance, but ordinarily, as in commonplace phenomena, this leads to failure.

Using this term, I would say that in the realm of *montage imagery* the American cinema wins no laurels for itself; and it is ideological "limitations" that are responsible for this.

This is not affected by technique, nor by scope, nor by dimensions.

The question of montage imagery is based on a definite structure and system of thinking; it derives and has been derived only through collective consciousness, appearing as a reflection of a new (socialist) stage of human society and as a thinking result of ideal and philosophic education, inseparably connected with the social structure of that society.

We, our epoch—*sharply ideal* and *intellectual*—could not read the content of a shot without, before all else, having read its ideological nature, and therefore find in the *juxtaposition of shots an arrangement of a new qualitative element*, a new *image*, a new *understanding*.

Considering this, we could not help rushing into sharp excesses in this direction.

In *October* we cut shots of harps and balalaikas into a scene of Mensheviks addressing the Second Congress of Soviets. And these harps were shown not as harps, but as an imagist symbol of the mellifluent speech of Menshevik opportunism at the Congress. The balalaikas were not shown as balalaikas, but as an image of the tiresome strumming of these empty speeches in the face of the gathering storm of historical events. And placing side by side the Menshevik and the harp, the Menshevik and the balalaika, we were *extending the frame of parallel montage into a new quality, into a new realm:* from the sphere of *action* into the sphere of *significance.**

The period of such rather naive juxtapositions passed swiftly enough. Similar solutions, slightly "baroque" in form, in many ways attempted (and not always successfully!) with the available palliative means of the silent film to anticipate that which is now done with such ease by the music track in the sound-film! They quickly departed from the screen.

However, the chief thing remained—an understanding of montage as not merely a means of producing effects, but above all as a means of *speaking*, a means of *communicating* ideas, of communicating them by way of a special film language, by way of a special form of film *speech*.

* Further analysis of this error can be found on page 58.—EDITOR.

The arrival at an understanding of normal film-speech quite
naturally went through this *stage of excess in the realm of
the trope and primitive metaphor.* It is interesting that in this
direction we were covering methodological ground of great
antiquity. Why, for example, the "poetic" image of the cen-
taur is nothing more than a combination of man and horse with
the aim of expressing *the image of an idea, directly un-repre-
sentable by a picture* (but its exact meaning was that people
of a certain place were "high speed"—swift in the race).

Thus the very production of simple meanings rises as a
process of juxtaposition.

Therefore *the play of juxtaposition* in montage also has such
a deep background of influence. On the other hand, it is exactly
through elementary *naked juxtaposition* that must be worked
out a system of the complicated inner (the outer no longer
counts) juxtaposition that exists in each phrase of ordinary
normal literate montage speech.

However, this same process is also correct for the production of *any kind of speech* in general, and above all *for that
literary speech,* of which we are speaking. It is well known
that the metaphor is an abridged simile.

And in connection with this Mauthner has very acutely
written about our language:

Every metaphor is witty. A people's language, as it is spoken
today, is the sum total of a million witticisms, is a collection of
the points of a million anecdotes whose stories have been lost. In
this connection one must visualize the people of the language-
creating period as being even wittier than those present-day wags
who live by their wits. . . . Wit makes use of distant similes.
Close similes were captured immediately into concepts or words.
A change in meaning consists in the conquest of these words, in
the metaphorical or witty extension of the concept to distant
similes. . . .[27]

And Emerson says of this:

As the limestone of the continent consists of infinite masses of the
shells of animalcules, so language is made up of images, or tropes,

* no, metaphor is a whole different
perception of the interrelatedness of reality
as filtered through a perceiving consciousness.

which now, in their secondary use, have long ceased to remind us of their poetic origin.[28]

At the threshold of the creation of language stands the simile, the trope and the image.

All meanings in language are imagist in origin, and each of these may, in due time, lose its original imagist source. Both these states of words—imagery and non-imagery—are equally natural. If the non-imagery of a word was considered derivative as something elementary (which it is always), that derives from the fact that it is a temporary latency of thought (which imagery is its new step), but movement attracts more attention and is more provocative of analysis than is latency.

The calm observer, reviewing a prepared transferred expression of a more complicated poetic creation, may find in his memory a corresponding non-imagist expression, more imagistically corresponding to his (the observer's) mood of thought. If he says that this non-imagery is *communis et primum se offerens ratio* then he attributes his own condition to the creator of imagist expression. This is as if one were to expect that in the midst of a heated battle it is possible thus calmly to deliberate, as at a chess-board, with an absent partner. If one should transfer into the condition of the speaker himself, that would easily reverse the assertion of the cold observer and he would decide that *primum se offerens,* even if not *communis,* is exactly imagist. . . .[29]

In Werner's work on the metaphor he thus places it in the very cradle of language, although for other motives—he links it not with the tendency to *perceive* new regions, familiarizing the unknown through the known, but, on the contrary, with the tendency to *hide,* to substitute, to replace in customary usage that which lies under some oral ban—and is "tabu." [30]

It is interesting that the "fact word" itself is *naturally* a rudiment of the poetic trope:

Independently from the connection between the primary and derivative words, any word, as an aural indication of meaning, based on the combination of sound and meaning in simultaneity or succession, consequently, is metonymy.[31]

And he who would take it into his head to be indignant and rebel against this would inevitably fall into the position of the pedant in one of Tieck's stories, who cried out:

". . . When a man begins to compare one object with another, he lies directly. 'The dawn strews roses.' Can there be any thing more silly? 'The sun sinks into the sea.' Stuff! . . . 'The morning wakes.' There is no morning, how can it sleep? It is nothing but the hour when the sun rises. Plague! The sun does not rise, that too is nonsense and poetry. Oh! If I had my will with language, and might properly scour and sweep it! O damnation! Sweep! In this lying world, one cannot help talking nonsense!" [32]

The *imagist* transference of thought to simple *representation* is also echoed here. There is in Potebnya a good comment on this:

The image is more important than the representation. There is a tale of a monk who, in order to prevent himself from eating roast suckling during Lent, carried on himself this invocation: "Suckling, transform thyself into a carp!" This tale, stripped of its satirical character, presents us with a universal historical phenomenon of human thought: word and image are the spiritual half of the matter, its essence. [33]

Thus or otherwise the primitive metaphor necessarily stands at the very dawn of language, closely linked with the period of the production of the first transfers, that is, the first words to convey meanings, and not merely *motor* and *objective* understanding, that is, with the period of the birth of the first tools, as the first means of "transferring" the functions of the body and its actions from man himself to the tool in his hands. It is not astonishing, therefore, that the period of the birth of articulate montage speech of the future had also to pass through a sharply metaphorical stage, characterized by an abundance, if not a proper estimation, of "plastic sharpness"!

However, these "sharpnesses" very soon became sensed as excesses and twistings of some sort of a "language." And attention was gradually shifted from curiosity *concerning excesses* towards an interest in *the nature of this language itself.*

Thus the secret of the structure of montage was gradually revealed as a secret of *the structure of emotional speech*. For the very principle of montage, as is the entire individuality of its formation, is the substance of *an exact copy of the language of excited emotional speech*.

It is enough to examine the characteristics of similar speech, in order to be convinced, with no further commentary, that this is so.

Let us open to the appropriate chapter in Vendryes' excellent book, *Language:*

The main difference between affective and logical language lies in the construction of the sentence. This difference stands out clearly when we compare the written with the spoken tongue. In French the two are so far removed from each other that a Frenchman never speaks as he writes and rarely writes as he speaks. . . .

. . . The elements that the written tongue endeavours to combine into a coherent whole seem to be divided up and disjointed in the spoken tongue: even the order is entirely different. It is no longer the logical order of present-day grammar. It has its logic, but this logic is primarily affective, and the ideas are arranged in accordance with the subjective importance the speaker gives to them or wishes to suggest to his listener, rather than with the objective rules of an orthodox process of reasoning.

In the spoken tongue, all idea of meaning in the purely grammatical sense, disappears. If I say, *L'homme que vous voyez la-bas assis sur la greve est celui que j'ai rencontre hier à la gare* (The man that you see sitting down there on the beach is he whom I met yesterday at the station), I am making use of the processes of the written tongue and form but one sentence. But in speaking, I should have said: *Vous voyez bien cet homme—la-bas—il est assis sur la greve—eh bien! je l'ai rencontre hier, il etait à la gare.* (You see that man, down there—he is sitting on the beach—well! I met him yesterday, he was at the station.) How many sentences have we here? It is very difficult to say. Imagine that I pause where the dashes are printed: the words *la-bas* in themselves would form one sentence, exactly as if in answer to a question—"Where is this man?—*Down there.*" And even the sentence *il est assis sur la greve* easily becomes two if I pause between the two component parts: "*il est assis*," [*il est*] "*sur la greve*" (or "[*c'est*] *sur la greve* [*qu'*] *il est assis*"). The boundaries of the grammatical sentence are here so elusive that we had better give up all attempts to determine them. In a certain sense, there is but one sentence. The verbal image is one though it follows a kind of kinematical development. But whereas in the written tongue it is presented as a whole, when spoken it is cut up into short sections whose number and intensity correspond to the speaker's impressions, or to the necessity he feels for vividly communicating them to others.[34]

Isn't this an exact copy of what takes place in montage? And doesn't what is said here about "written" language seem a duplication of the clumsy "long shot," which, when it attempts to present something *dramatically*, always hopelessly looks like a florid, awkward phrase, full of the subordinate clauses, participles and adverbs of a "theatrical" *mise-en-scène*, with which it dooms itself?!

However, this by no means implies that it is necessary to chase at any cost after "montage hash." In connection with this one may speak of the *phrase* as the author of "A Discussion of Old and New Style in the Russian Language," the Slavophile Alexander Shishkov wrote of *words*:

In language both long and short words are necessary; for without short ones language would sound like the long-drawn-out moo of the cow, and without long ones—like the short monotonous chirp of a magpie.[35]

Concerning "affective logic," about which Vendryes writes and which lies at the base of spoken speech, montage very quickly realized that "affective logic" is the chief thing, but for finding all the fullness of its system and laws, montage had to make further serious creative "cruises" through the "inner monologue" of Joyce, through the "inner monologue" as understood in film, and through the so-called "intellectual cinema," before discovering that a fund of these laws can be found in a third variety of speech—not in *written*, nor in *spoken* speech, but in *inner speech*, where the affective structure functions in an even more full and pure form. But the formation of this *inner speech* is already inalienable from that which is enriched by *sensual thinking*.

Thus we arrived at the primary source of those interior principles, which already govern not only the formation of montage, but the inner formation of all works of art—of those basic *laws of the speech of art in general*—of those general *laws of form*, which lie at the base not only of works of film art, but of all and all kinds of arts in general. But of that—at another time.

Let us return now to that historical stage when montage in our field realized itself as a *montage trope*, and let us follow that path of development which it performed in the field of creating a unity of work, inseparable from that process, in which it became conscious of itself as an independent language.

Thus, in its way, montage became conscious of itself among us with the very first, not imitative, but independent steps of our cinema.

It is interesting that even in the interval between the old cinema and our Soviet cinema, researches were conducted exactly along the line of *juxtaposition*. And it is even more interesting that at this stage they naturally are known as . . . *contrasts*. Therefore on them above all else lies the imprint of *"contemplative dissection"* instead of an *emotional fusion* in some "new quality," as were already characterizing the first researches in the field of the Soviet cinema's own language. Such a speculative play of contrasts fills, for example, the film *Palace and Fortress* as if to carry the principle of contrast from its title into the very style of the work. Here are still constructions of a type of *un-crossed* parallelism: "here and there," "before and now." It is completely in the spirit of the posters of the time, split into two halves, showing on the left, a landlord's house *before* (the master, serfdom, flogging) and on the right—*now* (a school in the same building, a nursery). It is completely such a type of colliding shots that we find in the film: the "points" of a ballerina (the *Palace*) and the shackled legs of Beidemann (the *Fortress*). Similarly speculative in the *order of parallelism* is given also in the combination of shots—Beidemann behind bars and . . . a caged canary in the jailer's room.*

In these and other examples there is nowhere any further tendency towards *a union of representations in a generalized image:* they are united neither by a unity of composition nor by the chief element, emotion: they are presented in an even narrative, and not in that degree of emotional excitement when it is only natural for an imagist turn of speech to *arise*.

But pronounced without a corresponding emotional degree, without corresponding emotional preparation, the "image" inevitably sounds absurd. When Hamlet tells Laertes:

> I loved Ophelia; forty thousand brothers
> Could not, with all their quantity of love,
> Make up my sum. . . .

this is very pathetic and arresting; but try taking from this the expression of heightened emotion, transfer it to a setting of ordinary lifelike conversation, that is, consider the immediate objective content of this image, and it will evoke nothing but laughter!

Strike (1924) abounded in "trials" of this new and independent direction. The mass shooting of the demonstrators in the finale, interwoven with bloody scenes at the municipal slaughter-house, merged (for that "childhood" of our cinema this sounded fully convincing and produced a great impression!) in a film-metaphor of "a human slaughter-house," absorbing into itself the memory of bloody repressions on the part of the autocracy. Here already were not the simple "contemplative" *contrasts* of *Palace and Fortress*, but already—though still crude and still "hand-made"—a consistent and conscious attempt at *juxtaposition*.

Juxtaposition, striving to tell about an execution of workers

* This motif was placed on a considerably higher stage of meaning—in an image of Hopelessness—as it was later used by Pudovkin in *Mother* in the scene of the conversation between the mother and son in the prison, interrupted by shots of a cockroach pushed back into the sticky mass by the sentry's finger.

not only in representations, but further also through a generalized "plastic turn of speech," approaching a verbal image of "a bloody slaughter-house."

In *Potemkin* three *separate* close-ups of three different marble lions in different attitudes were merged into *one* roaring lion and, moreover, in another *film-dimension*—an embodiment of a metaphor: *"The very stones roar!"*

Griffith shows us an ice-break rushing along. Somewhere in the center of the splintering ice lies, unconscious, Anna (Lillian Gish). Leaping from ice-cake to ice-cake comes David (Richard Barthelmess) to save her.

But the parallel *race of the ice-break* and of *the human actions* are nowhere brought together by him in a unified image of *"a human flood,"* a mass of people bursting their fetters, a mass of people rushing onward in an all-shattering inundation, as there is, for example, in the finale of *Mother*, by Gorky-Zarkhi-Pudovkin.

Of course, on this path excesses also occur, and also bald failures; of course, in more than a few examples these were good intentions defeated by shortcomings in compositional principles and by insufficient reasons for them in the context: then, in place of a flashing unity of image, a miserable trope is left on the level of an unrealized fusion, on the level of a mechanical pasting together of the type of "Came the rain and two students."

But thus or otherwise the dual *parallel rows* characteristic of Griffith ran in our cinema on the way to realizing themselves in the future *unity of the montage image* at first as a whole series of plays of montage comparisons, montage metaphors, montage puns.

These were more or less stormy floods, all serving to make clearer and clearer the final main task in the montage side of creative work—the creation in it of an inseparable domination of the *image*, of *the unified montage image*, of *the montage-built image, embodying the theme*, as this was achieved in the "Odessa steps" of *Potemkin*, in the "attack of the Kappel Division" of *Chapayev*, in the hurricane of *Storm Over Asia*, in the

Dnieper prologue of *Ivan*, more weakly—the landing of *We Are from Kronstadt*, with new strength in "Bozhenko's funeral" in *Shchors*, in Vertov's *Three Songs About Lenin*, in the "attack of the knights" in *Alexander Nevsky*. . . . This is the glorious *independent* path of the Soviet cinema—the path of the creation of the *montage image-episode*, the *montage image-event*, the *montage image-film in its entirety*—of equal rights, of equal influence and equal responsibility in the perfect film—on an equal footing with the *image of the hero*, with the *image of man, and of the people*.

Our conception of montage has far outgrown the classic dualistic montage esthetic of Griffith, symbolized by the two never-convergent parallel racers, interweaving the thematically variegated strips with a view towards the mutual intensification of entertainment, tension and tempi.

For us montage became a means of achieving *a unity of a higher order*—a means *through the montage image of achieving an organic embodiment of a single idea conception, embracing all elements, parts, details of the film-work.*

And thus understood, it seems considerably broader than an understanding of narrowly cinematographic montage; thus understood, it carries much to fertilize and enrich our understanding of art methods in general.

And in conformity with this principle of our montage, *unity and diversity* are both sounded as principles.

Montage removes its last contradictions by abolishing dualist contradictions and mechanical parallelism between the realms of sound and sight in what we understand as audio-visual ("vertical") montage.*

It finds its final artistic unity in the resolution of the problems of the unity of audio-visual synthesis—problems that are now being decided by us, problems that are not even on the agenda of American researches.

Stereoscopic and color film are being realized before our eyes.

---

* See *The Film Sense*, particularly Chapters II-IV.

And the moment is drawing near when, not only through the method of montage, but also through the synthesis of *idea, the drama of acting man, the screen picture, sound, three-dimension and color,* that same great law of *unity and diversity*—lying at the base of our thinking, at the base of our philosophy, and to an equal degree penetrating the montage method from its tiniest link to the fullness of montage imagery in the film as a whole—passes into *a unity of the whole screen image.*

[1944]

APPENDIX A

A STATEMENT

THE DREAM of a sound-film has come true. With the invention of a practical sound-film, the Americans have placed it on the first step of substantial and rapid realization. Germany is working intensively in the same direction. The whole world is talking about the silent thing that has learned to talk.

We who work in the U.S.S.R. are aware that with our technical potential we shall not move ahead to a practical realization of the sound-film in the near future. At the same time we consider it opportune to state a number of principle premises of a theoretical nature, for in the accounts of the invention it appears that this advance in films is being employed in an incorrect direction. Meanwhile, a misconception of the potentialities within this new technical discovery may not only hinder the development and perfection of the cinema as an art, but also threatens to destroy all its present formal achievements.

At present, the film, working with visual images, has a powerful affect on a person and has rightfully taken one of the first places among the arts.

It is known that the basic (and only) means that has brought the cinema to such a powerfully affective strength is MONTAGE. The affirmation of montage, as the chief means of effect, has become the indisputable axiom on which the world-wide culture of the cinema has been built.

The success of Soviet films on the world's screens is due, to a significant degree, to those methods of montage which they first revealed and consolidated.

Therefore, for the further development of the cinema, the

important moments will be only those that strengthen and broaden the montage methods of affecting the spectator. Examining each new discovery from this viewpoint, it is easy to show the insignificance of the color and the stereoscopic film in comparison with the vast significance of SOUND.

Sound-recording is a two-edged invention, and it is most probable that its use will proceed along the line of least resistance, i.e., along the line of *satisfying simple curiosity*.

In the first place there will be commercial exploitation of the most saleable merchandise, TALKING FILMS. Those in which sound-recording will proceed on a naturalistic level, exactly corresponding with the movement on the screen, and providing a certain "illusion" of talking people, of audible objects, etc.

A first period of sensations does not injure the development of a new art, but it is the second period that is fearful in this case, a second period that will take the place of the fading virginity and purity of this first perception of new technical possibilities, and will assert an epoch of its automatic utilization for "highly cultured dramas" and other photographed performances of a theatrical sort.

To use sound in this way will destroy the culture of montage, for every ADHESION of sound to a visual montage piece increases its inertia as a montage piece, and increases the independence of its meaning—and this will undoubtedly be to the detriment of montage, operating in the first place not on the montage pieces, but on their JUXTAPOSITION.

ONLY A CONTRAPUNTAL USE of sound in relation to the visual montage piece will afford a new potentiality of montage development and perfection.

THE FIRST EXPERIMENTAL WORK WITH SOUND MUST BE DIRECTED ALONG THE LINE OF ITS DISTINCT NON-SYNCHRONIZATION WITH THE VISUAL IMAGES. And only such an attack will give the necessary palpability which will later lead to the creation of an ORCHESTRAL COUNTERPOINT of visual and aural images.

This new technical discovery is not an accidental moment in film history, but an organic way out of a whole series of im-passes that have seemed hopeless to the cultured cinematic avant-garde.

The FIRST IMPASSE is the sub-title and all the unavailing attempts to tie it into the montage composition, as a montage piece (such as breaking it up into phrases and even words, increasing and decreasing the size of type used, employing camera movement, animation, and so on).

The SECOND IMPASSE is the EXPLANATORY pieces (for example, certain inserted close-ups) that burden the montage composition and retard the tempo.

The tasks of theme and story grow more complicated every day; attempts to solve these by methods of "visual" montage alone either lead to unsolved problems or force the director to resort to fanciful montage structures, arousing the fearsome eventuality of meaninglessness and reactionary decadence.

Sound, treated as a new montage element (as a factor divorced from the visual image), will inevitably introduce new means of enormous power to the expression and solution of the most complicated tasks that now oppress us with the impossibility of overcoming them by means of an imperfect film method, working only with visual images.

The CONTRAPUNTAL METHOD of constructing the sound-film will not only not weaken the INTERNATIONAL CINEMA, but will bring its significance to unprecedented power and cultural height.

Such a method for constructing the sound-film will not confine it to a national market, as must happen with the photographing of plays, but will give a greater possibility than ever before for the circulation throughout the world of a filmically expressed idea.

(signed by) S. M. EISENSTEIN
V. I. PUDOVKIN
G. V. ALEXANDROV

[Note: This historic collective "Statement," generally assumed to have been initiated and composed by the first of its three signatories and endorsed by the other two, first appeared in the Leningrad magazine, *Zhizn Iskusstva*, on August 5, 1928. All previous English texts have been translated from a German publication of the statement later in that month. The above is the first direct translation into English from the original Russian text. As predicted by the Statement, progress in the technical development of the Soviet sound-film was slow. In September of that year, the Shorin sound-system was first tested in Leningrad, and these tests were exhibited in March of the following year; in Moscow the Tager system was tried out in July 1929. In August the Leningrad studio of Sovkino constructed the first sound-stage, which was first used for the synchronization of recently completed films. Following the release of *Old and New* in October, arrangements were made for Eisenstein, Alexandrov, and Tisse to go abroad to study the sound-film.]

APPENDIX B

NOTES FROM A DIRECTOR'S LABORATORY

(DURING WORK ON *Ivan the Terrible*)

1. The First Vision

THE MOST important thing is to have the vision. The next is to grasp and hold it. In this there is no difference whether you are writing a film-script, pondering the plan of the production as a whole, or thinking out a solution for some particular detail.

You must see and feel what you are thinking about. You must see and grasp it. You must hold and fix it in your memory and senses. And you must do it at once.

When you are in a good working mood, images swarm through your busy imagination. Keeping up with them and catching them is very much like grappling with a run of herring.

You suddenly see the outline of a whole scene and, rising simultaneously before this same inner eye, a close-up in full detail: a head nesting on a great white ruff.

Just as you are seizing from the passing figures in your imagination a characteristic bend of Tzar Ivan's back in the confessional, you must drop your pencil and take up your pen to sketch the dialogue for this scene, and before the ink of this is dry, your pencil is once more making a note of an image that came to you during the dialogue—of the priest's long white hair descending like a canopy over the Tzar's graying head. Before this mood has finished, you find yourself drawing with your pen and penciling notes for the dialogue—on the sheets of drawings.

261

Directions become drawings; the voices and intonations of various characters are drawn as series of facial expressions. Whole scenes first take shape as batches of drawings before they take on the clothing of words.

In this way mountains of folders, stuffed with drawings, accumulate around the writing of the script—these multiply as the production plans are conceived—and they become a storage problem as the details of sequences and *mises-en-scène* are worked out.

These are nothing more than attempts to grasp stenographically the features of those images that flash through your mind in thinking about the individual details of your film. These drawings cannot claim to be more than this, nor can they possibly make any claim as drawings!

But neither can they claim less than this! For in them are secured the principal, initial elements of those ideas that will later have to be worked on, developed and realized in the course of the coming weeks and months: through the work of the designer who will have to transform rough sketches into a system of blueprints for the settings, through the work of the make-up man who will have to fuss for hours with grease-paint and wigs to achieve the same effect on the screen that the light pressure of a pencil indicated so freely on paper.

For days we will struggle with the stubborn cloth, cutting and draping it to capture that rhythm of folds that suddenly struck me when I closed my eyes over that bit of brocade and envisioned a procession of boyars in heavy robes moving slowly to the chambers of the dying Tzar.

And Cherkasov's incomparably lithe and flexible body will practice long and tiringly to produce the tragic bend of Tzar Ivan's figure so spontaneously fixed on paper as camera set-ups. In intent these drawings are no more (but also no less) than those Japanese paper toys that, when cast into warm water, unfold and develop stems, leaves and flowers of fantastic and surprising shape.

Altogether, to change the image, they are no more than the corner of a veil lifted from the creative kitchen of film production.

Here a viewpoint on that suddenly rising head and ruff is calculated.

Here the characteristic position of fingers and hands in El Greco's paintings is analyzed.

And here is a trial for the most effective intersection of the curve of an arch by a tall, dark figure in the foreground.

Sometimes the hint fixed on paper will be developed and transferred to the screen. Sometimes it will be scrapped. Sometimes the contribution of an actor, or some unforeseen possibility (or more frequently, impossibility) of lighting, or any kind of production circumstance will alter or revise your first vision. But even here, by other means and methods, you will strive to convey in the finished work that invaluable seed that was present in your first vision of what you hoped to see on the screen.

2. Facing the Camera

The dream becomes reality.

It is no longer pen and pencil, notebooks, scraps torn from envelopes, backs of telegrams, announcements, invitations—all completely covered with sketches and notes—that lie before one.

The dream has grown up to be an unwieldy, massive thing.

The words of the script on the capture of Kazan have grown into a military camp.

The rays of the sun are so scorching that we are all compelled to wear sun helmets. No second under this sun can be spent in dream or fantasy. Fancy is now in harness.

The earlier free play of fantasy has now become depth of focus, choice of the properly dense filters for the lens, the clicking of the footage meter.

The cold glass of the lens looks out mercilessly on the hot chaos of tents, reflectors, armor and umbrellas—paying attention to nothing but that which has been called into being by the innocent pages of the script.

From the sun-scorched plains of Kazan the cameras move to the sound-stage. No longer do we face the dust of hundreds of galloping horses.

Now Tzar Ivan is swearing his vow over the coffin of his poisoned wife. At this moment he would seem to be absolutely alone with her body.

Nothing of the sort. The fearful steel cameras are recording his every movement, every trace of emotion on his face.

Eyes are watching him intently from every corner of the sound-stage: to make sure that he does not slide out of the compositional margins, that he does not slip out of focus, or out of the laboriously set lighting, that he does not raise his voice beyond the level that the sound-engineers have prepared for. . . .

A few days later in the same cathedral where the aging Tzar wept over the coffin of his Tzaritza, the same man, but now fifteen years younger, is being crowned Tzar!

It requires a great effort of creative will and imagination on the part of Cherkasov to transform himself from a mature man weighed down by cares, into an impassioned youth full of hope and boldly looking towards a glorious future.

And with the ruthlessness of H. G. Wells' "time machine," the same camera boom is wheeled into position to record, with the same objectivity and accuracy as for the stern words of the graying Tzar, the youthful speech and gestures of the newly crowned Tzar.

One of the absorbing aspects of film-making, compensating for much that is irksome, difficult and unpleasant, is the constant variety and novelty of the subject matter.

Today you film a record-breaking harvest. Tomorrow a

matador in the bull-ring. The next day, the Patriarch blessing the new Tzar.

And each subject requires its own peculiar and strict technique.

That the scythe may be more effective in the fields of the collective-farm, it must be handled with no less strict an observance of rule than that observed by the matador preparing his muleta and sword for the kill.

Equally strict is the ritual in the ceremonies and customs of the past which you resurrect when you bring the people of that past to the screen of today.

And so Father Pavel Tzvetkov, one of the deans of Moscow, himself dressed in civilian clothes, patiently teaches the actor who plays the rôle of the Metropolitan, the proper performance of the ritual of blessing of the Tzar. At the same time he instructs the young Tzar how to conduct himself at this solemn moment, in accordance with the ancient canons.

And here, in a deep bass (how deep, and what a bass!) the words of the prayer for the young Tzar's health pass from the pages of the script onto the sound-track.

Not only have we selected the best bass in our country, that of People's Artist Mikhailov, but we have also selected that version of the "Long Life" prayer that best suits the atmosphere of our sequence—the solemn coronation of the first Russian Autocrat—Tzar Ivan Vasilyevich IV.

[Note: These "Notes" were originally written to accompany sketches and production stills made during the preparation and filming of *Ivan the Terrible*.]

NOTES ON TEXTS AND TRANSLATIONS

"Through Theatre to Cinema" (Srednaya iz trekh, 1924-1929). Originally printed in *Sovyetskoye kino*, November-December 1934 (Moscow). The present translation, by the editor and Paya Haskelson, has been previously published in *Theatre Arts Monthly*, New York, September 1936.

"The Unexpected" (Nezhdannyi styk). Originally printed in *Zhizn iskusstva*, 19 August 1928 (Leningrad). The present translation is the first appearance in English of this essay.

"The Cinematographic Principle and the Ideogram" (Za kadrom). An afterword to *Yaponskoye kino*, by N. Kaufman (Moscow, 1929). Translated by Ivor Montagu and S. S. Nolbandov and revised by the author and Ivor Montagu, published as "The Cinematographic Principle and Japanese Culture (with a digression on montage and the shot)" in *Transition*, June 1930 (Paris). The present text employs this translation, with alterations based on the original Russian text.

"A Dialectic Approach to Film Form." The original German manuscript, deposited in the Eisenstein Collection at the Museum of Modern Art Film Library, New York, has been newly translated for this edition by John Winge. Only the first half of this essay has been previously translated by Ivor Montagu as "The Principles of Film Form," *Close Up*, September 1931 (London).

"The Filmic Fourth Dimension" (Kino chetyrekh izmerenii). Originally printed in *Kino*, 27 August 1929 (Moscow). Previously translated by W. Ray as "The Fourth Dimension in the Kino," *Close Up*, March 1930 (Territet). The translation for this edition has been newly made from the original Russian text.

"Methods of Montage," written in London to supplement the preceding essay, this essay was translated by W. Ray as "The Fourth Dimension in the Kino: II," *Close Up*, April 1930 (Territet). The present text is a revision of Miss Ray's translation.

"A Course in Treatment" (Odolzhaites!). Originally printed in *Proletarskoye kino*, No. 17-18, 1932 (Moscow). Previously translated by W. Ray as "Cinematography *with* Tears," *Close Up*, March 1933, and "An American Tragedy," *Close Up*, June 1933 (London). The translation for this edition has been newly made from the original Russian text, restoring omitted passages.

"Film Language" ("E!" o chistotye kinoyazyka). Originally printed in *Sovyetskoye kino*, May 1934 (Moscow). The present translation is the first appearance in English of this essay. (The portion of analysis was quoted in Vladimir Nilsen's *The Cinema as a Graphic Art*, translated by Stephen Garry, London, 1936.)

"Film Form: New Problems." The full text of this speech at the All-Union Creative Conference of Workers in Soviet Cinematography, Moscow, 8-13 January 1935, was published in *Za bolshoye kinoiskusstvo* (Moscow, 1935). The greater part of the speech was translated by Ivor Montagu as "Film Form, 1935—New Problems," *Life and Letters Today*, September-December 1935 (London). The present text employs this translation, with alterations based on the original Russian text.

"The Structure of the Film" (O stroyenii veshchei). Originally printed in *Iskusstvo kino*, June 1939 (Moscow). The present translation is the first appearance in English of this essay. A detailed mathematical analysis of ideal proportions (in relation to the inter-related parts of *Potemkin*), employing illustrations from the practice of architecture, poetry, and painting, has been omitted in this translation.

"Achievement" (Gordost). Originally printed in *Iskusstvo kino*, January-February 1940 (Moscow). Previously translated as "Pride," *International Literature*, April-May, 1940 (Moscow). The translation for this edition has been newly made from the original Russian text.

"Dickens, Griffith, and the Film Today" (Dikkens, Griffit i myi). An essay in *Amerikanskaya kinematografiya: D. U. Griffit*, Volume I in *Materialy po istorii mirovogo kinoiskusstva* (Moscow, 1944). The present translation has been made for this edition.

"Statement" (Zayavleniye). Originally printed in *Zhizn iskusstva*, 5 August 1928 (Leningrad). Previously translated from a German text in the New York *Herald Tribune* (September 21, 1928), the New York *Times* (October 7, 1928), and *Close Up* (October 1928). The present translation has been made for this edition from the original Russian text.

"Notes from a Director's Laboratory." Written for the VOKS *Film Chronicle*, February 1945 (Moscow), and published as "In a Regisseur's Laboratory." The present text is an adaptation of the earlier translation, based on the original Russian text.

SOURCES

"THROUGH THEATER TO CINEMA"

1. Gustave Flaubert, *Madame Bovary*, translated by Eleanor Marx-Aveling. New York, Alfred A. Knopf, 1929.
2. Andrei Belyi (Boris Nikolayevich Bugayev), *Masterstvo Gogolya.* Moscow, 1934.

"THE UNEXPECTED"

1. Quoted in *Haiku Poems, Ancient and Modern*, translated and annotated by Miyamori Asatarō. Tokyo, Maruzen Company, 1940.
2. From a collection of anecdotes about Vasili Ignatyevich Givochini.
3. "Montage of Attractions," *LEF*, 3, 1923; a translated excerpt appears in Appendix 2 of *The Film Sense*.
4. Zoë Kincaid, *Kabuki, The Popular Stage of Japan.* London, Macmillan and Co., 1925, pp. 199-200.
5. J. Ingram Bryan, *The Literature of Japan.* London, Thornton Butterworth Ltd., 1929, pp. 33-34.
6. Julius Kurth, *Japanische Lyrik*, p. iv.
7. Heinrich von Kleist, "Über das Marionettentheater," translated by Eugene Jolas, in *Vertical.* New York City, Gotham Book Mart, 1941.

"THE CINEMATOGRAPHIC PRINCIPLE AND THE IDEOGRAM"

1. Jean Pierre Abel Rémusat, *Recherches sur l'origine et la formation de l'écriture chinoise.* Paris.
2. Translation by Miyamori, op. cit.
3. Translation by Frederick Victor Dickins, in *Primitive & Mediaeval Japanese Texts.* Oxford, Clarendon Press, 1906.
4. Yone Noguchi, *The Spirit of Japanese Poetry.* London, John Murray, 1914, p. 53.
5. Julius Kurth, *Sharaku.* München, R. Piper, 2nd edition, 1922, pp. 78-79. The Sharaku print referred to is that numbered 24 in the catalogue by Harold G. Henderson and Louis V. Ledoux, *The Surviving Works of Sharaku.* Published by E. Weyhe, in behalf of the Society for Japanese Studies, 1939.
6. George Rowley, *Principles of Chinese Painting.* Princeton University Press, 1947, p. 56.
7. Ibid., p. 66.
8. Lev Kuleshov, *Iskusstvo Kino.* Leningrad, 1929.
9. Illustration No. 12, "How to choose composition," in *Jinjo Shogaku Shintei Gaten Dai Roku Gaku Nen Dan Sei Yo* (Elementary Grade Drawing Manual for Sixth Grade Boys). Tokyo, Board of Education, 1910.

"A DIALECTIC APPROACH TO FILM FORM"

1. In *Conversations with Eckermann* (5 June 1825), translated by John Oxenford.
2. Razumovsky, *Theory of Historical Materialism*, Moscow, 1928.
3. Ludwig Klages, *The Science of Character*, translated by W. H. Johnston, London, George Allen & Unwin Ltd., 1929.
4. Graham Wallas, *The Great Society, A Psychological Analysis*. Macmillan, 1928, p. 101.
5. In *Conversations with Eckermann* (23 March 1829).
6. In the preface to Baudelaire's *Les fleurs du mal*, illustrated by Auguste Rodin, Paris, Limited Editions Club, 1940.
7. Renoir's manifesto for *La Société des Irrégularistes* (1884) is thus synopsized by Lionello Venturi in his *Painting and Painters*, New York, Scribners, 1945; the original text can be consulted in *Les archives de l'Impressionisme*, edited by Lionello Venturi, Paris, Durand-Ruel, 1939, I, pp. 127-129.
8. Charles Baudelaire, *Intimate Journals* (13 May 1856), translated by Christopher Isherwood. New York, Random House, 1930.

"THE FILMIC FOURTH DIMENSION"

1. Albert Einstein, *Relativity, the Special and General Theory*, translated by Robert W. Lawson. Peter Smith, p. 65.

"METHODS OF MONTAGE"

1. *Memoirs of Goldoni*, translated by John Black, New York, Alfred A. Knopf, 1926.
2. Vladimir Ilyich Lenin, *Filosofskiye tetradi*. Moscow, Ogiz, 1947, pp. 192-193.

"A COURSE IN TREATMENT"

1. James Joyce, *Ulysses*, New York, Random House, 1934, p. 475.
2. Nikolai Gogol, "The Story of the Quarrel between Ivan Ivanovich and Ivan Nikiforovich."
3. "What 'The Friends of the People' Are," in Lenin, *Sochineniya*, Moscow, 1929.
4. Quoted in Herbert Gorman, *The Incredible Marquis*. New York, Farrar & Rinehart, 1929, p. 441.
5. Jean Lucas-Dubreton, *The Fourth Musketeer, the Life of Alexander Dumas*, translated by Maida Castelhun Darnton. New York, Coward-McCann, 1928, p. 145.
6. Ibid., p. 148.
7. Ibid., pp. 141-142.
8. "Maupassant" by Isaac Babel.
9. See *Last Plays of Maxim Gorky*, translated by Gibson-Cowan. New York, International Publishers, 1937.
10. Friedrich Engels, *Socialism: Utopian and Scientific*, translated by Edward Aveling. New York, International Publishers, 1935. Introduction, p. 18.

11. Theodore Dreiser, *An American Tragedy*, New York, Boni and Liveright, 1925, II, p. 78. (Note: Eisenstein's copy of this work, used in the preparation of his film treatment, is in the Eisenstein Collection of the Museum of Modern Art, New York.)
12. Translated by Stuart Gilbert as *We'll to the Woods No More*, Cambridge, New Directions, 1938.
13. See, particularly, René Bizet, *La double vie de Gérard de Nerval*. Paris, Plon, 1928.

"FILM LANGUAGE"

1. From a speech, "Soviet Literature," delivered at the First Soviet Writers' Congress. Proceedings published as *Problems of Soviet Literature*. New York, International Publishers, 1934.
2. Belyi, op. cit.
3. Book V, Chap. XXV of *Gargantua and Pantagruel*, "How We Disembarked at the Isle of Hodes, Where the Roads a-Roading Go," in *All the Extant Works of François Rabelais*, translated by Samuel Putnam. New York, Covici-Friede, 1929.
4. Translation by Miyamori, op. cit.
5. Emile Zola, *Germinal*, translated by Havelock Ellis. New York, Boni & Liveright, 1924.
6. Sebastien Mercier, *Paris pendant la Revolution* . . . Paris, Poulet-Malassis, 1862, I, p. 88.

"FILM FORM: NEW PROBLEMS"

1. "The Actor and the Image," in *Proceedings of the Moscow Club of Art Craftsmen*, No. 1, Moscow, 1934.
2. Wilhelm Wundt, *Elements of Folk Psychology*, translated by Edward Leroy Schaub. New York, Macmillan, 1928, p. 72.
3. This illustration, employed by Lévy-Bruhl in *Les fonctions mentales dans les sociétés inférieures*, is taken from *The Klamath Language*, by A. Gatschet (Contributions to *North American Ethnology*, ii, I); the previous illustration from the Bororo tribe, used by Lévy-Bruhl in the same work, is taken from *Unter den Naturvölkern Zentralbräsiliens*, by K. von den Steinen.
4. "The Philosophy of Style," in *Essays: Scientific, Political, and Speculative*. New York and London, D. Appleton and Co., 1916.
5. Engels, op. cit.
6. Engels, op. cit., p. 48.

"THE STRUCTURE OF THE FILM"

1. Maxim Gorky, essay on "Man."
2. Franz Kafka, "Reflections on Sin, Pain, Hope, and the True Way," in *The Great Wall of China*, translated by Willa and Edwin Muir. New York, Schocken Books, 1947.
3. Johann Nicolaus Forkel, "On Johann Sebastian Bach's Life, Genius, and Works," translated by Mr. Stephenson. In *The Bach Reader*, edited by Hans T. David and Arthur Mendel. New York, W. W. Norton & Company, 1945.

4. *The Works of Leo Tolstoy*, Oxford University Press, London, 1937 (Centenary Edition). *The Kreutzer Sonata*, translated by Louise and Aylmer Maude, Chap. XXIII.

5. Ibid., Vol. 9, *Anna Karenina*, translated by Louise and Aylmer Maude, Part II, Chap. XI.

6. V. Veresayev (Smidovich), *Vospominaniya* (second edition). Moscow, 1938.

7. *The Kreutzer Sonata*, ed. cit., Chap. XIII.

8. Ibid., Chap. XVI.

9. Lenin, loc. cit., Vol. XIII, pp. 302-303.

10. See Notes for *L'Assommoir* as described in the appendix to Matthew Josephson, *Zola and His Time*, New York, Macaulay, 1928; the full notes have been printed by Henri Massis in *Comment Zola composait ses Romans*, 1906.

11. Victor Shklovsky, *Ikh nastoyashcheye*. Moscow, Kinopechat, 1927.

12. See "P-R-K-F-V," Eisenstein's introduction to *Sergei Prokofiev*, by Israel Nestyev, New York, Alfred A. Knopf, 1945.

"ACHIEVEMENT"

1. Quoted in Léon Moussinac, *La décoration théâtrale*. Paris, F. Rieder, 1922, p. 13.

2. A. Gvozdëv, *Zapadno-yevropeiskii teatre na rubezhe XIX i XX stoletii*. Leningrad, Iskusstvo, 1939.

3. Quoted in Moussinac, op. cit., pp. 12, 14.

4. Gvozdëv, op. cit.

5. Moussinac, op. cit., p. 16.

6. Gvozdëv, op. cit.

7. The context of these opening titles can be found in the printed treatment of *Old and New*, in *Film Writing Forms*, edited by Lewis Jacobs. New York, Gotham Book Mart, 1934.

8. In *Novi Zritel*, No. 35, 1926.

"DICKENS, GRIFFITH, AND THE FILM TODAY"

1. George Bernard Shaw, *Back to Methuselah* (Preface). London, 1921.

2. Gilbert Keith Chesterton, *Charles Dickens, The Last of the Great Men*. New York, The Readers Club, 1942, p. 107.

3. Mrs. D. W. Griffith, *When the Movies Were Young*. New York, E. P. Dutton & Company, 1925, p. 66.

4. Stefan Zweig, *Three Masters: Balzac, Dickens, Dostoyevsky*, translated by Eden and Cedar Paul. New York, The Viking Press, 1930, pp. 51-53.

5. A Philadelphia newspaper, New York correspondent, December 1867.

6. Letters of January 5 and 9, 1868; quoted in John Forster, *The Life of Charles Dickens*. London, Chapman and Hall, 1892.

7. T. A. Jackson, *Charles Dickens; The Progress of a Radical*. New York, International Publishers, 1938, pp. 250-251, 297-298.

8. Zweig, op. cit.

9. George Henry Lewes, "Dickens in Relation to Criticism," *The Fortnightly Review*, February 1, 1872, p. 149.
10. Quoted in Forster, op. cit., p. 364.
11. Charles Dickens, *Nicholas Nickleby*, Chap. XXXII.
12. Charles Dickens, *Hard Times*, Book I, Chap. V.
13. Lewis Jacobs, *The Rise of the American Film*. New York, 1939, pp. 101-103.
14. Iris Barry, *D. W. Griffith, American Film Master*. New York, The Museum of Modern Art, 1940, p. 15.
15. Ibid., pp. 16-17.
16. This, and the following citations from Brady's reminiscences are quoted from his "Drama in Homespun," *Stage*, January 1937, pp. 98-100.
17. William A. Brady, *Showman*. New York, E. P. Dutton & Co., 1937.
18. This entire issue has been reproduced in *Phoenixiana*, edited by Francis P. Farquhar, San Francisco, The Grabhorn Press, 1937.
19. "Phoenix at Benicia" (first printed in the *Pioneer*, July 1855), ibid., p. 175.
20. V. A. Bogoroditzky, *General Course in Russian Grammar*. Moscow-Leningrad, 1935, p. 203.
21. Ivan I. Meshchaninov, *General Linguistics*. Leningrad, 1940.
22. Gilbert Seldes, *The Movies Come from America*. New York, Scribner's, 1937, pp. 23-24.
23. Gilbert Seldes, *The Seven Lively Arts*. New York, Harper & Brothers, 1924.
24. *The Shorter Oxford English Dictionary*.
25. Terry Ramsaye, *A Million and One Nights*. New York, Simon and Schuster, 1926.
26. Robert Edgar Long, *David Wark Griffith*. D. W. Griffith Service, 1920.
27. Fritz Mauthner, *Beitrage zu einer Kritik der Sprache: Zweiter Band, Zur Sprachwissenschaft.* Leipzig, Felix Meiner, 1923, pp. 487-488.
28. Ralph Waldo Emerson, "The Poet." In *Essays: Second Series*.
29. A. A. Potebnya, *From Notes on a Theory of Literature*. Kharkov, 1905.
30. Richard Maria Werner [?].
31. Potebnya, op. cit., p. 203.
32. Johann Ludwig Tieck, *Die Gemälde;* cited translation published London, 1825.
33. Potebnya, op. cit., p. 490.
34. Joseph Vendryes, *Language, A Linguistic Introduction to History*, translated by Paul Radin. New York, Alfred A. Knopf, 1925, pp. 145-146.
35. Alexander Semyonovich Shishkov, *Collected Works and Translations*. St. Petersburg, 1825, Part 5, p. 229.

The Film Sense

TRANSLATOR'S NOTE

Sergei Eisenstein's contribution to the film medium is a double one—as film-maker and as film-teacher. Since all but one of his six completed films have enjoyed wide circulation in this country, his contribution as a creative director is well-known. American and English film-makers have had, however, only scattered opportunities to appreciate his contribution in the field of theory. His Soviet pupils in the State Institute of Cinematography are his chief beneficiaries in this regard.

This film-maker's first book of theory is primarily for the use of other film-makers. Yet, without any paradoxical intent, it can be said that only such a professionally aimed book can to any appreciable extent inform the layman or the artist in another medium, or can encourage the reader to dive below the surface of general appreciation.

One factor is so taken for granted in Eisenstein's native land that it obviously seemed unnecessary to stress it in this text. He has discussed in detail certain means whereby the spectator's reactions can be fused with the creative process, producing a richer emotional expression of a film's theme. But the thoroughness with which he investigates these means should mislead no one into assuming that in his view they represent ends in themselves, or that an emotion or a sensation represents an end in itself. The purposive direction of the spectator's emotion is a social responsibility, and all art in the Soviet Union is conscious of that responsibility—in time of peace as well as of war. This social function—which today merits particular attention from our own film-makers—underlines every word of Eisenstein's film theory.

Although this is Eisenstein's first book, its uncompromising persistence of argument will not surprise readers who have followed his articles on film theory as they have appeared in American and English journals. For readers to whom the present work is an introduction to Eisenstein as analyst, a guide to his earlier writing has been provided among the appendices.

The choice of documents in the appendices has been governed largely by an effort to show the stages of a film concept on its way to completed film form—from the first sketched structure of *Que Viva Mexico*, through the notes for picture and sound images of *Sutter's Gold*, through the first full outline of a sequence in *An American Tragedy*, to the blueprint of *Ferghana Canal*—ready for final construction. (The searching reader will discover in this last fragment evidence that Eisenstein has employed the contents of this book to teach himself as well as others.) The analysis of *Alexander Nevsky* in Part IV, "Form and Content: Practice," covers that final stage.

Work on this book provided the kind of pleasure which leaves no room for discussion of difficulties. The only just complaints can come from the many friends

upon whom I imposed for the purpose of presenting in
its maximum clarity the material of the book. My greatest debt is to Miss Leda Swan for her unstinting contribution of her knowledge of the Russian language. In
the other language problems—the translations of the
French and German citations from Eisenstein's unlimited
field of reference—I am indebted to Helen Grayson,
Leonard Mins and Samuel Brody. The text has been
materially enriched by Muriel Rukeyser's translation of
Rimbaud's *Voyelles*, prepared for this volume. The
Chinese citation has been provided through the courtesy
of Dr. Chi-Chen Wang of Columbia University, the
characters themselves having been lent by the Yale University Press.

The translation has further benefited by the attention
and patience with which Lee Strasberg examined the
manuscript and Max Goberman's check on its musical
material. I owe thanks to Jack Rau for his adaptations
of the original Russian diagrams. A special kind of grati-
tude is due to the U.S.S.R. Society for Cultural Relations with Foreign Countries (VOKS) for their interest
and their facilitating this American edition.

Part I of this book is substantially as translated by
Stephen Garry as "Montage in 1938" in *Life and Letters
Today*, London, and it is through the kind permission
of translator and publisher that we are using it in this
form.

The section entitled Sources, beginning on page 276,
lists the books to which the author refers or the editions from which citations have been made. Acknowl-

edgment is due the publishing houses of Covici, Friede; Dodd, Mead; E. P. Dutton; Houghton Mifflin; International Publishing Company; Alfred A. Knopf; Little, Brown; Macmillan; Random House and Reynal & Hitchcock for permission to reprint from their books. Thanks are due *Theatre Arts Monthly* for their gracious loan of the engraving of *The Life of Sir Henry Unton*.

There is another debt—a basic debt—to be acknowledged: to those institutions whose profession is intelligent assistance. I want to thank at this time the staffs in the Libraries of Congress, of Columbia University, of the American-Russian Institute, of the Metropolitan Museum, of the Museum of Modern Art, of the Hispanic Society, of the Academy of Medicine and the Frick Art Reference Library. Literally all departmental staffs of the New York Public Library were generous with their time, undoubtedly through the force of generous habit.

J. L.

Although the author is himself of the profession and knows the things that long practice, aided by much special reflection, can teach him about it, he will not linger as much as might be thought over that part of the art which seems the whole of art to many mediocre artists, but without which art would not exist. He will thus seem to encroach on the domain of the critics of esthetic affairs, men who doubtless think that practice is not needed for them to rise to speculative consideration of the arts.

He will treat of philosophic more than of technical matters. That may seem singular in a painter who writes on the arts: many semi-erudite men have treated the philosophy of art. It would seem that their profound ignorance of technical matters was looked on by them as a title to respect, persuaded as they were that preoccupation with this matter, so vital to every art, debarred professional artists from esthetic speculation.

It would seem almost that they had imagined a profound ignorance of technical matters to be one reason more for rising to purely metaphysical considerations, in a word that preoccupation with a craft must render professional artists rather unfit to rise to the heights which are forbidden to the people outside esthetics and pure speculation.

EUGÈNE DELACROIX [1]

WORD AND IMAGE

Every word has been permeated, as every image has been transmuted, through the imaginative intensity of one compelling creative act. "Consider it well," says Abt Vogler of the musician's analogous miracle:

> Consider it well: each tone of our scale in itself is nought;
>> It is everywhere in the world—loud, soft, and all is said:
>
> Give it to me to use! I mix it with two in my thought:
>> And, there! Ye have heard and seen: consider and bow the head!

Give Coleridge one vivid word from an old narrative; let him mix it with two in his thought; and then (translating terms of music into terms of words) "out of three sounds he [will] frame, not a fourth sound, but a star."

JOHN LIVINGSTON LOWES [2]

THERE was a period in Soviet cinema when montage was proclaimed "everything." Now we are at the close of a period during which montage has been regarded as "nothing." Regarding montage neither as nothing nor everything, I consider it opportune at this juncture to recall that montage is just as indispensable a component feature of film production as any other element of film effectiveness. After the storm "for montage" and the battle "against montage," we must approach its problems simply and afresh. This is all the more necessary because in the period of "renunciation" of montage, its most incontrovertible aspect, the one really immune to challenge, was also repudiated. The point is that the creators of a number of films in recent years have so completely "discarded" montage that they have forgotten even its basic aim and function: that rôle set itself by every work of art, *the need for connected and sequential exposition of the theme, the material, the plot, the action,* the movement within the film sequence and within the film drama as a whole. Aside from the *excitement* of a story, or even its logic or continuity, the simple matter of telling *a connected story* has often been lost in the works of some outstanding film masters, working in various types of films. What we need, of course, is not so much an individual criticism of those masters, but

3

primarily an organized effort to recover the montage culture that so many have lost. This is all the more necessary since our films are faced with the task of presenting not only a narrative that is *logically connected*, but one that contains a *maximum of emotion and stimulating power*.

Montage is a mighty aid in the resolution of this task.

Why do we use montage at all? Even the most fanatical opponent of montage will agree that it is not merely because the film strip at our disposal is not of infinite length, and consequently, being condemned to working with pieces of restricted lengths, we have to stick one piece of it on to another occasionally.

The "leftists" of montage saw it from the opposite extreme. While playing with pieces of film, they discovered a certain property in the toy which kept them astonished for a number of years. This property consisted in the fact *that two film pieces of any kind, placed together, inevitably combine into a new concept, a new quality, arising out of that juxtaposition*.

This is not in the least a circumstance peculiar to the cinema, but is a phenomenon invariably met with in all cases where we have to deal with juxtaposition of two facts, two phenomena, two objects. We are accustomed to make, almost automatically, a definite and obvious deductive generalization when any separate objects are placed before us side by side. For example, take a grave, juxtaposed with a woman in mourning weeping beside it, and scarcely anybody will fail to jump to the conclusion: *a widow*. It is precisely on this feature of our perception that the following miniature story by Ambrose Bierce bases its effect. It is from his *Fantastic Fables* and is entitled "The Inconsolable Widow":

A Woman in widow's weeds was weeping upon a grave. "Console yourself, madam," said a Sympathetic Stranger. "Heaven's mercies are infinite. There is another man somewhere, besides your husband, with whom you can still be happy."

"There was," she sobbed—"there was, but this is his grave." [3]

The whole effect of this is built upon the circumstance that the grave and the woman in mourning beside it lead to the inference, from established convention, that she is a widow mourning her husband, whereas in fact the man for whom she is weeping is her lover.

The same circumstance is often found in riddles—for example, this one from international folk-lore: "The raven flew, while a dog sat on its tail. How can this be?" We automatically combine the juxtaposed elements and reduce them to a unity. As a result, we understand the query as though the dog were sitting on the tail of the raven, while actually, the riddle contains two unrelated actions: the raven flies, while the dog sits on its own tail.

This tendency to bring together into a unity two or more independent objects or qualities is very strong, even in the case of separate words, characterizing different aspects of some single phenomenon.

An extreme instance of this can be found in that inventor of the "portmanteau word," Lewis Carroll. His modest declaration of his invention, of "two meanings packed into one word like a portmanteau," concludes his introduction to *The Hunting of the Snark:*

For instance, take the two words "fuming" and "furious." Make up your mind that you will say both words, but leave it unsettled which you will say first. Now open your mouth and speak. If your thoughts incline ever so little towards "fuming," you will say "fuming-furious"; if they turn, by even a hair's breadth, towards "furious," you will say "furious-fuming"; but if you have that rarest of gifts, a perfectly balanced mind, you will say "frumious." [4]

Of course, in this instance we do not gain a new concept, or a new quality. The charm of this "portmanteau" effect is built upon the sensation of duality residing in the arbitrarily formed single word. Every language has its "portmanteau" practitioner—the American language has its Walter Winchell. Obviously, the greatest manipulation of the portmanteau word is to be found in *Finnegans Wake.*

Essentially, therefore, Carroll's method is a *parody* of a natural phenomenon, a part of our common perception—the formation of qualitatively new unities; hence it is a basic method of building comic effects.

This comic effect is achieved through the perception of both the new result and its two independent parts—all at the same time. Instances of this kind of wit are innumerable. I shall cite here only three such examples that one can find — in Freud:

During the war between Turkey and the Balkan States, in 1912, *Punch* depicted the part played by Roumania by representing the latter as a highwayman holding up the members of the Balkan alliance. The picture was entitled: *Kleptoroumania*. . . .

A naughty jest of Europe has rebaptized a former potentate, Leopold, into *Cleopold* because of his relation to a lady surnamed Cleo. . . .

In a short story . . . one of the characters, a "sport," speaks of the Christmas season as the *alcoholidays*. By reduction it can be easily seen that we have here a compound word, a combination of *alcohol* and *holidays*. . . .[5]

I think it is apparent that the phenomenon we are discussing is more than widespread—it is literally universal.

Hence there is nothing surprising in the circumstance that a film audience also draws a definite inference from the juxtaposition of two strips of film cemented together.

We are certainly not criticizing all these facts, nor their noteworthiness, nor universality, but simply the false deductions and conclusions that have been drawn from them. On this basis it will be possible to make the necessary corrections.

Of what omission were we guilty when we first remarked the undoubted importance of the above phenomenon to an understanding and mastery of montage? What was true, and what false, in our enthusiastic declarations at that time?

The basic fact was true, and remains true to this day, that the juxtaposition of two separate shots by splicing them together resembles not so much a simple sum of one shot plus another shot—as it does a *creation*. It re-

sembles a creation—rather than a sum of its parts—
from the circumstance that in every such juxtaposition
the result is qualitatively distinguishable from each component element viewed separately. At this late date no
one need really be reminded that quantity and quality
are not two different properties of a phenomenon but
only different aspects of the same phenomenon. This
law of physics is just as true in other spheres of science
and in art. Of the many fields to which it can be applied,
Professor Koffka's application of it to the field of behavior is apropos to our discussion:

It has been said: The whole is more than the sum of its
parts. It is more correct to say that the whole is something
else than the sum of its parts, because summing is a mean-
ingless procedure, whereas the whole-part relationship is
meaningful.[6]

The woman, to return to our first example, is a representation, the mourning robe she is wearing is a representation—that is, both are *objectively representable.*
But "*a widow,*" arising from a juxtaposition of the two
representations, is objectively unrepresentable—a new
idea, a new conception, a new image.

What was the "distortion" in our attitude at that time
to this indisputable phenomenon?

The error lay in placing the main emphasis on the
possibilities of juxtaposition, while less attention seemed
to be paid to the problem of *analyzing* the *material* that
was juxtaposed.

My critics did not fail to represent this as a lack of
interest in the *content* of the film shot-pieces, confusing

research in one aspect of a problem with the attitude of the researcher to the representation of reality.

I leave them to their consciences.

The trouble arose from my having been charmed primarily with that newly revealed feature of the film strips—that, no matter how unrelated they might be, and frequently despite themselves, they engendered a "third something" and became correlated when juxtaposed according to the will of an editor.

Hence I was preoccupied by a potentiality untypical in normal film construction and film composition.

Operating at the outset with such material and such occurrences, it was natural to speculate principally upon the potentialities of juxtaposition. Less attention was given to an *analysis* of the actual nature of the pieces juxtaposed. Such attention would not have been sufficient in itself. History has proven that such attention, directed solely to the content of single shots, led in practice to a decline of montage to a level of "special effects," "montage sequences," etc., with all the consequences this involved.

What should have been the proper emphasis, what should have received the principal attention, in order that neither element would be unduly exaggerated?

It was necessary to turn to that fundamental basis which equally determines both the content enclosed by single frames and the compositional juxtaposition of these separate contents with each other, i.e., to the content of the *whole*, of the general and *unifying* needs.

One extreme consisted in distraction with problems of

the technique of unification (the methods of montage), the other—with the unified elements (the content of the shot).

We should have occupied ourselves more with an examination of the nature of the *unifying principle* itself. This is precisely that principle which should determine both the content of the shot and that content which is revealed through a given *juxtaposition of these shots.*

But with this in mind it was necessary for the researcher's interest to be turned primarily not in the direction of paradoxical cases, where this whole, general, final result is not *foreseen* but emerges unexpectedly. We should have turned to those cases where the shot-pieces are not only not unrelated to each other, but where this *final,* this *general,* this *whole* result is not merely foreseen, but itself predetermines both the individual elements and the circumstances of their juxtaposition. Such cases are normal, generally accepted and frequent in occurrence. In such cases the whole emerges perfectly as "a third something." The full picture of the whole, as determined both by the shot and by montage, also emerges, vivifying and distinguishing both the content of the shot and the content of the montage. It is cases of this kind that are typical for cinematography.

With montage considered in this light, both single shots and their juxtaposition fall into a correct mutual relationship. In addition to this, the very nature of montage not only ceases to be divorced from the principles of realistic film delineation, but serves as one of the most coherent and practical resources for realistic narration of film content.

What is essentially involved in such an understanding of montage? In such a case, each montage piece exists no longer as something unrelated, but as a given *particular representation* of the general theme that in equal measure penetrates *all* the shot-pieces. The juxtaposition of these partial details in a given montage construction calls to life and forces into the light that *general* quality in which each detail has participated and which binds together all the details into a *whole*, namely, into that generalized *image*, wherein the creator, followed by the spectator, experiences the theme.

If *now* we consider two pieces of film placed together, we appreciate their juxtaposition in a rather different light. Namely:

Piece *A* (derived from the elements of the theme being developed) and piece *B* (derived from the same source) in juxtaposition give birth to the image in which the thematic matter is most clearly embodied.

Expressed in the imperative, for the sake of stating a more exact working formula, this proposition would read:

Representation A and *representation* B must be so selected from all the possible features within the theme that is being developed, must be so sought for, that their *juxtaposition*—that is, the juxtaposition of *those very elements* and not of alternative ones—shall evoke in the perception and feelings of the spectator the most complete *image of the theme itself*.

Into our discussion of montage two new terms have entered: "representation" and "image." I want to define the demarcation between these terms before we proceed further.

We turn to an example for demonstration. Take a white circular disc of average size and smooth surface, its circumference divided into sixty equal parts. At every fifth division is set a figure in the order of succession of 1 to 12. At the center of the disc are fixed two metal rods, moving freely on their fixed ends, pointed at their free ends, one being equal to the radius of the disc, the other rather shorter. Let the longer pointed rod have its free end resting at the figure 12, and the shorter, in succession, have its free end pointing toward the figures 1, 2, 3, and so on up to 12. This will comprise a series of *geometrical* representations of successive relations of the two metal rods to one another expressed in the dimensions 30, 60, 90 degrees, and so on up to 360 degrees.

If, however, this disc be provided with a mechanism that imparts steady movement to the metal rods, the geometrical figure formed on its surface acquires a special meaning: it is now not simply a *representation*, it is an *image* of time.

In this instance, the representation and the image it evokes in our perception are so completely fused that only under special conditions do we distinguish the geometrical figure formed by the hands on the dial of the clock from the concept of time. Yet this can happen

to any one of us, given, admittedly, the unusual circumstances.

It happened to Vronsky after Anna Karenina tells
him that she is pregnant:

> When Vronsky looked at his watch on the Karenins'
> verandah he was so agitated and so preoccupied that he
> saw the hands and the face of the watch without realizing
> the time.[7]

In his case, the *image* of time created by the watch
did not arise. He saw only the geometrical representation formed by the watch dial and the hands.

As we can see in even so simple an instance, where
the question touches only astronomical time, the hour,
the representation formed by the clock dial is insufficient in itself. It is not enough merely to see—something has to happen to the representation, something
more has to be done with it, before it can cease to be
perceived as no more than a simple geometrical figure
and can become perceptible as the image of some particular "time" at which the event is occurring. Tolstoy
points out to us what happens when this process does
not take place.

What exactly is this process? A given order of hands
on the dial of a clock invokes a host of representations
associated with the time that corresponds to the given
order. Suppose, for example, the given figure be five.
Our imagination is trained to respond to this figure by
calling to mind pictures of all sorts of events that occur
at that hour. Perhaps tea, the end of the day's work, the

beginning of rush hour on the subway, perhaps shops closing, or the peculiar late afternoon light . . . In any case we will automatically recall a series of pictures (representations) of what happens at five o'clock.

The image of five o'clock is compounded of all these individual pictures.

This is the full sequence of the process, and it is such at the point of assimilating the representations formed by the figures which evoke the images of the times of day and night.

Thereafter the laws of economy of psychic energy come into force. There occurs "condensation" within the process above described: the chain of intervening links falls away, and there is produced instantaneous connection between the figure and our perception of the time to which it corresponds. The example of Vronsky shows us that a sharp mental disturbance can cause this connection to be destroyed, and the representation and the image become severed from each other.

We are considering here the *full* presentation of the process which takes place when an image is formed from a representation, as described above.

These "mechanics" of the formation of an image interest us because the mechanics of its formation in *life* turn out to be the prototype of the method of creating images in art.

To recapitulate: between the representation of an hour on the dial of the clock and our perception of the image of that hour, there lies a long chain of linked representations of separate characteristic aspects of that hour. And we repeat: that psychological habit tends to reduce this intervening chain to a minimum, so that only the beginning and the end of the process are perceived.

But as soon as we need, for any reason, to establish a connection between a representation and the image to be evoked by it in the consciousness and feelings, we are inevitably compelled to resort again to a chain of intervening representations, which, in aggregate, form the image.

Consider first an example approximating closely the other example from everyday life.

In New York City most of the streets have no names. Instead, they are distinguished by numbers—Fifth Avenue, Forty-second Street, and so on. Strangers find this method of designating streets extraordinarily difficult to remember at first. We are used to streets with names, which is much easier for us, because each name at once brings up an image of the given street, i.e., when you hear the street name, this evokes a particular complex of sensations and, together with them, the image.

I found it very difficult to remember the *images* of New York's streets and, consequently, to recognize the streets themselves. Their designations, neutral numbers like "Forty-second" or "Forty-fifth," failed to produce images in my mind that would concentrate my perception on the general features of one or the other street. To produce these images, I had to fix in my memory a set of objects characteristic of one or another street, a set of objects aroused in my consciousness in answer to the signal "Forty-second," and quite distinct from

those aroused by the signal "Forty-fifth." My memory
assembled the theaters, stores and buildings, characteristic of each of the streets I had to remember. This
process went through definite stages. Two of these
stages should be noted: in the first, at the verbal designation: "Forty-second Street," my memory with great
difficulty responded by enumerating the whole chain of
characteristic elements, but I still obtained no true perception of the street because the various elements had
not yet been consolidated into a single image. Only in
the second stage did all the elements begin to fuse into
a single, emerging image: at the mention of the street's
"number," *there still arose this whole host of its separate
elements, but now not as a chain, but as something single*
—as a whole characterization of the street, *as its whole
image.*

Only after this stage could one say that one had really
memorized the street. The image of the given street began to emerge and live in the consciousness and perception exactly as, in the course of creating a work of art,
its single, recognizable whole image is gradually composed out of its elements.

In both cases—whether it be a question of memorizing
or the process of perceiving a work of art—the procedure of entering the consciousness and feelings through
the whole, the whole *through the image*, remains obedi-
ent to this law.

Further, though the image enters the consciousness
and perception *through aggregation*, every detail is preserved in the sensations and memory *as part of the*

whole. This obtains whether it be a sound image—some rhythmic or melodic sequence of sounds, or whether it be a plastic, a visual image, embracing in pictorial form a remembered series of separate elements.

In one way or another, the series of ideas is built up in the perception and consciousness into a whole image, storing up the separate elements.

We have seen that in the process of remembering there are two very essential stages: the first is the *assembling* of the image, while the second consists in the *result* of this assembly and its significance for the memory. In this latter stage it is important that the memory should pay as little attention as possible to the first stage, and reach the result after passing through the stage of assembling as swiftly as possible. Such is practice in life in contrast to practice in art. For when we proceed into the sphere of art, we discover a marked displacement of emphasis. Actually, to achieve its result, a work of art directs all the refinement of its methods to the *process*.

A work of art, understood dynamically, is just this process of arranging images in the feelings and mind of the spectator.* It is this that constitutes the peculiarity of a truly vital work of art and distinguishes it from a lifeless one, in which the spectator receives the represented result of a given consummated process of creation, instead of being drawn into the process as it occurs.

* Later we shall see that this same dynamic principle lies at the base of all truly vital images, even in such an apparently immobile and static medium as, for example, painting.

This condition obtains everywhere and always, no matter what the art form under discussion. For example, the lifelike acting of an actor is built, not on his representing the copied results of feelings, but on his causing the feelings to *arise, develop, grow into other feelings— to live before the spectator.*

Hence the image of a scene, a sequence, of a whole creation, exists not as something fixed and ready-made. It has to arise, to unfold before the senses of the spectator.

In the same way a character (both in the writing and in the performing of a rôle), if it is to produce a genuinely living impression, must be built up for the spectator in the course of the action, and not be presented as a clockwork figure with set *a priori* characteristics.

In drama it is particularly important that the course of the action should not only build up an *idea* of the character, but also should build up, should "image," *the character itself.*

Consequently, in the actual method of creating images, a work of art must reproduce that process whereby, *in life itself,* new images are built up in the human consciousness and feelings.

We have just shown the nature of this in our example of the numbered streets. And we should be correct in expecting an artist, faced with the task of expressing a given image by factual representation, to resort to a method precisely like this "assimilation" of the streets of New York.

We also used the example of the representation

formed by the dial of a clock, and revealed the process
whereby the image of time arises in consequence of this
representation. To create an image, a work of art must
rely upon a precisely analogous method, the construction of a chain of representations.

Let us examine more broadly this example of time.

With Vronsky, above, the geometrical figure failed
to come to life as an image of time. But there are cases
when what is important is not to perceive the hour of
twelve midnight chronometrically, but to experience
midnight in all the associations and sensations the author
chooses to evoke in pursuance of his plot. It may be an
hour of the anxious awaiting of a midnight assignation,
an hour of death at midnight, the hour of a fateful midnight elopement, in other words it may well be far from
a simple representation of the chronometrical hour of
twelve midnight.

In such a case, *from a representation of the twelve
strokes* must emerge the image of midnight as a kind of
"hour of fate," charged with significance.

This can also be illustrated by an example—this time
from Maupassant's *Bel Ami*. The example has an additional interest in that it is auditory. And yet another
because, in its nature pure montage, by the correctly
chosen method of its resolution it is presented in the
story as a narration of actual events.

The scene is the one where Georges Duroy (who
now writes his name Du Roy) is waiting in the cab for
Suzanne, who has agreed to flee with him at midnight.

Here twelve o'clock at night is only in the slightest

degree the chronometrical hour and is in the greatest degree the hour at which all (or at any rate a very great deal) is at stake. (*"It is all over. It is a failure. She won't come."*)

This is how Maupassant drives into the reader's consciousness and feelings the image of this hour and its *significance,* in distinction from a mere description of the particular time of night:

He went out towards eleven o'clock, wandered about some time, took a cab, and had it drawn up in the Place de la Concorde, by the Ministry of Marine. From time to time he struck a match to see the time by his watch. When he saw midnight approaching, his impatience became feverish. Every moment he thrust his head out of the window to look. A distant clock struck twelve, then another nearer, then two together, then a last one, very far away. When the latter had ceased to sound, he thought: "It is all over. It is a failure. She won't come." He had made up his mind, however, to wait till daylight. In these matters one must be patient.

He heard the quarter strike, then the half-hour, then the quarter to, and all the clocks repeated "one," as they had announced midnight. . . .[8]

In this example, we see that when Maupassant wanted to chisel into the reader's consciousness and sensations the *emotional* quality of the midnight hour, he did not confine himself to saying merely that first midnight struck and then one. He forced us to experience the sensation of midnight by making twelve o'clock strike in various places on various clocks. Combining in our perception, these individual groups of twelve strokes are built up into a general sensation of midnight. *The separate representations are built up into an image.* This was done entirely through montage.

The example from Maupassant can serve as a model for the most polished kind of montage scripting, where "12 o'clock" in sound is denoted by means of a whole series of shots "from different camera-angles": "distant," "nearer," "very far away." This striking of the clocks, recorded at various distances, is like the shooting of an object from various camera set-ups and repeated in a series of three different shot-pieces: "long shot," "medium shot," "distant shot." Moreover, the actual striking or, more correctly, the varied striking of the clocks is chosen not in the least for its virtue as a naturalistic detail of Paris at night. The primary effect of this conflicting striking of clocks in Maupassant is the insistent stressing of the emotional image of the "fateful midnight hour," not the mere information that it is "12:00 P.M."

If his object had been merely to convey the information that it was then twelve o'clock at night, Maupassant would scarcely have resorted to such a polished piece of writing. Just as, without a carefully chosen creative-montage solution of this kind, he would never have achieved, by such simple means, so palpable an emotional effect.

While we are on the subject of clocks and hours, I am reminded of an example from my own practice. During the filming of *October*, we came across, in the Winter Palace, a curious specimen of clock: in addition to the main clock dial, it possessed also a wreath of small dials ranged around the rim of the large one. On each of the dials was the name of a city: Paris, London, New York, Shanghai, and so on. Each told the time as it happened to be in each city, in contrast with the time in Petrograd shown by the main face. The appearance of this clock stuck in our memory. And when in our film we needed to drive home especially forcefully the historic moment of victory and establishment of Soviet power, this clock suggested a specific montage solution: we repeated the hour of the fall of the Provisional Government, depicted on the main dial in Petrograd time, throughout the whole series of subsidiary dials recording the time in London, Paris, New York, Shanghai. Thus this hour, unique in history and in the destiny of peoples, emerged through all the multitudinous variety of local readings of time, as though uniting and fusing all peoples in the perception of the moment of victory. The same concept was also illuminated by a rotating movement of the wreath of dials itself, a movement which, as it grew and accelerated, also made a plastic fusion of all the different and separate indices of time in the sensation of one single historic hour. . . .

At this point I hear a question from my invisible opponents: "That's all very well for you to say, but what about a single unbroken, uncut strip of film containing the performance of an actor—what has this to do with montage? Doesn't his acting, of itself, make an impression? Doesn't the performance of a rôle by Cherkasov *

* Nikolai Cherkasov, as Prof. Polezhayev in *Baltic Deputy*, the Tzarevich Alexei in *Peter the First*, and as Alexander Nevsky.

or Okhlopkov,* Chirkov † or Sverdlin ‡ also make an impression?" It is futile to suppose that this question inflicts a mortal blow on the conception of montage. The principle of montage is far broader than such a question assumes. It is entirely incorrect to assume that if an actor acts in a single unbroken strip of film, uncut by the director and cameraman into different camera-angles, that such a construction is untouched by montage! By no means!

In such a case all we have to do is look for montage elsewhere, in fact, *in the performance of the actor.* And the question of the extent to which the principle of the "inner" technique of acting is related to montage we shall discuss later. At the moment it will be sufficient to let a leading artist of the stage and screen, George Arliss, contribute to this question:

I had always believed that for the movies, acting must be exaggerated, but I saw in this one flash that *restraint* was the chief thing that the actor had to learn in transferring his art from the stage to the screen. . . . The art of restraint and suggestion on the screen may any time be studied by watching the acting of the inimitable Charlie Chaplin.[9]

To emphasized representation (exaggeration), Arliss counterposes restraint. He sees the degree of this re-

* Nikolai Okhlopkov, as Vasili in *Lenin in October* and *Lenin in 1918,* and as Vasili Buslai in *Alexander Nevsky.*

† Boris Chirkov, as Maxim in the *Maxim* Trilogy, and as *The New Teacher.*

‡ Lev Sverdlin, as the spy Tzoi, in *In the Far East,* Colonel Usizhima in *The Defense of Volochayevsk,* and as Chubenko in *Guerrilla Brigade.*

straint in the reduction of actuality to suggestion. He rejects not merely the exaggerated representation of actuality, but even the representation of actuality in entirety! In its place he counsels suggestion. But what is "suggestion" if it not be an element, a detail of actuality, a "close-up" of actuality, which, in juxtaposition with other details, serves as a determination of the entire fragment of actuality? Thus, according to Arliss, the fused effective piece of acting is nothing but a juxtaposition of determining close-ups of this kind; combined, they create the image of the acting's content. And, to proceed further, the actor's acting may have the character of a flat representation or of a genuine image according to the method he uses to construct his performance. Even though his performance be shot entirely from a single set-up (or even from a single seat in a theater auditorium), none the less—in a felicitous case—the performance will itself be "montage" in character.

It should be remarked that the second example of montage cited above (from *October*) is not an example of everyday montage, and that the first example (from Maupassant) illustrates only a case where an object is shot from various set-ups with various camera-angles.

Another example that I will cite is quite typical for cinematography, no longer concerned with an individual object, but instead, with an image of a whole phenomenon—composed, however, in exactly the same way.

This example is a certain remarkable "shooting-script." In it, from a cumulative massing of contributory details and pictures, an image palpably arises before us.

It was not written as a finished work of literature, but simply as a note of a great master in which he attempted to put down on paper for his own benefit his visualization of The Deluge.

The "shooting-script" to which I refer is Leonardo da Vinci's notes on a representation of The Deluge in painting. I choose this particular example because in it the *audio-visual* picture of The Deluge is presented with an unusual clarity. Such an accomplishment of sound and picture co-ordination is remarkable coming from any painter, even Leonardo:

Let the dark, gloomy air be seen beaten by the rush of opposing winds wreathed in perpetual rain mingled with hail, and bearing hither and thither a vast network of the torn branches of trees mixed together with an infinite number of leaves.

All around let there be seen ancient trees uprooted and torn in pieces by the fury of the winds.

You should show how fragments of mountains, which have been already stripped bare by the rushing torrents, fall headlong into these very torrents and choke up the valleys,

until the pent-up rivers rise in flood and cover the wide plains and their inhabitants.

Again there might be seen huddled together on the tops of many of the mountains many different sorts of animals, terrified and subdued at last to a state of tameness, in company with men and women who had fled there with their children.

And the fields which were covered with water had their waves covered over in great part with tables, bedsteads, boats and various other kinds of rafts, improvised through necessity and fear of death,

upon which were men and women with their children, massed together and uttering various cries and lamentations, dismayed by the fury of the winds which were causing the waters to roll over and over in mighty hurricane, bearing with them the bodies of the drowned;

and there was no object that floated on the water but was covered with various different animals who had made truce and stood huddled together in terror, among them wolves, foxes, snakes and creatures of every kind, fugitives from death.

And all the waves that beat against their sides were striking them with repeated blows from the various bodies of the drowned, and the blows were killing those in whom life remained.

Some groups of men you might have seen with weapons in their hands defending the tiny footholds that remained to them from the lions and wolves and beasts of prey which sought safety there.

Ah, what dreadful tumults one heard resounding through the gloomy air, smitten by the fury of the thunder and the lightning it flashed forth, which sped through it, bearing ruin, striking down whatever withstood its course!

Ah, how many might you have seen stopping their ears with their hands in order to shut out the loud uproar caused through the darkened air by the fury of the winds mingled together with the rain, the thunder of the heavens and the raging of the thunderbolts!

Others were not content to shut their eyes but placing their hands over them, one above the other, would cover them more tightly in order not to see the pitiless slaughter made of the human race by the wrath of God.

Ah me, how many lamentations!

How many in their terror flung themselves down from the rocks! You might have seen huge branches of the giant oaks laden with men borne along through the air by the fury of the impetuous winds.

How many boats were capsized and lying, some whole, others broken in pieces, on the top of men struggling to escape with acts and gestures of despair which foretold an awful death.

Others with frenzied acts were taking their own lives, in despair of ever being able to endure such anguish;

some of these were flinging themselves down from the lofty rocks,

others strangled themselves with their own hands;

some seized hold of their own children,

and with mighty violence slew them at one blow;

some turned their arms against themselves to wound and slay; others falling upon their knees were commending themselves to God.

Alas! how many mothers were bewailing their drowned sons, holding them upon their knees, lifting up open arms to heaven, and with divers cries and shrieks declaiming against the anger of the gods!

Others with hands clenched and fingers locked together gnawed and devoured them with bites that ran blood, crouching down so that their breasts touched their knees in their intense and intolerable agony.

Herds of animals, such as horses, oxen, goats, sheep, were to be seen already hemmed in by the waters and left isolated upon the high peaks of the mountains, all huddling together,

and those in the middle climbing to the top and treading on the others, and waging fierce battles with each other, and many of them dying from want of food.

And the birds had already begun to settle upon men and other animals, no longer finding any land left unsubmerged which was not covered with living creatures.

Already had hunger, the minister of death, taken away their life from the greater number of animals, when the dead bodies already becoming lighter began to rise from out the bottom of the deep waters, and emerged to the surface among the contending waves; and there lay beating one against another, and as balls puffed up with wind rebound back from the spot where they strike, these fell back and lay upon the other dead bodies.

And above these horrors the atmosphere was seen covered with murky clouds that were rent by the jagged course of the raging thunderbolts of heaven, which flashed light hither and thither amid the obscurity of the darkness. . . .[10]

The foregoing was not intended by its author as a poem or literary sketch. Péladan, the editor of the French edition of Leonardo's *Trattata della Pittura*, regards this description as an unrealized plan for a picture, which would have been an unsurpassed "chef d'œuvre of landscape and the representation of elemental struggles." [11] None the less the description is not a chaos but is executed in accordance with features that are characteristic rather of the "temporal" than of the "spatial" arts.

Without appraising in detail the structure of this extraordinary "shooting-script," we must point, however, to the fact that the description follows a quite definite *movement*. Moreover, *the course of this movement* is not in the least fortuitous. The movement follows a definite order, and then, in corresponding *reverse order*, returns to phenomena matching those of the opening. Beginning with a description of the heavens, the picture ends with a similar description, but considerably increased in intensity. Occupying the center is the group of humans and their experiences; the scene develops from the heavens to the humans, and from the humans to the heavens, passing groups of animals. The details of largest scale (the close-ups) are found in the center, at the climax of the description (". . . *hands clenched and fingers locked together . . . bites that ran blood . . .*"). In perfect clarity emerge the typical elements of a montage composition.

The content within each frame of the separate scenes is enforced by the increasing intensity in the action.

Let us consider what we may call the "animal theme": animals trying to escape; animals borne by the flood; animals drowning; animals struggling with human beings; animals fighting one another; the carcasses of drowned animals floating to the surface. Or the progressive disappearance of terra firma from under the feet of the people, animals, birds, reaching its culmination at the point where the birds are forced to settle on the humans and animals, not finding any unsubmerged and unoccupied land. This passage forcibly recalls to us that the distribution of details in a picture on a single plane also presumes movement—a compositionally directed movement of the eyes from one phenomenon to another. Here, of course, movement is expressed less directly than in the film, where the eye *cannot* discern the succession of the sequence of details in any other order than that established by him who determines the order of the montage.

Unquestionably though, Leonardo's exceedingly sequential description fulfills the task not of merely listing the details, but of outlining the trajectory of the future movement of the attention over the surface of the canvas. Here we see a brilliant example of how, in the apparently static simultaneous "co-existence" of details in an immobile picture, there has yet been applied exactly the same montage selection, there is exactly the same ordered succession in the juxtaposition of details, as in those arts that include the time factor.

Montage has a realistic significance when the separate pieces produce, in juxtaposition, the generality, the synthesis of one's theme. This is the image, incorporating the theme.

Turning from this definition to the creative process, we shall see that it proceeds in the following manner. Before the inner vision, before the perception of the creator, hovers a given image, emotionally embodying his theme. The task that confronts him is to transform this image into a few basic *partial representations* which, in their combination and juxtaposition, shall evoke in the consciousness and feelings of the spectator, reader, or auditor, that same initial general image which originally hovered before the creative artist.

This applies both to the image of the work of art as a whole and the image of each separate scene or part. This holds true in precisely the same sense for the actor's creation of an image.

The actor is confronted with exactly the same task: to express, in two, three, or four features of a character or of a mode of behavior, those basic elements which in juxtaposition create the integral image that was worked out by the author, director and the actor himself.

What is most noteworthy in such a method? First and foremost, its dynamism. This rests primarily in the fact that the desired image is *not fixed or ready-made, but arises—is born*. The image planned by author, director and actor is concretized by them in separate representational elements, and is assembled—again and finally —in the spectator's perception. This is actually the final aim of every artist's creative endeavor.

Gorky put this eloquently in a letter to Konstantin Fedin:

You say: You are worried by the question, "how to write?" I have been watching for 25 years how that question worries people . . . Yes, it is a serious question; I have worried about it myself, I do worry about it, and I shall go on worrying about it to the end of my days. But for me the question is formulated: How must I write so that the man, no matter who he may be, shall emerge from the pages of the story about him with that strength of physical palpability of his existence, with that cogency of his *half-imaginary* reality, with which I see and feel him? That is the point as I understand it, that is the secret of the matter. . . .[12]

Montage helps in the resolution of this task. The strength of montage resides in this, that it includes in the creative process the emotions and mind of the spectator. The spectator is compelled to proceed along that selfsame creative road that the author traveled in creating the image. The spectator not only sees the represented elements of the finished work, but also experiences the dynamic process of the emergence and assembly of the image just as it was experienced by the author. And this is, obviously, the highest possible degree of approximation to transmitting visually the author's perceptions and intention in all their fullness, to transmitting them with "that strength of physical palpability" with which they arose before the author in his creative work and his creative vision.

Relevant to this part of the discussion is Marx's definition of the course of genuine investigation:

Not only the result, but the road to it also, is a part of truth. The investigation of truth must itself be true, true investigation is unfolded truth, the disjuncted members of which unite in the result.[13] *

* Zur Wahrheit gehört nicht nur das Resultat, sondern auch der Weg. Die Untersuchung der Wahrheit muss selbst wahr sein, die wahre Untersuchung ist die entfaltete Wahrheit, deren auseinander gestreute Glieder sich im Resultat zusammenfassen.

The strength of the method resides also in the circumstance that the spectator is drawn into a creative act in which his individuality is not subordinated to the author's individuality, but is opened up throughout the process of fusion with the author's intention, just as the individuality of a great actor is fused with the individuality of a great playwright in the creation of a classic scenic image. In fact, every spectator, in correspondence with his individuality, and in his own way and out of his own experience—out of the womb of his fantasy, out of the warp and weft of his associations, all conditioned by the premises of his character, habits and social appurtenances, creates an image in accordance with the representational guidance suggested by the author leading him to understanding and experience of the author's theme. This is the same image that was planned and created by the author, but this image is at the same time created also by the spectator himself.

One might think that nothing could be more definite and clear than the almost scientific listing of the details of The Deluge as they pass before us in Leonardo's "shooting-script." Yet how personal and individual are the resulting images that arise in the mind of each reader, deriving from a specification and juxtaposition of details which are shared by all readers of such a document. Each is just as similar and as dissimilar as would be the rôle of Hamlet or Lear played by different actors of different countries, periods, or theaters.

Maupassant offers every reader the same montage construction for the striking of the clocks. He knows that this particular construction will evoke in the perception more than mere information of the hour of night. An experience of the significance of the hour of midnight will be evoked. Each reader hears the striking of the hour identically. But in each reader is born an image of his own, his own representation of midnight and its significance. Each such representation is, in the image sense, individual, dissimilar, and yet identical thematically. And each such image of midnight, while being for every reader at the same time also that of the author, is also equally his own—living, close, intimate.

The image planned by the author has become flesh of the flesh of the spectator's risen image. . . . Within me, as a spectator, this image is born and grown. Not only the author has created, but I also—the creating spectator —have participated.

At the beginning of this chapter I spoke of an emotionally exciting and moving story as distinguished from a logical exposition of facts—as much difference as there is between an experience and an affidavit.

An *affidavit-exposition* would be the corresponding *non-montage* construction in each of the examples that have been cited. In the case of Leonardo da Vinci's notes for The Deluge, an affidavit-exposition would not have taken into consideration as he did the various scales and perspectives to be distributed over the surface of the finished picture, according to his calculations of the trajectory of the spectator's eyes. It would have been

satisfied by a mere display of the dial of a clock telling
the exact time of the overthrow of the Provisional Government. If Maupassant had used such a method in the
passage of Duroy's appointment, it would have been a
curt item of information that the hour of twelve struck.
In other words such an approach conveys bare documentary information, not raised by means of art to a
created exciting force and emotional affect. As affidavit-
expositions, these examples would all be, in film terms,
representations shot from a single set-up. But, as fashioned by artists, they constitute *images*, brought to life
by means of *montage construction*.

And now we can say that it is precisely the *montage*
principle, as distinguished from that of *representation*,
which obliges spectators themselves to *create* and the
montage principle, by this means, achieves that great
power of inner creative excitement * in the *spectator*
which distinguishes an emotionally exciting work from
one that stops without going further than giving information or recording events.

Examining this distinction we discover that the montage principle in films is only a sectional application of

* It is quite obvious that the *theme as such* is capable of exciting
emotionally, independently of the form in which it is presented. A
brief newspaper report of the victory of the Spanish Republicans at
Guadalajara is more moving than a work by Beethoven. But we are
discussing here how, by means of art, to raise a given theme or subject, that may already be exciting "in itself," to a maximum degree
of affectiveness. It is further quite obvious that montage, as such, is
in no way an exhaustive means in this field, though a tremendously
powerful one.

the *montage principle in general*, a principle which, if fully understood, passes far beyond the limits of splicing bits of film together.

As stated above, the compared montage methods of *creation by the spectator* and *creation by the actor* can lead to absorbing conclusions. In this comparison a meeting occurs between the montage method and the sphere of the *inner* technique of the actor; that is, the form of that *inner process* through which the actor creates a living feeling, to be displayed subsequently in the truthfulness of his activity on the stage or on the screen.

A number of systems and doctrines have been erected upon the problems of the actor's performance. More accurately, there are really two or three systems with various offshoots. These offshoot schools are distinguished one from the other not merely by differences in terminology, but chiefly by their varying conceptions of the principal rôle played by *different* basic points of acting technique. Sometimes a school almost completely forgets an entire link in the psychological process of image-creation. Sometimes a link that is *not basic* is raised to the foremost place. Within even such a monolith as the method of the Moscow Art Theatre, with all its body of basic postulates, there are independent offshoots in the interpretation of these postulates.

I have no intention of delving into the nuances of either essential or terminological differences in methods of training or creation with the actor. Our purpose here is to consider those features of inner technique which enter necessarily and directly into the technique of the actor's work and enable it to achieve results—seizing the imagination of the spectator. Any actor or director is, as a matter of fact, in a position to deduce these features from his own "inner" practice, if he would but manage to halt that process in order to examine it. The techniques of the *actor* and the *director* are, in regard to this section of the problem, indistinguishable, since the director in this process is also, to some extent, an actor. From observations of this "actor's share" in my own directorial experience, I shall try to outline this inner technique we are considering through a concrete example. In so doing there is no intention of saying anything *new* on *this* particular question.

Let us suppose that I am faced with the problem of playing the "morning after" of a man who, the night before, has lost government money at cards. Suppose the action to be full of all kinds of matters, including, let us say, a conversation with a completely unsuspecting wife, a scene with a daughter gazing intently at her father whose behavior seems strange, a scene of the embezzler nervously awaiting the telephone call that is to call him to account, and so on.

Suppose that a series of such scenes leads the embezzler into an attempt to shoot himself. The task before the actor is to act the final fragment of the climax, where he arrives at this realization that there is only one solution —suicide—and his hand begins to fumble in the drawer of his writing-table, searching for the revolver. . . .

I believe that it would be almost impossible to find

an actor of any training today who in this scene would start by trying to "act the feeling" of a man on the point of suicide. Each of us, instead of sweating and straining to imagine how a man would behave under such circumstances, would approach the task from quite another direction. We should compel the appropriate consciousness and the appropriate feeling to *take possession* of us. And the authentically felt state, sensation, experience would, in direct consequence, "manifest" itself in true and emotionally correct movements, actions, general behavior. This is the way towards *a discovery of the initiating elements* of correct behavior, correct in the sense that it is appropriate to a genuinely experienced state or feeling.

The next stage of an actor's work consists in compositionally sorting these elements, cleansing them of every fortuitous accretion, refining the premises to the furthest degree of expressiveness. But this is the *following* stage. Our concern here is with the stage *preceding* this.

We are interested in that part of the process in which the actor becomes *possessed* by the feeling. How is this achieved? We have already said that it cannot be done with the "sweating and straining" method. Instead we pursue a path that should be used for all such situations.

What we actually do is compel our imagination to depict for us a number of concrete pictures or situations appropriate to our theme. The aggregation of the pictures so imagined evokes in us the required emotion, the feeling, understanding and actual experience that we are seeking. Naturally the material of these imagined pictures will vary, depending on the particular characteristics of the character and image of the person being played by the actor at the time.

Suppose that a characteristic feature of our embezzler be fear of public opinion. What will chiefly terrify him will not be so much the pangs of conscience, a consciousness of his guilt or the burden of his future imprisonment, as it will be "what will people say?"

Our man, finding himself in this position, will imagine first of all the terrible consequences of his act in these particular terms.

It will be these imagined consequences and their combinations which will reduce the man to such a degree of despair that he will seek a desperate end.

This is exactly how it takes place in life. Terror resulting from awareness of responsibility initiates his feverish pictures of the consequences. And this host of imagined pictures, reacting on the feelings, increases his terror, reducing the embezzler to the utmost limit of horror and despair.

The process is exactly similar to that by which the actor induces a similar state in the conditions of the theater. A difference exists only in his use of will to force his imagination to paint the same pictured consequences that in life a man's imagination would awake spontaneously.

The methods whereby the imagination is induced to do this on the basis of presumed and imaginary circumstances are not at the moment pertinent to my exposition. We are dealing with the process from the point where the imagination is already depicting whatever is necessary for the situation. It is not necessary for the actor to force himself to feel and experience the foreseen consequences. Feeling and experience, like the actions that flow from them, arise of themselves, called to life by the pictures his imagination paints. The living feeling will be evoked by the pictures themselves, by their aggregation and juxtaposition. In seeking ways of waking the required feeling, one can depict to oneself an innumerable quantity of relevant situations and pictures that all advance the theme in various aspects.

By way of example I shall take the first couple of situations that come to me from the multiplicity of imagined pictures. Without weighing them carefully I shall try to record them here as they occur to me. "I am a criminal in the eyes of my former friends and acquaintances. People avoid me. I am ostracized by them," and so on. To feel this through all my senses I follow the process outlined above by depicting to myself concrete situations, actual pictures of the fate that awaits me.

The first situation in which I imagine myself is the courtroom where my case is being tried. The second situation will be my return to normal life after serving my sentence. These notes will attempt to reproduce the plastic and graphic qualities that such multifold fragmentary situations naturally possess when our imagination is fully functioning. The manner in which such situations arise differs with each actor.

This is merely what came to *my* mind when I set *myself* the task:

The courtroom. My case is being tried. I am on the stand. The hall is crowded with people who know me—some casually, some very well. I catch the eye of my neighbor fixed upon me. For thirty years we lived next door to each other. He notices that I have caught him staring at me. His eyes slip past me with feigned abstraction. He stares out of the window, pretending boredom. . . . Another spectator in court—the woman who lives in the apartment above mine. Meeting my look, she drops her gaze terrified, while watching me out of the corners of her eyes. . . . With a clearly motivated half-turn my usual billiards partner presents his back to me. . . . There are the fat owner of the billiards parlor and his wife—staring at me with set insolence. . . . I try to shrink by gazing at my feet. I see nothing, but all around me I hear the whisper of censure and the murmur of voices. Like blow upon blow fall the words of the prosecuting attorney's summing-up. . . .

I imagine the other scene with the same vividness—my return from prison:

The clang of the gates closing behind me as I am released . . . The astonished stare of the servant girl, who stops cleaning the windows next door when she sees me enter my old block . . . There is a new name on the mail-box. . . . The floor of the hall has been newly varnished and there is a new mat outside my door. . . . The door of the next apartment opens. People whom I have never seen look out suspiciously and inquisitively. Their children huddle against them; they instinctively withdraw from my appearance. From below, his spectacles awry on his nose, the old janitor, who remembers me from the past, stares up the stair-well. . . . Three or four faded letters sent to my address before my shame was generally known . . . Two or three coins jingling in my pocket . . . And then—my door is closed in my face by the former acquaintances who now occupy my apartment. . . . My legs reluctantly carry me up the stairs towards the apartment of the woman I used to know and then, when there are only two further steps to go, I turn back. The hurriedly raised collar of a passer-by who recognizes me . . .

And so on. The above is the result of merely jotting down all that crowds through my consciousness and feelings when, either as director or actor, I try to get an emotional grasp of the proposed situation.

After mentally placing myself in the first situation and then mentally passing through the second, doing the same with two or three other relevant situations of various intensities, I gradually arrive at a genuine perception of what awaits me in the future and hence—at a real experiencing of the hopelessness and tragedy of my position. The juxtaposition of the details of the first imagined situation produces one shade of this feeling. The juxtaposition of the details of the second situation—another. Nuance of feeling is added to nuance of feeling, and from all these the image of hopelessness begins to arise, linked inseparably with the sharp emotional experience of actually feeling such hopelessness.

In this way, without straining to act the feeling itself, it is successfully evoked by the assembly and juxtaposition of deliberately selected details and situations from all those that first crowded into the imagination.

It is quite irrelevant here whether the description of this process, as I have outlined it above, tallies or not in its mechanical details with that laid down by this or the other existing school of acting technique. Here the important matter to be settled is that a stage similar to that which I have described exists on every path to the *shaping and intensification* of emotion, whether in real life or in the technique of the creative process. We can convince ourselves of this by a minimum of self-observation, whether in the conditions of creation or in the circumstances of real life.

Another important matter here is the fact that the technique of creation recreates a life process, conditioned only by those special circumstances required by art.

It should be appreciated, of course, that we have been dealing not with the entire body of acting technique, but only with a single link in its system.

We have, for instance, not touched here at all on the nature of the imagination itself, particularly the technique of "warming" it to the point where it paints the pictures we wish it to, those demanded by the particular theme. Lack of space does not allow an examination of these links, though an analysis of them would only confirm the soundness of the assertions made here. For the present we confine ourselves to the point already made, while keeping in mind that the link we have analyzed occupies no greater place in the actor's technique than does montage among the expressive resources of the film. Nor can we assume that montage occupies any lesser place, either.

The question will be asked, In what way does the above presentation in the sphere of the actor's inner technique differ in practice or in principle from that which we had previously outlined as the essence of film montage? The distinction here is in the sphere of application and not in essential method.

Our latter question was how to make the living feelings and experience emerge within the actor.

The former question was how to evoke for the spectator's feelings an emotionally experienced image.

In both questions the static elements, the given factors and the devised factors, all in juxtaposition with one another, give birth to a dynamically emerging emotion, a dynamically emerging image.

We see this as not in the least different in principle from the montage process in film: here is the same sharp concretization of the theme being made perceptible through determining details, the resulting effect of the juxtaposition of the details being the evocation of the feeling itself.

As for the actual nature of these component "visions" that appear before the "inner eye" of the actor, their plastic (or auditory) features are completely homogeneous with the characteristics that are typical of the film shot. The terms "fragments" and "details" as applied above to these visions were not idly chosen, since the imagination does not call up completed pictures, but the decisive and determining properties of these pictures. For if we examine the crowd of "visions" noted down almost automatically above, which I honestly tried to record with the photographic accuracy of a psychological document, we shall see that these "visions" have a positively film-like order—with camera-angles, set-ups at various distances, and rich montage material.

One shot, for example, was chiefly that of a man turning his back, obviously a composition cut by the frame-lines of his back rather than of the whole figure. Two heads with a glassy-eyed and stubborn stare are in contrast to the lowered eyelashes from under which the woman of the apartment above me stole sidelong glances at me—obviously requiring a distinction in the distance of the camera from the subjects. There are several obvious close-ups—of the new mat before the door, of the three envelopes. Or, employing another sense that is just as much a part of our medium—the sound long-shot of the whispering visitors in the courtroom, contrasting with the few coins jingling in my pocket, etc. The mental lens works like this with variety—it enlarges the scale or diminishes it, adjusting as faithfully as a film camera to varying frame requirements—advancing or drawing away the microphone. All that is lacking to turn these imagined fragments into a typical shooting-script is to set numbers before each of the fragments!

This example reveals the secret of writing shooting-scripts with genuine emotion and movement, instead of a mere sprinkling of a numbing alternation of close-ups, medium shots, and long-shots!

The basic validity of the method obtains in both spheres. The first task is the creative breaking-up of the theme into determining representations, and then combining these representations with the purpose of bringing to life *the initiating image of the theme*. And the process whereby this image is perceived is identical with the original experiencing of the theme of the image's content. Just as inseparable from this intense and genuine experience is the work of the director in writing his shooting-script. This is the only way that suggests to him those decisive representations through which the whole image of his theme will flash into creative being.

Herein lies the secret of that emotionally exciting quality of exposition (as distinguished from the affidavit-exposition of mere information) of which we spoke earlier, and which is just as much a condition of a living performance by an actor as of living film-making.

We shall find that a similar crowd of pictures, carefully selected and reduced to the extreme laconism of two or three details, is to be found in the finest examples of literature.

Take Pushkin's narrative poem, *Poltava*—the scene of Kochubei's execution. In this scene the theme of "Kochubei's end" is expressed with unusual vividness in the image of "the end of Kochubei's execution." But the actual image of this end of the execution arises and grows out of the juxtaposition of three almost "documentarily" selected representations of three detail incidents from the episode:

> "Too late," someone then said to them,
> And pointed finger to the field.
> There the fatal scaffold was dismantled,
> A priest in cassock black was praying,
> And onto a wagon was being lifted
> By two cossacks an oaken coffin. . . .[14] *

* In the majority of the following citations from Russian poets a translation has been made to preserve the original relation of sense and line, important to the context. In these translations an effort has

It would be difficult to find a more effective selection
of details to convey the sensation of the image of death
in all its horror, than these from the conclusion of the
execution scene.

The validity of choosing a realistic method to produce
and achieve an emotional quality can be confirmed by
some very curious examples. Here, for instance, is another scene from Pushkin's *Poltava*, in which the poet
magically causes the image of a nocturnal flight to rise
before the reader in all its picturesque and emotional
possibilities:

> But no one knew just how or when
> She vanished. A lone fisherman
> In that night heard the clack of horses' hoofs,
> Cossack speech and a woman's whisper. . . .[15]

Three shots:
1. Clack of horses' hoofs.
2. Cossack speech.
3. A woman's whisper.

Once more three objectively expressed representations (in sound!) come together in an emotionally expressed unifying image, distinct from the perception
of the separate phenomena if encountered apart from
their association with each other. The method is used
solely for the purpose of evoking the necessary emotional experience in the reader. The emotional experience only, because the information that Marya has

been made to preserve also the quantities, but the rhyme is ignored.
Whenever the quotation serves a more general purpose, a recognized
translation is used.—Editor.

vanished has been given in a previous single line (*"She vanished. A lone fisherman"*). Having told the reader that she had vanished, the author wanted to give him the experience as well. To achieve this, he turns to montage. With three details selected from all the elements of flight, his image of nocturnal flight emerges in montage fashion, imparting the experience of the action to the senses.

To the three sound pictures he adds a fourth picture. It has the effect of a full stop. To attain this effect he chooses his fourth picture from another sense. This last "close-up" is not in sound, but in sight:

> . . . And eight horseshoes had left their traces
> Over the meadow morning dew. . . .

Thus Pushkin uses montage in creating the images of a work of art. But Pushkin uses montage just as skillfully when he creates the image of a character, or of an entire *dramatis personae*. With a superlative combination of various aspects (i.e., "camera set-ups") and of different elements (i.e., montage pieces of pictorially represented things, clarified by the framing of the shot) Pushkin gains astonishing reality in his delineations. Man, indeed, complete and feeling, emerges from the pages of Pushkin's poems.

When Pushkin works with a large quantity of montage pieces, his use of montage grows more intricate. Rhythm, constructed with successive long phrases and phrases as short as a single word, introduces a dynamic characteristic to the image of the montage construction.

This rhythm serves to establish the actual temperament of the character being depicted, giving us a dynamic characterization of his behavior.

One can also learn from Pushkin how an orderly succession in transmitting and disclosing a man's characteristics and personality can heighten the total value of the image. An excellent example in this connection is his description of Peter the Great in *Poltava*:

I. . . . And then with highest exaltation
II. There sounded, ringing, Peter's voice:
III. "To arms, God with us!" From the tent,
IV. By crowding favorites surrounded,
V. Peter emerges. His eyes
VI. Are flashing. His look is terrible.
VII. His movements swift. Magnificent he,
VIII. In all his aspect, wrath divine.
IX. He goes. His charger is led him.
X. Fiery and docile faithful steed.
XI. Scenting the fray's fire
XII. It quivers. It turns its eyes aslant
XIII. And dashes into the fight's dust,
XIV. Proud of its mighty rider.[16]

The above numbering is of the poem's lines. Now we shall write out this same passage again as a shooting-script, numbering the "shots" as edited by Pushkin:

1. And then with highest exaltation there sounded, ringing, Peter's voice: "To arms, God with us!"
2. From the tent, by crowding favorites surrounded,
3. Peter emerges.
4. His eyes are flashing.
5. His look is terrible.
6. His movements swift.

7. Magnificent he,
8. In all his aspect, wrath divine.
9. He goes.
10. His charger is led him.
11. Fiery and docile faithful steed.
12. Scenting the fray's fire it quivers.
13. It turns its eyes aslant
14. And dashes into the fight's dust, proud of its mighty rider.

The number of *lines* and the number of *shots* prove to be *identical*, fourteen in each case. But there is almost no internal congruence between the lay-out of the lines and the lay-out of the shots; such congruence occurs only twice in the entire fourteen lines: VIII = 8 and X = 11. Furthermore the content of a shot varies as much as two complete lines (1, 14) and as little as a single word (9).*

This is very instructive for film-workers, particularly those specializing in sound.

Let us examine how Peter is "edited":

Shots 1, 2, 3 contain an excellent example of the *significant* presentation of a figure in action. Here three degrees, three stages of his appearance, are absolutely distinct: (1) Peter is not yet shown, but is introduced in sound—his voice. (2) Peter has emerged from the tent, but he is not yet visible. All we can see is the group of favorites surrounding his emergence from the tent. (3) At last, only in a third stage, is Peter actually seen as he comes from the tent.

* In Russian "he goes" is a single word, *idët* (phonetically, "id-yót").

These are followed by *flashing eyes,* as the most important detail in his general appearance (4). And then—the whole face (5). Only then his full figure is displayed (although very likely cut at the knees by the lower frame-line of a traveling shot) to show his movements, their swiftness and brusqueness. The rhythm of the movement and the character it illuminates are expressed "impetuously" by the clash of short phrases. The full display of the full figure is given only in Shot 7, and now in a manner beyond the conveyance of information —vividly, as an image: "Magnificent he." In the following shot this description is strengthened and heightened: "In all his aspect, wrath divine." Only in this eighth shot does Pushkin reveal Peter with the full power of a plastic representation. This eighth shot, obviously, contains Peter at full height, emphasized by all the resources of shot composition, with a crown of clouds above him, with tents and people surrounding him at his feet. After this broad shot the poet at once returns us to the realm of movement and action with the single word: "He goes" (*idët*). It would be difficult to seize more vividly Peter's second decisive characteristic: Peter's stride—the most important since the "flashing eyes." The laconic "He goes," completely conveys the feeling of that enormous, elemental, impetuous stride of Peter, who always made such difficulties for his suite in keeping up with him. It was in as masterly a manner that Valentin Serov seized and impressed that "stride of Peter" in his celebrated picture of Peter at the construction of St. Petersburg.[17]

I believe that the presentation above is a correct film reading of the passage. In the first place, such an "introduction" of a Pushkin character is generally typical of his style. Take, for example, another brilliant passage of exactly the same type of "presentation," that of the ballerina Istomina in *Eugene Onegin.** A second proof of the correctness of the above reading is the determination of the order of the words that, with absolute exactitude, in turn *order the successive appearance* of each element, all of which finally fuse into the image of the character, plastically "revealing" it.

Shots 2 and 3 would be constructed quite differently if, instead of:

> . . . From the tent,
> By crowding favorites surrounded,
> Peter emerges. . . .

the text had read:

> . . . Peter emerges,
> By crowding favorites surrounded,
> From the tent. . . .

If the emergence had begun with, instead of leading up to, Peter, the impression would have been quite dif-

---

* The theatre's full, the boxes glitter,
The stalls are seething, the pit roars,
The gallery claps and stamps, atwitter;
The curtain rustles as it soars;
A fairy light about her playing,
The magic of the bow obeying,
A. crowd of nymphs around her—lo!
Istomina on lifted toe . . .[18]

ferent. As Pushkin wrote it, it is a model of expressiveness, achieved by a purely montage method and with purely montage means. For every instance there is available a different expressive construction. But the expressive construction chosen for each instance prescribes and outlines in advance that "only right arrangement of the only suitable words," about which Tolstoy wrote in *What Is Art?* [19]

The sound of Peter's voice and his words are arranged with just the same quality of logical succession that pervades the pictorial images (see Shot 1). For Pushkin did not write:

> . . . "To arms, God with us!"
> Sounded Peter's voice, ringing,
> And with highest exaltation.

but:

> And then with highest exaltation
> There sounded, ringing, Peter's voice:
> "To arms, God with us!" . . .

If we, as film-makers, should be faced with the task of building up the expressiveness of such an exclamation, we, too, must transmit it so that there is an ordered succession, revealing first its *exaltation*, then its ringing quality, followed by our *recognition of the voice* as Peter's, and finally, to distinguish *the words* that this exalted, ringing voice of Peter *utters:* "To arms, God with us!" It seems clearly evident that in "staging" such a passage, the solution of the opening could simply be resolved by hearing first a phrase of exclamation coming from the tent, in which the words could not be distinguished, but which would already resound the exalted and ringing qualities which we would later recognize as characteristic of Peter's voice.

As we see, this has enormous importance in connection with the problem of enriching the expressive resources of film.

The example is a model of the most complex type of sound-picture, or audio-visual composition. It seems amazing that there are those who think it hardly necessary to seek assistance from such media, and that one can accumulate quite enough experience in the study of co-ordination of music and action exclusively from the opera or ballet!

Pushkin even teaches us how to work so that the picture shots avoid a mechanical coincidence with the beats on the music track.

To consider only the simplest of circumstances—noncoincidence of the measures (in this case, the poetic lines) with the ends, beginnings and lengths of the separate plastic pictures. In a rough diagram this would appear something like this:

MUSIC	I	II	III	IV	V	VI	VII	VIII	IX	X	XI	XII	XIII	XIV
PICTURE	1		2		3	4	5	6	7	8	9	10	11	12	13	14

The upper row is occupied by the fourteen lines of the passage. The lower row—by the fourteen pictures carried through the lines.

The diagram indicates their relative distribution through the passage.

This diagram makes it clearly evident what exquisite contrapuntal writing of sound-picture elements Pushkin employs to achieve the remarkable results of this polyphonic passage of poetry. As we have already noted, with the exception of VIII $= 8$ and X $= 11$, we do not encounter in the remaining twelve lines a single case of identical correspondence of line and picture.

Moreover picture and line coincide in regard to order only once: VIII $= 8$. This cannot be accidental. This single exact correspondence between the articulations of the music and the articulations of the pictures marks the most significant montage-piece in the whole composition. Of its particular type it is unique: within this eighth shot the features of Peter are fully developed and fully revealed and, in addition to this, it is the only line to employ a pictorial comparison: "In all his aspect, wrath divine." We see that this device of coinciding stress of music with stress of representation is used by Pushkin for his strongest blow in the passage. This is exactly what would be done in film by an experienced editor—as a composer in audio-visual co-ordinations.

In poetry the carrying-over of a picture-phrase from one line to another is called "enjambement." In his *Introduction to Metrics*, Zhirmunsky writes:

When the metrical articulation does not coincide with the syntactic, there arises the so-called carry-over (*enjambement*). . . . The most characteristic sign of a carry-over is the presence within a line of a *syntactic pause* more significant than that at the beginning or end of the given line. . . .[20]

Or, as one can read in Webster's *Dictionary:*

ENJAMBEMENT . . . Continuation of the sense in a phrase
beyond the end of a verse or couplet, the running over
of a sentence from one line into another, so that closely
related words fall in different lines. . . .

A good example of enjambement may be recalled
from Keats' *Endymion:*

> . . . Thus ended he, and both
> Sat silent: for the maid was very loth
> To answer; feeling well that breathed words
> Would all be lost, unheard, and vain as swords
> Against the enchased crocodile, or leaps
> Of grasshoppers against the sun. She weeps,
> And wonders; struggles to devise some blame
> To put on such a look as would say, *Shame*
> *On this poor weakness!* but, for all her strife,
> She could as soon have crush'd away the life
> From a sick dove. At length, to break the pause,
> She said with trembling chance: "Is this the cause?" . . .

Zhirmunsky also speaks of a particular one of the
compositional *interpretations* of this type of construction that is also not without a certain interest for our
audio-visual co-ordinations in film, where the picture
plays the rôle of syntactical phrase and the musical construction the rôle of rhythmical articulation:

Any non-coincidence of the syntactic articulation with
the metrical is an artistically deliberate dissonance, which
reaches its resolution at the point where, after a series of
non-coincidences, the syntactic pause at last coincides with
the bounds of the rhythmic series.[21]

This can be illustrated by an example, this time from Shelley:

> He ceased, and overcome leant back awhile, ||
> Then rising, with a melancholy smile
> Went to a sofa, || and lay down, || and slept
> A heavy sleep, || and in his dreams he wept
> And muttered some familiar name, || and we
> Wept without shame in his society. . . .*

In Russian poetry "enjambement" takes on particularly rich forms in the work of Pushkin.

In French poetry the most consistent use of this technique is in the work of Victor Hugo and André Chénier, although the clearest example that I have ever found in French poetry is in a poem by Alfred de Musset:

> L'antilope aux yeux bleus, | est plus tendre peut-être
> Que le roi des forêts; || mais le lion répond
> Qu'il n'est pas antilope, | et qu'il a nom || lion.[22]

"Enjambement" enriches the work of Shakespeare and Milton, reappearing with James Thomson, and with Keats and Shelley. But of course the most interesting poet in this regard is Milton, who greatly influenced Keats and Shelley in their use of this technique.

He declared his enthusiasm for enjambement in the introduction to *Paradise Lost:*

. . . true musical delight . . . consists onely in apt Numbers, fit quantity of Syllables, and the sense variously drawn out from one Verse into another . . .[23]

---

* *Julian and Maddalo.*

Paradise Lost itself is a first-rate school in which to study montage and audio-visual relationships. I shall quote several passages from different parts of it—firstly, because Pushkin in translation can never succeed in giving the English or American reader the direct delight in the peculiarities of his composition obtained by the Russian reader from such passages as those analyzed above. This the reader can successfully get from Milton. And secondly, because I doubt whether many of my British or American colleagues are in the habit of dipping often into *Paradise Lost*, although there is much in it that is very instructive for the film-maker.

Milton is particularly fine in battle scenes. Here his personal experience and eye-witness observations are frequently embodied. Hilaire Belloc justly wrote of him:

Everything martial, combining as such things do both sound and multitude, had appealed to Milton since the Civil Wars. . . . His imagination seized especially upon the call of its music and the splendour of its colour. . . .[24]

And, consequently, he frequently described the heavenly battles with such strongly earthly detail that he was often the subject of serious attacks and reproaches.

Studying the pages of his poem, and in each individual case analyzing the determining qualities and expressive effects of each example, we become extraordinarily enriched in experience of the audio-visual distribution of images in his sound montage.

But here are the images themselves:

(The Approach of the "Host of Satan")
> . . . at last
> Farr in th' Horizon to the North appeer'd
> From skirt to skirt a fierie Region, stretcht
> In battailous aspect, and neerer view
> Bristl'd with upright beams innumerable
> Of rigid Spears, and Helmets throng'd, and Shields
> Various, with boastful Argument portraid,
> The banded Powers of *Satan* hasting on
> With furious expedition. . . .[25]

Note the cinematographic instruction in the third full line to *change the camera set-up:* "neerer view"!

(The Corresponding Movement of the "Heavenly Hosts")
> . . . that proud honour claim'd
> *Azazel* as his right, a Cherube tall:
> Who forthwith from the glittering Staff unfurld
> Th' Imperial Ensign, which full high advanc't
> Shon like a Meteor streaming to the Wind,
> With Gemms and Golden lustre rich imblaz'd,
> Seraphic arms and Trophies: all the while
> Sonorous mettal blowing Martial sounds:
> At which the universal Host upsent
> A shout that tore Hells Concave, and beyond
> Frighted the Reign of *Chaos* and old Night.
> All in a moment through the gloom were seen
> Ten thousand Banners rise into the Air
> With Orient Colours waving: with them rose
> A Forrest huge of Spears: and thronging Helms
> Appear'd, and serried Shields in thick array
> Of depth immeasurable: Anon they move
> In perfect *Phalanx* to the *Dorian* mood
> Of Flutes and soft Recorders; such as rais'd
> To hight of noblest temper Hero's old
> Arming to Battel, . . .[26]

And here is a section from the battle itself. I will give it in the same two types of transcription as I did the passage from Pushkin's *Poltava*. First, *as broken by Milton into lines*, and then arranged in accordance with the various compositional set-ups, as a shooting-script, where each number will indicate a new montage-piece, or shot.

First transcription:

```
       . . . in strength each armed hand
   I. A Legion, led in fight, yet Leader seemd
  II. Each Warriour single as in Chief, expert
 III. When to advance, or stand, or turn the sway
  IV. Of Battel, open when, and when to close
   V. The ridges of grim Warr; no thought of flight,
  VI. None of retreat, no unbecoming deed
 VII. That argu'd fear; each on himself reli'd,
VIII. As onely in his arm the moment lay
  IX. Of victorie; deeds of eternal fame
   X. Were don, but infinite: for wide was spred
  XI. That Warr and various; somtimes on firm ground
 XII. A standing fight, then soaring on main wing
XIII. Tormented all the Air; all Air seemd then
 XIV. Conflicting Fire: long time in eeven scale
  XV. The Battel hung. . . .²⁷
```

Second transcription:

1. led in fight, yet Leader seemd each Warriour single as in Chief,
2. expert when to advance,
3. or stand,
4. or turn the sway of Battel,
5. open when,
6. and when to close the ridges of grim Warr;

7. no thought of flight,
8. none of retreat, no unbecoming deed that argu'd fear;
9. each on himself reli'd, as onely in his arm the moment lay of victorie;
10. deeds of eternal fame were don, but infinite:
11. for wide was spred that Warr and various;
12. somtimes on firm ground a standing fight,
13. then soaring on main wing tormented all the Air;
14. all Air seemd then conflicting Fire:
15. long time in eeven scale the Battel hung. . . .

As in the Pushkin quotation, here also there proves to be an identical number of lines and shots. Again as in Pushkin, there is built up here a contrapuntal design of non-coincidences between the limits of the representations and the limits of the rhythmical articulations.

One is moved to exclaim, in the words of Milton himself—from another part of the poem:

. . . mazes intricate,
Eccentric, intervolv'd yet regular
Then most, when most irregular they seem. . . .[28]

One more passage from Book VI, where the rebellious angels are cast into Hell:

Yet half his strength he put not forth, but check'd
His Thunder in mid Volie, for he meant
Not to destroy, but root them out of Heav'n:
I. The overthrown he rais'd, and as a Heard
II. Of Goats or timerous flock together throngd
III. Drove them before him Thunder-struck, pursu'd
IV. With terrors and with furies to the bounds
V. And Chrystall wall of Heav'n, which op'ning wide,
VI. Rowld inward, and a spacious Gap disclos'd

VII. Into the wastful Deep; the monstrous sight
VIII. Strook them with horror backward, but far worse
　IX. Urg'd them behind; headlong themselves they threw
　　X. Down from the verge of Heav'n, Eternal wrauth
　XI. Burnt after them to the bottomless pit.

　　　　. . .
　　　Nine dayes they fell . . .[29]

And as a shooting-script:

　1. The overthrown he rais'd, and
　2. as a Heard of Goats or timerous flock together throngd
　3. drove them before him Thunder-struck,
　4. pursu'd with terrors and with furies to the bounds and Chrystall wall of Heav'n,
　5. which op'ning wide, rowld inward,
　6. and a spacious Gap disclos'd
　7. into the wastful Deep;
　8. the monstrous sight strook them with horror backward,
　9. but far worse urg'd them behind;
10. headlong themselves they threw down from the verge of Heav'n,
11. Eternal wrauth burnt after them to the bottomless pit.

　It would be possible to find in Milton as many such instructive examples of co-ordination as might be desired.

　The formal outline of a poem usually observes the form of stanzas internally distributed according to metrical articulation—in lines. But poetry also provides us with another outline, which has a powerful advocate in Mayakovsky. In his "chopped line" the articulation is carried through not to accord with the limits of the line, but with the limits of the "shot."

　Mayakovsky does not work in lines:

Emptiness. Wing aloft,
Into the stars carving your way.

He works in shots:

Emptiness.
Wing aloft,
Into the stars carving your way.*

Here Mayakovsky cuts his line just as an experienced
film editor would in constructing a typical sequence of
"impact" (the *stars*—and *Yesenin*). First—the one. Then
—the other. Followed by the impact of one against the
other.

1. *Emptiness* (if we were to film this "shot," we
   should take the stars so as to emphasize the void,
   yet at the same time making their presence felt).
2. *Wing aloft.*
3. And only in the *third* shot do we plainly portray
   the contents of the first and second shots in the
   circumstances of impact.

As we can see, and as could be multiplied by other
instances, Mayakovsky's creation is exceedingly graphic
in this respect of montage. In general, however, in this
direction it is more exciting to turn back to the classics,
because they belong to a period when "montage" in this
sense was not dreamt of. Mayakovsky, after all, belongs
to that period in which montage thinking and montage
principles had become widely current in all the border-
arts of literature: in the theater, in the film, in photo-
montage, and so on. Consequently, examples of realistic

* *To Sergei Yesenin.* The poem is in memoriam.

montage writing taken from the treasury of our classic inheritance, where interactions of this nature with bordering spheres (for example, with the film), were either less, or else entirely non-, existent, are the more pointed and more interesting and, perhaps, the most instructive.

However, whether in picture, in sound, or in picture-sound combinations, whether in the creation of an image, a situation, or in the "magical" incarnation before our eyes of the images of the *dramatis personae*— whether in Milton or in Mayakovsky—everywhere we find similarly present this same method of montage.

What conclusion can be drawn from what has been said up to this point?

The conclusion is that there is no inconsistency between the method whereby the poet writes, the method whereby the actor forms his creation *within himself*, the method whereby the same actor acts his rôle *within the frame of a single shot*, and that method whereby his actions and whole performance, as well as the actions surrounding him, forming his environment (or the whole material of a film) are made to flash in the hands of the director through the agency of the montage exposition and construction of the entire film. At the base of all these methods lie in equal measure the same vitalizing human qualities and determining factors that are inherent in every human being and every vital art.

No matter how opposed the poles in which each of these spheres may appear to move, they meet in the final kinship and unity of a method such as we now perceive in them.

These premises place before us with new force the issue that workers in the art of film should not only study playwriting and the actor's craft, but must give equal attention to mastering all the subtleties of montage creation in all cultures.

II

SYNCHRONIZATION OF SENSES

. . . indeed the more the arts develop the more they depend on each other for definition. We will borrow from painting first and call it pattern. Later we will borrow from music and call it rhythm.

E. M. FORSTER [1]

He gradually melted into the Infinite—already his bodily senses were left behind, or at any rate all mixed up: so that the little green tables of the café only penetrated to him as a tinkling arpeggio to the blaring bass of the sunlight, the booming sky outside: while the rattle of a passing bullock-cart was translated into a series of vivid flashes of colour, and the discomfort of the rickety chair he sat on smelt bitter in his nostrils. . . .

RICHARD HUGHES [2]

MONTAGE has been defined above as:

Piece *A*, derived from the elements of the theme being developed, and piece *B*, derived from the same source, in juxtaposition give birth to the image in which the thematic matter is most clearly embodied.

Or:

Representation A and *representation* B must be so selected from all the possible features within the theme that is being developed, must be so sought for, that their *juxtaposition*— the juxtaposition of *those very elements* and not of alternative ones—shall evoke in the perception and feelings of the spectator the most complete *image of the theme itself*.

This formulation was presented in this way, without our limiting ourselves by attempting any determination of the *qualitative* degrees of A or of B, or by fixing any system of measuring A or B. The formulation stands, but we must develop its *qualities* and its *proportions*.

"From all the possible features within the theme that is being developed." This phrase was not included in the formulation by chance.

Granted that the single, unifying image that is determined by its component parts plays the decisive rôle in creative film work, we want to point out at the outset of this part of the discussion that the means of expression can be drawn from any number of various fields in order to enrich the image further.

There should be no arbitrary limits set on the variety of expressive means that can be drawn upon by the film-maker. I should think that this has been conclusively demonstrated by the examples above drawn from Leonardo da Vinci and Milton and Mayakovsky.

In Leonardo's notes for The Deluge, all its various elements—those that are purely plastic (the visual element), those indicating human behavior (the dramatic element), and the noise of crashing and crying (the sound element)—all equally fuse into a single, unifying, definitive image of a deluge.

Keeping this in mind, we see that the transition from silent montage to sound-picture, or audio-visual montage, changes nothing *in principle*.

The conception of montage that has been presented here encompasses equally the montage of the silent film and of the sound-film.

However, this does not mean that in working with sound-film, we are not faced with new tasks, new difficulties, and even entirely new methods.

On the contrary!

That is why it is so necessary for us to make a thorough analysis of the nature of audio-visual phenomena. Our first question is: Where shall we look for a secure foundation of experience with which to begin our analysis?

As always, the richest source of experience is Man

himself. The study of his behavior and, particularly in this case, of his methods of perceiving reality and of forming images of reality will always be our determinant.

Later in our examination of strictly compositional questions, we shall see that Man and the relations between his *gestures* and the *intonations* of his voice, which arise from the same emotions, are our models in determining audio-visual structures, which grow in an exactly identical way from the governing image. Of this —later. Until we go into further detail about that parallel, this thesis will be sufficient: In selecting the montage material which is to be fused into this or that particular image which is to be made manifest, we must study ourselves.

We must keep sharp notice of the means and the elements through which the image forms itself in our consciousness.

Our first and *most spontaneous* perceptions are often our most valuable ones, because these sharp, fresh, lively impressions *invariably derive from the most widely various fields.*

Therefore, in approaching the classics, it is useful to examine not only finished works, but also those sketches and notes in which the artist endeavored to set down his first vivid and immediate impressions.

For this reason a sketch is often more alive than the resulting finished canvas—a fact noted by Byron in his criticism of a fellow-poet:

. . . Campbell smells too much of the oil: he is never satisfied with what he does; his finest things have been spoiled by over-polish—the sharpness of the outline is worn off. Like paintings, poems may be too highly finished. The great art is effect, no matter how produced.[3]

Leonardo's The Deluge was not a sketch in the sense of a "sketch from life," but certainly a sketch in which he strove to jot down all those features of the image as it passed before his inner eye. This accounts for the profusion in his description not only of graphic and plastic elements, but also of sound and dramatic elements.

Let us examine another sketch, containing all the "palpitation" of our first, immediate impressions.

This is from the Goncourt Journals—a footnote to the entry of September 18, 1867:

I find a description of the *Athletic Arena* in the notebook for our *future novels*, which haven't been realized, alas!
. . . In the deep shadow of the two ends of the hall, the scintillation of the buttons and sword hilts of the policemen.
The glistening limbs of wrestlers darting into the full light.—Challenging eyes.—Hands slapping flesh in coming to grips.—Sweat smelling of the wild beast.—Paleness blending with blonde moustaches.—Bruised flesh growing pink.—Backs sweating like the stone walls of a steam-bath.—Advancing by dragging on their knees.—Whirling on their heads, etc. etc.[4]

The scene has been brought close to us by a combination of well-chosen "close-ups," and by the unusually tangible image rising from their juxtaposition. But what is most remarkable about it? It is that in these few lines of description the different shots—the "montage elements"—touch literally every sense—except perhaps that of taste, which is, however, present in implication:

1. The sense of *touch* (backs sweating like the stone walls of a steam-bath)
2. The sense of *smell* (sweat smelling of the wild beast)
3. The sense of *sight*, including both
    light (the deep shadow, and the glistening limbs of wrestlers darting into the full light; the buttons and sword hilts of the policemen gleaming in the deep shadow) and
    color (paleness blending with blonde moustaches, bruised flesh growing pink)
4. The sense of *hearing* (hands slapping flesh)
5. The sense of *movement* (advancing on knees, whirling on their heads)
6. *Pure emotion*, or drama (challenging eyes)

Countless examples of this kind could be cited, but all would illustrate, to a greater or a lesser degree, the thesis presented above, namely:

There is no fundamental difference in the approaches to be made to the problems of purely visual montage and to a montage that links different spheres of feeling —particularly the visual image with the sound image, in the process of creating a single, unifying sound-picture image.

As a principle this was known to us as far back as 1928 when Pudovkin, Alexandrov and I issued our "Statement" on the sound-film.*

But a principle is no more than a principle, while our

* See item number 4, Bibliography.

present urgent task is to find the correct approach to this new kind of montage.

My search for this approach has been closely linked with the production of *Alexander Nevsky*. And this new kind of montage, associated with this film, I have named:

vertical montage.

What are the origins of this term—and why this particular term?

Everyone is familiar with the appearance of an orchestral score. There are several staffs, each containing the part for one instrument or a group of like instruments. Each part is developed horizontally. But the vertical structure plays no less important a rôle, interrelating as it does all the elements of the orchestra within each given unit of time. Through the progression of the *vertical* line, pervading the entire orchestra, and interwoven horizontally, the intricate harmonic musical movement of the whole orchestra moves forward.

When we turn from this image of the orchestral score to that of the audio-visual score, we find it necessary to add a new part to the instrumental parts: this new part is a "staff" of visuals, succeeding each other and corresponding, according to their own laws, with the movement of the music—and *vice versa.*

This correspondence, or relationship, could be just as successfully described if, for the image of the orchestral score, we had substituted the montage structure of the silent film.

In order to do this, we will have to draw from our silent film experience an example of *polyphonic* montage, where shot is linked to shot not merely through one indication—movement, or light values, or stage in the exposition of the plot, or the like—but through a *simultaneous advance* of a multiple series of lines, each maintaining an independent compositional course and each contributing to the total compositional course of the sequence.

Such an example may be found in the montage structure of the "procession" sequence in *Old and New*.

In this sequence the several interdependent lines virtually resemble a ball of vari-colored yarn, with the lines running through and binding together the entire sequence of shots.

These were the sequence lines:

1. The line of heat, increasing from shot to shot.

2. The line of changing close-ups, mounting in plastic intensity.

3. The line of mounting ecstasy, shown through the dramatic content of the close-ups.

4. The line of women's "voices" (faces of the singers).

5. The line of men's "voices" (faces of the singers).

6. The line of those who kneel under the passing ikons (increasing in tempo). This counter-current gave movement to a larger counter-stream which was threaded through the primary theme—of the bearers of ikons, crosses and banners.

7. The line of groveling, uniting both streams in the general movement of the sequence, "from heaven to the dust." From the radiant pinnacles of the crosses and banners against the sky to the prostrate figures beating their heads in the dust. This theme was announced at the opening of the sequence with a "key" shot: a swift camera pan downwards from the belfry cross glittering in the sky down to the church base from where the procession is moving.

The general course of the montage was an uninterrupted interweaving of these diverse themes into one unified movement. Each montage-piece had a double responsibility—to build the *total line* as well as to continue the movement within *each of the contributory themes*.

Occasionally a montage-piece would contain all the lines, and sometimes only one or two, excluding the other lines for a moment; at times one of the themes would take a necessary step backwards only to make more effective its two steps forward, while the other themes proceeded ahead in equal quantities, and so forth. But the value of a montage-piece was gauged, not by *one* feature alone, but always by the *whole series of features*, before its place in the sequence could be fixed.

One piece, satisfactory in its *intensity* for the heat line, would be out of place in that particular "*chorus*" into which it would have fallen if gauged alone by its intensity. While the *dimensions* of a close-up face might fit one place, the face's *expression* would better suit another place in the sequence. The difficulty of this work should not surprise anyone, because the process is exactly analogous to the preparation of the most unassuming orchestration. Its chief difficulty was of course that the work was being done with the far less flexible material of film, and that the amount of variation was limited by the demands of *this particular sequence.*

On the other hand, we must keep in mind that this polyphonic structure made up of many separate lines achieves its *final form* not alone from the plan for it that was determined beforehand. This final form depends just as much on the character of the film sequence (or complete film) as a complex—*a complex composed of film strips containing photographic images.*

It was exactly this kind of "welding," further complicated (or perhaps further simplified?) by another line—the sound-track—that we tried to achieve in *Alexander Nevsky,* especially in the sequence of the attacking German knights advancing across the ice. Here the lines of *the sky's tonality—clouded or clear,* of the accelerated *pace* of the riders, of their *direction,* of *the cutting back and forth* from Russians to knights, of the faces in close-up and the *total* long-shots, the *tonal* structure of the music, its *themes,* its *tempi,* its *rhythm,* etc.—created a task no less difficult than that of the silent sequence above. Many hours went into the fusing of these elements into an *organic* whole.

It is naturally helpful that, aside from the individual elements, the polyphonic structure achieves its total effect through the *composite sensation of all the pieces as a whole.* This "physiognomy" of the finished sequence is a summation of the individual *features* and the *general sensation* produced by the sequence. On the occasion of the release of *Old and New*, I wrote of this quality of polyphonic montage in relation to the "future" sound-film.[5]

In matching music with the sequence, this *general sensation* is a decisive factor, for it is directly linked with the *imagery perception* of the music as well as of the pictures. This requires constant corrections and adjustments of the individual features to preserve the important general effect.

In order to diagram what takes place in *vertical montage*, we may visualize it as *two* lines, keeping in mind that each of these lines represents *a whole complex of a many-voiced scoring*. The search for correspondence must proceed from the intention of matching both picture and music to the general, complex "imagery" produced by the whole.

Diagram 2 reveals the new "vertical" factor of inter-correspondence, which arises the moment that the pieces of the sound-picture montage are connected.

From the viewpoint of montage structure, we no longer have a simple horizontal succession of pictures, but now a new "super-structure" is erected vertically over the horizontal picture structure. Piece for piece these new strips in the "super-structure" *differ in length* from those in the picture structure, but, needless to say, they are equal in total length. Pieces of sound do not fit into the picture pieces in sequential order, but in simultaneous order.

DIAGRAM 1

DIAGRAM 2

It is interesting to note that *in principle* these sound-picture relationships do not differ from relationships within music, nor do they differ from relationships within the structure of silent montage.

Putting aside for the while our discussion of music relationships, let us speak first of the solution to the question of correspondence in silent montage. Here the effect comes not from the simple sequence of the film strips, but from their actual *simultaneity*, resulting from the impression derived from one strip being mentally superimposed over the following strip. The technique of "double-exposure" has merely materialized this basic phenomenon of cinematic perception. This phenomenon exists on the higher levels of film structure as well as on the very threshold of film illusion, for "persistence of vision" from frame to frame of the film strip is what creates the illusion of film movement. We shall see that a similar superimposition occurs even at the *highest stage* of montage development—audio-visual montage. The "double-exposed" image is just as inherently characteristic of audio-visual montage as it is for all other cinematic phenomena.

Long before we even dreamt of sound, I resorted to this particular technique when I wanted to create the effect of sound and music through purely plastic means:

. . . in *Strike* (1924) there are experiments in this direction. There is a short sequence showing a meeting of the strikers under the guise of a casual stroll with an accordion.

This sequence ended in a shot where we tried to create an aural effect through purely visual means.

The two tracks of the future — picture and sound — were, in this instance, both picture tracks, a double-exposure. In the first exposure a pond could be seen at the bottom of a hill, up which were moving towards the camera a throng of strollers with their accordion. The second exposure was of the huge accordion in close-up, filling the entire screen with its moving bellows and its high-lighted keys. This movement, seen from different angles, over the other continuous exposure, created the full sensation of a melodic movement, which drew together the whole sequence.[6]

Diagrams 1 and 2 show how the compositional joining in a silent film (1) is distinguished from that of the sound-film (2). It appears as a diagram of a *splice*, for montage is actually a *large, developing thematic movement*, progressing through a continuing diagram of individual splices.

The compositional structure of related movements as indicated by Diagram 2 (A_1–B_1–C_1) is familiar in music.

And the laws of compositional movement (A–B–C) have been evolved in the practice of the *silent film*.

The new problem facing the audio-visual cinema is to find a system for co-ordinating A–A_1; A_1 B_1 C_1; B–B_1; C–C_1, etc.—a system which will determine the intricate plastic and aural movements of a theme through all the diverse correspondences of A–A_1–B_1–B–C–C_1, etc. (see diagrams on page 79).

Our present problem is to find the key to these newly discovered *vertical splices*, A–A_1, B–B_1, learning to bring them together and to separate them as rhythmically as is now possible within the highly developed medium of music, or within the highly developed medium of visual montage. Both these media of cultural activity long since learned how to handle the lengths of A_1, B_1, etc., with complete assurance.

This leads us to the primary question of finding those means of *establishing the proportions between pictures and sound*, and of perfecting the compasses, rulers, tools and methods that will make it practicable. This is actually a question of finding *an inner synchronization between the tangible picture and the differently perceived sounds*. We have already mastered the problem of physical synchronization, even to the point of detecting the discrepancy of a single frame in the matching of lips and speech!

But this co-ordination is far beyond that external synchronization that matches the boot with its creaking— we are speaking of a "hidden" inner synchronization in which the plastic and tonal elements will find complete fusion.

To relate these two elements, we find a natural language common to both—movement. Plekhanov has said that all phenomena in the final analysis can be reduced to movement. Movement will reveal all the substrata of inner synchronization that we wish to establish in due course. Movement will display to us in a concrete form the *significance and method* of the fusion process. Let us move from exterior and descriptive matters to matters of an inner and deeper character.

The rôle of movement in this problem of synchronization is self-evident. Let us examine a number of different·approaches to synchronization in logical order. These are the A B C's of every sound-cutter, but their examination is essential.

The first will be in that sphere of synchronization properly outside the realm of artistic concern—a purely *factual* synchronization: the sound-filming of natural things (a croaking frog, the mournful chords of a broken harp, the rattle of wagon wheels over cobblestones).

In this case art begins only at that moment of synchronization when the natural connection between the object and its sound is not merely *recorded*, but is *dictated* solely by the demands of the expressive work in progress.

In the more rudimentary forms of expression both elements (the picture and its sound) will be controlled by an identity of *rhythm*, according to the content of the scene. This is the simplest, easiest and most frequent circumstance of audio-visual montage, consisting of shots cut and edited together to the rhythm of the music on the parallel sound-track. Whether movement exists in these shots is not of serious consequence. If movement happens to be present, the only demand upon it is that it conform with the rhythm fixed by the parallel track.

However, it is evident that even on this comparatively low plane of synchronization there is a possibility for creating interesting and expressive compositions.

From these simplest circumstances—simple "metrical" coincidence of accent (film "scansion")—it is possible to arrange a wide variety of syncopated combinations and a purely rhythmical "counterpoint" in the controlled play of off-beats, shot-lengths, echoed and repeated subjects, and so on.

Which step follows this second level of synchronized surface movement? It may possibly be one that will enable us to show not only rhythmic movement, but *melodic movement* as well.

Lanz spoke correctly of melody when he said:

. . . strictly speaking, one does not "hear" a melody. We are able or unable to follow it, which means that we either have or have not the ability to organize the tones into a higher unity. . . .[7]

From all the plastic means of expression at our disposal we can surely find those whose movement harmonizes not only with the movement of the rhythmic pattern, but also with the movement of the melodic *line*. We already have some idea as to what these means might be, but since we are about to deal with this question in full detail, we will mention at this point that we can assume that these elements will probably be drawn basically from a "linear" element of plastic art.

"The higher unity" into which we are capable of organizing the *separate tones* of the sound-scale may be visualized as a line that unites them through movement. The tonal *changes* on this line may also be characterized as movement, no longer as an intermingling movement, but as a *vibrating* movement, whose characteristics we can perceive as sounds of varying pitch and tone.

What visual element echoes this new type of "movement" introduced to our discussion by tones? Obviously it will be an element that also moves in vibrations (although of a differing physical formation), and is also characterized by tones. This visual equivalent is color. (In a rough analogy pitch can correspond to the play of *light*, and tonality to *color*.)

Pausing for a moment to recapitulate, we see that we have demonstrated that synchronization can be "natural," metric, rhythmic, melodic and tonal.

Matching of picture and sound may achieve a synchronization that fulfills all these potentialities (although this is a very rare occurrence), or it may be built upon a combination of unlike elements, without attempting to conceal the resulting dissonance between the aurals and the visuals. This occurs frequently. When it does, we explain that the visuals "exist for themselves," that the music "exists for itself": sound and picture each run on independently, without uniting in an organic whole. It is important to keep in mind that our conception of synchronization does not presume consonance. In this conception full possibilities exist for the play of both corresponding and non-corresponding "movements," but in either circumstance the relationship must be *compositionally controlled*. It is apparent that any one of these synchronization approaches may serve as the "leading," determining factor in the structure, dependent on the need. Some scenes would require rhythm as a determining factor, others would be controlled by tone, and so on.

But let us turn back to those varying forms, or more accurately, various fields of synchronization.

We observe that these varying forms coincide with those varying forms of silent montage which were established in 1928-29, and which we later included in the program for teaching film direction.*

At that time these "terms" may have seemed to some of my colleagues unnecessarily pedantic or playful analogies to other media. But even then we pointed out the importance of such an approach to the "future" problems of the sound-film. Now this is obviously and concretely a sensible part of our experiments in audio-visual relationships.

* See item number 49, Bibliography.

These forms included "overtonal" montage. This kind of synchronization has been touched upon, above, in connection with *Old and New*. By this perhaps not altogether exact term, we are to understand an intricate polyphony, and a perception of the pieces (of both music and picture) *as a whole*. This totality becomes the factor of perception which synthesizes that original image towards the final revelation of which all of our activity has been directed.

This brings us to the basic and primary matter that forms *the definitive inner synchronization—that between the image and the meaning of the pieces.*

The circuit is complete. From the same formula that unites the *meaning* of the whole piece (whether whole film or sequence) and the *meticulous, cunning selection* of the pieces, *emerges the image* of the theme, *true to its content.* Through this fusion, and through that fusion of the logic of the film's subject with the *highest form* in which to cast this subject, comes the full *revelation* of the film's meaning.

Such a premise naturally serves as a source and departure for the whole series of varying approaches to synchronization. For each "different" kind of synchronization is embraced by the organic whole, and embodies the basic image through its own specifically defined limits.

Let us begin our investigation in the field of color, not only because color is the most immediate and stimulating problem of the film today, but chiefly because color has long been (and still is) used in *deciding* the question of *pictorial and aural correspondence, whether absolute or relative*—and as an indication of specific *human emotions*. This would certainly be of cardinal importance to the problems and principles of the audio-visual image. The most graphic and effective development of a *method* of investigation would be in the field of *melodic synchronization* for the convenience of graphic analysis and our primary field of black and white reproduction.

So we first turn to the question of associating music with color, which will lead us in turn to consideration of that form of montage which may be called chromophonic, or color-sound montage.

To remove the barriers between sight and sound, between the seen world and the heard world! To bring about a unity and a harmonious relationship between these two opposite spheres. What an absorbing task! The Greeks and Diderot, Wagner and Scriabin—who has not dreamt of this ideal? Is there anyone who has made no attempt to realize this dream? Our survey of dreams cannot begin here, however.

Our survey must lead us to some method of fusing sound with sight, to some investigation of the preliminary indications leading towards this fusion.

We will begin by observing the forms taken by these dreams of a picture and sound fusion that have disturbed mankind for so long. Color has always received more than an average share of these dreams.

The first example is not too remote, drawn from no

further back than the borderline between the eighteenth and the nineteenth centuries. But it is a very graphic example. We first give the floor to Karl von Eckartshausen, author of *Disclosures of Magic from Tested Experiences of Occult Philosophic Sciences and Veiled Secrets of Nature:* [8]

I have long tried to determine the harmony of all sense impressions, to make it manifest and perceptible.

To this end I improved the ocular music invented by Père Castel.[9]

I constructed this machine in all its perfection, so that whole color chords can be produced, just like tonal chords. Here is the description of this instrument.

I had cylindrical glasses, about half an inch in diameter, made, of equal size, and filled them with diluted chemical colors. I arranged these glasses like the keys of a clavichord, placing the shades of color like the notes. Behind these glasses I placed little lobes of brass, which covered the glasses so that no color could be seen. These lobes were connected by wires with the keyboard of the clavichord, so that the lobe was lifted when a key was struck, rendering the color visible. Just as a note dies away when the finger is removed from a key, so the color disappears, since the metal lobe drops quickly because of its weight, covering the color. The clavichord is illuminated from behind by wax candles. The beauty of the colors is indescribable, surpassing the most splendid jewels. Nor can one express the visual impression awakened by the various color chords. . . .

A THEORY OF OCULAR MUSIC

Just as tones of music must harmonize with the playwright's words in a melodrama, so must colors likewise correspond with the words.

I set down an example to make this more understandable. I wrote a little poem, which I accompany with my color music. It reads:

WORDS: *Sadly she wandered, loveliest of maidens* . . .
MUSIC: The notes of a flute, plaintive.
COLOR: Olive, mixed with pink and white.

WORDS: . . . *in flowery meadows—*
MUSIC: Gay, rising tones.
COLOR: Green, mixed with violet and daisy yellow.

WORDS: *Singing a song, joyful as a lark.*
MUSIC: Soft notes, rising and gently falling in quick succession.
COLOR: Dark blue streaked with scarlet and yellowish-green.

WORDS: *And God, in the temple of creation, hears her.*
MUSIC: Majestic, grand.
COLOR: A mixture of the most splendid colors—blue, red and green—glorified with the yellow of the dawn and purple—dissolving into soft green and pale yellow.

WORDS: *The sun rises over the mountains* . . .
MUSIC: A majestic bass, from which middle tones rise imperceptibly!
COLOR: Bright yellows, mixed with the color of the dawn—dissolving into green and whitish yellow.

WORDS: *And shines upon the violet in the valley* . . .
MUSIC: Softly descending tones.
COLOR: Violet, alternating with varied greens.

This should be sufficient to prove that colors also hold the power of expressing the emotions of the soul. . . .

If this citation should be thought too unfamiliar, let us next choose one of the best-known examples—Arthur Rimbaud's famous "color" sonnet, *Voyelles*, whose scheme of color-sound correspondences has disturbed so many intellects:

Vowels : black *A*, white *E*, red *I*, green *U*, blue *O*,
Someday I shall name the birth from which you rise:
A is a black corset and over it the flies
Boil noisy where the cruel stench fumes slow,

Shadow-pits; *E*, candor of mists and canopies,
Shiver of flowers, white kings, spears of the glacial snow:

I, purples, blood spit out, laugh of lips so
Lovely in anger or penitent ecstasies;

U, cycles, divine vibrations of green seas;
The peace of animal pastures, peace of these
Lines printed by alchemy on the great brows of the wise;

O, the great Trumpet strange in its stridencies,
The angel-crossed, the world-crossed silences:
— O the Omega, the blue light of the Eyes!

(Translation by Muriel Rukeyser)

Rimbaud's scheme occasionally approaches that of René Ghil,[10] although for the most part these two diverge sharply:

oû, ou, oui, iou, oui	Bruns, noirs à roux
ô, o, io, oi	Rouges
â, a, aï, ai	Vermillons
eû, eu, ieu, euï, eui	Orangés à ors, verts
û, u, iu, uï, ui	Jaunes, ors, verts
e, è, é, ei, eï	Blancs, à azurs pâles
ie, iè, ié, î, i, i, ii	Bleus, à azurs noirs

It was after Helmholtz had published the results of his experiments in correlating the timbres of voices and instruments [11] that Ghil "perfected" his own chart, introducing not only consonants and instrumental timbres, but also a whole catalog of emotions, premises and hypotheses which were to be understood as maintaining an absolute correspondence.

In an analysis of romanticism, Max Deutschbein concluded that "syntheses of the various sensations" is one of the fundamental indications of a romantic work of art.[12]

In complete harmony with this definition is the chart of correspondences between vowels and colors determined by A. W. Schlegel (1767-1845):

A represents the light, clear red (*das rote lichthelle A*), and signifies Youth, Friendship and Radiance. *I* stands for celestial blue, symbolizing Love and Sincerity. *O* is purple; *U* stands for violet, and *OO* is adorned in navy blue.[13]

Later in this century another romanticist gave a great deal of attention to this problem. Lafcadio Hearn, however, does not attempt any "classification," and even criticizes departures from a spontaneous approach towards such a system, as we can see in his letter of June 14, 1893,[14] in which he disapproves of John Addington Symonds' newly published *In the Key of Blue*.

But in this same letter, written to his friend, Basil Hall Chamberlain, he tells him:

. . . *you* immediately illustrated the values for me. When you wrote of "the deep bass" of that green I could see, feel, smell, taste, and chew the leaf; it was rather bitter in taste, and dense, and faintly odorous. . . . I have been thinking of soprano, alto, contralto, tenor, and baritone colours. . . .

A few days before this he had exploded in a passionate outburst for this cause:

Recognizing the ugliness of words, however, you must also recognize their physiognomical beauty. . . . For me words have colour, form, character; they have faces, parts, manners, gesticulations; they have moods, humours, eccentricities;—they have tints, tones, personalities. . . .[15]

Further, in an attack on magazine editors who object to such a style, he says they claim:

"The readers do not feel as you do about words. They can't be supposed to know that you think the letter A is blush-crimson, and the letter E pale sky-blue. They can't be supposed to know that you think KH wears a beard and a turban; that initial X is a mature Greek with wrinkles. . . ."

Here Hearn gives his answer to these critics:

Because people cannot see the colour of words, the tints of words, the secret ghostly motions of words:—
Because they cannot hear the whispering of words, the rustling of the procession of letters, the dream-flutes and dream-drums which are thinly and weirdly played by words:—
Because they cannot perceive the pouting of words, the frowning of words and fuming of words, the weeping, the raging and racketing and rioting of words:—
Because they are insensible to the phosphorescing of words, the fragrance of words, the noisesomeness of words,

the tenderness or hardness, the dryness or juiciness of words,—the interchange of values in the gold, the silver, the brass and the copper of words:—

Is that any reason why we should not try to make them hear, to make them see, to make them feel? . . .

Elsewhere he speaks of the variability of words:

Long ago I said that words are like lizards in their power of changing colour with position.[10]

This refinement in Hearn is not accidental. It can be partially explained by his near-sightedness, which had sharpened his perceptions in these matters. A fuller explanation lies in his long residence in Japan where the faculty of finding audio-visual correspondence had been developed with especial acuteness.*

Lafcadio Hearn has brought us to the East where audio-visual relationships are not only part of the Chinese educational system, but are actually incorporated into the code of law. They derive from the principles of Yang and Yin, upon which is based the entire system of Chinese world-outlook and philosophy.† According to Sung tradition this law (ho t'u) was delivered to the world in the form of a diagram (see page 94), brought up dripping from the river, in the mouth of a dragon-horse.[17]

* Eisenstein's analysis of the Kabuki theater's sense-appeals appeared in *Zhizn Iskusstva* (Moscow), No. 34, August 19, 1928.

† Yang and Yin—depicted as a circle, locked together within it *yang* and *yin—yang*, light; *yin*, dark—each carrying within itself the essence of the other, each shaped to the other—*yang* and *yin*, forever opposed, forever united. An exceptionally pertinent principle for a film-maker to study.

Even more interesting than the correspondence between certain sounds and colors is the analogous reflection of the *artistic tendencies* of certain "epochs" *in the structure both of music and painting.*

From the increasing and interesting literature in this field, first mapped by Wölfflin, we choose an article by the late René Guilleré on the "jazz age," *Il n'y a plus de perspective:*

Formerly the science of esthetics rested content on the principle of fused elements. In music—on the continuous

melodic line threaded through harmonic chords; in literature—on the fusion of a sentence's elements through con-
junctions and transitions; in art—on a continuity of plastic
forms and structures of combinations of these forms.

Modern esthetics is built upon the disunion of elements,
heightening the contrast of each other: repetition of identical elements, which serves to strengthen the intensity of
contrast. . . .[18]

A necessary comment on this opinion is that *repetition*
may well perform two functions.

One function is to facilitate the creation of an organic
whole.

Another function of repetition is to serve as a means
of developing that mounting intensity which Guilleré
mentions. We need not seek far for examples of both
these functions. Both may be found in films.

The first function is found in operation in *Potemkin*—
in the repetition of "Brothers!", first occurring on the
quarter-deck before the marines refuse to fire; next not
as a sub-title but as the sequence of the sail-boats that
merge shore and ship, and last, again as a sub-title,
"Brothers!" when the squadron permits the Potemkin
to pass unattacked.

Alexander Nevsky contains an example of the second
function of repetition—mounting intensity. Instead of
repeating a single measure of the music *four* times as
written in the score, I multiplied this by three, achieving *twelve* exact repeats of the measure. This occurs in
the sequence where the peasant militia cuts into the rear

of the German wedge. The resultant effect of growing excitement never fails to win the spectators' approval.

To continue from Guilleré's article:

. . . in the form of jazz, if we look into its musical element and into its method of composition—we find a typical expression of this new esthetic.

Its basic parts: syncopation and a dominance of rhythm. This cancels out smoothly curving lines—curlicues, phrases in the form of a lock of curling hair, characteristic of Massenet, and all slow arabesques. Rhythm is stated by angle—protruding edge, sharp profile. It has a rigid structure—firmly constructed. It strives towards plasticity. Jazz seeks volume of sound, volume of phrase. Classical music was based on planes (not on volumes)—planes arranged in layers, planes erected atop one another, planes horizontal and vertical, creating an architecture of truly noble proportions: palaces with terraces, colonnades, flights of monumental steps—all receding into a deep perspective. In jazz all elements are brought to the foreground. This is an important law that can be found in painting, in stage design, in films, and in poetry of this period. Conventional perspective with its fixed focus and its gradual vanishing point has abdicated.

In both art and literature creation proceeds through several perspectives, simultaneously employed. The order of the day is intricate synthesis—bringing together viewpoints of an object from below and viewpoints from above.

Antique perspective presented us with geometrical concepts of objects—as they could be seen only by an ideal eye. Our perspective shows us objects as we see them with both eyes—gropingly. We no longer construct the visual world with an acute angle, converging on the horizon. We open up this angle, pulling representation against us, upon us, toward us. . . . We take part in this world. That is why we are not afraid to use close-ups in films: to portray a man as he sometimes seems to us, out of natural proportions, suddenly fifty centimeters away from us; we are not afraid to use metaphors, that leap from the lines of a poem, or to allow the piercing sound of a trombone to swoop out of the orchestra, aggressively.

In antique perspective the planes behaved much like the wings of a stage setting—receding in a funnel towards the depths where the vista closes on a colonnade or on a monumental stair-case. Similarly in music the theatre wings formed by the double basses, the cellos and the violins are shaped in like planes, one after the other, like the stairs of a great approach, with the eye carried over terraces towards the triumphant sunset of the brasses. In literature the same structure dominated the milieu—built in elegant promenades from one tree to the next; each character described minutely—from the color of his hair. . . .

In our new perspective there are no steps, no promenades. A man enters his environment—the environment is seen through the man. Both function through each other.

In other words, in our new perspective—there is no perspective. Volumes are no longer created through perspective; different intensities, varying color saturations now create the volumes. Musical volume is no longer created through receding planes, with a sound foreground and appropriate recessions. Its volume is now created by the volume of sound. There are no more great canvases painted with sound in the manner of theatre backdrops. Jazz is volume. It doesn't employ voices with accompaniments, similar to figures against a background. Everything works. Each instrument performs its solo while participating in the whole. The orchestra has even lost its impressionist divisions—with all the violins, for instance, playing the same theme on harmonic notes to create greater richness of sound.

In jazz each man plays for himself in a general ensemble. The same law applies to art: the background is itself a volume. . . .

The above excerpt is interesting for the picture it provides of equivalent structures in musical and graphic arts, particularly that of architecture, although the questions raised here are chiefly concerned with spatial and proportional concepts. However, we have only to glance at a group of cubist paintings to convince ourselves that what takes place in these paintings has already been heard in jazz music.

This relationship is just as evident in the architectural landscape—classic architecture bearing the same relation to the classicists in music composition as the modern urban landscape bears to jazz.

Indeed, Roman squares and villas, Versailles' parks and terraces could be "prototypes" for the structure of classical music.

The modern urban scene, especially that of a large city at night, is clearly the plastic equivalent of jazz. Particularly noticeable here is that characteristic pointed out by Guilleré, namely, the absence of perspective.

All sense of perspective and of realistic depth is washed away by a nocturnal sea of electric advertising. Far and near, small (in the *foreground*) and large (in the *background*), soaring aloft and dying away, racing and circling, bursting and vanishing—these lights tend to abolish all sense of real space, finally melting into a single plane of colored light points and neon lines moving over a surface of black velvet sky. It was thus that people used to picture stars—as glittering nails hammered into the sky!

Headlights on speeding cars, highlights on receding rails, shimmering reflections on the wet pavements—all mirrored in puddles that destroy our sense of direction (which is top? which is bottom?), supplementing the mirage above with a mirage beneath us, and rushing between these two worlds of electric signs, we see them no longer on a single plane, but as a system of theater wings, suspended in the air, through which the night flood of traffic lights is streaming.

This reminds us of another starry sky above and below, for the characters in Gogol's story *A Terrible Revenge*, imagined that the world floated down the Dnieper River between the real starry sky above them and its reflection in the water.

The preceding impressions were those of at least one visitor to the streets of New York during the hours of evening and night.*

Guilleré's article gains added interest through its description, not only of the correspondence between musical and graphic arts, but also through its presentation

---

* Similar impressions have been recorded by Antoine de Saint Exupéry in describing an aerial encounter with a storm: "Horizon? There was no longer a horizon. I was in the wings of a theatre cluttered up with bits of scenery. Vertical, oblique, horizontal, all of plane geometry was awhirl. A hundred transversal valleys were muddled in a jumble of perspectives. . . . For a single second, in a waltzing landscape like this, the flyer had been unable to distinguish between vertical mountainsides and horizontal planes. . . ." (*Wind, Sand and Stars*, Reynal and Hitchcock, 1941, page 83.)

of the idea that these arts, fused together, correspond to the very *image of an epoch and the image of the reasoning process* of those who are linked to the epoch. Isn't this picture familiar to us, with that "absence of perspective," reflecting the lack of historical perspective in a large part of the world today, or in the image of an orchestra where each player is on his own, straining to break up this *inorganic* whole of many units by taking an independent course—but bound together in an ensemble only by the *iron necessity* of a common rhythm?

It is interesting to note that all the traits mentioned by Guilleré have been encountered before in the course of art history. Each time these traits reappear in history, one finds them aspiring towards *a unified whole, a higher unity*. It is only in periods of decadence in the arts that this *centripetal movement* changes to a *centrifugal* movement, hurling apart all unifying tendencies— tendencies that are incompatible with an epoch that places an over-emphasis on individualism. We recall Nietzsche:

. . . What is the characteristic of all *literary décadence?* It is that life no longer resides in the whole. The word gets the upper hand and jumps out of the sentence, the sentence stretches too far and obscures the meaning of the page, the page acquires life at the expense of the whole—the whole is no longer a whole. . . . The whole has ceased to live altogether; it is composite, summed up, artificial, an unnatural product.[19]

The fundamental and characteristic feature lies precisely here and not in separate particulars. Aren't the

Egyptian bas-reliefs valid works even though they were done without a knowledge of linear perspective? Didn't Dürer and Leonardo deliberately make simultaneous use of several perspectives and several vanishing points when it suited their purposes.* And in his painting of Giovanni Arnolfini and his wife,[20] Jan van Eyck employed fully *three* vanishing points (see illustration on page 102). In his case this may have been an unconscious method, but what a wonderful *intensity of depth* this painting gains thereby!

Isn't it perfectly legitimate for Chinese landscape paintings to avoid leading the eye into a single depth, stretching out the viewpoint instead along the entire panorama, so that their mountains and water-falls all appear to be moving towards us?

Haven't Japanese prints used *super-close-up* foregrounds and effectively disproportionate features in *super-close-up* faces?

One may object that our business has not been to uncover the tendencies of previous epochs towards unity, but simply to demonstrate a less important and merely supplementary diapason in our comparison with a decadent epoch.

Where, for example, can we also find in the past such a degree of simultaneity of viewpoints from above and below, of mixed vertical and horizontal planes, as we found when we looked for the examples of "intricate synthesis" above?

* In the familiar *Last Supper* the objects on the table have a vanishing point at variance with that of the room. The Dürer engraving (page 102) is typical of his use of double perspective.

Joseph Kern

Karl Rapke

Diagram (*left*) of Jan van Eyck's *Giovanni Arnolfini and His Wife*, showing three vanishing points (S, F', F''). Diagram (*right*) of an engraving from *Die Kleine Passion* by Albrecht Dürer, showing his deliberate use of a double horizon line (H) to increase dramatic content. See page 101.

Modern "simultaneous" stage settings have their ancestors, too, such as those designed by Yakulov [21] in the "cubist tradition," cutting through widely separated locales of action, cutting interiors through exteriors. Their exact prototypes can be found in the theater technique of the sixteenth and seventeenth centuries, where we may see designs of single settings that offered the manager a desert, a palace, a hermit's cave, a king's throne-room, a queen's dressing-room, a sepulcher and various skies—all for the price of one! Such ingenuity immediately recalls certain works of Picasso, both in his cubist and more recent periods, where a face or a figure is presented from multiple viewpoints, and at varying stages of an action.

The copperplate frontispiece to a seventeenth-century Spanish biography of St. John of the Cross shows the saint at the moment he beholds the miraculous appearance of the crucifix. With striking effect, there is incorporated into the same plate a second view in perspective of the same crucifix—as seen from the saint's viewpoint.

If these examples are too special, then let us turn to El Greco. He provides an instance for us of an artist's viewpoint leaping furiously back and forth, fixing on the same canvas details of a city seen not only from various points outside the city, but even from various streets, alleys, and squares!

All this is done with such a full consciousness of his right to work thus, that he has even recorded, on a map inserted into the landscape for this purpose, a description of this procedure. He probably took this step to avoid any misunderstanding on the part of people who knew the city of Toledo too well to see his work except as a form of capricious "leftism."

The painting is his *View and Plan of Toledo*, finished some time between 1604 and 1614, and now in Toledo's Greco Museum. It contains a general view of Toledo from approximately the distance of a kilometer eastwards. At the right a young man displays the map of the city. On this map Greco instructed his son to write these words:

It has been necessary to put the Hospital of Don Juan Tavera in the form of a model [that on the cloud] because it not only so happened as to conceal the Visagra gate, but thrust up its dome or cupola in such a manner that it overtopped the town; once put thus as a model, and removed from its place, I thought it would show the façade before any other part of it; how the rest of it is related to the town will be seen on the map. . . .[22] *

What difference has this made? *Realistic proportions* have been altered, and while part of the city is shown

---

* The full text as it appears in the painting:

Ha sido forçoso poner el hospital de Don Joan Tauera en forma de modelo porque no solo venia a cubrir la puerta de visagra mas subia el cimborrios o copula de manera que sobrepujaua la çiudad y asi vna vez puesto como modelo y mouido de su lugar me pareçio mostrar la haz antes que otra parte y en lo demas de como viene con la çiudad se vera en la planta.

Tambien en la historia de nra Señora que trahe la casulla a S. Illefonso para su ornato y hazer las figuras grandes me he valido en çierta manera de ser cuerpos çelestiales como vemos en las luçes que vistas de lexos por pequeñas que sean nos pareçen grandes.

from *one* direction, one detail of it is shown from *exactly the opposite direction!*

That is why I insist upon including El Greco among the forefathers of film montage. In this particular instance he appears as a forerunner of the newsreel, for his "re-editing" is rather more informational here than in his other *View of Toledo* (painted in the same period).[23] In this latter work he accomplished no less radical a *montage revolution* of realistic landscape, but here it has been done through an *emotional* tempest, which has immortalized this painting.

El Greco brings us back to our principal theme, for his painting has a precise musical equivalent in one portion of Spain's many-sided folk music. El Greco walks into our problem of color-sound montage, for it would have been impossible for him not to have known this music—so close is his painting in spirit to the characteristics of the so-called *cante jondo.**

This spiritual kinship (naturally without reference to cinematography!) is brought out by Legendre and Hartmann in the introduction to their monumental catalog of El Greco's works.

They begin by citing Jusepe Martínez' testimony to the effect that El Greco often invited musicians to his home. (Martínez criticized such behavior as an "unnecessary luxury.") We cannot help imagining that an affinity of music to painting would be natural in the work of an artist who had so personal a love for music.

* Or *cante hondo;* literally, "a deep song."

Legendre and Hartmann openly declare:

. . . we readily believe that El Greco loved the *Cante
Jondo*, and we shall endeavor to explain how his work rep-
resents in painting the counterpart to that which *Cante
Jondo* represents in music.[24]

In searching for a description and analysis of *cante
jondo*, we find the splendid brochure on this subject,
issued anonymously by Manuel de Falla on the occasion
of the *cante jondo* festival organized at Granada by the
composer and Federico Garcia Lorca.[25] This brochure
has been summarized and quoted in J. B. Trend's work
on Falla. After tracing elements of the Byzantine chant,
the Arabian song, and gipsy music in *cante jondo* . . .

. . . Falla finds analogies with certain types of melody
found in India and elsewhere in the East. The positions of
the smaller intervals in the scale are not invariable; their
production depends upon the raising or lowering of the
voice due to the expression given to the word which is
being sung . . . ; further, each of the notes susceptible of
alteration is divided and subdivided, resulting in certain
cases in the alteration of the notes of attack and resolution
of some fragments of the phrase. To this may be added the
portamento of the voice—that manner of singing which produces the infinite gradations of pitch existing between two
notes, whether next to each other or far apart. "Summing
up what has been said, we may affirm, firstly, that in *cante
hondo* (as equally in the primitive melodies of the East) the
musical scale is the direct consequence of what might be
called the oral scale. . . . Our tempered scale only permits
us to change the functions of one note; while in 'modulation by enharmonism,' properly so-called, that tone is

modified according to the natural necessities of its functions. . . ."

Another peculiarity of *cante hondo* is the employment of a compass which rarely exceeds the limits of a sixth. "This sixth, of course, is not composed solely of nine semitones as is the case with our tempered scale. By the employment of the enharmonic genus, there is a considerable increase in the number of tones which the singer can produce."

Thirdly, *cante hondo* provides examples of the repetition of the same note—to the point of obsession—frequently accompanied by an appoggiatura from above or below. . . .

Although gipsy melody is rich in ornamental figures, these (as in primitive oriental music) are only employed at determinate moments as lyrical expansion or as passionate outbursts suggested by the strong emotions described in the text. "They may be considered, therefore, as extended vocal inflexions rather than as ornamental figures, although they assume the latter on being translated into the geometrical intervals of the tempered scale." [26]

Legendre and Hartmann leave the reader in no doubt as to their analogy between *cante jondo* and El Greco.

. . . when we contemplate those subtly subdivided "intervals" of color, where the modulations of essentials prolong themselves into infinity, these violent viewpoints, these explosive gestures, these violent contortions which so shock mediocre and colorless minds—we hear the *Cante Jondo* of painting—an expression of Spain and the East—of the Occident and the Orient. . . . [27]

Other Greco scholars, such as Maurice Barrès, Meier-Graefe, Kehrer, Willumsen and others, without actually referring to music, have nevertheless described *in almost* *these exact words* this effect of Greco's paintings. How lucky are those who may confirm these impressions with their own eyes! *

Unsystematized but very curious evidence on this question is provided in Yastrebtzev's memoirs of Rimsky-Korsakov. In the entry for April 8, 1893:

> During the course of the evening the conversation turned to the question of tonality and Rimsky told how harmonies in sharps had the personal effect on him of *colors*, while harmonies in *flats* conveyed moods of "greater or lesser degrees of warmth" to him. C sharp minor followed by D flat major in the "Egypt" scene of *Mlada* was "deliberately introduced to convey a *feeling of warmth*, just as the color red arouses *sensations of heat*, while *blue and purple* suggest *cold and darkness.* "This is possibly why," he said, "that the strange tonality (E minor) of Wagner's inspired Prelude of *Das Rheingold* always has such a depressing effect on me. I would have transposed this Prelude in the key of E major." [28]

In passing, we should remember James McNeill Whistler's "color symphonies"—*Harmony in Green and Blue, Nocturne in Blue and Silver, Nocturne in Blue and Gold*, and his *Symphonies in White.* [29]

Audio-color associations have occupied even so little respected a figure as Böcklin:

> To him, who always pondered the secret of color, all colors spoke—as Floerke reports—and in turn, everything he perceives, both inwardly and outwardly, is translated

---

* American public collections now contain a wealth of El Greco's work. There are paintings of first importance in New York, Chicago, Boston, Washington and Philadelphia.—Editor.

into color. I am convinced that to him a trumpet blast, for example, is cinnamon red.[30]

Considering the prevalence of this phenomenon, Novalis' demand is quite relevant:

Plastic works of art should never be viewed without music; musical works, on the other hand, should be heard only in beautifully decorated halls.[31]

As for an absolute "color alphabet," unfortunately we must agree with François Coppée, that philistine whom I thoroughly despise, when he writes:

Rimbaud, fumiste réussi,
—Dans un sonnet que je déplore—
Veut que les lettres O. E. I.
Forment le drapeau tricolore.
En vain le *Décadent* pérore. . . .[32]

The question must, nevertheless, be undertaken, for the problem of achieving such absolute correspondence is still disturbing many minds, even those of American film producers. Only a few years ago I came across in an American magazine quite serious speculations as to the absolute correspondence of the piccolo's tone to— yellow!

But let this yellow color, allegedly produced by the piccolo, serve us as a bridge to the problems, not of "non-objective abstractions" but those problems encountered by the artist in his creative work with color.

III

COLOR AND MEANING

Forms, colors, densities, odors—what is it in me
that corresponds with them?

WALT WHITMAN [1]

IN THE preceding section we gave a rather thorough consideration to that question of *finding* "absolute" relations between sound and color. For further clarification let us examine another problem tangent to this, namely: the question of "absolute" relations between particular emotions and particular colors.

For variety's sake, let us approach this question less through "authorities" with their reasonings and opinions, and more through the living emotions and impressions that artists have left us in this matter.

And for convenience' sake, let us confine our examples to one color tonality. Let us compose our own "rhapsody in yellow."

Our first example is an extreme case.

When we speak of "inner tonality" and "inner harmony of line, form and color," we have in mind a harmony with *something*, a correspondence with *something*. The inner tonality must contribute to the *meaning* of an inner feeling. As vague as this feeling may be, in its turn it is always directed finally to something concrete, which finds an outer expression in colors, lines and forms.

Nevertheless, there are those who claim that such an approach denies the "freedom" of feeling. To counter our views and opinions, they propose an aimless, vague, "absolutely free" inner tonality (*der innere Klang*), neither as a direction nor as a means, but as *an end in itself*, as the summit of achievement, as finality.

Such a view of "freedom" only frees us from reason. This is truly a rare, unique freedom, the only one *absolutely* attainable among our fascist neighbors.

A leading exponent and life-long advocate of the above ideal is the painter Kandinsky—the source of the first measures of our "rhapsody in yellow."

The following is an excerpt from "The Yellow Sound," [2] a theater-composition by Kandinsky, which concludes the volume entitled *Der blaue Reiter*—practically a manifesto of the group of this name—and of considerable influence in the subsequent tendencies of modern European art.

This "Yellow Sound" is actually a "program" for a scenic presentation of its author's feelings regarding the play of colors as of music, of the play of music as of colors, of the play of people in some way or other, and so on.

Within its obscurity and bewildering elusiveness one eventually senses the presence of some mystic "seed"— although it would be very difficult to arrive at any clear definition of it. Finally, in the sixth scene, it is revealed, almost religiously:

Dull blue background. . . .
In the center of the stage is a bright yellow giant with a blurred white face and big, round, black eyes. . . .

He slowly raises his arms alongside his body (palms down), growing in height as he does so.

At the moment he attains the full height of the stage, and his figure resembles a cross, the stage is *suddenly* darkened. The music is expressive, following the action on the stage.

The contents of this work cannot be satisfactorily conveyed, due to the total absence of content—as well as theme.

The most we can do for the author is to present a few examples of his feelings, winding around the "yellow sounds":

Scene 2.

The blue haze gradually gives way to the light, which is completely and harshly white. Upstage a mound, entirely round, as bright green as possible.

The background is violet, rather bright.

The music is harsh, stormy, with constantly recurring *A*'s and *B*'s and *A* flats. These individual notes are finally swallowed up by the loud tempestuousness. Suddenly total stillness ensues. A pause. Again *A* and *B* moan, complainingly, but definite and sure. This lasts for some time. Then again a pause.

At this moment the background suddenly turns dirty brown. The mound turns dirty green. And at the very center of the mound an indefinite black spot is formed, alternately becoming clearer and then blurry gray. At the left on the mound a *large* yellow flower suddenly becomes visible. It remotely resembles a big crooked cucumber and constantly grows brighter. Its stem is long and thin. A single spiny, narrow leaf grows out of the middle of the stem and is turned toward the side. A long pause.

Later, *in dead silence*, the flower very slowly swings

from right to left. Still later the leaf joins in the oscillation, but not in unison with the flower. Later still they both oscillate in uneven tempo. Then they again swing to and fro separately, a very thin *B* sounding with the motion of the flower, and a very deep *A* with the leaf's motion. Then both swing in unison, both notes sounding with them. The flower trembles violently and is still. The two musical notes continue to sound. At the same time many persons enter from the left in garish, long, formless clothes (one all in blue, another in red, the third in green, etc.—only yellow is lacking). They have very large white flowers in their hands, similar to the flower on the mound. . . . They speak a recitative in mixed voices. . . .

First the whole stage suddenly grows blurred in dull red light. Secondly, complete darkness alternates with harsh white light. Thirdly, everything suddenly turns a faded gray (all colors disappear!). Only the yellow flower shines ever brighter!

The orchestra gradually begins and covers the voices. The music grows restless, falling away from fortissimo to pianissimo. . . . At the instant that the first figure becomes visible, the yellow flower trembles as if in a cramp. Then it suddenly vanishes. Just as suddenly all the white flowers turn yellow. . . .

Finally they throw away the flowers, which seem to be soaked in blood, and, forcibly freeing themselves from their rigidity, run toward the footlights, closely packed shoulder to shoulder. They often look about them. Sudden darkness.

Scene 3.

Upstage: two big reddish-brown rocks, one of them pointed, the other rounded and larger than the first. Background: black. The giants (of Scene 1) stand between the rocks and silently whisper to one another. Sometimes they whisper in pairs, sometimes they approach with all their heads together. Their bodies remain motionless. In rapid succession fall from all sides harshly colored beams of light (blue, red, violet, green—alternating several times). These beams meet at the center of the stage, where they mix. Everything is motionless. The giants are almost wholly invisible. Suddenly all the colors vanish. The stage is black for an instant. Then a dull yellow light floods the stage, gradually growing more intense, until the whole stage is bathed in garish lemon-yellow. As the light increases, the music grows deeper and becomes darker and darker (these movements remind one of a snail forcing itself into its shell). During these two movements nothing but light should be visible on the stage—no objects. . . .

Etc., etc.

The method employed here is clear—to abstract "inner tonalities" of all "external" matter.

Such a method *consciously attempts to divorce all formal elements from all content elements;* everything touching theme or subject is dismissed, leaving only those extreme formal elements that in *normal creative work* play only a partial rôle. (Kandinsky formulates his theory elsewhere in the volume cited.)

We cannot deny that compositions of this kind evoke *obscurely disturbing* sensations—but no more than this.

But to this day attempts continue to be made to arrange these subjective and largely personal sensations into meaningful relationships, that are, frankly, just as vague and remote.*

---

* Both Remy de Gourmont and Humpty-Dumpty adopted this course. The one claims, "To erect into laws one's personal impressions, this is the great effort of a man if he is sincere." The other: "When *I* use a word, it means just what I choose it to mean—neither more nor less."

The following will demonstrate how Paul Gauguin dealt with similar "inner tonalities" in a notebook entitled *Genèse d'un tableau*,[3] concerning his painting "Manao Tupapau—The Spirit of the Dead Watching": [4]

A young Tahitian girl is lying on her belly, revealing a part of her frightened face. She reposes on a bed covered with a blue *pareo* and a light chrome yellow sheet. There is a background of purple violet, strewn with flowers similar to electric sparks; a somewhat strange figure stands by the bed.

Charmed by a form, a movement, I paint this with no other concern than to do a nude. As it now stands, it is a slightly indecent sketch in the nude. What I want to do, however, is a chaste painting, expressing the Tahitian spirit, its character and its tradition.

I use the *pareo* as a bedspread because it is intimately bound to the life of a Tahitian. The sheet, with a texture of tree-bark, must be yellow—because this color suggests something unexpected to the beholder; and also because it suggests lamplight which spares me the trouble of producing this effect. I must have a slightly terrifying background. Violet is obviously necessary. The scaffolding of the musical aspect of the picture is now erected.

In this somewhat daring pose, what can a young Tahitian girl be doing stark naked on a bed? Preparing for love?— This would be characteristic for her, but it is indecent, and I don't want it. Sleeping?—The act of love would be ended, which is still indecent. I see only fear. What kind of fear?—Certainly not the fear of some Susanna surprised by the elders. This fear is unknown in Tahiti.

The *tupapau* (Spirit of the Dead) is the answer I am seeking. It is a source of constant fear for the Tahitians. At night, a lamp is always kept alight. When there is no moon, nobody walks along the road without a lantern, and even then they always walk in groups.

Having found my *tupapau*, I become completely attached to it and make it the motif of my picture. The nude takes on a secondary importance.

How does a Tahitian girl imagine a ghost? She has never been to the theatre, nor has she read novels, and when she thinks of a dead person, she can only think of one that she has already seen. My ghost can only be some little old woman. She extends her hand as though to clutch her prey.

A decorative sense leads me to strew flowers over the background. These are *tupapau* flowers, phosphorescences, indicating that the ghost is thinking of you. Tahitian beliefs.

The title *Manao tupapau* has two meanings: she can be thinking of the ghost, or the ghost is thinking about her.

Summing up. The musical element: undulating horizontal lines; harmonies of orange and blue woven together by yellows and violets and their derivatives, all lighted by greenish sparks. The literary element: the Spirit of a living girl bound to the Spirit of the dead. Night and Day.

This genesis is written for those who always insist on knowing the *whys* and *wherefores*.

Otherwise, it is simply a Tahitian nude study.

Here is everything we are seeking: "the scaffolding of the musical aspect of the picture is now erected;" an appraisal of the psychological values of colors—the "terrifying" use of violet, as well as of our yellow, here calculated to suggest "something unexpected to the beholder."

A close associate of Gauguin's has recorded a similar appraisal of our color. Vincent van Gogh describes his "Night Café" [5] which he has just finished, to his brother:

In my picture of the "Night Café" I have tried to express the idea that the café is a place where one can ruin one's self, run mad, or commit a crime. So I have tried to express as it were the powers of darkness in a low drink shop, by soft Louis XV green and malachite, contrasting with yellow green and hard blue greens, and all this in an atmosphere like a devil's furnace, of pale sulphur.[6]

Here is another artist speaking of yellow—Walther Bondy, writing of his designs for a production of Strindberg's *Brott och Brott* [7] in 1912:

In staging the Strindberg play we made an attempt to bring the settings and costumes directly into participation in the action of the play.

To do this it was necessary for every detail of the milieu to express something and to play its own specific rôle. In many cases, for example, particular colors would be employed for their direct effect on the spectator. There were several leit-motifs, conveyed through color, in order to show a more profound connection between separated moments of the play. Thus in the third scene (Act II, Scene 1) a yellow motif was introduced into the action. Maurice and Henriette are sitting in the "Auberge des Adrets"; the general tone of the scene is black, with a black cloth almost completely covering an enormous stained-glass window; on the table is a candelabra with three candles. In the necktie and gloves given him by Jeanne, now unwrapped by Maurice, the color of yellow appears for the first time. Yellow becomes the color motif of Maurice's "sinking into sin" (through this gift he is inescapably tied to Jeanne and Adolphe).

In the fifth scene (Act III, Scene 2) when Adolphe leaves the stage and Maurice and Henriette become aware of their crime, great bunches of yellow flowers are brought onto the stage. In the seventh scene (Act IV, Scene 1) Maurice and Henriette are sitting in the Luxembourg Gardens. The sky is brilliant yellow, and silhouetted against it are the thin bare black branches, the bench and the figures of Maurice and Henriette. . . . It should be noted that the treatment of the whole production was on a mystic plane. . . .

The premise here is that "particular colors exert specific influences" on the spectator. This is "substantiated" by the connection of yellow with sin, and the influence of this color on the psyche. Mysticism is also mentioned. . . .

It is interesting to see the same associative use made of this color by T. S. Eliot, particularly in his early poems:

> Sitting along the bed's edge, where
> You curled the papers from your hair,
> Or clasped the yellow soles of feet
> In the palms of both soiled hands.[8]

Well! and what if she should die some afternoon,
Afternoon grey and smoky, evening yellow and rose . . .[9]

The yellow fog that rubs its back upon the window-panes,
The yellow smoke that rubs its muzzle on the window-
      panes
Licked its tongue into the corners of the evening,
Lingered upon the pools that stand in drains. . . .[10]

Mr. Eliot's pointed use of yellow extends even to substances and objects of this color. In *Sweeney Among the Nightingales:*

> : . . the man with heavy eyes
> Declines the gambit, shows fatigue,
>
> Leaves the room and reappears
> Outside the window, leaning in,
> Branches of wistaria
> Circumscribe a golden grin. . . .

And *Mr. Apollinax* ends on:

> I remember a slice of lemon, and a bitten macaroon.

To make the color of yellow thoroughly "frightening" we choose another example.

There are few writers as acutely sensitive to color as is Gogol. And few also are the writers of our time who understand Gogol as acutely as did the late Andrei Belyi.

In his painstaking analysis of Gogol's craftsmanship,[11] Belyi subjects the changes of Gogol's palette throughout his creative career to the most minute examination in the chapter, "The Spectrum of Gogol." What is revealed thereby? Following the yellow graph in Belyi's charts, we see our color increasing steadily from the joyous *Evenings in the Village*, through *Taras Bulba*, and making its greatest quantitative leap upwards in the second volume of *Dead Souls*.

Of all colors employed by Gogol in his first works, the average of yellow references is only 3.5%.

In the second group (of novels and comedies) this average rises to 8.5%, and in the third group (Volume I of *Dead Souls*) reaches 10.3%. And lastly (Volume II of

Dead Souls), yellow occupies 12.8% of Gogol's color attention. Being close to yellow, green moves correspondingly: 8.6–7.7–9.6–21.6%. Together, these two colors occupy *more than a third* of Gogol's palette in his last work.

Nor does this include the 12.8% of "golden" references. Belyi points out:

> . . . the gold of Volume II (of *Dead Souls*) is not the gold of gold-plate and gold thread, but the gold of cathedrals and crosses, heightening the influential rôle of the Orthodox Church; the ringing of "gold" is balanced against the "red ringing" of Cossack glory; with the red graph declining and the yellow and green graphs rising, this second volume moves away to a color world far removed from the spectrum of *Evenings in the Village* . . .

Even more terrifying seems the "fateful" tone of yellow, when we recall how this is exactly the chromatic scale that dominates another work of art, created in a tragic twilight—Rembrandt's self-portrait at the age of fifty-five.[12]

To avoid charges of personal prejudice in describing the color of this painting, I cite here, not my own, but Allen's description of this work, as he wrote of it in his article relating the problems of esthetics to those of psychology: [13]

> . . . the colors are all dark and dull, lightened only in the center. This center is a combination of dirty green and yellowed gray, mixed with faded brown; the rest is almost black. . . .

This yellow scale, melting into dirty greens and a faded brown, is emphasized by contrast with the lower portion of the canvas:

. . . only below some reddish tones can be seen; muffled and overlaid upon each other, but, more or less aided by thickness and their comparatively great color intensity, they create a clearly expressed contrast to the rest of the painting. . . .

In this connection it is impossible to forbear any reference to the unfortunate image of the aged Rembrandt presented by Alexander Korda and Charles Laughton in *Rembrandt*. As scrupulously costumed and made-up as Laughton was for these concluding scenes, no attempt was made to mirror this tragic *chromatic scale*, so typical of the late Rembrandt, with an equivalent cinematic *light-scale*.

It becomes apparent that many characteristics we ascribe to the color yellow derive from its immediate neighbor in the spectrum—green. Green, on the other hand, is directly associated with the symbols of life—young leaf-shoots, foliage and "greenery" itself—just as firmly as it is with the symbols of death and decay—leaf-mold, slime, and the shadows on a dead face.

There is no limit to the evidence we could bring in to this court, but have we not enough to make us ask ourselves, "Perhaps there *is* something sinister in the nature of the color of yellow?" Does this touch something more profound than mere conventional symbolism and habitual or accidental associations?

For answers to these questions we must turn to the

history of the evolution of symbolic meanings within certain colors. There is, fortunately, a very thorough work on this subject by Frédéric Portal, first published in 1857: *Des couleurs symboliques dans l'antiquité, le Moyen-Age, et les temps modernes.*

This authority on the "symbolic meaning" of color has this to say about the color that concerns us here—yellow, and how ideas of *perfidy, treason and sin* grew to be connected with it:

> Divine and sacred languages designated with the colors of gold and yellow the union of the soul with God and, by opposition, adultery in a spiritual sense. In profane speech, this was a materialized emblem representing legitimate love as well as carnal adultery that breaks the bonds of marriage. . . .
>
> The golden apple was, for the Greeks, the symbol of love and concord and, by opposition, it represented discord and all the evils in its train; the judgment of Paris proves this. Likewise Atalanta, while gathering the golden apples picked in the Garden of the Hesperides, is beaten in the race and becomes the victor's prize.[14]

Of particular interest is Portal's evidence of one feature to be found in all mythological matter attaching to this color: the *ambivalent* meanings that are read into it. This phenomenon can be explained by the fact that in early stages of evolution *the same concept, meaning or word equally represents two opposites that are mutually exclusive.*

Yellow, he shows, has equally strong connections with both "loving union" and "adultery."

Havelock Ellis provides a convincing explanation of

this phenomenon, that is, in the particular instance of *yellow:*

It was clearly the advent of Christianity that introduced a new feeling in regard to yellow. . . . In very large measure, no doubt, this was clearly the outcome of the whole of the Christian revulsion against the classic world and the rejection of everything which stood as the symbol of joy and pride. Red and yellow were the favorite colors of that world. The love of red was too firmly rooted in human nature for even Christianity to overcome it altogether, but yellow was a point of less resistance and here the new religion triumphed. Yellow became the color of envy.

Yellow became the color of jealousy, of envy, of treachery. Judas was painted in yellow garments and in some countries Jews were compelled to be so dressed. In France in the sixteenth century the doors of traitors and felons were daubed with yellow. In Spain heretics who recanted were enjoined to wear a yellow cross as a penance and the Inquisition required them to appear at public *autos de fe* in penitential garments and carrying a yellow candle.

There is a special reason why Christianity should have viewed yellow with suspicion. It had been the color associated with wanton love. In the beginning the association was with legitimate love. . . . But in Greece, and to a still more marked extent in Rome, the courtezan began to take advantage of this association.[15]

In one of the lectures which I happened to hear given by the late academician Marr,[16] he illustrated the basic phenomenon of ambivalence with the word-root "kon," which is a root for both the Russian word for *end*, "kon-yetz," and one of the oldest Russian words for *beginning*, "is-kon-i."

The ancient Hebrew language contains a similar example in the word קֹדֶשׁ "K°d°sh," which has both "holy" and "unholy" significance. The "clean" and "unclean" significance of the word *tabu* is already familiar to us. And Gauguin has already mentioned that "Manao tupapau" holds a dual meaning: "*she* is thinking of the *ghost*," and "the *ghost* is thinking about *her*."

Remaining within the circle of our present interest in ideas of yellow and gold, we can remark another case of ambivalence: gold, a symbol of *highest value*, also serves as a popular metaphor signifying—filth. This is true not only in a general way, as in the Western European examples below, but in the Russian language which contains the term "zolotar" ("zoloto," the root—gold), having the specific meaning of "cess-pool cleaner."

We will see also that a "*positive*" interpretation (in a "major key") of this color's golden or yellow gleam contains a *directly sensual* base, and that into this are woven entirely marginal associations (sun, gold, stars).

Even Picasso has remarked these particular associations:

There are painters who transform the sun into a yellow spot but there are others who with the help of their art and their intelligence transform a yellow spot into a sun.[17]

And van Gogh, for whom the color of yellow had special vitality, casts aside its evil associations which he exploited in his "Night Café," and takes the floor for the painters who "transform a yellow spot into a sun":

. . . instead of trying to reproduce exactly what I have before my eyes, I use colour arbitrarily so as to express myself forcibly. Well, let that be as far as theory goes, but I am going to give you an example of what I mean.

I should like to paint the portrait of an artist friend, a man who dreams great dreams, who works as the nightingale sings, because it is his nature. He'll be a fair man. I want to put into the picture my appreciation, the love I have for him. So I paint him as he is, as faithfully as I can, to begin with.

But the picture is not finished yet. To finish it I am now going to be the arbitrary colourist. I exaggerate the fairness of the hair, I come even to orange tones, chromes and pale lemon-yellow.

Beyond the head, instead of painting the ordinary wall of the mean room, I paint infinity, a plain background of the richest, intensest blue that I can contrive, and by the simple combination of the bright head against the rich blue background, I get a mysterious effect, like a star in the depths of an azure sky. . . .[18]

The positive source of yellow in the first instance was the *sun* (Picasso), and in the second—a *star* (van Gogh).

Let us take another image of the golden hue of yellow —finding it in "a man who dreams great dreams"—Walt Whitman himself, "speeding through space, speeding through heaven and the stars":

Painters have painted their swarming groups and the centre-
     figure of all,
From the head of the centre-figure spreading a nimbus of
     gold-color'd light,
But I paint myriads of heads, but paint no head without its
     nimbus of gold-color'd light,
From my hand from the brain of every man and woman
     it streams, effulgently flowing forever.[19]

Whitman must have loved the color, but loved it enough not to restrict its application to one use alone. His nature descriptions are full of a "positive" use of yellow, growing into great, warm, "positive" landscapes:

Sprouts take and accumulate, stand by the curb prolific
    and vital,
Landscapes projected masculine, full-sized and golden.[20]

I see the highlands of Abyssinia,
I see flocks of goats feeding, and see the fig-tree, tamarind,
    date,
And see fields of teff-wheat and places of verdure and
    gold.[21]

California gets special "golden" attention:

Always California's golden hills and hollows, and the silver
    mountains of New Mexico. . . .[22]

The flashing and golden pageant of California,
The sudden and gorgeous drama, the sunny and ample
    lands. . . .[23]

Among the important positive associations that Whitman makes with yellow is with a theme that concerned him even more than nature—the theme of work:

By the curb toward the edge of the flagging,
A knife-grinder works at his wheel sharpening a great
    knife,
Bending over he carefully holds it to the stone, by foot
    and knee,
With measur'd tread he turns rapidly, as he presses with
    light but firm hand.

Forth issue then in copious golden jets,
Sparkles from the wheel.²⁴

and from the *Song of the Broad-Axe:*

The butter-colored chips flying off in great flakes and
slivers. . . .

Despite the powerful major key in which these yellow
references are sounded, there is also a minor key—first
heard in the rural sunset passages, from which the transition to death and old age stems through direct images:

Ray'd in the limpid yellow slanting sundown,
Music, Italian music in Dakota.²⁵

Pictures of growing spring and farms and homes,
With the Fourth-month eve at sundown, and the gray
smoke lucid and bright,
With floods of the yellow gold of the gorgeous, indolent,
sinking sun, burning, expanding the air. . . .²⁶

Passing the yellow-speared wheat, every grain from its
shroud in the dark-brown fields uprisen,
Passing the apple-tree blows of white and pink in the
orchards,
Carrying a corpse to where it shall rest in the grave,
Night and day journeys a coffin.²⁷

and from *Old Age's Lambent Peaks:*

The calmer sight—the golden setting, clear and broad. . . .

And finally yellow becomes the color of the faces of
wounded men, of old women—and is added to the color-
scale of deathly decay:

I dress a wound in the side, deep, deep,
But a day or two more, for see the frame all wasted and
    sinking,
And the yellow-blue countenance see.[28]

It is my face yellow and wrinkled instead of the old
    woman's,
I sit low in a straw-bottom chair and carefully darn my
    grandson's stockings.[29]

and in *The Pallid Wreath:*

Somehow I cannot let it go yet, funeral though it is,
Let it remain back there on its nail suspended,
With pink, blue, yellow, all blanched, and the white now
    gray and ashy. . . .

But one can detect even among Whitman's broad,
varied uses of this color that he does make some distinc-
tions in his use of subtle differences of *shades* of yellow
—ranging all the way from golden to "yellow, all
blanched."

Returning to our authority, Portal tells us of a stage
in the evolution of "yellow traditions" in the Middle
Ages. The single color which in antiquity had been a
token of two opposites simultaneously, underwent a
"rationalizing process" and emerged as *two distinct
tones*, each representing *one half* of the former *double-
significance:*

. . . the Moors differentiated the two symbols by using
two different shades: golden yellow signified *wise and
good counsel*, and pale yellow signified treachery and de-
ceit. . . .[30]

The learned rabbis of medieval Spain gave an interpretation of added interest for us:

> . . . the rabbis held that the fruit of the forbidden tree was a lemon, by opposing its pale color and its acidity to the golden color and sweetness of the orange or golden apple, according to the Latin term.

This subdivision is carried further:

> In heraldry, gold is the emblem of love, of constancy and of wisdom and, by opposition, yellow still denotes, in our time, inconstancy, jealousy and adultery.

Thus came into existence the French tradition mentioned by Ellis of smearing yellow paint on the doors of traitors (such as Charles de Bourbon for his treason during the reign of Francis I). The official garment for an executioner in medieval Spain was prescribed as of two colors, yellow and red: yellow to symbolize the accused's treachery; red, retribution.

These are the "mystic" sources from which the symbolists tried to extract "eternal" color meanings, and determine the irrevocable influences of colors on the human psyche.

But what tenacity there has been in preserving traditions in this matter!

It is precisely these meanings that are preserved, for example, in Parisian "argot"—a language full of wit and folk imagery.

Open one of the many dictionaries of this argot to the word "jaune":

YELLOW—the color assigned to deceived husbands: cf. *Sa femme le peignait en jaune de la tête aux pieds*—his wife cuckolded him tremendously; *un bal jaune*—a ball where all the men are cuckolds.[31]

This is not all. The interpretation of treachery spreads further than this.

(*c*) YELLOW—a member of an anti-socialist trade union.

This use of the term is to be found in many countries. We often hear the Second International referred to as the "yellow international." "Yellow trade unions" is a familiar term in many places while America knows the "yellow dog contract." Yellow as the color of treachery has been preserved to the point of stigmatizing traitors to the working class! Through the medium of films Alberto Cavalcanti has brought into common usage an epithet for one of the most despicable of these traitors —*Yellow Caesar*.*

Close cousins of the Paris argot, the slang and "cant" of America and England have preserved the same associations for yellow.

A New Canting Dictionary of 1725 asserts that yellow, meaning *jealous*, was originally a term of the London underworld.[32]

In *Slang and Its Analogues Past and Present*, the parent of all modern slang dictionaries, the authors found older, broader interpretations for this color:

YELLOW, subs. (old colloquial). (1) Generic for jealousy, envy, melancholy. . . . Also in frequent proverbial

* A two-reel satire produced for Michael Balcon, 1941.

phrase: e.g., *to wear yellow hose* (*breeches or stock-ings*)—to be jealous; . . . *to wear yellow stockings*—to be cuckolded. . . .[33]

The authors bring Shakespeare to testify:

. . . civil as an orange, and something of that jealous com-plexion.   (*Much Ado About Nothing*, Act II, Scene 1)

. . . with a green and yellow melancholy . . .
(*Twelfth Night*, Act II, Scene 4)

. . . 'mongst all colours
No yellow in't, lest she suspect, as he does,
Her children not her husband's!
(*Winter's Tale*, Act II, Scene 3)

American slang is particularly colorful in this respect:

Yellow-livered—Cowardly.
Yellow streak—Cowardice, undependableness.
Yaller dog—A treacherous person, a cowardly person.[34]

Another meaning is found for yellow in the term "yellow stuff"—money (or, sometimes, counterfeit money). A fusion of this meaning and of the more "tra-ditional" meaning gave birth to that inspired phrase, formed from "bought" and "treachery"—"the yellow press."

However, the most interesting light cast on these "symbolic meanings" of yellow comes from the fact that, essentially it was not yellow, as a color, that deter-mined them.

We have shown that in antiquity this interpretation arose as an automatic antipode to the sun-motivated positive tone of yellow.

Its negative "reputation" in the Middle Ages was formed of the sum of *associative and no longer narrowly color indications*. The Arabs found "wanness" rather than "brilliance" in this color. The rabbis saw yellow as "pallor" rather than as "vividness," and gave first place to taste associations: the "treacherous" taste of the lemon as distinct from the sweetness of the orange!

This use was also preserved in the argot. There is a popular French expression—*rire jaune* (yellow laughter). In Balzac's *Paris Marié*, Chapter III is entitled "Les risettes jaunes." Pierre MacOrlan gives the title of *Le Rire Jaune* to a novel. The expression can also be found in the dictionary (*Parisisms*) quoted above. What is its meaning?

An exact counterpart can be found in both the English and Russian languages: a sour smile. (In German also: *ein saures Lächeln*.) The interesting fact here is that where the French use a *color* identification, these other languages use a corresponding designation of *taste*. That lemon of the Spanish rabbis furnishes us with a key to the code.

The tradition of dividing the meanings of yellow according to associations was continued by Goethe. Most of his concrete associations are with textures, but he introduces a psychological approach with a new pair of concepts: "noble" (*edel*) and "coarse" (*unedel*), which even ring of social motives!

In Part IV, entitled "Effect of colour with reference to moral associations," of Goethe's *Farbenlehre*, we read:

Yellow

765. This is the colour nearest the light. . . .

766. In its highest purity it always carries with it the nature of brightness, and has a serene, gay, softly exciting character.

767. In this state, applied to dress, hangings, carpeting, &c., it is agreeable. Gold in its perfectly unmixed state, especially when the effect of polish is superadded, gives us a new and high idea of this colour; in like manner, a strong yellow, as it appears on satin, has a magnificent and noble effect. . . .

770. If, however, this colour in its pure and bright state is agreeable and gladdening, and in its utmost power is serene and noble, it is, on the other hand, extremely liable to contamination, and produces a very disagreeable effect if it is sullied, or in some degree tends to the *minus* side. Thus, the colour of sulphur, which inclines to green, has something unpleasant in it.

771. When a yellow colour is communicated to dull and coarse surfaces, such as common cloth, felt, or the like, on which it does not appear with full energy, the disagreeable effect alluded to is apparent. By a slight and scarcely perceptible change, the beautiful impression of fire and gold is transformed into one not undeserving the epithet foul; and the colour of honour and joy reversed to that of ignominy and aversion. To this impression the yellow hats of bankrupts and the yellow circles on the mantles of Jews, may have owed their origin. . . .[35]

Before proceeding further on our "yellow path" (which seems to have landed us among Nazi revivals of medieval darkness!), let us note some facts about the color of green, the spectrum neighbor of yellow. The same picture appears here, too. If green, in its positive interpretation, fully coincides with the initial image which is presupposed above, then its "sinister" interpretation is also determined, like the "negative" side of yellow, not by direct associations, but with the same ambivalence.

In its first interpretation, green is a symbol of life, regeneration, spring, hope. In this the Christian, the Chinese and the Moslem religions agree. Mohammed is believed to have been attended in all critical moments of his life by "angels in green turbans," and so a *green banner* became the *Prophet's banner*.

Along with this a number of contradictory interpretations evolved. The color of hope was also the color of hopelessness and despair: in the Greek theater the dark green color of the sea conveyed a sinister meaning under certain conditions.

This tone of green contains a strong blue. And it is interesting that in the Japanese theater, where color symbolism is so "tightly" attached to particular imagery, blue is the color worn by sinister figures.

In a letter to me (October 31, 1931) Masaru Kobayashi, author of the definitive work on "kumadori" (makeup in the Kabuki theater) wrote:

. . . the basic colors employed in kumadori are red and blue. Red is warm and attractive. Blue, the opposite, is the color of villains, and among supernatural creatures, the color of ghosts and fiends. . . .

And Portal has this to say of green:

Green, like other colors, had a nefarious meaning; as it had been the symbol of the soul's regeneration and of wisdom, it also signified, by opposition, moral degradation and madness.

The Swedish theosophist, Swedenborg, gives green eyes to the madmen in hell. A window in Chartres Cathedral depicts the temptation of Jesus—Satan has a green skin and great green eyes. . . .

The eye, in the lore of symbolism, signifies intelligence, the light of the mind; man may turn it towards good or evil; Satan and Minerva, folly and wisdom, were both represented with green eyes.[36]

Abstracting green from green objects or the color of yellow from objects of this color, elevating green to an "eternal green" or yellow to a "symbolic yellow," the symbolist who performs this feat is remarkably akin to the madman of whom Diderot wrote to Madame Volland:

. . . a single physical quality can lead the mind preoccupied with it to an infinite variety of things. Let us take a color, yellow, for instance: gold is yellow, silk is yellow, anxiety is yellow, bile is yellow, straw is yellow; with how many other threads does not this thread connect? Insanity, dreams, rambling conversations consist in passing from one subject to the next by means of some common quality.

The madman is unaware of the transition. He holds a blade of shiny yellow straw in his hand, and he shouts that he has caught a sunbeam.[37]

This madman was an ultra-formalist, seeing as he did only the *form* of the sunbeam and the *yellowness* of the color, seeing only *line and color*. And to this color and line, completely independent of the *concrete content of the object*, he gives a meaning, determined by himself alone.

In this he resembles his ancestor of the period of magic beliefs. Then, too, meanings were determined for yellow "of itself."

The ancient Hindoos performed an elaborate ceremony, based on homeopathic magic, for the cure of jaundice. Its main drift was to banish the yellow colour to yellow creatures and yellow things, such as the sun, to which it properly belongs, and to procure for the patient a healthy red colour from a living, vigorous source, namely a red bull. With this intention, a priest recited the following spell: "Up to the sun shall go thy heart-ache and thy jaundice: in the colour of the red bull do we envelop thee! We envelop thee in red tints, unto long life. May this person go unscathed and be free of yellow colour! . . ." Then in order to improve his colour by thoroughly eradicating the yellow taint, he proceeded thus. He first daubed him from head to foot with a yellow porridge made of tumeric or curcuma (a yellow plant), set him on a bed, tied three birds, to wit, a parrot, a thrush, and a yellow wagtail, by means of a yellow string to the foot of the bed; then pouring water over the patient, he washed off the yellow porridge, and with it no doubt the jaundice, from him to the birds. . . . The ancients held that if a person suffering from jaundice looked sharply at a stone-curlew, and the bird looked steadily at him, he was cured of the disease. "Such is the creature," says Plutarch, "and such the temperament of the creature that it draws out and receives the malady which issues, like a stream, through the eyesight." . . . The virtue of the bird lay not in its colour but in its large golden eye, which naturally drew out the yellow jaundice. Pliny . . . mentions also a stone which was supposed to cure jaundice because its hue resembled that of a jaundiced skin. In modern Greece jaundice goes by the name of the Golden Disease, and very naturally it can be healed by gold.[38]

We must not fall into the error either of the madman or the Hindu magician, who see the sinister power of disease or the great power of the sun as solely reposing in the golden color.

Ascribing to a color such independent and self-sufficient meanings,

abstracting color from the *concrete phenomenon, which was its sole source for the attendant complex of concepts and associations,*

seeking absolute correlations of color and sound, color and emotion,

abstracting the concreteness of color into a system of colors that act "for their own sakes,"

we will get nowhere, or worse, we will arrive at the same destination as that of the French symbolists of the latter half of the nineteenth century, about whom Gorky wrote:

. . . We must, they tell us, attach to every letter a particular, specific sensation,—A with cold, O with longing, U with fear, etc.: then we are to paint these letters with colors, as Rimbaud has done, then give them sounds, bringing them to life, making out of each letter a tiny, living organism. This done, we can begin to combine these into words. . . .[39]

The harm consequent on such a method of playing with absolute correspondences is self-evident.

But if we look more carefully at the schemes for "absolute" relationships cited in the previous section, we will discover that in almost each citation, its author speaks not of "absolute correspondences," but of *images* to which he has attached *personal* color concepts. It is from these various image concepts that the various "meanings" have evolved, ascribed by these different authors to the same color.

Rimbaud begins very decidedly: "*A*, black; *E*, white," and so on. But in the following line he promises:

Someday I shall name the birth from which you rise. . . .

And in going further, he does reveal this "secret," not only the secret of the formation of his own *personal* sound-color correspondences, but of the very *principle* of any author's determination of such relationships.

Every vowel, as a result of his personal life and his private emotional experiences, belongs, for Rimbaud, to a definite group of image complexes, each of which has a color source.

"I" is not merely colored red. But:

> *I*, purples, blood spit out, laugh of lips so
> Lovely in anger or penitent ecstasies. . . .

"U" is not merely green. But:

> *U*, cycles, divine vibrations of green seas;
> The peace of animal pastures, peace of these
> Lines printed by alchemy on the great
> brows of the wise . . .

(We recall that, according to Lafcadio Hearn, above, a similar figure, of "a mature Greek with wrinkles," is indicated by the initial "X," and so on.)

Here color acts as nothing more than a stimulus, as in a conditioned reflex, which recalls a whole complex, in which it had once played a part, to the memory and the senses.

However, one opinion is that Rimbaud's *Voyelles* was inspired by his memories of the primer which he had used as a child. Such primers, familiar to all of us, consist of great letters of the alphabet, next to which appears the picture of some object or animal whose name begins with the same letter. Its purpose is to fasten the letter to the memory through the object or animal. Rimbaud's "vowels" very possibly grew according to this "image and likeness." With each letter Rimbaud associated the "picture" which, for him, was bound to the letter. These pictures are of various colors, so that these colors are therefore bound to particular letters.

This is exactly what takes place with other writers.

In general the "psychological" interpretation of color *qua* color is a very slippery business. It becomes even more absurd when this system of interpretation begins to claim social "associations."

How gratifying it would be, for example, to find in the fading colors and powdered wigs of the eighteenth-century French aristocracy a reflection "so to speak" of "the ebb of life force from the highest group in the social structure whose place in history the middle classes and the third estate are about to assume." How perfectly this fading scale of delicate (super-delicate!) colors of aristocratic costumes echoes this formulation! However, there is a much simpler explanation of this pastel color-scale: the powder that fell from the wigs onto costumes that were actually vivid in color. Thus this "scale of fading colors" penetrates the intelligence, becoming understood almost as "functional." This is 'protective coloration" in significance as much as is khaki; * the fallen powder is no longer a "dissonance" but is simply unnoticed.

The colors of red and white have long been posed as traditional opposites (and long before the Wars of the Roses). Later these colors move in the direction of *social* tendencies (along with the representation of divisions in parliamentary situations as "right" and "left"). Whites have been the émigrés and legitimists in both the French and Russian Revolutions. Red (the favorite color of Marx and Zola) is associated with revolution. But even in this case there are "temporary violations." Towards the end of the French Revolution, the survivors of the aristocracy, the most violent representatives of reaction, started a vogue for wearing red handkerchiefs and cravats. It was also at this time that the French aristocracy adopted a hair-dress exposing the nape of the neck. This hair-dress, remotely resembling that of the Emperor Titus, was called "à la Titus," but its actual origin had nothing to do with Titus, aside from the accidental resemblance. Essentially it was a symbol of implacable counter-revolutionary hatred, for it was intended to be a constant reminder of the shaving of the necks of those aristocrats condemned to the guillotine. Hence also the red kerchiefs, in memory of the neckerchiefs which wiped the blood from the "victims of the guillotine"—

* The Oxford Dictionary: KHAKI. Dust-coloured, dull-yellow . . . (Hindustani, dusty).

creating a relic that cried aloud for vengeance to every sympathetic beholder.

Thus when any segment of the color spectrum achieves a special vogue, we can look behind it for the *anecdote*, the concrete episode that binds a color to specifically associated ideas.

It may be rewarding to recall other color terminology of pre-revolutionary France—particularly that shade of brown that enjoyed a vogue at the time of the birth of one of the last Louis'—that shade that leaves no doubt as to its origin: "caca Dauphin." A variant of this was called "caca d'oie." Another self-revealing color-word is "puce." The popularity among Marie Antoinette's courtiers of the combination of yellow and red bore little relation to the Spanish executioner's robes that we mentioned above. This combination was called "cardinal sur la paille," and was a sign of the French aristocracy's protest over the imprisonment in the Bastille of Cardinal de Rohan in connection with the famous case of the Queen's Necklace.

In such examples, which are innumerable, lies this "anecdotal origin" which is at the base of those "special" interpretations of color meanings in which so many authors have indulged themselves. The anecdotes are so much more graphic and expressive than the mystic meanings given these colors!

Can we, on the basis of all this presented evidence, deny altogether the existence of relationships between emotions, timbres, sounds and colors? If not convincing relationships to all men, can they at least be established as common to special groups?

The Life of Sir Henry Unton, by an anonymous English painter of the second half of the sixteenth century. This work contains not only an echo of the "simultaneous" theater of the Middle Ages but also a reflection of the multiple-stage settings employed in the theater of the period (see page 103). Courtesy of *Theatre Arts Monthly*.

View and Plan of Toledo, El Greco. See pages 103 to 105 for Greco's remarks and Eisenstein's discussion.

It would be impossible to deny such relationships. Pure statistics themselves would prevent such a mechanical conclusion. Without referring to the special statistical literature in this field, we can quote again from Gorky's article:

. . . It is strange and difficult to understand [Rimbaud's attitude], until one remembers the research conducted in 1885 by an eminent oculist among the students of Oxford University. 526 of these students painted sounds as colors and *vice versa*—and they unanimously decided an equivalence between brown and the note of the trombone, between green and the tone of the hunting-horn. Perhaps this sonnet by Rimbaud has some psychiatric base. . . .[40]

It is clear that in purely "psychiatric" states these phenomena would be far more heightened and evident.

Within these bounds it is possible to speak of the connections between certain colors and certain "definite" emotions. In Havelock Ellis' color investigations he mentions certain color predilections established to his satisfaction:

. . . in the achromatopsia of the hysterical, as Charcot showed and as Parinaud has since confirmed, the order in which the colors usually disappear is violet, green, blue, red: . . . this persistence of red vision in the hysterical is only one instance of a predilection for red which has often been noted as very marked among the hysterical.[41]

These color reactions of hysterical persons have interested other experimenters, whose results concern us despite the antiquated terminology:

The experiments of Binet have established that the impressions conveyed to the brain by the sensory nerves ex-

ercise an important influence on the species and strength of
the excitation distributed by the brain to the motor nerves.
Many sense-impressions operate enervatingly and inhibi-
tively on the movements; others, on the contrary, make
these more powerful, rapid and active; they are "dynamogenous," or "force-producing." As a feeling of pleasure
is always connected with dynamogeny, or the production
of force, every living thing, therefore, instinctively seeks
for dynamogenous sense-impressions, and avoids enervating
and inhibitive ones. Now, red is especially dynamogenous.
"When," says Binet, in a report of an experiment on a
female hysterical subject who was paralyzed in one half of
her body, "we place a dynamometer in the anaesthetically
insensible right hand of Amélie Cle— the pressure of the
hand amounts to 12 kilogrammes. If at the same time she is
made to look at a red disc, the number indicating the pressure in kilogrammes is at once doubled. . . ."
If red is dynamogenous, violet is conversely enervating
and inhibitive. It was not by accident that violet was chosen
by many nations as the exclusive colour for mourning. . . .
The sight of this colour has a depressing effect, and the
unpleasant feeling awakened by it induces dejection in a
sorrowfully-disposed mind. . . .[42]

Similar qualities are ascribed by Goethe to the color
of red. These qualities led him to divide all colors into
active and passive groups (*plus* and *minus*). Such a division is connected with the popular grouping of "warm"
and "cold" colors.

When William Blake sought ironical instructions for
his *Advice to the Popes who succeeded the Age of
Rafael*,[43] he employed such a grouping:

Hire Idiots to Paint with cold light & hot shade . . .

If this data is perhaps insufficient for the formulation of a convincing "scientific code," nevertheless art has long since adopted this in a purely empirical manner, and employed it flawlessly.

Even though the reactions of a normal person are of course far less intense than those of Amélie Cle— while facing a red disc, the artist is quite confident of the effects he can expect to shape with his palette. For the *dynamic tempest* of his painting of "Peasant Women," Malyavin [44] didn't just *happen* to flood his canvas with a riot of *vivid red*.

Goethe has something to say on this score, too. He divides red into three shades: red, red-yellow and yellow-red. To this last shade, our *orange,* he ascribes an "ability" to exert psychic influence:

YELLOW-RED

775. The active side is here in its highest energy, and it is not to be wondered at that impetuous, robust, uneducated men should be especially pleased with this colour. Among savage nations the inclination for it had been universally remarked, and when children, left to themselves, begin to use tints, they never spare vermilion and minium.

776. In looking steadfast at a perfectly yellow-red surface, the colour seems actually to penetrate the organ. . . . A yellow-red cloth disturbs and enrages animals. I have known men of education to whom its effect was intolerable if they chanced to see a person dressed in a scarlet cloak on a grey, cloudy day. . . . [45]

As regards our primary interest, the correspondence of sounds and feelings not only to emotions, but also to each other, I had occasion to come upon an interesting fact outside the scientific or semi-scientific works.

Its source may not be exactly "legal," but it was direct and quite logically convincing to me.

I have an acquaintance, S., to whom I had been introduced by the late Professor Vygotsky and by Professor Luriya.[46] S., failing to find any other use for his unusual faculties, had worked for several years on the vaudeville stage, astonishing audiences with feats of memory. While a man of perfectly normal development, he had retained till his maturity all those traits of primary sensual processes which human beings ordinarily lose in their evolution of logical thought. In his case, particularly, was that boundless capacity for *memorizing* concrete objects through the visualization of their surroundings as well as *what is said* about them (in the evolution of the ability to *generalize*, this early form of thought, assisted by accumulated *single factors*, retained by the *memory*, becomes atrophied).

Thus S. could *at the same time* remember *any number* of figures or meaninglessly strung together words. He could then recite these from beginning to end—from end to beginning—skipping every second or third word, and so on. In addition to this, he would, upon meeting you a year and a half later, repeat the entire feat, and just as flawlessly. He could duplicate all the details of any conversation that he had ever overheard, and he could recite from memory all the experiments in which he had taken part (and the tables used in these experiments often contained several hundred words!). In short, he was a living, and naturally more amazing thereby, prototype of Mr. Memory in Hitchcock's *Thirty-Nine Steps*. "Eidetics" also figured in his talents—that is, an ability to make an exact reproduction, not consciously, but automatically, of any drawing of any complexity (this ability normally disappears with the evolution of an *understanding of relationships* in drawings or pictures, and of conscious examination of the objects depicted in them).

I repeat that all these traits and abilities were preserved in S. alongside the absolutely normal traits acquired through a full development of active consciousness and of thought processes.

S. was, of course, endowed far beyond any other being within my experience, with the power of *synesthesia*, or the production from one sense-impression of one kind of an associated mental image of a sense-impression of another kind. The particular examples of this cited above were limited to the ability *to see sounds in terms of color and to hear colors as sounds*. I once had an opportunity to discuss this with him. The most interesting fact to appear, for the authenticity of which I would be glad to vouch, was that the *scale of vowels* was seen by him *not as colors,* but as a scale of varying *light values.* Color, for him, *is summoned only* by the consonants. This seems much more convincing to me than all the calculations cited above.

We may say without fear of contradiction that purely physical relations do exist between sound and color vibrations.

But it can also be said, just as categorically, *that art*

has extremely little in common with such purely physical relationships.

Even if an absolute correspondence between colors and sounds were to be revealed to us, such a control over our making of films would bring us, under the most perfect conditions, to the same curious destination as that of the jeweler described by Jean d'Udine:

I know a goldsmith who, while very intelligent and cultivated, is certainly a mediocre artist. He is determined to design *original* vases and jewelry at any cost. Because he is empty of genuine creative impulse, he has come to believe that all natural forms are beautiful (which, by the way, is not true). In order to obtain the purest forms, he is content to copy exactly the curves produced by instruments in the study of physics, intended for the analysis of natural phenomena. His principal patterns are the light curves produced on a screen by the vibrations on a perpendicular plane of the mirror-tipped tuning forks used in physics to study the relative complexity of the various musical intervals. For instance he will copy on a belt buckle the figure eight, more or less elegant in contour, produced by two forks tuned to the octave. I think it would be difficult to convince him that the consonant octave tones which in music form a perfectly simple chord do not transmit a comparable emotion through the eye. When he designs a brooch by chiseling the particular curve produced by two tuning forks sounding at nine intervals from each other, he firmly believes that he is creating through plastic art an emotion which corresponds to the harmonies that M. Debussy has introduced into the art of music.[47]

In art it is not the *absolute* relationships that are decisive, but those *arbitrary* relationships within a system of images dictated by the particular work of art.

Photography performs, mechanically, a reproduction of more or less *absolute* relationships between object & image; yet the ambivalence is there, also, allowing of equally *arbitrary* representation & imagery.

The problem is not, nor ever will be, solved by a fixed catalog of color-symbols, but *the emotional intelligibility and function of color will rise from the natural order of establishing the color imagery of the work, coincidental with the process of shaping the living movement of the whole work.*

Even within the limitations of a color-range of black and white, in which most films are still produced, one of these tones not only evades being given a single "value" as an *absolute* image, but can even assume absolutely *contradictory* meanings, *dependent only upon the general system of imagery that has been decided upon for the particular film.*

It will be enough to note the thematic rôle played by the colors of black and white in *Old and New* and in *Alexander Nevsky.* In the former film black was associated with everything reactionary, criminal and outdated, while white was the color representative of happiness, life, new forms of management.

In *Nevsky*, the white robes of the Teuton *Ritter* were associated with the themes of cruelty, oppression and death, while the color of black, attached to the Russian warriors, conveyed the positive themes of heroism and patriotism. This deviation from the generally accepted image for these colors would have been less surprising to the critics and press abroad (whose objections were very interesting in themselves) if they had recalled an astonishing and powerful passage of literature which I have since found for myself—the chapter called "The Whiteness of the Whale," in Melville's *Moby Dick.*

A long time ago * I introduced this subject of *imagery relationships with color*, in analyzing the question of *relationships within the montage-image in general*.

If we have even a *sequence* of montage pieces:

> A gray old man,
> A gray old woman,
> A white horse,
> A snow-covered roof,

we are still far from certain whether this sequence is working towards "old age" or towards "whiteness."

Such a sequence of film-strips might proceed for some time before we would finally discover that guiding piece of film which immediately "identifies" the *whole* sequence in one way or another.

That is why it is advisable to place this "identifying" piece as near as possible to the beginning of the sequence (in an "orthodox" construction). Sometimes it even becomes necessary to do this with a sub-title.

This means that *we do not obey some "all-pervading law" of absolute "meanings" and correspondences between colors and sounds—and absolute relations between these and specific emotions*, but it does mean that *we ourselves decide which colors and sounds will best serve the given assignment or emotion as we need them*.

Of course, the "generally accepted" interpretation may serve as an impetus, and an effective one at that, in the construction of the color-imagery of the drama.

But the law laid down here will not legalize any abso-

* See Bibliography, No. 15.

lute correspondence "in general," but will demand that consistency in a definite tone-color key, running through the whole work, must be given by an imagery structure in strict harmony with the work's theme and idea.

IV

FORM AND CONTENT: PRACTICE

. . . if, to a composition which is already interesting through the choice of subject, you add a disposition of lines which augments the impression, if you add chiaroscuro which seizes the imagination, and color adapted to the characters, you have solved a more difficult problem—you have entered a realm of superior ideas, doing what the musician does when, to a single theme, he adds the resources of harmony and its combinations.

EUGÈNE DELACROIX [1]

I always took the score and read it carefully during the performance, so that, in time, I got to know the sound—the voice, as it were—of each instrument and the part it filled. . . . Listening so closely, I also found out for myself the intangible bond between each instrument and true musical expression.

HECTOR BERLIOZ [2]

A song by Shakespeare or Verlaine, which seems so free and living and as remote from any conscious purpose as rain that falls in a garden or the lights of evening, is discovered to be the rhythmic speech of an emotion otherwise incommunicable, at least so fitly.

JAMES JOYCE [2a]

IN PART II we discussed the new question posed by audio-visual combinations—that of solving a wholly new compositional problem. The solution to this compositional problem lies in finding *a key to the measured matching* of a strip of music and a strip of picture; such measured matching as would enable us to unite both strips *"vertically"* or *simultaneously:* matching each continuing musical phrase with *each phase* of the continuing parallel picture strips—our shots. This will be conditioned by our adherence to the letter of that law allowing us to *combine "horizontally"* or *continuously:* shot after shot in the silent film — phrase after phrase of a developing theme in music. We have brought to this question an analysis of existing theories on general correlations of aural and visual phenomena. We have also examined the question of correlating visual and aural phenomena with specific emotions.

With these problems in mind we discussed the question of correlating music and color. And we concluded that the existence of "absolute" sound-color equivalents—even if found in nature—cannot play a decisive rôle in creative work, except in an occasional "supplementary" way.

The decisive rôle is played by the *image structure* of the work, not so much by *employing* generally accepted correlations, but by *establishing* in our images of a *spe-cific creative work* whatever correlations (of sound and picture, sound and color, etc.) are dictated by the *idea and theme of the particular work.*

We turn now from all the preceding *general premises* to *concrete methods* of constructing relations between music and picture. These methods will not vary basically no matter how varying the circumstances: it makes no difference whether the composer writes music for the "general idea" of a sequence, or for a rough or final cutting of the sequence; or, if procedure has been or-ganized in an opposite direction, with the director build-ing the visual cutting to music that has already been written and recorded on sound-track.

I should like to point out that in *Alexander Nevsky* literally all these possible approaches were employed. There are sequences in which the shots were cut to a previously recorded music-track. There are sequences for which the entire piece of music was written to a final cutting of the picture. There are sequences that contain both approaches. There are even sequences that furnish material for the anecdotists. One such example occurs in the battle scene where pipes and drums are played for the victorious Russian soldiers. I couldn't find a way to explain to Prokofiev what precise effect should be "seen" in his music for this joyful moment. Seeing that we were getting nowhere, I ordered some "prop" instruments constructed, shot these being played (with-out sound) *visually*, and projected the results for Proko-fiev—who almost immediately handed me an exact "musical equivalent" to that visual image of pipers and drummers which I had shown him.

With similar means were produced the sounds of the great horns blown from the German lines. In the same way, but inversely, completed sections of the score sometimes suggested plastic visual solutions, which neither he nor I had foreseen in advance. Often these fitted so perfectly into the unified "inner sounding" of the sequence that now they seem "conceived that way in advance." Such was the case with the scene of Vaska and Gavrilo Olexich embracing before leaving for their posts, as well as a great part of the sequence of knights galloping to the attack—both of which sequences had effects that we were totally unprepared for.

These examples are cited to confirm the statement that the "method" we are proposing here has been tested "backwards and forwards" to check all its possible variations and nuances.

What then is this method of building audio-visual correspondences?

One answer, a naive one, to this problem would be to find equivalents to the *purely representational elements in music.*

Such an answer would be not only naive, but childish and senseless as well, inevitably leading to the confusions of Shershavin in Pavlenko's novel *Red Planes Fly East:*

Out of his wallet he pulled an exercise-book in a peeling oil-cloth binding, inscribed *Music. . . .*

"What is it?" she asked.

"My impressions of music. At one time I tried to reduce everything I heard to a system, to understand the logic of music before I understood the music itself. I took a fancy to a certain old man, a movie pianist, a former colonel of the Guards. What do instruments sound like? 'That's courage,' said the old man. 'Why courage?' I asked. He shrugged his shoulders. 'C major, B flat major, F flat major are firm, resolute, noble tones,' he explained. I made a habit of seeing him before the film began and treated him to my ration cigarettes—since I didn't smoke—and asked how music was to be understood. . . .

"I continued visiting him at the theatre, and on candy-wrappers he wrote down the names of the works he played and their emotional effect. Open the note-book and we'll laugh together." . . .

She read:

" 'Song of Maidens' from Rubinstein's *Demon:* sadness.

"Schumann's *Fantasiestuecke*, No. 2: inspiration.

"Barcarolle from Offenbach's *Tales of Hoffman:* love.

"Overture to Chaikovsky's *Pique Dame:* sickness."

She closed the book.

"I can't read any more," she said. "I'm ashamed of you."

He flushed, but did not yield.

"And, you know, I wrote and wrote, I listened and made notes, compared, collated. One day the old man was playing something great, inspired, joyous, encouraging, and I guessed at once what it connoted: it meant rapture. He finished the piece and threw me a note. It appeared that he had been playing Saint-Saëns' *Danse Macabre*, a theme of terror and horror. And I realized three things: first, that my colonel didn't understand a thing about music, second that he was as stupid as a cork, and third that only by smithing does one become a smith." [3]

Two of the shots from *Alexander Nevsky* shown to Prokofiev by Eisenstein (see pages 158-159), to which the composer wrote his "musical equivalent."

The Meeting of St. Anthony and St. Paul, Sassetta. An illustration
of the "path of the eye" (see pages 190-192) as linked to an advancing rather than a receding composition along a pictured road.

Besides such patently absurd definitions as these, any definitions that even touch this approach of a *narrowly representational comprehension of music* inevitably lead to visualizations of a most platitudinous character—if for any reason visualizations should be required:

"Love": a couple embracing.

"Illness": an old woman with a warming pad on her stomach.

If we also add to the pictures evoked by the "Barcarolle" a series of Venetian scenes, and to the *Pique Dame* Overture various St. Petersburg vistas—what then? The "illustration" of the lovers and the "illustration" of the old woman are blotted out.

But take from these Venetian "scenes" only the *approaching and receding* movements of the water combined with the reflected *scampering and retreating play of light* over the surface of the canals, and you immediately remove yourself, by at least one degree, from the series of "illustration" fragments, and you are closer to finding a response to the *sensed inner movement* of a barcarolle.

The number of "personal" images arising from this inner movement is unlimited.

And they will all reflect this inner movement, for all will be based upon the same sensation. This even includes the ingenious embodiment of the Offenbach "Barcarolle" in the hands of Walt Disney * where the visual solution is a peacock whose tail shimmers "musi-

* *Birds of a Feather* (a Silly Symphony, 1931).

cally," and who looks into the pool to find there the identical contours of its opalescent tail feathers, shimmering upside down.

All the approachings, recedings, ripples, reflections and opalescence that came to mind as a suitable essence to be drawn from the Venetian scenes have been preserved by Disney in the same relation to the music's movement: the spreading tail and its reflection approach each other and recede according to the nearness of the flourished tail to the pool—the tail feathers are themselves waving and shimmering—and so on.

What is important here is that this imagery in no way contradicts the "love theme" of the "Barcarolle." Only here there is a substitution for "pictured" lovers by a characteristic trait of lovers—an ever-changing opalescence of approaches and retreats from one another. Instead of a literal picture, this trait afforded a *compositional foundation*, both for Disney's style of drawing in this sequence and for the movement of the music.

Bach, for example, built his music on this same foundation, eternally searching for those *movement* means that gave expression to the fundamental movement characterizing his theme. In his work on Bach, Albert Schweitzer provides innumerable musical quotations to evidence this, including the curious circumstance to be found in the Christmas cantata No. 121: [4]

How far he will venture to go in music is shewn in the Christmas cantata *Christum wir sollen loben schon* (no. 121). The text of the aria "Johannis freudenvolles Springen erkannte dich mein Jesu schon" refers to the passage from the Gospel of St. Luke, "And it came to pass that when Elisabeth heard the salutation of Mary, the babe leaped in the womb." Bach's music is simply a long series of violent convulsions:

A similar but less willing search was confessed by a quite different type of composer, Giuseppe Verdi, in a letter to Léon Escudier:

Today I have sent off to Ricordi the last act of *Macbeth* finished and complete. . . .

When you hear it you will observe that I have written a *fugue* for the battle!!! A *fugue?* I, who detest everything that smacks of the schools and who have not done such a thing for nearly thirty years!!! But I'll tell you that in this instance that musical form is to the point. The repetition of subject and counter-subject, the jar of dissonances, the clashing sounds express a battle well enough. . . .[5]

Musical and visual imagery are actually not commensurable through narrowly "representational" elements. If one speaks of genuine and profound relations and proportions between the music and the picture, it can only be in reference to the relations between the *fundamental movements* of the music and the picture, i.e., compositional and structural elements, since the relations between the "pictures," and the "pictures" produced by the musical images, are usually so individual in perception and so lacking in concreteness that they cannot be fitted into any strictly methodological "regulations." The Bach example is eloquent proof of this.

We can speak only of what is actually "commensurable" i.e., the movement lying at the base of both the structural law of the given piece of music and the structural law of the given pictorial representation.

Here an understanding of the structural laws of the process and rhythm underlying the stabilization and development of both provides the only firm foundation for establishing a unity between the two.

This is not only because this understanding of regulated movement is "materialized" in equal measure through the particular specifics of any art, but is mainly because such a structural law is generally the first step towards the embodiment of a theme through an image or form of the creative work, regardless of the material in which the theme is cast.

This remains clear as long as we deal with theory. But what happens to this in practice?

Practice reveals this principle with even greater simplicity and clarity.

Practice is built somewhat along the following lines:

We all speak of particular pieces of music as "transparent," or as "dynamic," or as having a "definite pattern," or as having "indistinct outlines."

We do this because most of us, while hearing music, visualize some sort of plastic images, vague or clear, concrete or abstract, but somehow peculiarly related and corresponding to our own *perceptions* of the given music.

In the more rare circumstance of an abstract rather than a concrete or a dynamic visualization, someone's recollection of Gounod is significant. While listening to a Bach concert, Gounod suddenly and thoughtfully remarked, "I find something octagonal in this music. . . ."

This observation is less surprising when we remember that Gounod's father was "a painter of distinguished merit" and his mother's mother "a musician and poetess as well." [6] Both streams of impressions were so vivid throughout his childhood that he recorded in his memoirs his equally attractive opportunities for working in the plastic arts as well as in music.

But in a final analysis such "geometrism" may not be so exceptional.

Tolstoy, for example, made Natasha's imagination picture a much more intricate complex—a complete image of a man—by means of such a geometrical figure: Natasha describes Pierre Bezukhov to her mother as a "blue quadrant." [7]

Dickens, another great realist, occasionally shows the images of his characters by exactly this "geometrical means," and it is quite likely that in such cases it is only through such means that the full depth of the character may be revealed.

Look at Mr. Gradgrind on the opening page of *Hard Times*—a man of paragraphs, figures and facts, facts, facts:

The scene was a plain, bare, monotonous vault of a school-room, and the speaker's square forefinger emphasized his observations by underscoring every sentence with a line on the schoolmaster's sleeve. The emphasis was helped by

the speaker's square wall of a forehead, which had his eyebrows for its base, while his eyes found commodious cellar-
age in two dark caves, overshadowed by the wall. . . . The
speaker's obstinate carriage, square coat, square legs, square
shoulders—nay, his very neckcloth, trained to take him by
the throat with an unaccommodating grasp, like a stubborn
fact, as it was—all helped the emphasis.

"In this life, we want nothing but Facts, sir; nothing but
Facts!"

Another illustration of our normal visualization of
music is the ability of each of us, naturally with individual variations and to a greater or lesser degree of expressiveness, to "depict" with the movement of our
hands that movement sensed by us in some nuance of
music.

The same is true of poetry where rhythm and meter
are sensed by the poet primarily as images of movement.

How the poet feels about this identification between
meter and movement has been keenly expressed by
Pushkin in his ironic sixth stanza of *The Cottage in
Kolomna:*

> Pentameters demand caesural rest
> After the second foot, I do agree.
> If not, you oscillate 'twixt ditch and crest.
> Reclining on a sofa though I may be,
> I feel as though a driver with a jag on
> Were jolting me o'er cornfields in a wagon.[8]

And it is Pushkin who provides some of the best examples of translating the movement of a phenomenon
into verse.

For example, the splashing of a wave. The Russian

language lacks a word that adequately and tersely describes the whole action of a wave, rising in a curve and splashing as it falls. The German language is more fortunate: it has a compound word—*wellenschlag*—that conveys this dynamic picture with absolute accuracy. Somewhere Dumas *père* bewails the fact that the French language compels its authors to write: "the sound of water striking against the surface," while an English author has at his disposal the single rich word, "splash."

However, I doubt if any nation's literature contains a more brilliant *translation of the dynamics of splashing waves into the movement of poetry* than the flood passage of Pushkin's *Bronze Horseman*. Following the well-known couplet,

> Behold Petropol floating lie
> Like Triton in the deep, waist-high!

the flood surges in:

> A siege! the wicked waves, attacking
> Climb thief-like through the windows; backing,
> The boats stern-foremost smite the glass;
> Trays with their soaking wrappage pass
> And timbers, roofs, and huts all shattered,
> The wares of thrifty traders scattered,
> And the pale beggar's chattels small,
> Bridges swept off beneath the squall,
> Coffins from sudden graveyards—all
> Swim in the streets! [9] *

---

* Elsewhere I have described the exact "reconstruction" in these lines of the splashing, the rolling and breaking of a wave, in terms that would lose their point entirely with *any* English translation.

From the material presented above we can formulate a simple, practical approach to a method of audio-visual combinations.

We must know how to grasp the movement of a given piece of music, locating its path (its line or form) as our foundation for the plastic composition that is to correspond to the music.

There are already instances of this approach, building a plastic composition upon firmly determined musical lines, in the case of ballet choreography, where there is a full correspondence between the movement of the score and of the *mise-en-scène*.

However, when we have before us a number of shots of equal "independence," * at least insofar as their original flexibility was concerned, but differing in composition, we must, keeping the music before us, select and arrange only those shots that prove their correspondence to the music according to the above conditions.

A composer must proceed in the same way when he takes up a previously cut film sequence: he is obliged to analyze the visual movement both through its overall montage construction and the compositional line carried from individual shot to shot—even the compositions *within* the shots. He will have to base his musical imagery composition on these elements.

* "Independent" only in the sense that *thematically* they can be arranged in any sequence. The twelve shots of the "waiting sequence" developed below, were precisely of this sort. In their purely *thematic and narrative-informational* nature they might have been arranged in any order. Their final arrangement was determined by purely interpretive and emotional requirements of construction.

The movement which lies at the base of a work of art is not abstract or isolated from the theme, but is the generalized plastic embodiment of that image through which the theme is expressed.

"Striving upwards," "expanding," "broken," "well-knit," "limping," "smoothly developing," "patchy," "zig-zagging"—are terms used to define this movement in the more abstract and generalized instances. We will see in our example how such a line can contain not only dynamic characteristics but also a whole complex of fundamental elements and meanings peculiar to *that* theme and *that* image. Sometimes the primary embodiment of the future image will be found in *intonation*. But this won't affect the basic conditions—for intonation is the *movement of the voice* flowing from the same *movement of emotion* which must serve as a fundamental factor in outlining the whole image.

It is precisely this fact that makes it so easy to describe an intonation with a gesture as well as a movement of the music itself. From the base of the music's movement all these manifestations spring with equal force—the intonation of the voice, the gesture, and the movement of the man who makes the music. Elsewhere we will consider this point in more detail.

Here we want to emphasize that *pure line*, that is, the specifically "graphic" outline of a composition, is only *one of the many* means of visualizing the character of a movement.

This "line"—the path of the movement—under differing conditions and in differing works of plastic art—can be drawn in other ways besides purely linear ones.

For example, movement can be drawn with the same success by means of changing nuances within the light- or the color-imagery structure, or by the successive unfolding of volumes and distances.

In Rembrandt the "movement line" is described by the shifting densities of his chiaroscuro.

Delacroix found this line through that path followed by the spectator's eye in moving from form to form, as the forms are distributed throughout the volume of the painting. He has recorded in his *Journal* his admiration for Leonardo's use of "le système antique du déssin par boules," [10] a method which his contemporaries tell us Delacroix himself used all his life.

In a remarkably close echo of Delacroix's thoughts on line and form, Balzac's Frenhofer (in *Le Chef-d'œuvre Inconnu*) says that the human body is not made up of lines and, strictly speaking, "Il n'y a pas de lignes dans la nature ou tout est plein."

In opposition to such a view, we can call upon that "contour" enthusiast—William Blake, whose pathetic plea,

O dear Mother outline, of knowledge most sage . . . [11]

can be found among his bitter polemics against Sir Joshua Reynolds, and against Sir Joshua's insufficient regard for the firmness of outline.

It should be clear that our argument is not over the *fact of movement* in the work of art, but over the *means* by which that movement is *embodied,* which is what characterizes and distinguishes the work of different painters.

In the work of Dürer, such movement is often expressed by the *alternation of mathematically precise formulae through the proportions* within his figures.

This is not very remote from the expression of other painters, Michelangelo in particular, whose rhythm flows dynamically through the undulating and swelling muscles of his figures, serving thus to voice not only the movement and position of these figures, but primarily to voice the whole flight of the artist's emotions.*

Piranesi reveals no less emotional a flight with his particular line—a line built from the movements and variations of *"counter-volumes"*—the broken arcs and vaults of his *Carceri,* with their intertwined lines of movement woven with the lines of his endless stairs—breaking the accumulated *spatial fugue* with a *linear fugue.*

Van Gogh similarly expresses the movement of his line with thick running slashes of color, as though in a desperate effort to weld the flight of his line with a flying explosion of color. In his own way he was carrying out a law of Cézanne's which he could not have known

---

* We can recall what Gogol said of him: "For Michelangelo, the body served only as a revelation of the strength of the soul, of its suffering, of its cry aloud, of its invincible nature—and for him mere plastics were discarded, and man's contour assumed gigantic proportions in its function as a symbol; the result is not man, but man's passions." [12]

—a law carried out in an entirely different aspect by Cézanne himself:

Le déssin et la couleur ne sont point distincts . . .[18]

Moreover, any "communicator" realizes the existence of such a "line." A practitioner in any medium of communication has to build his line, if not from plastic elements, then certainly from "dramatic" and thematic elements.

In this we must bear in mind that in cinema, the selection of "correspondences" between picture and music must not be satisfied with any one of these "lines," or even with a harmony of several employed together. Aside from these general formal elements the same law has to determine the selection of *the right people, the right faces, the right objects, the right actions, and the right sequences,* out of all the equally possible selections within the circumstances of a given situation.

Back in the days of the silent film, we spoke of the "orchestration" of *typage* faces * in repeated instances (for example, in producing the mounting "line" of grief by means of intensified close-ups in the sequence of "mourning for Vakulinchuk" in *Potemkin*).

Similarly, in sound-films there arise such moments as that mentioned above: the *farewell embrace* between Vaska and Gavrilo Olexich in *Alexander Nevsky*. This

---

* *Typage,* as a term and as a method, might be defined as "type-casting" (of non-actors), elevated by Eisenstein to the level of a conscious creative instrument, just as *montage,* a simple term for a physical process of film editing, has been transformed to a broader term and a deeper process by the Russian film-makers.—Editor.

could occur only at one *precise* point in the musical score, in the same way that the close-up shots of the German knights' helmets could not be used before the point where they were finally employed in the attack sequence, for only at that point does the music change its character from one that can be expressed in long shots and medium shots of the attack to one that demands rhythmic visual beats, close-ups of galloping and the like.

Alongside this, we cannot deny the fact that the most *striking* and immediate impression will be gained, of course, from *a congruence of the movement of the music with the movement of the visual contour*—with the graphic composition of the frame; for this contour or this outline, or this line is the most vivid "emphasizer" of the very idea of the movement.

But let us turn to the object of our analysis and try, through one fragment from the beginning of Reel 7 of *Alexander Nevsky*, to demonstrate how and why a certain series of shots in a certain order and of a certain length was related in a specific way, rather than any other way, with a certain piece of the musical score.

We will try to discover here that "secret" of those sequential *vertical correspondences* which, step by step, relate the music to the shots *through an identical motion* that lies at the base of the musical as well as the pictorial movement.

Of particular interest in this case is the fact that the music was composed to a completely finished editing of the pictorial element. The visual movement of the theme

was fully grasped by the composer to the same degree
that the completed musical movement was caught by
the director in the subsequent scene of the attack, where
the shots were matched to the previously recorded
music-track.

However, it is an exactly identical method of binding
organically *through movement* that is used in either case.
Therefore, methodologically, it is absolutely immaterial
from which element the process of determining audio-
visual combinations begins.

The audio-visual aspect of *Alexander Nevsky* achieves
its most complete fusion in the sequence of the "Battle
on the Ice"—particularly in the "attack of the knights"
and the "punishment of the knights." This aspect becomes a decisive factor also, because of all the sequences
of *Alexander Nevsky*, the attack seemed the most impressive and memorable to critics and spectators. The
method used in it of audio-visual correspondence is that
used for any sequence in the film. So for our analysis we
will choose a fragment which can be somewhat satisfactorily reproduced on a printed page—some fragment
where a whole complex is resolved by almost *motionless*
frames, in which a minimum would be lost by showing
its shots on a page rather than on a screen. It is such a
fragment that we have chosen for analysis.

These are the twelve shots of that "dawn of anxious
waiting" which precedes the beginning of the attack and
battle, and which follows a night full of trouble and
anxiety, on the eve of the "Battle on the Ice." The

thematic content of these twelve frames has a simple unity: Alexander on Raven Rock and the Russian troops at the foot of the Rock on the shore of the frozen Lake Chudskoye, peering into the distance from which the enemy is to appear.

A diagram inserted in the back of this book shows four divisions. The first two describe the succession of shot-frames and musical measures which together express the situation. XII frames; 17 measures. (This particular disposition of the pictures and the measures will be clarified in the process of analysis; this disposition is connected with the chief inner components of music and picture.)

Let us imagine these XII shots and these 17 measures of music—not as we see them in the diagram, but as we experienced them from the screen. What part of this audio-visual continuity exerted the greatest pull on our attention?

The strongest impression seems to come from Shot III followed by Shot IV. We must keep in mind that such an impression does not come from the photographed shots alone, but is an *audio-visual impression* which is created by the combination of these two shots together with the corresponding music—which is what one experiences in the auditorium. These two shots, III and IV, correspond to these measures of music—5, 6 and 7, 8.

That this is the most immediate and most impressive audio-visual group can be checked by playing the four measures on the piano "to the accompaniment" of the reproduced corresponding two shots. This impression was confirmed in the appraisal of this excerpt during the students' screening at the State Institute of Cinematography.

Take these four measures and try to describe in the air with your hand that line of movement suggested by the movement of the music.

The first chord can be visualized as a "starting platform."

The following five quarter-notes, proceeding in a scale upwards, would find a natural gesture-visualization in a *tensely rising line*. Therefore, instead of describing this passage with a simple climbing line, we will tend slightly to arch our corresponding gesture—*ab:*

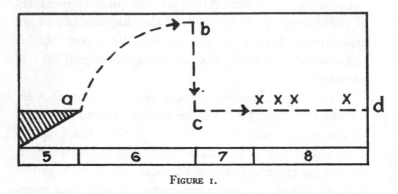

FIGURE 1.

The next chord (at the beginning of measure 7), preceded by a sharply accented sixteenth, will in these circumstances create an impression of an abrupt fall—*bc.**
The following row of four repeats on a single note—in

* Melodically the sensation of the "fall" is achieved by a leap from B to G sharp.

eighths, separated by rests—can be described naturally by a *horizontal gesture*, in which the eighths are indicated by even accents between *c* and *d*.

Draw this line (on Figure 1: *bc* and *cd*) and place this graph of the music's movement over the corresponding measures of the score.

Now let us describe the *graph of the eye's movement* over the main lines of Shots III and IV which "correspond" to this music.

This can also be described by a gesture of your hand, which will present us with the following drawing representing the *motion* within the linear composition of the two frames:

FIGURE 2.

From *a* to *b* the gesture "arches" upwards—drawing an arc through the outlined dark cloud, hanging over the lighter lower part of the sky.

From *b* to *c*—an abrupt *fall of the eye downwards:* from the upper frame-line of Shot III almost to the lower frame-line of Shot IV—the maximum fall possible in this vertical position.

From *c* to *d—evenly horizontal—*with neither an ascending nor a descending movement, but twice interrupted by the points of the flags that stand over the horizontal line of the troops.

Now let us collate the two graphs. What do we find? Both graphs of movement correspond absolutely, that is, we find a *complete correspondence between the movement of the music and the movement of the eye over the lines of the plastic composition.*

In other words, *exactly the same motion lies at the base of both the musical and the plastic structures.*

I believe that this motion can also be linked with the emotional movement. The rising tremolo of the cellos in the scale of C minor clearly accompanies the increasingly tense excitement as well as the increasing atmosphere of watching. The chord seems to break this atmosphere. The series of eighth-notes seems to describe the motionless line of the troops: the feelings of the troops spread along the entire front; a feeling which grows again in Shot V, with renewed tenseness in Shot VI.

It is interesting to note that Shot IV, which corresponds to measures 7 and 8, contains two flags, while the music contains four eighth-notes. The eye appears to pass over these two flags twice, so that the front seems twice as broad as that which we actually see before us in the frame. Passing from left to right, the eye "taps off" the eighth-notes with flags, and the two remaining notes lead the perception away beyond the frame-line to the right, where the imagination continues indefinitely the front-line of the troops.

Now it becomes clear why these two shots in juxtaposition arrested our attention particularly. The plastic element of movement and the musical movement coincide here, with a maximum of descriptiveness.

Let us, however, proceed further, to find what catches our "second" attention. Running over this sequence again, we are attracted by Shots I, VI-VII, IX-X.

Looking more closely at the music with these shots, we will find a structure similar to the music of Shot III. (Generally speaking, the music for this entire fragment consists, actually, of two two-measure phrases A and B, alternating with each other in a certain way. The distinguishing factor here is that while they belong structurally to the same A phrase, they vary in tonality: the music with Shots I and III belong to one tonality [C minor], while the music of Shots VI-VIII and IX-X belong to another [C sharp minor]. The relation of this tonal change to the thematic meaning of the sequence will be brought out in the analysis of Shot V.)

Thus the music for Shots I, VI-VII and IX-X will duplicate the graph of movement that we found in Shot III (see Figure 1).

But in looking at the shot-frames themselves, do we find the same graph of linear composition, which with the line of musical movement "welded" together Shots III and IV with their music (measures 5, 6, 7, 8)?

No.

And yet the sensation of an audio-visual unity seems just as powerful in these combinations.

Why?

The explanation can be found in our previous discussion of the various possible expressions of the line of movement. The graph of movement that we found for Shots III and IV need not be confined to the line *a-b-c alone*, but may be expressed *through any* plastic means at our disposal. Thus we encounter in practice the hypothetical cases suggested above.

Let us supplement our previous discussion with the aid of our three new cases—I, VI-VII, IX-X.

CASE 1. Photography cannot convey the full sensation of Shot I, for this shot *fades into sight:* appearing from the darkness we first see on the left a dark group of men with a banner, and then gradually revealed is a mottled sky, irregularly spotted with clouds.

We can see that the movement inside this shot is absolutely identical with our description of the movement within Shot III. The lone difference lies in the fact that the movement of Shot I is not linear, but is a movement of gradual lighting of the frame—a movement of increasing degree of lightness.

So that our "starting platform" *a*, which corresponded to the initial chord of Shot III, is here found in the darkness before the fade-in begins—a "water-line" of darkness from which the degrees of gradual lightening of the frame can be counted. The "arching" here is formed from the progressive chain of differing frames—each of which is lighter than the preceding frame. The *arching* of Shot III is reflected here by the curve of gradual lightening of the full frame. The individual stages are marked by the appearance of more and clearer cloud spots. In the emergence of the fully lit frame, the darkest spot (the one in the center of the frame) appears first. This is followed by a somewhat lighter one above. Then we grow aware of the whole sky of a general light tone—with a darker "fleece" in the lower right center and in the upper left corner.

We see that the curved line of movement is duplicated here, down to a detail, but not expressed through the *contour* of the plastic composition, but through a "line" of *light tonality*.

We can thus declare a correspondence between Shot I and Shot III, in their identical basic motion, a correspondence, in the former case, in *tone*.

CASE 2. Examine the pair of shots—VI-VII. These should be examined as a pair, for the musical phrase *A* which falls entirely within Shot I (over *one picture*), here covers fully *two pictures*. The variation of phrase *A* that is over Shots VI-VII can be identified as *A1*. (See the general diagram of the whole fragment.)

Let us check this combination according to our perception of the music.

This is what we see in the first of the two shots: four warriors with shields and upright spears stand at the left; behind them, further to the left edge, the contour of the high rock can be seen; into the further distance, but towards the right edge—ranks of warriors stretching into the distance.

Without checking the reactions of others, the impression always made upon me by the first chord of measure 10 is of a heavy mass of sound, rolling down along the lines of spears from the top of the frame to the bottom:

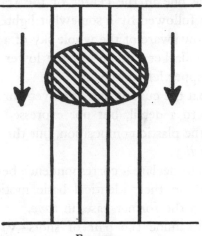

FIGURE 3.

(Subjective as this impression may have been, it was precisely due to it that I felt the need for giving this shot its particular place in the montage.)

Behind the group of four spearmen the line of warriors stretches out in stages of depth, to the right. The most prominent "stage" is the transition from the entirety of Shot VI to the entirety of Shot VII, which continues the line of warriors in the same direction, further into the distance. The dimensions of the warriors in Shot VII are somewhat greater, but the general movement into depth (in stages) carries on the movement of Shot VI. In the second shot there is another clearly defined stage: the white line of empty horizon on the right edge of the frame. This element in Shot VII breaks the continuous line of warriors and introduces us to a new sphere—towards the horizon where the sky merges with the frozen surface of Lake Chudskoye.

Let us graph this basic movement through both frames by means of stages:

FIGURE 4.

We have diagrammed the troop groupings as though they were the receding wings of a theater set—1, 2, 3, 4 inwards. Our *starting surface* is formed by the four spearmen of Shot VI. These coincide with our screen's surface, from which all the *inward* movement stems. Drawing a line to unify these "theater wings," we obtain a certain curve *a*, 1, 2, 3, 4. Where have we seen a strikingly similar curve? This is still the same curved line of our "arc," but now found not along the *vertical surface* of the frame, as in Shot III, but moving in *horizontal* perspective into the depth of the frame.

This curve has exactly the same *starting surface*, our

wing of four standing warriors. In addition to this, the several phases have defined limits, giving sharp edges to the succeeding wings, that can be enclosed by four vertical lines: the three warrior figures that stand away from the troop-line in Shot VII (x, y, z)—and the line that separates Shot VI from Shot VII.

Can we find a correspondence in the music to that glimpsed cut of horizon in VII?

A fact to be considered in this connection: the music of phrase $A1$ does not extend over the entirety of Shots VI and VII, so that the phrase $B1$ begins to be heard during Shot VII. This beginning includes three-quarters of measure 12.

What do these three-quarters contain?

Exactly that chord preceded by a sharply accented sixteenth, which in Shot III corresponded to the feeling of an abrupt fall downward from Shot III into Shot IV.

In the former case the whole movement was placed along a vertical surface, and the abrupt musical break was visualized as a fall (from the upper right corner of frame III to the lower left corner of frame IV). Here the whole movement is horizontal—into the depth of the frame. The plastic equivalent to such a sharp break in the music can be assumed under these conditions to appear as an analogous jolt—now not from top to bottom, but perspectively, inwards. *The "jolt" in Shot VII from the line of warriors to the horizon line is exactly such a jolt.* Again we attain a "maximum break," since in landscape the horizon represents the limit of depth!

We are justified in considering this strip of horizon

to the right of Shot VII as a visual equivalent to the musical "jolt" between measure 11 and three-quarters of measure 12.

We should add that from a purely psychological viewpoint, this audio-visual correspondence conveys a full and precise feeling to the audience, whose attention is pulled beyond the horizon to some unseen point from which they are expecting the foe to attack.

Thus we see that like strips of music—such as the "jolt" at the beginning of measures 7 and 12—can be plastically solved by varying the means of the *plastic break*.

In one case it is a break along a vertical line during the transition from shot to shot—III-IV. In the other case—a break along *a horizontal line, within the frame of Shot VII* at point *M*. (See Figure 4.)

But this is not all that can be found in these two pairs of shots. In III our "arc" sprang across the *surface*. In VI-VII it sprang inwards in perspective, that is, spatially. Along this second "arc" was strung our system of theater wings, unfolding into space itself. This recession from the surface of the screen (wing *a*) into the space of the screen, accompanies the scale of upward climbing sounds.

Thus in the case of VI-VII, we can point to another kind of correspondence between music and picture—solved through the same graph—and with the same motion. This is—*spatial* correspondence.

Let us draw a general graph of this new variant of corresponding music and pictorial representation. To complete our picture we should finish phrase *B* in the score (by adding one measure and a quarter-note). This will give us a full repeat of the musical phrase that we examined with Shots III and IV. But our pictorial line will demand the addition of Shot VIII to VI-VII—for this repeat of phrase *B* (actually *B1* here) closes with the completion of Shot VIII.

So Shot VIII demands our inspection at this point.

Plastically it can be divided into three parts. In the foreground our attention is caught by the first *close-up* to appear thus far in the sequence of eight shots—Vasilisa in a helmet. This occupies only a part of the frame, leaving the rest to the front-line of troops, placed in the frame in much the same way as in the preceding frames. Shot VIII serves as a transition shot, since it contains, first, a plastic completion of the motif in VI-VII. (We should not forget that the further recession inwards of Shot VII has the effect of an *enlargement*, in relative size to Shot VI, providing an opportunity for a further change in Shot VIII to a close-up.) The three shots—VI-VII-VIII—are further tied together organically by their correspondence with the musical sequence *A1-B1*. The *furthest* margins of these four measures 10, 11, 12, 13 coincide with the furthest edges of the pair of shots —VI-VIII, although within this grouping, the divisions between Shots VII and VIII do not coincide with the divisions between measures 11 and 12. (See the general diagram.)

Shot VIII completes the phrase of *medium shots* of

troops (VI-VII-VIII) and introduces the phrase of *close-ups* (VIII-IX-X) which now appears.

In this same way the phrase of *the prince on the rock* was carried through Shots I-II-III, and was followed by a new phrase of *long shots of warriors at the foot of the rock.* This second phrase was introduced not by a *crossing* in a single shot, but through a *montage crossing.*

Following Shot III comes the phrase "the troops," shown in a long shot (IV), followed by "the prince on the rock" *again*—also shown in a long shot (V).

This *essential* transition from "prince" to "troops" is marked by an *essential* musical change—a transition from one tonality to another (C minor to C sharp minor).

A less important transition—not *from one theme* (prince) *to another theme* (troops), but *within* a theme —from a middle shot of warriors to close-ups of them— is not solved through a *montage crossing* (as in III-IV-V-VI) but *within one shot*—Shot VIII.

This solution is by means of a composition containing *two planes:* the new theme is shown in close-up, emerging in the foreground, while the fading theme (the long shot of the front-line) recedes into the background. One may note, besides this fact, that the "fading" of the preceding theme is also expressed by filming the troops (in the second plane of distance) with a deliberate avoidance of depth of focus, so that this slightly out-of-focus receding line provides a background for Vasilisa's close-up.

This close-up of Vasilisa introduces the other close-ups—of Ignat and Savka (IX-X) which, joined to the

last two shots of this fragment (XI-XII), will give us a
new plastic interpretation for our graph of motion.

But this part of our analysis has to wait for our next
step.

On our examination of Shot VIII depends the completion of our graph for the group of shots (VI-VII-
VIII).

The three divisions of Shot VIII can be described
thus:

In the foreground—Vasilisa's face in close-up. Further
to the right in the frame is a long row of troops—photographed without sharply defined focus, which results in
emphasizing the high-lights on their helmets. In the narrow section between Vasilisa's head and the left edge of
the frame can be seen part of the line of troops, topped
by a banner.

What corresponds to this in the musical score?

This shot is covered by one whole musical measure
and a quarter-note—the end of measure 12 and the whole
of measure 13. This musical fragment contains three distinct elements, of which the middle one—the chord that
opens measure 13—comes to the foreground. This chord
has the "impact" of a full fusion with the close-up in
our shot.

From the middle of this measure start four eighth-
notes, interrupted by rests. Just as this even horizontal
musical movement was accompanied by the tiny flags
of Shot IV, the slightly shifting high-lights on the helmets of the troop-line in Shot VIII accompany these
notes like little stars.

Only our left edge lacks its musical "correspondence."

But—we have forgotten the eighth-note, remaining over from the preceding measure 12, and which "on the left" precedes the opening chord of measure 13; it is this eighth-note that "corresponds" to the narrow strip of frame to the left of Vasilisa's head.

This analysis of Shot VIII and its corresponding musical movement can be diagrammed thus:

FIGURE 5.

At this point I expect to hear a quite natural exclamation—"Hold on there! Isn't it a little far-fetched to match a line of music so exactly to a pictorial representation? Doesn't the *left* of a measure of music and the *left* of a picture signify absolutely *different* things?"

A *motionless* picture exists *spatially*, that is, *simultaneously*, and neither its left, nor its right, nor its center can be thought of as occupying *any order in time*, while the musical staff contains a definite *order moving in time.* In the staff the left always signifies *"before,"* while the right signifies *"after."*

All the above objections would carry weight if our shot contained elements that *appeared in succession,* as indicated by the diagram (Figure 6) opposite.

The objections at first sound quite reasonable.

And then we realize that an extremely important factor has been ignored, namely, that *the motionless whole of a picture and its parts do not enter the perception simultaneously* (with the exception of those cases where the composition is calculated to create just such an effect).

The art of plastic composition consists in leading the spectator's attention through the exact path and with the exact sequence prescribed by the author of the composition. This applies to the eye's movement over the surface of a canvas if the composition is expressed in painting, or over the surface of the screen if we are dealing with a film-frame.

It is interesting to note here that at an earlier stage of graphic art, when the conception of "the path of the eye" was still difficult to separate from a physical image —that paths were introduced into pictures *as paths of the eye, concrete picturizations of roads* along which were distributed the events that the artist wished to portray in particular sequence. One of the most dramatic (and cinematic) of all illuminated manuscripts is the Greek manuscript of the sixth century known as the Vienna Genesis [14]—in which this device is employed repeatedly. There it was solely concerned with a sequence

FIGURE 6.

of scenes which, often in this period, were depicted in one painting. Development of this device continued into the era of perspective, where the scenes were placed in the different planes of a painting, similar to the effect of a path. Thus, Dirk Bouts' painting of *The Dream of Elijah in the Desert* shows Elijah sleeping in the foreground, while another Elijah departs on a path that winds into the depth of the picture. In *The Adoration of the Shepherds* by Domenico Ghirlandaio, the Infant surrounded by shepherds occupies the foreground, and on a road that twists forward from the background appear the Magi; so that the road ties together events which are, in subject, thirteen days apart (December 24 —January 6).

Memling used this same device, but in a far more complex (and exciting) composition, in distributing all the consecutive Stations of the Cross through the streets of a city, in his *Passion of Christ*, now in Turin.

Later on, when such jumps in time disappear, the physical road, as one of the means of plotting the spectator's view of a painting, also disappears.

The *road* is transformed into the *path of the eye*, transferred from a sphere of *representation* to one of *composition*.

The means employed in this further stage of development are varied, although they have one characteristic in common: there is usually something in a painting which attracts attention before all other elements. From this point the attention moves along that path desired by the artist. This path can be described either by a movement-line, or as a path of graduated tones, or even by grouping or the "play" of personages in the picture. A classic case of deciphering in this regard is Rodin's analysis of Watteau's *L'Embarquement pour Cythère* which I cannot forbear quoting here:

In this masterpiece the action, if you will notice, begins in the foreground to the right and ends in the background to the left.

What you first notice in the front of the picture, in the cool shade, near a sculptured bust of Cypris garlanded with roses, is a group composed of a young woman and her adorer. The man wears a cape embroidered with a pierced heart, gracious symbol of the voyage that he would undertake.

Kneeling at her side, he ardently beseeches his lady to yield. But she meets his entreaties with an indifference perhaps feigned, and appears absorbed in the study of the decorations on her fan. Close to them is a little cupid, sitting half-naked upon his quiver. He thinks that the young woman delays too long, and he pulls her skirt to induce her to be less hard-hearted. But still the pilgrim's staff and the script of love lie upon the ground. This is the first scene.

Here is the second: To the left of the group of which I have spoken is another couple. The lady accepts the hand of her lover, who helps her to arise. She has her back to us, and has one of those blonde napes which Watteau painted with such voluptuous grace.

A little further away is the third scene. The lover puts his arm around his mistress's waist to draw her with him. She turns towards her companions, whose lingering confuses her, but she allows herself to be led passively away.

Now the lovers descend to the shore and all push laughing towards the barque; the men no longer need to entreat, the women cling to their arms.

Finally the pilgrims help their sweethearts on board the little ship, which, decked with flowers and floating pennons of red silk, rocks like a golden dream upon the water. The sailors, leaning on their oars, are ready to row away. And already, borne by the breezes, little cupids fly ahead to guide the travellers towards that azure isle which lies upon the horizon.[15]

Have we any right to claim that our film-frames also can gauge the movement of the eye over a determined path?

We can give an affirmative answer to this, and add further—that in the twelve shots we are analyzing that this movement proceeds precisely *from left to right* through *each* of the *twelve shots identically*, and *fully corresponds* in its pictorial character with the character of the *music's movement*.

We have said the music has two phrases—*A* and *B* —alternating throughout the length of the entire fragment.

A is constructed thus:

FIGURE 7.

B is constructed thus:

FIGURE 8.

First, a chord. Then against the background of the resonance of the chord, is an ascending scale,* moving in an "arc," or else, a recurrence of one note in a *horizontal* movement.

Plastically all the frames are constructed in the same way (except IV and XII, which do not really function as independent shots, but as continuations of the movement of preceding shots).

Actually they each have on the left a darker, more solid, heavy plastic "chord" which commands the eye's attention first.

In Shots I-II-III this "chord" is a group of dark figures, placed on the heavy mass of the rock. These attract our attention for another reason: they are the only living people in the frame.

In Shot V—these figures, but with a greater mass of rock.

In Shot VI—the four spearmen in the foreground.

In Shot VII—the mass of the troops, and so on.

And in each of these shots there is something to the

---

* For example, along with Shot III is a *tremulous* movement of the cellos, rising in a C minor scale.

right of the frame which occupies the secondary attention: something light, airy, consecutively "moving" which compels the eye to follow it.

In Shot III—the *upward* "arc."

In Shots VI-VII—the "theater wings" of the troops, *inward*.

So that for the entire plastic system of frames the left side is "before," while the right is "later," for the eye has been directed in a particular way from left to right through each of these motionless frames.

In the process of dividing up the frame compositions along a vertical line, this gives us the right to mark our musical beats and measures among the various plastic elements that make up these frames.

It was upon our perception of this circumstance that we based our montage of this particular sequence—and made our audio-visual correspondences more precise. This analysis, certainly as painstaking for the reader as it was for its writer, could only be done, of course, *post factum*, but it is worth doing to prove to what degree compositional "intuition" is responsible for correct audio-visual structures—and how those senses of "instinct" and "feeling" can materialize sound-picture montage. It hardly seems necessary to point out that this is premised wholly on a wish for truth in the choice of theme, and a desire for vitality in its treatment.

From frame to frame in our sequence, the eye becomes accustomed to "read" the picture from left to right.

Moreover, this continuous horizontal reading of the sequence induces horizontal reading in general, so that frames are *psychologically* perceived as placed side by side *upon a horizontal line* in the same left-to-right direction.

This is what allows us not only to divide each frame "in time" upon our vertical line, but also *to place frame after frame upon a horizontal line*, and describe their correspondence to the music in this precise way.

Let us continue to take advantage of this circumstance by describing in one gesture the succession of Shots VI-VII-VIII, along with the movement of the music that is fused with these shots, and the movement of that total plastic motion upon which both picture and music are based. (See general diagram.) This is the same motion that goes through the combination of Shots III-IV. An interesting distinction here between the motion through two shots and the same motion through three shots, is that the effect of a "fall" is, in the latter case, placed *within* the frame (Shot VII), rather than at the *transition* between two shots (Shot III to IV).*

Upon this graph and with the addition of the remaining frames, we can construct the general graphic diagram for the whole fragment. Comparing the III-IV graph with the VI-VII-VIII graph, we can see how

* The differing diagrammed lengths of the musical measures (10 and 12, for example) bear no relation to the content, either of the music or of the frames. This, and the occasional stretching of the notes within the frame limits have been conditioned exclusively by the exigencies of diagramming.

much more complicated in the case of the latter is the audio-visual development of "variations" on a basic line of movement.

We have noted that the movement from left to right through each frame has given a psychological suggestion that the frames are actually set next to one another upon a horizontal line running in one direction—to the right. This peculiarity permitted the arrangement of our diagram in the way you see it.

In connection with this, another much more important factor of a different type is now revealed. The psychological effect of left-to-right combines the total sequence into a focused shaping of the attention, directed from somewhere at the left towards somewhere at the right.

This underlines our dramatic "indicator"—which is a direction of the eyes of all personages in these shots towards one point—with only one exception, the close-up of Ignat in IX.

In Shot IX Ignat looks to the left, but precisely because of this our general direction of attention towards the right is thereby strengthened.

This close-up emphasizes our general direction, which is developed by the "triple-sounding" of close-ups VIII-IX-X, where it holds a middle position for the shortest period of time—only three-quarters of a measure—while Shots VIII and X occupy a measure plus an eighth and a measure plus a quarter respectively.

This turn towards the left replaces what would have been a monotonous series

FIGURE 9.

with a nervous series:

FIGURE 10.

in which the third close-up (Shot X) acquires, instead of a general, vaguely expressive direction, which the first arrangement would have produced, even sharper emphasis for its rightward direction by being photographed with a 180° lens.

Examples can be found of Pushkin's adherence to a similar construction. In *Ruslan and Ludmila* he tells of those who were killed in battle against the Pechenegs: one struck by an arrow, another smitten by a mace, and a third trampled by a horse.

A sequence of *arrow, mace, horse* would have corresponded with a direct crescendo.

Pushkin, however, gives a different arrangement. He distributes the "weight" of the blow, not in a simple ascending line, but with a "recoil" in the middle link in the chain:

not: arrow—mace—horse,
but: mace—arrow—horse.

That one, felled by a mace's blow;
And that—struck by an arrow;
Another, pressed to his shield,
Crushed by a frenzied horse. . . .[16]

So these separate movements of the eye from left to right throughout the sequence add up to a feeling of something on the left, striving "with all its soul" in a direction somewhere to the right.

This is precisely the feeling that the entire complex of twelve shots was seeking: the prince on the rock, the army at the foot of the rock, the general air of expectation—all directed to that point, to the right, into the distance, somewhere beyond the lake, from which the as yet invisible enemy will appear.

At this point the enemy is shown only through the Russian army's expectation of it.

Following these twelve shots are three empty frames of the deserted icy surface of the lake.

In the middle of the second of these three shots the enemy appears "in a new quality"—through the sounding of his horn. The sound of the horn ends upon a shot of Alexander's group—to give a feeling that the sound "came from afar" (the series of deserted landscapes) and finally "reached" Alexander (or "fell upon the picture of the Russians").

The entrance of the sound is *in the middle* of a shot of empty landscape, so that the sound is heard as if from the middle of the picture—*head on*. It is then heard *head on* in the shot of the group of Russians (facing the enemy).

The following shot discloses the distant cavalry line of German knights, moving *head on*, appearing to flow from the horizon with which it at first seemed to be merged. (This theme of a *head on* attack is prepared long in advance by Shots IV and XII—both *head on* shots—which was their chief rôle in the sequence, apart from their function as plastic equivalents of the music at these points.)

To all that has been said a basic reservation must be added.

It is perfectly obvious that a horizontal reading of a sequence of frames, attached to each other in a horizontal conception, is not always pertinent. As we have shown, in this case it flows entirely from the total image sensation that is required of the sequence: a sensation bound to a direction of the attention from left to right.

This particular feature of our desired image is achieved fully by both picture and music, and by genuine inner synchronization of both. (Even the music seems to expand, moving away from the heavy chords of the "left" side. Try to imagine for a moment the effect that would result from these chords being placed to the "right," i.e., *ending* the phrases with chords; there could be no sensation of "flight" to beyond the spaces of Lake Chudskoye, such as is now achieved.)

In working to achieve *other images*—in other cases—the composition of the frames can "train" the eye for an entirely different plastic reading.

The eye may be trained, not to attach one frame to

another as in our fragment, but to place frame upon frame—as layers.

This would produce either a sensation of being drawn into a depth or a sensation of pictures rushing towards the spectator.

Imagine, for instance, a sequence of four close-ups of increasing size, each of a different person, each placed centrally in its frame. A natural perception of this series of shots would not be as diagrammed in the upper drawing, but as in the lower:

FIGURE 11.

This would not be a movement past the eye—from left to right, but a movement either away from the eye in a sequence of 1, 2, 3, 4—or towards the eye, 4, 3, 2, 1.

What we have just noted is a second type of movement in our analysis of the horn-sound and the change to a *head on* movement into a depth—which follows our first sequence.

The sound falls on a shot similar to Shot XII—such a shot as could be read just as well ("by inertia") from left to right, as into a depth:

FIGURE 12.

But two things help us to switch attention to a depth.

First, the sound bursts from the *temporal* center of the shot, so that our perception, guided by analogy and a sense of space, places the sound in the *spatial* center of the shot.

Second, a step-like movement of the grayish-white streaks of snow, moving upward from the bottom frame-line.

FIGURE 13.

This "ladder" carries the eye upward, but this upward movement over the surface is at the same time an approach to the horizon; it can thus be read psychologically as a spatial movement towards the horizon, or into the depth, which is exactly what we need here. This movement is further strengthened by the following shot, which has an almost identical composition, but with a lowered horizon-line—so that the increased expanse of sky induces the eye to perceive an even greater distance. Later this conditioned direction of the eye is materialized —first audibly (with an approaching sound), and then concretely (with the galloping riders) as the moment of the attack draws nearer.

With a systematic distribution of forms, lines or

movements, it is just as possible to train the eye for vertical reading, or in any desired direction.

There is a little more to add to our analysis of Shots IX-X and XI-XII. As already mentioned, Shots IX-X fall on phrase A_1 (equal to A, but in a new tonality). We may note that Shots XI-XII fall on phrase B_1 in the same way.

The general diagram shows that, unlike Shots III and IV where one picture covers each two measures of the phrases A and B, two pictures cover each two measures of the phrases A_1 and B_1.

Let us see whether Shots IX-X-XI-XII repeat the graph of motion that we determined for Shots III-IV. If so, in what new aspect? The first three-quarters of the first measure fall on the close-up, IX. These three-quarters include the introductory chord—"the starting platform," as we called it on other occasions. The picture that accompanies this chord seems almost like an enlargement of part of Shot VI: the close-up of a bearded man (Ignat) against a background thick with spears might have been a closer camera set-up on the four spearmen of Shot VI. The remaining five-quarters of the phrase fall over Shot X—the background of which is relatively free of spears, compared to the background of Shot IX. This "simplification" resembles that of Shot VI, if you compare the left side of that frame with its right side. Our "jolt" also can be found in this close-up —but here expressed in an entirely new manner—as puffs of breath in the cold air, exhaled from a nervously tense throat. The "arc" in this instance is built upon a main element of growing suspense, now "acted"—increasing the excitement.

A new embodiment of our "motion" is revealed—a psychological factor of play, of acting—woven into the rising emotion.

Along with this factor, we may visualize Shot X as having volume. In the transition from Shot X to Shot XI, analogous to the "fall" of III-IV, we have no less sharp a jolt from a rounded volume—Savka's young face in close-up—to a long shot of small figures, with their backs to the camera, peering into the distance. This jolt is produced not only through an abrupt decrease of dimensions, but also through the full about-face of the personages.

These two shots—X and XI—are analogous to the right and left sides of Shot VII. Each half of Shot VII is given here a whole frame, producing its own effect. Naturally these are enriched and given more weight (compare VII and XI, or the strip of horizon in VII with the whole frame of deserted frozen lake in Shot XII).

Echoes of the other elements can be found here, also. The tapping off of flags that we remarked in Shot IV, and the moving high-lights of Shot VIII here appear as vertical streaks, alternating white and gray, stretching across the icy surface.

Thus we can find the same graph of motion that determined the synchronization of the inner movement of music and picture, reappearing in varying plastic means:

Tonally (Shot I)

Lineally (Shot III)

Spatially (the wings of Shots VI-VII)

Dramatically and substantially (by the acting in
Shots IX-X and by the plastic transition from the
close-up volume of Shot X to the reduced volumes
of Shot XI)

And, too, the anxious awaiting of the enemy was itself expressed through several kinds of variations: by
vague, "general" half-uttered means through the light
of Shot I, then the line of Shot III, then by *mise-en-
scène* and the grouping of Shots VI-VII, and finally by
a fully edited integration of Shots VIII-IX-X.

There is one shot that we have not yet touched in
our analysis—Shot V. In referring to it above we called
it a "transitional" shot. Thematically this is an exact description: a transition from the prince on the rock to
the troops at its foot.

This shot also contains a musical transition—and its
change from one tonality to another is consistent with
its thematic function, and with the plastic character of
the shot. This is the only frame in the sequence where
the "arc" is transposed from the right of the frame to the
left side. Here it serves to outline, not the airy part of
the frame, but the heavy, solid part: here the arc does
not move upward, but downward—all of which is in
full correspondence with the music: a clarinet in the
bass expressing a movement downward against a background of violins, tremolo.

Despite these differences this frame cannot be freed
completely from its responsibilities to the whole se-

quence. In theme this shot is completely linked with the other shots.

The different character of this shot could be explained without any hesitation if it contained some antagonistic element—if, for example, the German knights appeared, in any aspect, in this shot. Such a sharp cut, deliberately breaking up the general texture of the sequence, would have been in such a case not only "desirable," but actually necessary. The enemy theme does break in thus, with a harsh, new sound, a few shots later, as described above. Later the "clashing" themes of the two foes cross in a combat of clashing shots: in a clash of montage strips, sharply differing in composition and structure—white German knights—black Russian troops; immobile Russian troops—galloping riders; open, living emotional Russian faces—German faces hidden by the visors of iron masks.

This clashing of the two foes is first shown as a clash of shots assembled by means of contrast—solving the introductory phase of the battle without as yet bringing the troops into contact. A filmic battle has already begun, however, by means of this clash of the plastic elements that characterize the antagonists for us.

But no such full clash takes place between Shot V and the other shots. Despite the fact of a difference between the features of Shot V and the features of the other shots, V does not break away from their unity.

How is this achieved?

Since we have seen that the features of Shot V are torn away from the features of the other shots in almost every respect, we will, apparently, have to look beyond the limits of this frame alone for the answer.

Examining the entire series of pictures, we shall quickly discover two frames which, to a lesser degree, describe the same inverted curved arc that characterizes the descending line of the rock in Shot V.

We find that Shot V is placed roughly half-way between these two.

One shot prepares for the appearance of Shot V. The other cancels it out.

These two shots, so to speak, "amortize" the appearance and disappearance of Shot V, whose coming and going without them would have been too abrupt.

These two shots are II and VIII.

In fact, if we draw a directional line of their two main masses, we can see a coincidence with the rock contour of Shot V:

SHOT II   SHOT VIII

FIGURE 14.

Shot V differs from Shots II and VIII in that this line is not *physically* drawn, but functions as a construction line along which the main shapes of II and VIII arise.

In addition to this more fundamental welding of Shot V to the other shots, there are also curious "clamps" that hold V to its immediate neighbors—IV and VI.

It is tied to Shot IV by the tiny banner fluttering above the rock, continuing the play of flags over the troop-line in Shot IV; the last musical accent of the flags actually coincides with the appearance of the banner in Shot V.

Shot V is tied to Shot VI by the black contour of the rock, whose base occupies the left of frame VI.

This rock base has an importance other than the considerations of its plastic-compositional elements. It conveys topographical information—proving that the army is really at the foot of Raven Rock. The lack of such "information trifles" too often leads to a lack of definite topographical and strategic logic, allowing most film battles to melt into an hysterical chaos of skirmishes through which it is impossible to discern the general picture of the whole developing event.

Aside from these elements, we should note here another means of achieving compositional unity—through a mirror type of contrast. The same unity can be felt in Shot V that can be felt *quantitatively* by representing the same quantity with a *plus* and with a *minus* sign.

Our perception of this shot would be entirely different if, for example, Shot V had contained not only the same (though *inverted*) curve of the arc, but also a *broken* or a *straight* line. Then we would have sought its relationships among such opposites as black-white, immobile-moving, etc., where we would be dealing with *qualities* that are diametrically opposite rather than with equal quantities equipped with differing *indications*.

However, such general considerations could lead us very far afield.

Let us instead exploit our established fact—that we may draw a general diagram of audio-visual correspondence and a motion graph of this correspondence through our entire analyzed sequence. (During this résumé of the analysis it is advisable to follow the argument while keeping an eye on the general diagram.)

For this stage of the discussion we will overlook the details of how the repeats and variations are interwoven harmoniously. In this respect the diagram is quite clear in itself, both through its spacing and its figures.

There is another question that has not yet been touched in the analysis.

At the beginning of Part II we laid down a general principle, according to which audio-visual unity and correspondence is to be achieved. We defined this as a unity of both elements in an "image," i.e., through a unifying image.

We have just discovered that the "unifier" of the plastic and the music elements is the impulse of a movement that frequently and repeatedly passes through an entire sequence construction. Isn't there a contradiction here? Or may we, on the other hand, maintain that within our typical linear figure (that is, typical for a certain part of the work) there is a definite "imagery," and that that imagery is firmly connected with the "theme" of the part?

Does this appear in our general graph of motion, as shown in Figure 1?

If we try to read this graph emotionally in conjunction with the thematic matter of the sequence, checking one against the other, we can find a "seismographical" curve of a certain process and rhythm of *uneasy expectation*.

Beginning with a state of relative calm, it develops into an increasing upward movement—which can be read as a period of tenseness—waiting.

Near the summit of this tension, there is a sudden discharge, a complete fall—like an escaping sigh.

This similarity cannot really be considered accidental, because the apparently similar structure of the emotional graph is actually the prototype of the motion graph itself, which, like every living compositional graph, is a fragment of the activity of man, colored in a certain emotional way—a fragment of the regularity and the rhythm of this activity.

The line *a-b-c* on Figure 1 very clearly reproduces the state of "holding one's breath," holding in the exhalation until the chest is ready to burst—to burst not only with the increasing intake of air, but also with the increasing emotion that is bound to the physical act. —"Any moment now the enemy will appear on the horizon." And then, "No, he is not yet in sight." And you sigh with relief: the expanding chest suddenly collapsing with the deep exhalation. . . . Even here, in a simple description, one involuntarily places after this action . . . —three dots: the three dots of a pulsing anti-climax reacting to the previously increased tension.

Here something else catches our attention in the graph. A repeated stationary feeling matched to the introductory chord of the new musical phrase before again climbing to suspense—then a fall—and so on. And so the entire process moves ahead, rhythmically, invariably repeating itself with the very monotony that makes suspense so unbearable for those who are experiencing it. . . .

Deciphered in this way, our graph of curved ascensions, falls and horizontal resonances may be rightly considered as the limits to be reached by a graphic *embodiment* of that image which fuses the process of a certain state of excited suspense.*

Such a construction can obtain realistic fullness, and the *full imagery* of "suspense" only through the fullness of the shot-frames—only when these frames are filled with a plastic *representation* that is composed according to the most *generalized* graph of our theme.

---

* ". . . as Osmin's rage gradually increases, there comes (just when the aria seems to be at an end) the allegro assai, which is in a totally different measure and in a different key; this is bound to be very effective. For just as a man in such a towering rage oversteps all the bounds of order, moderation and propriety and completely forgets himself, so must the music too forget itself. But as music . . . must never cease to be *music*, I have gone from F (the key in which the aria is written), not into a remote key, but into a related one, not, however, into its nearest relative D minor, but into the more remote A minor." Mozart, in a letter to his father, September 26, 1781, regarding *Die Entführung aus dem Serail*.[17]

Along with a firm *generalized graph* of the sequence's emotional content sounded several times in the musical score, the element of the changing *pictorial representations* carries the responsibility for increasing the theme of suspense.

In our sequence we see a growing intensity of varying *representations* passing consecutively through a series of varying dimensions:

1. Tonal I.
2. Linear III-IV.
3. Spatial VI-VII-VIII.
4. Substantial (the masses of the close-ups) and, at the same time: Dramatic (the playing of these close-ups on through IX-X-XI-XII).

The very order in which these dimensions change forms a definitely growing line—from unsubstantial, vaguely alarming "play of light" (the fade-in) up to the clear, concrete *human action*, the activity of realistic characters, realistically awaiting a realistic foe.

One question remains to be answered—a question asked by every listener or reader for whom any picture of the regularity of compositional structures is laid out for the first time: "Did you know all this *beforehand?* Did you anticipate it *beforehand?* Did you really calculate this in such detail *beforehand?*"

This sort of question usually betrays an ignorance in the questioner as to the true manner in which the creative process proceeds.

It is a mistake to think that with the composition of a shooting-script, no matter how "ironclad" or "foolproof" it might be judged, the creative process is ended. Unfortunately this is an opinion I very often hear expressed—that the creative job is ended as soon as the compositional formulae are drawn up, and that it is thus that all the subtleties of construction are pre-determined.

This is far from a true picture of the process—and at the most, only to a certain degree is it even a possible picture.

It is especially far from the truth in respect to those scenes and sequences of a "symphonic" construction, where the shots are connected by a dynamic process, developing a broad emotional theme, rather than by some sequence of the plot's phases, which may develop only in that definite order and that definite sequence dictated by common sense.

This is connected with another circumstance—that during the period of work one rarely *formulates* these "hows" and "whys" which determine this or that choice of "correspondence." In the work period the basic selection is transmuted, not into *logical evaluation*, as in a post-analysis of this sort, but into *direct action*.

Build your thought not through inference, but lay it out directly in frames and in the course of composition.

I involuntarily recall Oscar Wilde's denial that an artist's ideas are born "naked," and only later dressed in marble, paint and sound.

The artist thinks directly in terms of manipulating his resources and materials. His thought is transmuted into direct action, formulated not by a formula, but by a form.

Even in this "spontaneity" the necessary laws, bases, motivations for *precisely such and no other* distribution of one's elements pass through the consciousness (and are sometimes even uttered aloud), but *consciousness does not stop to explain these motivations*—it hurries on *towards completion of the structure itself.* The pleasure of deciphering these "bases" remains to post-analysis, which sometimes occurs years after the "fever" of the creative "act" has passed—that "act" which Wagner, at the height of his creative rise in 1853, referred to in refusing to contribute to a review devoted to musical theory which was being organized by his friends: "When you create—you do not explain." [18]

The laws governing the fruits of the creative "act" are in no sense relaxed or reduced thereby—as we have endeavored to demonstrate in the above analysis.

1. THE WORK OF EISENSTEIN

(1920-1947)

(Note to Revised Edition: This list has been corrected and supplemented by Ivor Montagu.)

This record has been compiled with the intention of providing a fully rounded picture of Eisenstein's creative career, beginning with his work as designer in the theater. The list includes not only his six finished films, but also the unrealized projects and unachieved dreams without which the record of any artist's career is incomplete. The titles in **bold-face** are those of the six completed films.

Sergei Mikhailovich Eisenstein was born in 1898 and educated in St. Petersburg. A student of engineering and architecture, his interest in the theater did not become active until the Civil War, when as an engineer attached to a Red Army fortification corps he organized an amateur theater group. After demobilization, he found work as a theater designer in Moscow.

THE MEXICAN (1920-1921)

An adaptation of a story by Jack London, prepared by B. Arbatov for the First Workers' Theatre of the Proletkult. Directed by Valeri Smishlayev and Eisenstein. Designed by Eisenstein. An "agit-poster," staged in the Central Arena of Proletkult, Moscow.

KING HUNGER (1921)

A play by Leonid Andreyev. Directed by V. Tikhonovich. Designed by Eisenstein. Staged in the Central Arena of Proletkult, Moscow.

MACBETH (1921)

A play by Shakespeare. Directed by V. Tikhonovich. Designed by Eisenstein. Produced in the Polenov Theatre, Moscow.

VAUDEVILLES (1921-1922)

Including *A Good Relation to Horses* (V. Mass), *Thieving Children* (Dennery), and *The Phenomenal Tragedy of Phetra* (a parody by Foregger of Tairov's production of Racine's *Phedra*). Directed by N. Foregger for his Free Studio, Moscow. Designed by Eisenstein.

HEARTBREAK HOUSE (1922)

A play by Bernard Shaw. Directed by Vsevolod Meyerhold. Designed by Eisenstein. This production was prepared, but not staged.

PRECIPICE (1922)

A play by Valeri Pletnyov. Directed by M. Altman. Designed by Eisenstein. Staged in the Proletkult Theatre, Moscow.

THE WISE MAN (1922-1923)

Premiere March, 1923. An adaptation by Eisenstein for the Proletkult Theatre of Ostrovsky's play, *Enough Simplicity in Every Wise Man*. Directed and designed by Eisenstein. Cast:

Glumov ....Gregori Alexandrov
Mamayev ....Maxim Shtraukh
Mamayeva .... Vera Yanukova

A short comic film representing Glumov's diary and photographed by B. Frantzisson, was especially produced for incorporation into this first of Eisenstein's independent theatrical productions.

LISTEN, MOSCOW! (1923)

Premiere in the summer of 1923. An "agit-Guignole" by Sergei Tretiakov, written for the Prolekult Theatre. Directed and designed by Eisenstein.

GAS MASKS (1923-1924)

A play by Sergei Tretiakov. Directed and designed by Eisenstein Staged in the Moscow Gas Factory.

For detailed analysis of rôle played by his theater work in Eisenstein's development, see item 47, Bibliography.

STRIKE (1924)

Produced by Goskino (1st Studio), Moscow. Released February 1, 1925; 8 reels, 1,969 meters. Scenario by Valeri Pletnyov, Eisenstein and the Proletkult Collective. Directed by Eisenstein. Photographed by Edward Tisse. Settings by Vasili Rakhals. Cast:

Organizer ....A. Antonov
Worker ....Mikhail Gomarov
Spy ....Maxim Shtraukh
Foreman ....Gregori Alexandrov
Lumpenproletariat.......Judith Glizer, Boris Yurtzev
and other Proletkult actors

The first of a proposed series of films on pre-revolutionary working-class activities. Its original intent was almost purely educational, but the finished film was as dynamic and experimental as might be expected of Eisenstein's first film. It was one of the prize-winning Soviet films at the 1925 Exposition des Arts Décoratifs in Paris, and it was commercially exhibited in Germany, but it has not been seen in America or England.

1905 (1925)

Produced by Goskino (1st Studio), Moscow. Scenario by Nina Agadzhanova-Shutko. Directed by Eisenstein. Photographed by Edward Tisse.

A large panoramic film in celebration of the 1905 Revolution, half-completed in shooting before Eisenstein decided to concentrate on the expansion of one episode in it—the mutiny of the sailors on the Battleship Potemkin. The other episodes were never edited or released.

POTEMKIN [The Battleship Potemkin] (1925)

Produced by Goskino, Moscow. Premiere in the Bolshoi Theatre, Moscow, January 1, 1926; 5 reels, 1,740 meters. Scenario by Eisenstein, from an outline by Nina Agadzhanova-Shutko. Directed by Eisenstein, assisted by Gregori Alexandrov. Photographed by Edward Tisse. Direction assistants: A. Antonov, Mikhail Gomarov, A. Levshin, Maxim Shtraukh. Group manager: Yakov Bliokh. Sub-titles by Nikolai Aseyev. Cast: Sailors of the Black Sea Fleet of the Red Navy, citizens of Odessa, members of the Proletkult Theatre; and

Vakulinchuk ....A. Antonov
Chief Officer Giliarovsky........Gregori Alexandrov
Captain Golikov.....................Vladimir Barsky
Petty Officer...........................A. Levshin
A sailor ....Mikhail Gomarov

Filmed in the city and port of Odessa and in Sevastopol. The only American prints of *Potemkin* that reproduce exactly its original state are available through the Museum of Modern Art Film Library, New York.

FIRST CAVALRY ARMY

A proposed film which was to celebrate the rôle played in the Civil War by Budyonny's cavalry division. Material was also to be drawn from Isaac Babel's stories published under a similar title.

THE GENERAL LINE

Produced by Sovkino, Moscow. Scenario and direction by Eisenstein and Gregori Alexandrov. Photography by Edward Tisse.

A detailed film on the changes in Russia's agricultural scene as a result of the policy of collectivization. Its production was interrupted by Eisenstein's assignment to the largest of the several films being made in celebration of the October Revolution. On the crew's return to the subject a year later, it was completely reorganized, rewritten and rephotographed as *Old and New*.

OCTOBER [*Ten Days That Shook the World*] (1928)

Produced by Sovkino, Moscow. Released January 20, 1928; 7 reels, 2,800 meters. Scenario and direction by Eisenstein and Gregori Alexandrov. Photography by Edward Tisse. Direction assistants: Maxim Shtraukh, Mikhail Gomarov, Ilya Trauberg. Camera assistants: Vladimir Nilsen, Vladimir Popov. The cast, drawn largely from the people of Leningrad, included:

Lenin	Nikandrov
Kerensky	N. Popov
A cabinet minister	Boris Livanov

A reconstruction of the critical days between February and October, 1917, ending on the fall of the Provisional Government. Photographed almost entirely in Leningrad. Known abroad and in America as *Ten Days That Shook the World*.

OLD AND NEW (1929)

Produced by Sovkino, Moscow. Released September, 1929; 6 reels, 2,469 meters. Scenario and direction by Eisenstein and Gregori Alexandrov. Photography by Edward Tisse. Direction assistants: Maxim Shtraukh, Mikhail Gomarov. Camera assistants: Vladimir Nilsen, Vladimir Popov. Settings by V. Kovrigin; architecture by Andrei Burov. Cast:

The Woman	Marfa Lapkina
Komsomol	Vasya Buzenkov
Tractor Driver	Kostya Vasiliev
The Kulak	Chukhmarev
The Priest	Father Matvei
The Peasant	Khurtin
The Witch	Sukhareva

A film entirely different from the half-completed *General Line*, employing a more concentrated and personal story than originally proposed. See treatment in item 38 of Bibliography. Shown in England as *The General Line*.

CAPITAL

A planned film-dramatization of Karl Marx's analysis. See item 9 in Bibliography.

THE STORMING OF LA SARRAZ

This unfinished film was the result of Eisenstein, Tisse and Alexandrov attending an international film congress held in the ancient chateau of La Sarraz in Switzerland. One of the delegates (Jeannine Bhoussinousse, clad in a white robe with two empty film-reels for breastplates) was suspended with ropes from the topmost tower where, as "the spirit of the artistic film," she was the object for contention of two armies: that of Commerce, led by Bela Balasz in full armor, and that of Independence, led by Eisenstein, mounted on a projection table and tilting with both lance and projection apparatus. Other remembered warriors were Léon Moussinac as Wallenstein, Hans Richter as General Tilly, and Walter Ruttmann as St. George. This riot was "directed" by Eisenstein, Richter and Montagu, and Richter is credited with most of the improvised script. Tisse had to shoot the entire allegorical jest in a single day, because the outraged hostess demanded a stop to the congress's eccentricities. The short but uncut film was lost in some Berlin film vault.

THE ROAD TO BUENOS AIRES

The reportage by Albert Londres was proposed to a French company by Eisenstein and he worked over it for a while with Montagu before the project evaporated. Eisenstein privately explained his choice of the subject by his belief in type-casting, for he would not have been able to make a film in France without employing the lady friends of the film's financiers.

ZAHAROFF

Eisenstein was attracted by a currently published biography of Sir Basil Zaharoff, and suggested it to French and English companies at this time as well as, later, to Paramount and to other American firms.

[*Romance Sentimentale*]

A musical short film made by Alexandrov and Tisse in Paris. Its producer would only put up the money for the production (which included salaries for three) if Eisenstein would agree to be named as co-director on it. Eisenstein did agree, in advance. He also later wrote defending the production from criticism as though it were indeed one of his own, although his actual participation was not more than as an occasional consultant.

ARMS AND THE MAN

George Bernard Shaw offered his play to Eisenstein if he could get an American producer to do it and it was later mentioned to Paramount, though without interest.

THE WAR OF THE WORLDS

When Eisenstein signed the contract with Paramount in Paris, Jesse Lasky proposed to him the H. G. Wells novel, but the project was soon dropped as too costly.

GLASS HOUSE

Possibly suggested by Eugene Zamiatin's novel *We*. Eisenstein outlined the idea to Lasky, who was interested, but the combined efforts of Eisenstein, Alexandrov and Montagu, plus some writers from the Paramount lot (including Oliver Garrett), to find a story to express the idea, produced nothing.

SUTTER'S GOLD

The next project submitted to Paramount. Along with a treatment by Eisenstein, Alexandrov and Montagu (see Appendix 5) a detailed production schedule to demonstrate how economically the film could be made (now in the Eisenstein Collection at the Museum of Modern Art Film Library) was turned in to Lasky.

AN AMERICAN TRAGEDY

The most completely developed of the several projects submitted to Paramount. This adaptation and treatment of Theodore Dreiser's novel was approved by the author but rejected by Paramount. See Appendix 4 and item 34 in Bibliography. Ivor Montagu thus ascribes the authorship of this and the previous *Sutter's Gold* scripts: "The scripts of both these subjects should be ascribed to S.M.E., G.V.A. and I.M. After a lot of research, of which E. of course did overwhelmingly the most and initiated everything, he and A. got out the first draft, which we then had translated, whereupon he and I got out the second, the actual writing of this being my job (as the writing of the first had been A.'s), the actual planning—general and detail—of both being E.'s."

BLACK MAJESTY

A film of the Haitian Revolution was considered at various times, and as early as Paris, before the Paramount contract was signed. In addition to the John Vandercook novel of this name, material was also to be drawn from Anatoli Vinogradov's *The Black Consul* and Otten's play *Der Schwarze Napoleon*. The idea of starring Paul Robeson was also absorbed into the continuing project.

ONCE IN A LIFETIME

Eisenstein obtained the Russian theatrical rights from Sam H. Harris to the play by Moss Hart and George S. Kaufman, with a view to staging it on his return to Moscow.

"A FILM IN JAPAN"

As the return home was first planned via Japan, a production there was contracted by letter exchange. This was cancelled by the change in traveling plans and the Mexican film.

QUE VIVA MEXICO!

> Independently produced, through Upton Sinclair. Scenario and direction by Eisenstein and Gregori Alexandrov. Photographed by Edward Tisse.

The footage shot for this film was utilized in 1933 by Sol Lesser to make *Thunder Over Mexico* (based on one episode of the complete plan) and two short films, *Death Day* and *Eisenstein in Mexico*. In 1939 Marie Seton used additional footage to release *Time in the Sun* (edited by Roger Burnford from extant outlines for *Que Viva Mexico!*). Eisenstein himself has never seen his full footage nor any uses that others have made of sections of it. See Appendix 6 and item 39 in Bibliography.

"A TRAVEL FILM OF RUSSIA"

A project mentioned on Eisenstein's journey back to Moscow.

"A MODERN *GÖTTERDÄMMERUNG*"

Another mentioned project, to be centered around the story of Ivar Kreuger.

MMM

A comedy prepared by Eisenstein immediately upon his return to Moscow. Although tentatively cast with Maxim Shtraukh and Judith Glizer, this did not get beyond the scenario stage.

MOSCOW

An ambitious historical film, planned to cover four centuries of Moscow's existence as a leading Russian city. Co-incidental with this plan was to be Eisenstein's return to the stage, as director of a play by his co-scenarist, Natan Zarkhi —*Moscow the Second*. Both film and play were halted by Zarkhi's death in 1934. See item 37 in Bibliography.

LA CONDITION HUMAINE

This proposed film was to be based on Malraux's own adaptation of his novel.

BEZHIN MEADOW

Produced by Mosfilm, Moscow. Original scenario by Alexander Rzheshevsky, based on Turgenev's short story of this name, and on the life of Pavel Morozov; later revisions by Eisenstein and Isaac Babel. Direction by Eisenstein. Photographed by Edward Tisse. Cast included Vitya Kartashov, Boris Zakhava, Elena Telesheva.

After several delays and revisions, the uncompleted film was shelved. See item 52 in Bibliography.

"A FILM OF THE CIVIL WAR IN SPAIN"

Mentioned by Vishnevsky in his pamphlet on Eisenstein.

"A FILM ON THE ORGANIZATION OF THE RED ARMY IN 1917"

Also mentioned by Vishnevsky. This may be identified with a scenario written by Vishnevsky, *We, the Russian People*.

ALEXANDER NEVSKY (1938)

Produced by Mosfilm, Moscow. Released November 23, 1938;
12 reels, 3,044 meters. Scenario by Eisenstein and Piotr Pavlenko.
Directed by Eisenstein, with the collaboration of D. I. Vasiliev.
Photographed by Edward Tisse. Music by Sergei Prokofiev.
Lyrics by Vladimir Lugovsky. Settings and costumes executed
from Eisenstein's sketches by Isaac Shpinel, Nikolai Soloviov,
K. Yeliseyev. Sound: B. Volsky, V. Popov. Direction assistants:
B. Ivanov, Nikolai Maslov. Camera assistants: S. Uralov, A. Asta-
fiev, N. Bolshakov. Consultant on work with actors: Elena
Telesheva. Cast:

Prince Alexander Yaroslavich Nevsky.........Nikolai Cherkasov
Vasili Buslai...................................Nikolai Okhlopkov
Gavrilo Olexich ....Alexander Abrikosov
Ignat, master armorer............................Dmitri Orlov
Pavsha, Governor of Pskov.....................Vasili Novikov
Domash Tverdislavich...........................Nikolai Arsky
Amelfa Timofeyevna, mother of Buslai.....Varvara Massalitinova
Olga, a Novgorod girl...........................Vera Ivasheva
Vasilisa, a girl of Pskov..........................Anna Danilova
Von Balk, Grand Master of the Livonian
   Order ....Vladimir Yershov
Tverdilo, traitorous mayor of Pskov.............Sergei Blinnikov
Ananias ....Ivan Lagutin
The Bishop ....Lev Fenin
The Black-robed Monk........................Naum Rogozhin

Work on the scenario was begun in the summer of 1937,
and the shooting was completed during the summer of
1938. Prokofiev has written a cantata based on his score,
also entitled *Alexander Nevsky*.

PEREKOP

A film-project to reconstruct Frunze's drive on the White
Guard forces of Baron Wrangel from the Crimean Penin-
sula in 1920. Script by Eisenstein and Fadeyev.

FERGHANA CANAL

A planned history of Central Asia from antiquity to the present day. There was one exploratory filming expedition to the chief location before the project was dropped. This footage was edited into a short documentary film on the opening of the Canal. The full script was by Pavlenko and Eisenstein (see Appendix 7). The preliminary photography was by Tisse, and a score was sketched by Sergei Prokofiev.

DIE WALKÜRE

The second opera of Richard Wagner's *Ring of the Nibelung.* Staged at the Bolshoi Opera Theatre, Moscow. Directed by Eisenstein. Settings and costumes designed by Peter Williams after sketches by Eisenstein. Conducted by Vasili Nebolsin. Premiere November 21, 1940. Cast:

Sieglinde	N. D. Schpiller
Brünnhilde	Marguerite Butenina
Fricka	Elena Slivinskaya
Siegmund	Alexander Khanayev
Hunding	Vasili Lubentzov
Wotan	Innocent Redikultzev

See item 60 in Bibliography.

MOSCOW FIGHTS BACK

The preparation of *Ivan the Terrible* was interrupted to work on a newsreel feature-length film with the collaboration of Quentin Reynolds. This project was variously called *War Against the Nazis* and *The Face of Fascism,* and was halted by the removal of Reynolds to Kuibyshev with the other correspondents at the end of 1941.

IVAN THE TERRIBLE: Part I (1944)

Produced by the Central Cinema Studio, Alma-Ata. Released December 30, 1944; 12 reels, 2745 meters. Scenario and direction by Eisenstein. Photographed by Edward Tisse (exteriors) and Andrei

Moskvin (interiors). Music by Sergei Prokofiev. Lyrics by Vladimir Lugovsky. Settings and costumes executed from Eisenstein's sketches by Isaac Shpinel, L. Naumov, V. Goryunov. Sound: V. Bogdankevich, B. Volsky. Direction assistants: B. Sveshnikov, L. Indenbom. Camera assistant: V. Dombrovsky.

Ivan IV ....Nikolai Cherkasov
Anastasia, his bride...........Ludmila Tzelikovskaya
The Boyarina Staritzkaya..........Scraphima Birman
Vladimir Andreyevich, her son....Piotr Kadochnikov
Prince Andrei Kurbsky................M. Nazvanov
Prince Fyodor Kolychov........Alexander Abrikosov
Archbishop Pimen......................A. Mgebrov
Nikola, the fanatic...............Vsevolod Pudovkin
Malyuta Skuratov....................Mikhail Zharov
Alexei Basmanov.....................Alexei Buchma
Fyodor, his son...................Mikhail Kuznetzov

This is the first of a projected series of three films, planned before the Nazi invasion, but not begun until after the evacuation of the Mosfilm Studio to Alma-Ata. The full treatment (then in two parts) was published in 1944, and thereupon translated into English (see item 67 in Bibliography).

IVAN THE TERRIBLE (Part II)

Most of this Part II of the projected trilogy was shot during the production of Part I, but its cutting (including sequences in color) was not completed until the beginning of 1946. Immediately upon the completion of the cutting, Eisenstein suffered an almost fatal heart-attack, confining him to a hospital for the remainder of the year. During this time screenings of his work-print aroused considerable critical controversy, of which he was unaware until his release from the hospital. At present he is completing Part II for release in 1948.

2. MONTAGE OF ATTRACTIONS

This is an excerpt from Eisenstein's first published article, printed in the magazine *Lef* in 1923. This statement was made in connection with the preparation of his production of Ostrovsky's play *Enough Simplicity in Every Wise Man*, staged in the Proletkult Arena. Of particular interest in the article is its formulation of a direction in Eisenstein's theater work that was not to find complete realization until practiced in the film medium. This direction has developed so consistently since Eisenstein entered films that a comparison between this and his latest work in this volume reveals no fundamental contradiction.

THE basic materials of the theater arise from the spectator himself—and from our guiding of the spectator into a desired direction (or a desired mood), which is the main task of every functional theater (agit, poster, health education, etc.). The weapons for this purpose are to be found in all the left-over apparatus of the theater (the "chatter" of Ostuzhev no more than the pink tights of the prima-donna, a roll on the kettledrums as much as Romeo's soliloquy, the cricket on the hearth no less than the cannon fired over the heads of the audience). For all, in their individual ways, bring us to a single ideal—from their individual laws to their common quality of *attraction*.

The attraction (in our diagnosis of the theater) is every aggressive moment in it, i.e., every element of it that brings to light in the spectator those senses or that psychology that influence his experience—every element that can be verified and mathematically calculated to produce certain emotional shocks in a proper order within the totality—the only means by which it is possible to make the final ideological conclusion perceptible. The way to knowledge—"Through the living play of the passions"—applies specifically to the theater (perceptually).

Sensual and psychological, of course, in the sense of efficient action—as directly active as in the Theatre Guignole, where an eye is gouged out, an arm or leg amputated before the very eyes of the audience; or a telephone communication is incorporated into the action to describe a horrible event that is taking place ten miles away; or a situation in which a drunkard, sensing his approaching end, seeks relief in madness. Rather in this sense than in that branch of the psychological theater where the attraction rests in the theme only, and exists and operates *beneath* the action, although the theme may be an extremely urgent one. (The mistake made by most agit-theaters is in their satisfaction with those attractions that already exist in their scripts.)

I establish attraction as normally being an independent and primary element in the construction of a theatrical production—a molecular (i.e., compound) unity of the *efficiency* of the theater and of *theater in general*. This is fully analogous with the "pictorial storehouse" employed by George Grosz, or the elements of photographic illustration [photo-montage] employed by Rodchenko.

As difficult as "compound" may be to limit, it certainly ends with that fascinating noble hero (the psychological moment) and begins with the concentrated moment of his personal charm (i.e., his erotic activity), for the lyric effect of certain Chaplin scenes does not in the least detract from the attractions communicated by the specific mechanics of his movement; it is just as difficult to fix the boundary line where religious pathos moves into sadist satisfaction during the torture scenes of the miracle plays.

The attraction has nothing in common with the trick. Tricks are accomplished and completed on a plane of pure craftsmanship (acrobatic tricks, for example) and include that kind of attraction linked to the process of giving (or in circus slang, "selling") one's self. As the circus term indicates, inasmuch as it is clearly from the viewpoint of the performer himself, it is absolutely opposite to the attraction —which is based exclusively on the reaction of the audience.

Approached genuinely, this basically determines the possible principles of construction as "an action construction" (of the whole production). Instead of a static "reflection" of an event with all possibilities for activity within the limits of the event's logical action, we advance to a new plane— free montage of arbitrarily selected, independent (within the given composition and the subject links that hold the influencing actions together) attractions—all from the stand of establishing certain final thematic effects—this is montage of attractions.

The theater is confronted with the problem of transforming its "illusory pictures" and its "presentations" into a montage of "real matters" while at the same time weaving into the montage full "pieces of representation" tied to the plot development of the subject, but now not as self-enforced and all-determining, but as consciously contributing to the whole production and selected for their pure strength as active attractions.

It is not in a "revelation" of the playwright's purpose, or the "correct interpretation of the author," or a "true reflection of an epoch" that a production can base itself. The only true and solid base for the action of a production can be found in attractions and in a system of attractions. With all details gathered together in the hand of the director, the attraction is always, in some way, intuitively employed, but not on a plane of montage or construction, but as part of a "harmonic composition" (from which de-

rives a whole jargon—"effective curtains," "a rich exit," "a
good stunt," etc.), but this exists solely within the frame
of the subject's plausibility, chiefly unconsciously and in
the pursuit of something entirely different (usually something that is present in the rehearsals from the beginning).
What remains to us in reworking the system of staging is
to shift the center of attention to that which is necessary,
scrutinizing everything for its value as a transitional, clari-
fying or factual exposition of the basic intentional line of
the staging, rather than for its ties to logical, natural and
literary traditional piety. *Our job is to establish this way
as a production method* (which has been the work of the
Proletkult Workshop since the autumn of 1922).

Schooling for the *montageur* can be found in the cinema,
and chiefly in the music-hall and circus, which invariably
(substantially speaking) puts on a good show—from the
spectator's viewpoint. This schooling is necessary in order
to build a strong music-hall-circus program, resulting from
the situation found at the base of a play. . . .

(*Lef*, No. 3, 1923)

3. A SEQUENCE FROM *STRIKE*

The following list of shots is a record * made of the
completed final sequence of Eisenstein's first film. This oft-
quoted example of an early montage conception has never
been seen on American or English screens, and its publication in this form may be of interest. Technical abbrevia-

* As published by Alexander Belenson in his *Cinema Today*
(Moscow, 1925), p. 59.

tions used here and in the subsequent script fragments: Close-up (*c.u.*), Medium Shot (*m.s.*), and Long Shot (*l.s.*).

1　The head of a bull jerks out of the shot, beyond the upper frame-line, avoiding the aimed butcher's knife.

2　(*c.u.*) The hand holding the knife strikes sharply—beyond the lower frame-line.

3　(*l.s.*) 1,500 persons roll down a slope—in profile.

4　50 persons raise themselves from the ground, arms outstretched.

5　Face of a soldier taking aim.

6　(*m.s.*) A volley of gun-fire.

7　The shuddering body of the bull (*head outside the frame*) rolls over.

8　(*c.u.*) Legs of the bull jerk convulsively. The hooves beat in a pool of blood.

9　(*c.u.*) The bolts of a rifle.

10　The bull's head is fastened with rope to a bench.

11　1,000 persons rush past the camera.

12　From behind bushes, a chain of soldiers appears.

13　(*c.u.*) The bull's head dies under unseen blows (the eyes glaze).

14　A volley (*l.s.*) seen from behind the soldiers' backs.

15　(*m.s.*) The bull's legs are bound together, in preparation for the slicing of meat.

16　(*c.u.*) People roll over a cliff.

17　The bull's throat is slit—the blood gushes out.

18　(*m.c.u.*) People lift themselves into the frame, arms outstretched.

19 The butcher moves past the camera (*panning*) swinging his bloody rope.

20 A crowd runs to a fence, breaks through it, and hides behind it (*in two or three shots*).

21 Arms fall into the frame.

22 The head of the bull is severed from the trunk.

23 A volley.

24 The crowd rolls down a slope into the water.

25 A volley.

26 (*c.u.*) The bullets can be seen leaving the gun-barrels.

27 Soldiers' feet walk away from the camera.

28 Blood floats on the water, discoloring it.

29 (*c.u.*) Blood gushes from the slit throat of the bull.

30 Blood is poured from a basin (held by hands) into a pail.

31 Dissolve from a truck loaded with pails of blood—to a passing truck loaded with scrap-iron.

32 The bull's tongue is pulled through the slit throat (to prevent the convulsions from damaging the teeth).

33 The soldiers' feet walk away from the camera (*seen at a further distance than previously*).

34 The bull's skin is stripped off.

35 1,500 bodies at the foot of the cliff.

36 Two skinned bulls' heads.

37 A hand lying in a pool of blood.

38 (*c.u.*) Filling the entire screen: the eye of the dead bull.

39 (*title*) THE END.

4. A SEQUENCE FROM
AN AMERICAN TRAGEDY

A copy of the "first treatment" of this script, dated October 9, 1930, and signed S. M. Eisenstein and Ivor Montagu, is in the Eisenstein Collection at the Museum of Modern Art Film Library, New York. The following sequence is from Reel 10 of this script.

17 The surface of Big Bittern Lake.

    Pools of the inky black surface of the silent water. The dark reflection of the pines.

    Boats trembling on the motionless surface of the silent water. Their gunwales against a rude landing stage at the foot of steps rising to the small hotel. The beautiful panorama of the lake.

18 Standing by the landing stage are Clyde and Roberta. They have just descended from the auto bus.

    "How pretty—how beautiful it is!" exclaims Roberta.

    Suddenly the hotel proprietor appears from behind the bus. Sprung up as if by magic, he busily praises the weather, greets his guests.

    Clyde notices that there are few people about and none to be seen upon the lake. Too late, he notices that the proprietor, praising his kitchen, has taken the grip from him and that Roberta is following him into the hotel.

He makes a movement as if to get the grip back, but thinks better of it, and with a strange, hypnotized step, follows them.

19 Open, the white pages of the hotel register stare threateningly at him.

Clyde grows paler; settling himself, he signs a fictitious name—"Carl Golden"—keeping his initials (C.G.) and adding "and wife." Roberta, noting this, feels a pang of joy that she hides before those in the hotel.

"It's very hot. I'll leave my hat and jacket here—we'll be coming back early," says Roberta and she leaves both on a hanger in the hall.

20 Losing his head and ignoring these incidents, Clyde takes his grip from the surprised proprietor and goes towards the boat stand. As he places the grip in a boat, he explains to the man: "We have our lunch in it."

Too preoccupied to note a remark by the boatman, he helps Roberta in and, taking hold of the oars, pulls off from the shore.

21 Thick pine forests line the shore, and behind them are to be seen the tops of the hills.

The water of the lake is calm and dark.

"What peace, what tranquillity"—says Roberta.

Rowing, then stopping, Clyde listens to this silence, looks about him. There is no one around.

22 As the boat glides into the darkness of the lake, so Clyde glides into the darkness of his thoughts. Two voices

struggle within him—one: "Kill—kill!" the echo of his dark resolve, the frantic cry of all his hopes of Sondra and society; the other: "Don't—don't kill!" the expression of his weakness and his fears, of his sadness for Roberta and his shame before her. In the scenes that follow, these voices ripple in the waves that lap from the oars against the boat; they whisper in the beating of his heart; they comment, underscoring, upon the memories and alarums that pass through his mind; each ever struggling with the other for mastery, first one dominating then weakening before the onset of its rival.

They continue to murmur as he pauses on his oars to ask: "Did you speak to anyone in the hotel?"

"No. Why do you ask?"

"Nothing. I thought you might have met someone."

23 The voices shudder as Roberta smiles and shakes her head in answer, playfully letting her hand fall into the water.

"It isn't cold," she says.

Clyde stops rowing and also feels the water. But his hand springs back as though it had received an electric shock.

24 As he photographs her, the voices preoccupy him. While they picnic, or pick water-lilies, they possess him. As he jumps ashore a moment to put down his grip, the voices rise and torment him.

25 "Kill—kill," and Roberta happy, freshened by her faith in him, is radiant with the joy of living. "Don't kill—

don't kill," and as the boat drifts almost soundlessly by
the dark pines and Clyde's face is racked by the struggle
within him, there rises the long-drawn-out booming cry
of a waterbird.

26 "Kill—kill" triumphs, and there passes through his mind
the memory of his mother. "Baby—baby" comes the
voice of his childhood and as "Don't kill—don't kill"
rises he hears "Baby boy—baby boy" in the so different
voice of Sondra, and at the image of Sondra and the
thought of all that surrounds her "Kill—kill" grows
harder and insistent, and with the thought of Roberta
importunate it grows still harsher and shriller, and then
the face of Roberta now, aglow with faith in him and
her great relief, and the sight of the hair he has so loved
to caress and "Don't—don't kill" grows and tenderly
supplants the other and now is calm and firm and final.
Ending the conflict. Sondra is lost forever. Never, never
now will he have the courage to kill Roberta.

27 And we see Clyde as he sits in blank despair and the
misery of renunciation. He raises his face from his
hands.

An oar drags in the water. In his left hand he holds
the camera.

And Clyde's face is so wild with misery and so stricken
by the struggle that has passed behind it that Roberta
crawls anxiously towards him and takes his hand in hers.

28 Clyde opens his eyes suddenly and sees near him her
anxious, tender face. With an involuntary movement of
revulsion he pulls back his hand and jumps up quickly.

As he does so the camera, quite accidentally, strikes her in the face. Roberta's lip is cut; she cries out and falls back in the stern of the boat.

"I'm sorry, Roberta, I didn't mean to," and he makes a natural movement towards her. Roberta is afraid. She tries to get up, loses her balance, and the boat overturns.

29 Once more rings out the long-drawn booming cry of the bird. The overset boat floats on the surface of the water.

Roberta's head appears above the surface.

Clyde comes up. His face showing terrible fright, he makes a movement to help Roberta.

Roberta, terrified by his face, gives a piercing cry and, splashing frantically, disappears under the water. Clyde is about to dive down after her, but he stops, and hesitates.

30 And a third time the long-drawn booming cry of the far-away bird.

On the mirror-like calmness of the water floats a straw hat.

The wilderness of forest, the motionless hills. Dark water barely lapping against the shore.

31 A noise of water is heard and Clyde is seen swimming to the shore. Reaching it, he first lies upon the earth, then slowly sits up, forgetting to lift one foot out of the water.

Gradually he begins to shiver, the shivering increases, he pales and makes a familiar gesture, that gesture that he makes when frightened or suffering. He shrinks into himself and hides his head in his shoulders. He notices the foot in the water and lifts it out. He begins to think, and with that, stops trembling. And the voice of his thought.

"Well, Roberta is gone—as you desired—and you didn't kill her—an accident—liberty—life—"

And then very low, tenderly, as if whispering into his ear, the voice says:

"Sondra."

And Clyde closes his eyes. And in the darkness:

"Sondra."

Her laughter and her tender voice.

"Sondra."

32 Clyde is feverishly clothing himself in the dry suit from his grip. Into the grip he packs the soaked suit, and then, getting up from his knees, he stretches to his full height, standing in the rays of the setting sun.

33 The sun vanishes behind the hills, behind the forest. The reflection vanishes from the lake, and all becomes darker and darker.

34 Through the increasing dread of the darkling forest, Clyde is making his way, his grip in his hand. He starts, alarmed by every noise, he is frightened by the cries of the night birds, he fears the moonlight penetrating be-

tween the thick branches of the trees, he fears his own
shadows and the shadows of the fantastic forest.

He desires to see the time on his watch in the moonlight,
but, when the lid is opened, water falls from it and he
finds out that it has stopped. . . .

A working sketch by Eisenstein in connection with his development
of the "inner monologue" in the foregoing sequence from *An American Tragedy*. The sketch specifically relates to a break-down of the
material included in nos. 22 and 23.

5 · A SEQUENCE FROM
SUTTER'S GOLD

The following fragment is Reel 4 of a synopsis or a draft treatment of this proposed subject. This manuscript and a detailed production plan for the film are both in the above-mentioned Eisenstein Collection.

Title: FRIDAY

Rain beats mercilessly and ceaselessly upon the ground.

Title: JANUARY 28

The deluge continues.

Title: 1848

The deluge.

Sutter is seated, working, at an old writing desk.

The rain beats hopelessly on the windows.

Galloping horse's hooves are heard through the beat of the rain.

Sutter lifts his head, gets up and, gun in hand, goes to the window.

The sound of the galloping hooves comes closer.

The door is flung open and, along with a gust of rain, a man soaked by the downpour rushes into the room, overturning two chairs.

"Marshall!"

—shouts Sutter, and runs to meet him.

Marshall is in a frenzy of excitement—and out of breath. Exhausted by his furious ride, he cannot speak at first.

But through his broken and choked sounds, it becomes clear that his news is secret—he motions for the door to be shut.

Sutter closes the door.

Marshall manages to take a package from his pocket, and tries to unfold it with his trembling fingers.

The door is opened—by one of Sutter's clerks in search of something.

Marshall hastily thrusts the package back into his pocket—glaring at the man.

Innocently and unhurriedly the clerk finds what he needs and leaves.

Marshall shuts the door after him, comes close to Sutter and again takes out the little package, starting to unfold it.

A servant girl comes into the room.

Marshall hides the package.

This time he thrusts the girl out of the room, slamming the door.

Failing to find a key, Marshall shoves a table against the door.

Marshall's trembling fingers are holding the unfolded paper, showing some tiny grains of metal.

Title: GOLD?

Title: GOLD?

Title: GOLD?

As hands complete a chemical test on the grains, Sutter's voice answers quietly and certainly:

"Gold."

Sutter stands at the table—the gold and reagent are in his hands, and grief fills his face. He repeats—even more quietly:

"Gold."

Title: GOLD. As the word zooms forward, filling the screen, we hear in a parallel rising inhuman roar— "Gold!"

"Gold!"

—shrieks Marshall at the top of his voice—overturning the table, he flings the door open and rushes into the yard.

Sutter rushes to the window, opens it, and into the rain that drives in, shouts after Marshall:

"Stop. Stop!"

Unheeding, Marshall gallops away through the downpour.

In the center of the room—with its overturned table, its leaning cupboard, its scattered papers tossed by the wind that is blowing in the rain through the open window and the door swinging on its hinges—stands Sutter, staring with foreboding at the gold on the table.

A gust of wind blows out the light. The dim outlines of the wind-swept room slowly fade out.

In a long fade-in—

—a gray and misty morning.

Sutter dismounts from horseback near his Coloma sawmill at the spot where the first gold was discovered.

At the mill the Indian workers are in the grip of superstitious horror.

They say that the gold belongs to the devil—they have always known of it, and avoided it—and they implore Sutter not to touch it.

Sutter replies that the first job is to complete the construction of his sawmill—no matter what happens.

He urges them to keep the discovery secret.

They all pledge secrecy.

And Sutter, on his way home—

—passes through the prosperous landscapes of a happy countryside.

Wealth, fertility and contentment can be sensed everywhere.

The rain has ceased, nature's garment is soft and sparkling. Myriads of raindrops shimmer in the sunshine.

Suddenly he meets a group of working people with picks, and pans for gold-washing.

Astonished, Sutter follows them with his eyes, then turns his horse and gallops towards the fort.

The store-keeper from near the fort comes up to Sutter to show him gold dust in the palm of his hand.

He asks Sutter if this is really gold or not.

Sutter nods slowly.

The man shouts: "Gold! Gold!"—and runs into his store.

Sutter, nervous and shaken, rides through the gate of the fort.

The store-keeper nails up the door of his store.

Everything he owns is flung into a wagon.

His helper steals two of Sutter's horses from the corral.

The store-keeper drives off furiously towards the Gold.

Two Indians have stopped their work in the fields to listen to a woman who, with much gesticulation, is telling them the news.

Flinging down their hoes, the Indians follow the store-keeper.

The herdsman deserts his animals.

A husband abandons his wife and children. They weep and plead, but he abandons them.

The schoolmaster leaves his school and his pupils.

Whole groups of Sutter's workers set out on the road.

More and more people stop working to join the human flood.

Fields and homes are empty, deserted.

Sutter places on his finger a ring with the inscription: FIRST GOLD FOUND 1848.

Engraved upon the ring is the coat-of-arms of his native town.

Picks, shovels and crowbars begin to bite into the earth.

The sound of sand moving in the wooden working-pans, the swash of the swinging water, begins to be heard through the forests and fields.

The noise of picks, and of stones cast from the working-pans, grows louder and louder, ever more and more insistent.

These sounds pervade the whole land.

And beneath this tearing sound, the dominion of Sutter falls to waste and rot from its own fertility and luxuriance.

The boughs of fruit-trees are cracking with their burden of ripe fruit.

Barrels are exploding with an over-fermentation of their wine and beer.

Horses, untended and unfoddered, break down the bars of their corrals and rush into the wheat-fields.

Cows fill the air with their lowings of pain, and maddened by their unrelieved udders, burst through the walls of the stables, trampling flowers and vegetables.

High-piled sacks of grain burst with the tension of their stacked weight, and the spilt running grain scatters in the wind.

The dams are taut with their heavy loads, the canal locks are shattered, and the waters rush through their old courses.

Sutter wanders alone through this desolation, listening to the incessant sound of the gold-seekers.

"Gold." The word rings through the forest, and echoes through the hills and canyons.

And then, from the depths of these canyons, a new theme of the noise symphony can be heard.

The sounds of thousands of feet trampling over stones.

The sounds of endless trails of creaking wagons.

The mixed sounds of horses' hooves and screeching wagon wheels.

And the murmur of limitless crowds.

The first of the wagons appears near the fort.

A savage-looking man tears out some flowers by the roots, and stabs his sharpened tent-pole into the earth.

The sound of the approaching procession grows louder and nearer.

Sutter sits on a hill.

His old dog is huddled against him.

The sounds are nearer—he can distinguish human voices.

They tell of the great distances that they have come—and he realizes that there is no end to this human flood.

Through these sounds can be heard the chopping of axes, falling trees, the whistling of saws, crashing trees.

Pigs are screaming, and frightened ducks quack frantically as they are pursued by the invaders.

Sutter is driven wild by these sounds. The picks grow louder, and now the sound of stone striking stone—stones piled high from out of the river-bed, stones burying the fertile fields. Stones growing into mountains that crush all the fertility that preceded this terrible symphony of sounds.

Darkness, and the crackling of a little fire that lights the silent face of Sutter.

The sounds of destruction swell to colossal proportions.

Sutter is in an agony of despair.

And the saws continue to whine, and the axes to chop, and the trees to crash and the picks to hammer upon the stones.

The gold-diggers curse in the fever of their hunt.

These things madden Sutter, and he takes refuge in the darkness of the forest. . . .

6. FIRST OUTLINE OF
QUE VIVA MEXICO!

This incomplete autograph draft of an outline sent to
Upton Sinclair before beginning the production of *Que
Viva Mexico!* is now in the Eisenstein Collection at the
Museum of Modern Art Film Library. Compare with item
39 of the Bibliography.

ROUGH OUTLINE OF THE MEXICAN PICTURE
(and *"plausum date"* for style, orthography, etc.!)

Do you know what a "Serape" is? A Serape is the striped
blanket that the Mexican indio, the Mexican charro—every
Mexican wears. And the Serape could be the symbol of
Mexico. So striped and violently contrasting are the cultures
in Mexico running next to each other and at the same time
being centuries away. No plot, no whole story could run
through this Serape without being false or artificial. And
we took the contrasting independent adjacence of its violent colors as the motif for constructing our film: 6 episodes following each other—different in character, different
in people, different in animals, trees and flowers. And still
held together by the unity of the weave—a rhythmic and
musical construction and an unrolling of the Mexican spirit
and character.

Death. Skulls of people. And skulls of stone. The horrible
Aztec gods and the terrifying Yucatan deities. Huge ruins.
Pyramids. A world that was and is no more. Endless rows
of stones and columns. And faces. Faces of stone. And

faces of flesh. The man of Yucatan today. The same man who lived thousands of years ago. Unmovable. Unchanging. Eternal. And the great wisdom of Mexico about death. The unity of death and life. The passing of one and the birth of the next one. The eternal circle. And the still greater wisdom of Mexico: the *enjoying* of this eternal circle. Death-Day in Mexico. Day of the greatest fun and merriment. The day when Mexico provokes death and makes fun of it—death is but a step to another cycle of life —why then fear it! Hat stores display skulls wearing top and straw hats. Candy takes the shape of skulls in sugar and coffins of confectionery. Parties go to the cemetery, taking food to the dead. Parties play and sing on the graves. And the food of the dead is eaten by the living. The drinking and the singing grow louder. And night covers Death Day. Death Day that is becoming birth day for new lives, for new arrivals. And from beneath the terrifying skull of the grotesque death masquerade and fiesta peeps the smiling face of a new baby establishing the unmovable law of death following life and life following death.

Life. . . . The moist, muddy, sleepy tropics. Heavy branches of fruits. Dreamy waters. And the dreamy eyelids of girls. Of girls. Of future mothers. Of the fore-mother. Like the queen-bee, the mother rules in Tehuantepec. The female tribal system has been miraculously preserved here for hundreds of years till our time. Like serpents are the branches of strange trees. And like serpents are the waves of black and heavy hair around the big dreamy eyes of the female waiting for the male. Activity is on the side of the woman in Tehuantepec. And from girlhood the woman starts the building of a new cell of a new family. Weaving. Cutting fruits. Selling. Sitting hours and hours in the market. The overflowing, slowly moving market of Tehuantepec. Day after day. Coin after coin. Until the neck of the girl bends under the weight of a golden chain. A golden

chain with hanging golden coins. Coins of the States. Coins
of Guatemala. Coins with the Mexican eagle. Dowry and
bank. Fortune and liberty. New home and wedding. Wedding called in Spanish "casamiento" in its highest biological
meaning—foundation of a new casa. New home. New family. Through picturesque fiestas. With survivals of most
ancient customs—like marking the face with red colonial
irons—in memory of the Spanish invaders who branded
cattle and Indians. Through dances in ancient fashioned
robes, gold, silk and embroidery—follows the love story of
the young woman. Through customs and rites the story
moves from love to wedding. And from the wedding "San-
dunga" (dance) to the lucky palm-shaded new home. A
new home overshadowed by the snowy white "weepeel"—
the mountain-like headdress of the triumphant mother and
wife.

The snowy serenity.

Snowy like the gray-haired Popocatepetl.

But harsh, rough, cruel and thorny is the vegetation at
his feet. Cruel, rough and harsh like the male tribe of
"charros," farmers, Mexican cowboys and hacendados who
live among it. The endless field of maguey—the prickling
sharp-leaved cactus. Leaves through which in an endless
effort the indio sucks the sap of the earth's heart—the
sweet honey-like "aguamiel"—which when treated becomes
"pulque." Relief of sorrows—the Mexican brandy. And sorrows are abundant. There is nothing of the aguamiel's
sweetness in the tall and bony hacendado, his guards and
his major-domos. And lower bends the back of the indio
with his little donkey that all day drags the precious load
of aguamiel from the boundless fields to the fortress-like
hacienda. These are the days of Diaz (before the Revolution of 1910—which changed entirely the living conditions

of the indio. We give a glimpse of his state of pure slavery in about 1905-6 to explain why there were always revolutionary "troubles" in Mexico). Living in the twentieth century but medieval in ways and habits. *Jus prima noctis*. The right of the land-owner to the wife of him who works on his fields. And the first conflict in the male tribe. One woman. The bride of a hacienda indio. One woman. And the tribe around her. The right of the land-owner, the outburst of protest and the cruelty of repression. And the triangular shadows of indios repeating the shape of the eternal triangle of Teotihuacan. The great pyramid of the Sun, near Mexico City. Waiting for better days. Days of Obregón.

Controlling their hate under the grimly smiling pagan faces of stone tigers and serpents, worshiped by their ancestors—the Aztecs. (N.B. Quite different from the Yucatan sculpture, people and edifices in part one. And quite different in handling and treatment.)

But the grotesque laughing of the stone heads becomes still more grotesque in the cardboard "piñata" faces—Christmas dolls. And then becomes voluptuous in the suffering smile of the Catholic polychrome saints. Statues of saints that were erected on the sites of pagan altars. Bleeding and distorted like the human sacrifices that were made on the top of these pyramids. Here, like imported and anemic flowers bloom the iron and fire of the Catholicism that Cortes brought. Catholicism and paganism. The Virgin of Guadalupe worshiped by wild dances and bloody bullfights. By tower-high Indian hair-dresses and Spanish mantillas. By exhausting hours-long dances in sunshine and dust, by miles of knee-creeping penitence, and the golden ballets of bull-fighting cuadrillas. . . .

A typical sketched break-down, into particular frame-compositions, in Eisenstein's preparation of the shooting-script for *Que Viva Mexico!* This page of sketches is a development of the transition passage noted on page 253 from the luxuriant tropical matriarchy of Tehuantepec to the harsh landscape and male dominion of the plateau at the feet of Popocatepetl.

7. FERGHANA CANAL

A shooting-script by Eisenstein, from a treatment by Piotr Pavlenko and Eisenstein. This first draft of the unproduced script is dated August 1-2-3, 1939. Of the published 657 shot indications, only the first 145 are reproduced below, forming a fourteenth-century prologue to the modern drama of Soviet Uzbekistan's reclamation of its desert wastes. In the film's Tamerlane will be found more resemblance to Adolf Hitler than to the heroic figure of Marlowe's tragedy.

1 (*m.s.*) The singer Tokhtasin sings, gazing into the desert . . .

2 (*m.s.*) . . . singing a song of a flowering land, such as was known in the days of the ancient land of Kharesm . . .

3 (*l.s.*) Before Tokhtasin spreads the endless desert . . .

4 (*l.s.*) The infinite sands of the desert . . . Over the words of the song, *dissolve to* . . .

4a (*c.u.*) . . . a spray of a delicately flowering bush . . .

5 (*m.s.*) . . . surrounded by young trees, clipped and blossoming . . .

6 (*l.s.*) And lo! before us a whole shady oasis is disclosed . . .

7 (*m.s.*) . . . its trees reflected in a broad artificial lake . . .

8 (*c.u.*) . . . an aqueduct flows into the lake . . .

9 (*l.s.*) . . . and irrigation-canals are filled from the lake, carrying away the water in a network of little channels.

10 (*l.s.*) Intricate patterns of silvery channels irrigate fertile fields.

11 (*l.s.*) Again we see the aqueduct flowing into the lake. And this time we see in the lake the inverted reflection of a sky-blue cupola . . .

12 (*l.s.*) The lake reflects the domes of the mosque, the shrine, the academy . . . And Tokhtasin sings of the great city of Urganj, whose beauty surpassed all the cities of Asia, and whose riches were uncounted.

13 (*m.s.*) The intricate pattern of silvery channels dissolves into the complex arabesques of the ornamental tiles on the façade of a magnificent mosque, and before us . . .

14 (*l.s.*) . . . is the square of the rich ancient city—busy in its many-colored movement . . .

15 (*l.s.*) Water pours from huge reservoirs. It is caught in jars . . .

16 (*m.s.*) . . . and from these jars it is poured into large vessels . . .

17 (*l.s.*) Streams of people pour over the monumental staircase of the ancient city.

18 (*m.s.*) Suspended in the sky are the pale blue domes of the academy, the mosque, the shrine . . .

19 (*m.s.*) Gleaming tiled streets are lined with splendid shrines. The crowd, richly robed, moves rhythmically through them.

20 (*m.s.*) White and black veils float through the throng. Dozing water-carriers. Placidly splashing fountains.

21 (*m.s.*) A silvery channel runs into the rectangular pool sunk in the courtyard of the magnificent mosque.

22 (*l.s.*) White-turbaned worshipers fill the courtyard, gradually occupying the whole space with their rich oriental robes and their kneeling figures.

23 (*m.s.*) Praying, kneeling figures, robed in wide silk gowns.

24 (*l.s.*) Rhythmically, throughout the courtyard of the mosque, prayers are offered. The melody of Tokhtasin's song takes a sharp, unexpected turn and, as if they too heard it, the hundreds of supplicants in the broad courtyard suddenly stretch out their arms towards the mosque.

25 (*l.s.*) Into the sky towers the heavy minaret of the mosque. With the song's melody the camera glides up the towering form.

26 (*m.s.*) Tokhtasin begins his song anew. Now he sings of Tamerlane the terrible warrior—Tamerlane who long held the city of Urganj under siege.

27 (*l.s.*) The words of the song soar over the black tents of Tamerlane's encampment, from where Urganj can be seen in the distance.

28 (*l.s.*) Black and white streamers flap over the tents, which are ringed with upright spears, topped with the heads of the vanquished. Before his mounted marshals, against a background of the tents and the army stands "he who limps, the iron one" . . .

29 (*m.s.*) Tamerlane . . .

30 (*c.u.*) . . . with narrowed eyes. He strokes a sparse beard. Not tall, he is slender—almost feeble in appearance. In his simple robe and plain black skull-cap, a common handkerchief for girdle, he seems quite ordinary.

31 (*l.s.*) Turned towards distant Urganj, like a fearsome wall, stands the army of Tamerlane.

32 (*m.s.*) Without looking towards his standing officers— young and old—Tamerlane quietly speaks:

"Water is the strength of that city."

After a moment of silence, he adds:

"Take away the water from Urganj . . ."

And without pause we hear the cracking of whips in the air . . .

33 (*m.s.*) Tamerlane stands surrounded by his officers. Through the air the cracking whips whistle shrilly. A wind shakes the tents . . .

34 (*l.s.*) The pavilion of Tamerlane in the distance. The foreground is filled with running half-naked laborers carrying mattocks and spades. Driving them on are the warriors of Tamerlane, cracking their long whips.

35 (*m.s.*) The frightened faces of the diggers run past the camera.

36 (*l.s.*) The crowded stooping backs of the running slaves. Long whips lash them forward.

37 (*m.s.*) The singer Tokhtasin continues his sad song. He sings of the great distress and privation of the city of Urganj, besieged by Tamerlane. His song carries over on to . . .

38 (*fade-in*) . . . water trickling from the channels . . .

39 (*m.s.*) . . . the emptied lake . . .

40 (*c.u.*) . . . a shriveled water-skin . . .

41 (*l.s.*) The half-demolished wall of the citadel, strewn with the bodies of the city's defenders, dying of thirst. Captives are barely able to drag themselves and the bricks upon their backs to the repair work on the huge . gaps in the wall.

42 (*m.s.*) Scattered over the ground near the wall lie empty water-skins. Crazed with thirst, a man seeks in vain a drop of water in them.

43 (*l.s.*) A street of the city, piled high with corpses. Captives are carrying beams through the street. One of the carriers loses his hold—and falls.

44 (*m.s.*) Pits, filled with dry lime. Around them stand perplexed masons, with helplessly hanging hands—there is nothing with which to mix the mortar. In the background slaves are throwing beams behind the broken wall.

45 (*m.s.*) Captains and masons. Among them is a tall mason —the foreman.

46 (*c.u.*)His long black hand scoops up a handful of dusty lime. His voice:

"There's nothing with which to mix the mortar!"

47 (*m.s.*) Wounded fighters lie dying in the courtyard of the mosque.

48 (*m.s.*) A silent crowd of mothers in another corner of the mosque.

49 (*m.s.*) A crowd of bound captives near the mosque's arcade . . .

50 (*c.u.*) . . . Captives dying of thirst . . .

51 (*c.u.*) . . . Faces of sullen Mongol captives . . .

52 (*l.s.*) Under a high arch of the mosque can be seen the
kneeling figure of the Emir of Kharesm—praying.

53 (*m.s.*) Young, handsome, languid, clothed in his golden
robes of kingship, the Emir of Kharesm kneels on his
royal carpet. The suppliant elders approach him with
decorum. A captain comes to the Emir's side. Humbly
bowing, he whispers: "Emir—there is no water to mix
the mortar."

54 (*m.s.*) The figure of a warrior runs into the frame with
a cry:
    "Emir—there is no water!"
And he falls at the feet of his lord . . .

55 (*m.s.*) Frenzied mothers cry:
    "Emir—there is no water!"

56 (*m.s.*) "Water, water!"—the wounded groan.

57 (*m.s.*) "Water! Water! Water!" — different voices
throughout the square take up the cry.

58. (*m.s.*) "Water! Water!"—the bound captives strain towards the Emir.

59 (*m.s.*) The Emir looks towards the captives. The captains repeat:
    "No water to mix the mortar! What are we to do!?"
The cry rises from the square:
    "Water! Water!"

60 (*c.u.*) The Emir tersely commands:
    "Mix the mortar with their blood."

61 (*m.s.*) In deathly fear the captives shrink from the Emir's arch. Warriors throw themselves upon the captives.

62 (*m.s.*) The warriors of the Emir seize the captives . . .

63 (*m.s.*) The Emir again kneels on his carpet, continuing his prayer.

64 (*c.u.*) Scimitars flash through the frame . . .

65 (*c.u.*) A curved knife flashes through the frame . . .

66 (*c.u.*) The stretched neck of a prisoner.

67 (*c.u.*) Blood drips into a tub . . .

68 (*c.u.*) Blood drips into a tub . . .

69 (*m.s.*) A line of bound captives is dragged through the frame.

70 (*c.u.*) A heap of lime with an empty gutter above.

71 (*m.s.*) Prisoners pushed to their knees . . .

72 (*c.u.*) A warrior (*outside the frame*) slashes his scimitar . . .

73 (*c.u.*) A lime pit. Through the empty gutter flows a thick black liquid . . .

74 (*c.u.*) Greedy hands hastily mix the dark mortar.

75 (*m.s.*) Beams and stones speedily fill the breech in the wall.

76 (*l.s.*) With a last effort, the besieged feverishly repair the citadel wall. Suddenly from the distance can be heard the roar of the enemy. The numbed masons throw themselves onto the wall to defend their city.

77 (*l.s.*) Crowds of people run in panic up the broad stairs. The enemy's roar comes nearer.

78 (*l.s.*) The court of the great mosque. The frightened people huddle together. The roar grows close.

79 (*m.s.*) The Emir rises from his knees. People crowd about him.

80 (*l.s.*) Onto the citadel walls stagger the last defenders of the city.

81 (*l.s.*) From the desert comes the black cloud of the attacking army of Tamerlane.

81a (*l.s.*) The hordes of Tamerlane ride across the plain.

81b (*l.s.*) Under the walls of Urganj drives Tamerlane's army.

82 (*l.s.*) Against a background of his attacking warriors—the lame figure of Tamerlane.

83 (*c.u.*) His eyes blaze. A smile plays upon his thin lips.

84 (*m.s.*) Those near him glance towards him, trembling.

85 (*c.u.*) Tamerlane's eyes blaze with a merry flame. He cries out:
"He who controls water, holds power!"

86 (*l.s.*) Fresh hordes roll under the citadel walls.

87 (*m.s.*) The weakened defenders retreat from the walls.

88 (*l.s.*) Slowly retreating from the invisible enemy, the defenders cross the square . . .

89 (*l.s.*) . . . and run towards the mosque, scattering the dead beneath their feet. (*The camera pans up the minaret.*) The distant roar of the victorious foe.

90 (*m.s.*) On the platform of the minaret, the Emir, leaning on his sword-bearer, looks over the picture of the city's death.

91 (*l.s.*) From above can be seen the courtyard of the mosque, filled with dead.

    One group of people, seeing him, stretch out their arms, asking him to relieve their thirst.

92 (*m.s.*) The city square is strewn with dead. In the middle of the square a single crawling figure strains upwards, crying: "Water!"

93 (*m.s.*) Turning slowly towards his sword-bearer, the Emir speaks, as if in answer to the dying man:

    "Water—is blood . . ."

    A young guard is dying on the steps leading from the platform. Without looking at him, the Emir descends the steps of the minaret.

94 (*l.s.*) The warriors of Tamerlane burst through the breech in the city wall, laying waste to everything in their path.

95 (*m.s.*) Hanging across the wall are the defenders, dead of thirst . . .

96 (*l.s.*) Others who have died of thirst are strewn over the flight of broad stairs . . .

97 (*m.s.*) The dried-up lake. At its bottom are more bodies . . .

98 (*m.s.*) More dead—beside empty water-vessels.

99 (*m.s.*) Dead—beside shriveled water-skins.

100 (*m.s.*) In the midst of jewelry and precious stones lies a merchant, dead of thirst . . .

101 (*m.s.*) In a half-darkened cell of the old academy, an old scholar has died—resembling a mummy, bent over his withered parchment.

102 (*l.s.*) The imprisoned wives of the Emir are dying in their harem, like quail in festive cages. The rooms have doors of rare woods and windows of mica.

103 (*m.s.*) Motionless, they lie naked or dressed in splendid gowns, upon the rugs and divans of the harem.

104 (*m.s.*) At the edge of a dried sunken basin, a young wife of the Emir is dying of thirst. At the bottom of the basin are some dead fish. Over all these pictures of death expands the music of roaring and crashing sound.

105 (*c.u.*) Two of the Emir's wives have died in each other's arms.

106 (*m.s.*) In the depths of the great hall of the harem sits the Emir.

107 (*m.s.*) The Emir stares before him, whispering:
"He who controls water—is the victor . . ."
He dies.

108 (*l.s.*) Tamerlane's warriors gallop into the square of Urganj . . .

109 (*l.s.*) They push their way up the broad stairs—their race upwards is accompanied by the music of the attack.

110 (*l.s.*) A group of the last defenders together with an old mason are hiding at the head of a street. In the

distance we see an advance company of the conquerors. We hear the music of Tokhtasin's song (but without words).

111 (*m.s.*) A group of masons dives through the gap in the wall . . .

112 (*m.s.*) . . . running in the concealing shadows of a cemetery, dodging among the ancient tombs of believers.

113 (*l.s.*) Diverted from the city of Urganj, the river that once kept the city alive flows turbulently through the channel walls of a temporary canal. It is guarded by Tamerlane's sentinels. In the distance his army is entering the city.

114 (*m.s.*) The water is guarded by his sentinels . . .

115 (*m.s.*) From the shadows the group of masons throw themselves upon the guards . . .

116 (*l.s.*) The army of Tamerlane is passing through the gate of the conquered city. Battle elephants move in the midst of the throng.

117 (*l.s.*) Onto the vanquished square Tamerlane enters, surrounded by a dusty retinue.

118 (*m.s.*) Having rendered the guards harmless, the masons break down the walls of the canal.

119 (*l.s.*) Water rushes through the gap, which rapidly widens. The whole canal wall collapses and the river bursts overflowing onto the sand.

120 (*c.u.*) "So take our water—that you took from us!"—cry the masons, as they themselves are engulfed by the swirling waters of the freed river.

121 (*l.s.*) The wild torrents of water rush towards the army of Tamerlane, still passing through the city gate.

122 (*m.s.*) The throng of dusty warriors is swept up in the rushing water . . .

123 (*m.s.*) The water dashes against the horsemen, rising over them . . .

124 (*m.s.*) In the swirling torrents are caught camels, men, pavilions . . .

125 (*l.s.*) In uncontrollable panic the army fights against the water . . .

126 (*m.s.*) All is washed away in the powerful flood . . .

127 (*m.s.*) . . . of the rising water.

128 (*m.s.*) Surrounded by his captains, Tamerlane speaks:
The theme of his speech is that no strength is greater than the strength of Nature . . .
Turning and seeing the fate of his army, he flees with his retinue, head bent down between his shoulders . . .

129 (*l.s.*) Tamerlane's army retreats in confusion before the onrushing water.

130 (*l.s.*) The water rushes over the desert towards the horizon. People, horses, camels, sheep are swimming and drowning in the flood . . .

131 (*m.s.*) The battle elephants circle deliberately. Drowning men try to climb onto them.

132 (*l.s.*) A tremendous mass of water flows over the desert. Cutting through the noise of the water is a new noise—the howl of a wind . . . of an approaching sand-storm . . .

133 (*l.s.*) Howling and whistling the sand-storm attacks the water . . .

134 (*l.s.*) The walls of the dead city. There the dead defenders fearlessly gaze with wide eyes and, as though slightly smiling, listen to the duel of the water and sand.

135 (*l.s.*) The blowing sand gradually veils the water from sight . . .

136 (*m.s.*) . . . The water sinks into the sand . . .

137 (*m.s.*) . . . As the sand runs with the wind, it forms broad curving dunes . . .

138 (*l.s.*) Over the curving sand-dunes we can see in the distance the dead city . . .

139 (*l.s.*) The city is buried in sand.

140 (*l.s.*) The ruined mosque, engulfed by sand . . .

141 (*l.s.*) The endless desert . . .

142 (*m.s.*) . . . The scattered skeletons of people, horses . . .

143 (*m.s.*) . . . skeletons of camels, half covered with bricks.

144 (*m.s.*) An overturned chest—scattered gold coins.

145 (*c.u.*) The gold coins sliding over the sand make an unexpectedly loud sound . . .

8. BIBLIOGRAPHY
OF EISENSTEIN'S WRITINGS
AVAILABLE IN ENGLISH

The following list is an attempt to collate all signed articles and published interviews in which Eisenstein's ideas have appeared in this language. Of these, his most basic writings have been starred (*) for the benefit of those who may wish to review the theoretical development of Eisenstein.

1927

1. Interview, *Eisenstein, Creator of "Potemkin."* The American Hebrew, January 28, 1927.

* 2. *MASS MOVIES.* The Nation, November 9, 1927. Another English translation appeared in the New York Times, December 25, 1927, as translated from Die Weltbühne (Berlin), December 6, 1927. Written by Louis Fischer on the basis of conversations with Eisenstein.

1928

3. Interview with Joseph Wood Krutch, *The Season in Moscow (III): Eisenstein and Lunacharsky.* The Nation, June 27, 1928.

* 4. *THE SOUND FILM* (a joint statement by Eisenstein, Pudovkin and Alexandrov). Close Up (London), October; 1928. Two previous appearances in English were a translation from the Berlin Vossische Zeitung, included in a dispatch by William L. McPherson to the New York Herald Tribune, September 2, 1928; and in the New York Times, October 7, 1928. Originally published as "Statement" in the magazine Zhizn Iskusstva (Leningrad), No. 32, 1928.

5. *Two Scenes Out of USSR Film "October"* (Fragments of the Scenario); written in collaboration with G. Alexandrov. The Daily Worker, November 3, 1928.

6. Interview with Theodore Dreiser, in "Dreiser Looks at Russia," Liveright, 1928.

1929

7. Interview with Alfred Richman, *Serge M. Eisenstein*. Dial, April, 1929. An interview given in 1926.

8. *The New Language of Cinematography*. Close Up, May, 1929. Originally published as a foreword to the Russian edition of Guido Seeber's "Der Trickfilm" (Moscow, 1929).

9. *The Man Who Put Karl Marx on the Screen*. New York Herald Tribune, December 22, 1929. A partial translation by William L. McPherson of an article written by Eisenstein for the Berlin Vossische Zeitung on a planned film treatment of Marx's "Capital."

1930

★ 10. *THE SOVIET FILM*, in "Voices of October," Vanguard, 1930. Manuscript dated 1928. Written especially for incorporation into Joseph Freeman's essay on Soviet films in this volume.

11. Amsterdam interview, *M. Eisenstein's Next Film*. New York Times, February 16, 1930. Translation of an interview given to the newspaper Het Volk, on the occasion of Eisenstein's trip to Holland to lecture to the Film-Liga.

12. Interview with H. W. L. Dana, *Revolution in the World of Make-Believe; Eisenstein, Russian Master of the Screen, Sets Forth His Theories*. Boston Evening Transcript, March 1, 1930. An interview given in 1929.

★ 13. *A RUSSIAN VIEW OF SCENARIOS*. New York Times, March 30, 1930. A partial translation of Eisenstein's German preface ("Drehbuch? Nein: Kinonovelle!") to the published treatment of *Old and New*—"Der Kampf um die Erde" (Berlin, 1929).

14. Interview with Mark Segal, *Filmic Art and Training*. Close Up, March, 1930.

★ 15. *THE FOURTH DIMENSION IN THE KINO: I*. Close Up, March, 1930. Dated August 19, 1929, translated by W. Ray, originally published in the newspaper Kino (Moscow), No. 34, 1929.

✱ 16. *THE FOURTH DIMENSION IN THE KINO: II.* Close Up, April, 1930. Dated Moscow-London, Autumn, 1929, translated by W. Ray.

17. Report by Samuel Brody, *Paris Hears Eisenstein.* Close Up, April, 1930. A résumé of Eisenstein's lecture at the Sorbonne University, entitled "Les Principes du Nouveau Cinéma Russe," on February 17, 1930. The full text is printed in La Revue du Cinéma, April, 1930.

18. Interview with Harry Alan Potamkin, *Eisenstein Explains Some Things That Make Sovkino.* The Daily Worker, May 24, 1930.

19. New York interview, *Eisenstein in America.* Today's Cinema News and Property Gazette (London), May 27, 1930.

✱ 20. *THE CINEMATOGRAPHIC PRINCIPLE AND JAPANESE CULTURE; WITH A DIGRESSION ON MONTAGE AND THE SHOT.* Transition (Paris), No. 19, Spring-Summer, 1930. Translated by Ivor Montagu and S. S. Nolbandov; reprinted in Experimental Cinema, No. 3, 1932. Originally published as an afterword entitled "Outside the Frame," in Nikolai Kaufman's brochure "Japanese Cinema" (Moscow, 1929).

21. *Doing Without Actors.* Written in collaboration with Alexandrov, Cinema, June, 1930. Translated by Ivor Montagu and S. S. Nolbandov.

22. Interview with Mark Segal, *The Future of the Film.* Close Up, August, 1930.

1931

✱ 23. *THE DYNAMIC SQUARE.* Close Up, March, June, 1931. An article based on the speech made by Eisenstein during a discussion on the wide film in relation to motion picture technique at a meeting organized by the Technicians Branch of the Academy of Motion Picture Arts and Sciences, in conjunction with the Directors and Producers branches, Fox Hills Studio, Hollywood, September 17, 1930. This also appears, in a condensed version, in Hound and Horn, April, 1931.

✱ 24. *THE PRINCIPLES OF FILM FORM.* Close Up, September, 1931. Dated Zurich, 2/11/29; translated by Ivor Montagu. Reprinted in Experimental Cinema, No. 4, 1932.

25. *The Intellectual Cinema.* Left (Davenport, Iowa), Autumn, 1931. Translated from the German by Christel Gang.

26. Interview with Morris Helprin, *Eisenstein's New Film, Russian Director in Mexico at Work on "Que Viva Mexico!"* New York Times, November 29, 1931.

27. *A Mexican Film and Marxian Theory; a communication.* New Republic, December 9, 1931. A reply to Edmund Wilson's article, "Eisenstein in Hollywood," New Republic, November 4, 1931.

1932

28. Interview with Lincoln Kirstein, *Que Viva Méjico!* Arts Weekly, April 30, 1932.

29. New York interview, *Eisenstein's Monster.* Time, May 2, 1932.

30. Berlin interview, *Eisenstein's Plans.* Living Age (Boston), July, 1932.

✶31. *OCTOBER AND ART.* Soviet Culture Review, No. 7-9, 1932. Reprinted in International Literature (Moscow), October, 1933, in a section, "Autobiographies," and in The Daily Worker, January 29, 1934.

✶32. *DETECTIVE WORK IN THE GIK.* Close Up, December, 1932. The first of three articles written for Close Up, and dated Moscow, October, 1932; translated by W. Ray. The series of three articles, all on the State Institute of Cinematography, are an expansion of an article, "Much Obliged," published in Proletarskoye Kino (Moscow), No. 17-18, 1932.

1933

✶33. *CINEMATOGRAPHY WITH TEARS.* Close Up, March, 1933. Translated by W. Ray. Second of a series of three articles on GIK.

✶34. *AN AMERICAN TRAGEDY.* Close Up, June, 1933. Translated by W. Ray. Third of a series on GIK.

35. Interview with Marie Seton, *Eisenstein Aims at Simplicity.* Film Art (London), Summer, 1933.

36. *The Cinema in America; impressions of Hollywood, its life and values.* International Literature, July, 1933. Translated by S. D.

Kogan. Originally published as "Overtake and Surpass" in Proletar-skoye Kino, No. 15-16, 1932.

37. Interview with Bella Kashin, *Career of Sergei Eisenstein, Who Is Now Preparing His Film, "Moscow."* New York Times, December 17, 1933.

1934

★38. *OLD AND NEW;* written in collaboration with Alexandrov. In Lewis Jacobs' "Film Writing Forms," Gotham Book Mart, 1934. The original treatment for the film, as translated from the German edition, "Der Kampf um die Erde" (Berlin, Schmidt, 1929).

★39. *QUE VIVA MEXICO!* written in collaboration with Alex-androv. Experimental Cinema, 1934. Synopsis of the proposed film, written in 1931.

40. *The Difficult Bride.* Film Art, Spring, 1934. Translated by Marie Seton. Originally published in Literaturnaya Gazeta (Moscow), No. 30, July 11, 1933.

★41. *ON FASCISM, THE GERMAN CINEMA, AND REAL LIFE* (An open letter to the German Minister of Propaganda Göbbels). International Theatre (Moscow), October, 1934. A reply to the propaganda minister's address to German film producers in February, 1934. This also appears, in another translation, as "Open Letter to Dr. Goebbels" in Film Art, Winter, 1934. A partial trans-lation, from the Pariser Tageblatt, appeared in the New York Times, December 30, 1934.

1935

42. *The New Soviet Cinema; entering the fourth period.* New Theatre, January, 1935. Translated by Leon Kutman. Originally pub-lished as "At Last!" in Literaturnaya Gazeta, No. 154, November 18, 1934.

43. Interview, *Eisenstein's New Film.* International Literature, May, 1935.

★44. *FILM FORM, 1935—NEW PROBLEMS.* Life and Letters To-day (London), September; December, 1935. Based on material sub-mitted to the All-Union Creative Conference on Cinematographic Questions, Moscow, January, 1935. Translated by Ivor Montagu.

Reprinted in New Theatre and Film, April, May, June, 1936, as "Film Forms: New Problems."

45. *The Enchanter from the Pear Garden.* Theatre Arts Monthly, October, 1935. Originally published in a brochure issued in connection with Mei Lan-Fang's Moscow performances.

46. Interview with Louis Fischer, in "Soviet Journey," Smith & Haas, 1935.

1936

★ 47. *THROUGH THEATRE TO CINEMA.* Theatre Arts Monthly, September, 1936. Translated by Jay Leyda and Paya Haskell. Originally published as "The Middle of Three (1924-1929)," in Sovietskoye Kino (Moscow), No. 11-12, November-December, 1934.

48. Interview with Leo Lania, *Films in Birth.* Living Age, November, 1936. Translated from Die Neue Weltbühne (Prague), June 4, 1936.

★ 49. *PROGRAMME FOR TEACHING THE THEORY AND PRACTICE OF FILM DIRECTION.* Life and Letters Today, No. 6, No. 7, 1936. The syllabus adopted as the basis for the course in Film Direction at the Higher State Institute of Cinematography (V.G.I.K.). Translated by Stephen Garry, with Ivor Montagu. Originally published in Iskusstvo Kino (Moscow), April, 1936.

50. *Foreword.* In Vladimir Nilsen's "The Cinema as a Graphic Art" (on a theory of representation in the cinema), London, Newnes, 1936. Translated by Stephen Garry. Reprinted in Theatre Arts Monthly, May, 1938.

51. Interview with Joseph Freeman, in "An American Testament," Farrar & Rinehart, 1936. The meeting recorded here took place in 1927.

1937

★ 52. *THE MISTAKES OF BEZHIN LUG.* International Literature, No. 8, 1937. Originally published in the pamphlet "About the Film *Bezhin Lug* of Eisenstein" (Moscow, 1937).

53. *The Epic in Soviet Film.* International Literature, No. 10, 1937.

1938

54. *Director of "Alexander Nevsky" Describes How the Film Was Made.* Moscow News, December 5, 1938. Reprinted in The Daily Worker, March 19, 1939.

1939

★ 55. *THE SOVIET SCREEN.* Moscow, Foreign Languages Publishing House, 1939. A pamphlet written for a series, issued in connection with the Soviet pavilion's exhibit at the New York World's Fair.

★ 56. *MY SUBJECT IS PATRIOTISM.* International Literature, No. 2, 1939. Reprinted in The Daily Worker, April 1, 1939.

57. *Foreword.* In "Soviet Films 1938-1939," Moscow, State Publishing House for Cinema Literature, 1939. Dated April, 1939.

★ 58. *MONTAGE IN* 1938. Life and Letters Today, June, July. August, September, October, November, 1939. Translated by Stephen Garry; technical check by Ivor Montagu. Reprinted with alterations in this volume as *Word and Image.* Originally published in Iskusstvo Kino, January, 1939.

1940

★ 59. *PRIDE.* International Literature, April-May, 1940. Reprinted as edited by Ivor Montagu in The Anglo-Soviet Journal, April, 1941. Originally published in Iskusstvo Kino, January-February, 1940.

60. *Eisenstein Makes His Debut in Opera; Noted Film Director Discusses His Work on "The Valkyrie."* Moscow News, November 28, 1940.

61. *To the Editors of "International Literature"; a communication.* International Literature, November-December, 1940. Reprinted in The Daily Worker, January 14, 1941.

1941

★ 62. *FASCISM MUST AND SHALL BE DESTROYED.* In "In Defense of Civilization Against Fascist Barbarism," Moscow, VOKS, 1941. Reprinted in a condensed version in New Masses, November 25, 1941.

1942

63. *American Films Reflect Fighting Qualities of American People.* Information Bulletin, Embassy of the USSR (Washington), 1942 (Special Supplement). Partial text of a speech read at the Conference on American and British Cinema, Moscow, August 21-22, 1942.

64. *"Ivan Grozny."* VOKS Bulletin, No. 7-8, 1942.

1945

65. *How We Filmed "Ivan the Terrible."* Film Chronicle (Moscow), February, 1945.

✱66. *IN A REGISSEUR'S LABORATORY.* Film Chronicle, February, 1945. Notes made during the preparation and production of *Ivan the Terrible:* "The First Vision," and "On the Set."

✱67. *IVAN THE TERRIBLE, A FILM SCENARIO.* Life and Letters, November, December, 1945; January, February, April, May, June, July, 1946. A translation, by Herbert Marshall, of the published treatment for Parts I and II, as originally planned for *Ivan the Terrible.*

1946

68. *P-R-K-F-V.* An introduction (translated by Jay Leyda) for "Sergei Prokofiev: His Musical Life," by Israel Nestyev. New York, Alfred A. Knopf, 1946. The introduction is dated Alma-Ata, November 1942—Moscow, November 1944.

69. *Charlie the Kid.* Sight and Sound, Spring 1946; *Charlie the Grown Up.* Sight and Sound, Summer 1946. A translation, by Herbert Marshall, of Eisenstein's contribution to "Charles Spencer Chaplin," Moscow, 1945.

SOURCES

1. *The Journal of Eugène Delacroix,* translated from the French by Walter Pach. Covici-Friede, 1937. This appears in the entry for January 13, 1857, and is a draft preface for Delacroix's proposed Dictionary of the Fine Arts.

PART I: *Word and Image*

2. John Livingston Lowes, *The Road to Xanadu.* Houghton Mifflin, 1930, p. 330.
3. Ambrose Bierce, *The Monk and the Hangman's Daughter: Fantastic Fables,* Boni, 1925, p. 311.
4. *The Complete Works of Lewis Carroll.* Random House, 1937.
5. Sigmund Freud, *Wit and Its Relation to the Unconscious,* translated by A. A. Brill. Dodd, Mead, 1916, pp. 22-23.
6. Kurt Koffka, *Principles of Gestalt Psychology.* Harcourt, Brace, 1935, p. 176.
7. *The Works of Leo Tolstoy.* Oxford University Press, 1937 (Centenary Edition). Vol. 9, *Anna Karenina,* translated by Louise and Aylmer Maude. Part II, Chapter 24, p. 216.
8. Guy de Maupassant, *Bel Ami,* translated by Ernest Boyd. Knopf, 1923, p. 335.
9. George Arliss, *Up the Years from Bloomsbury.* Little, Brown, 1927, p. 289.
10. *The Notebooks of Leonardo da Vinci,* arranged and rendered into English by Edward MacCurdy. Garden City Publishing Company, 1941. The broken arrangement of this passage represents Eisenstein's adaptation into script form.
11. Leonardo da Vinci, *Traité de la Peinture.* Paris, Delagrave, 1921. Footnote by Joséphin Péladan, p. 181.
12. Published in *Literaturnaya Gazeta* (Moscow), No. 17, March 26, 1938.
13. *Bemerkungen ueber die neueste preussische Zensurinstruktion,* Von ein Rheinlander. In Karl Marx, *Werke und Schriften. Bis Anfang 1844, nebst Briefen und Dokumenten.* Berlin, Marx-Engels Gesamtausgabe. Section 1, Vol. I, semi-volume 1.

277

14. Alexander Sergeyevich Pushkin, *Polnoye Sobraniye Sochinenii.* Leningrad, Academia, 1936. Vol. II, p. 403.
15. Ibid., p. 377.
16. Ibid., pp. 409-10.
17. *Peter I,* gouache painted in 1907, in the collection of the State Tretiakov Gallery, Moscow.
18. Pushkin, edition cited. Vol. III, Chapter 1, stanza XX (cited translation by Babette Deutsch, in *The Works of Pushkin,* Random House, 1936).
19. Tolstoy, edition cited. Vol. 18, *What Is Art?,* p. 201.
20. Viktor Maksimovich Zhirmunsky, *Vvedeni v Metriku, Teoria Stikha.* Leningrad, Academia, 1925, pp. 173-4.
21. Ibid., p. 178.
22. Not found in de Musset's collected works.
23. *The Works of John Milton.* Columbia University Press, 1931. Vol. II, *Paradise Lost, The Verse.*
24. Hilaire Belloc, *Milton.* Lippincott, 1935, p. 256.
25. Milton, edition cited. Book VI, lines 78-86.
26. Ibid., Book I, lines 531-53.
27. Ibid., Book VI, lines 231-46.
28. Ibid., Book V, lines 622-24.
29. Ibid., Book VI, lines 853-71.

PART II: *Synchronization of Senses*

1. E. M. Forster, *Aspects of the Novel.* Harcourt, Brace, 1927, p. 213.
2. Richard Hughes, "Lochinvarovic." In *A Moment of Time.* London, Chatto & Windus, 1926, p. 26.
3. Thomas Medwin, *Journal of the Conversations of Lord Byron: Noted During a Residence with His Lordship at Pisa, in the Years 1821 and 1822.* Baltimore, E. Mickle, 1825, pp. 73-74.
4. *Journal des Goncourt,* Vol. 3, Paris, Charpentier, 1888.
5. S.M.E., "The Future of Sound Films." Sovietski Ekran (Moscow), No. 32, 1928.
6. S.M.E., "Not Colored, but of Color." Kino Gazeta (Moscow), May 24, 1940.
7. Henry Lanz, *The Physical Basis of Rime.* Stanford University Press, 1931, p. 271.
8. Karl von Eckartshausen, *Aufschlüsse zur Magie aus geprüften Erfahrungen über verborgene philosophische Wissenschaften und*

verdeckte Geheimnisse der Natur, Vol. 1. München, Lentner, 1791. (Second Edition, pp. 336-39.)

9. Louis-Bertrand Castel, *Esprit, Saillies et Singularités du P. Castel*. Amsterdam, 1763, pp. 278-348. A guide to the voluminous literature of color-music is provided by the *Oxford Dictionary of Music*.

10. René Ghil, *En Methode à l'Oeuvre* (first published in 1891). In *Oeuvres Complètes*, Vol. 3. Paris, Albert Messein, 1938, p. 239.

11. Hermann L. F. Helmholtz, *Physiological Optics*. Rochester, Optical Society of America, 1924.

12. Max Deutschbein, *Das Wesen des Romantischen*. Cöthen, Otto Schulze, 1921, p. 118.

13. Cited in Lanz, op. cit., p. 167.

14. *The Japanese Letters of Lafcadio Hearn*, edited by Elizabeth Bisland. Houghton Mifflin, 1910.

15. Ibid., letter of June 5, 1893.

16. Ibid., letter of June 14, 1893.

17. Diagram reproduced from the *T'u Shu Chi Ch'eng*, a small reprint of the *K'ang Hsi* encyclopedia. Vol. 1116, Chapter 51.

18. In Le Cahier Bleu, No. 4, 1933. The translation in the text has not been made from the French original.

19. *The Works of Friedrich Nietzsche*. Vol. XI, *The Case of Wagner*, translated by Thomas Common. Macmillan, 1896, pp. 24-25.

20. In the collection of the National Gallery, London.

21. Georgi Bogdanovich Yakulov (1884-1928). There are some plates of this artist's work for the Kamerny Theatre, Moscow, in *The Russian Theatre*, by Joseph Gregor and René Fülöp-Miller.

22. Frank Rutter, *El Greco*. Weyhe, 1930, p. 67.

23. In the collection of the Metropolitan Museum, New York.

24. Maurice Legendre and A. Hartmann, *Domenikos Theotokopoulos called El Greco*. Paris, Editions Hyperion, 1937, p. 16.

25. (Manuel de Falla), *El "Cante Jondo" (Canto primitivo andaluz)*. Granada, Editorial Urania, 1922.

26. John Brande Trend, *Manuel de Falla and Spanish Music*. Knopf, 1929, p. 23 ff.

27. Legendre and Hartmann, op. cit., p. 27.

28. Vasili V. Yastrebtzev, *Moi vospominaniya o Nikolaye Andreyeviche Rimskom-Korsakove*. Petrograd, 1915.

29. All these cited "color symphonies" are in the collection of the Freer Gallery of Art, Washington, D. C.

30. Max Schlesinger, *Geschichte des Symbols, ein Versuch*. Berlin, Leonhard Simion, 1912. (Cited from Gustav Floerke, *Zehn Jahre mit Böcklin*. München, F. Bruckmann, 1902.)

31. (Friedrich Leopold Hardenberg), *Novalis Schriften.* Vol. II. Berlin, G. Reimer, 1837, p. 172.

32. François Coppée, Ballade. Cited in "Le Sonnet des Voyelles," R. Etiemble. Revue de Littérature Comparée, April-June, 1939.

PART III: *Color and Meaning*

1. Walt Whitman, *Leaves of Grass,* "Locations and Times," Double-day, Doran (Inclusive and Authorized Edition).

2. Der gelbe Klang. Eine Bühnenkomposition von Kandinsky. In *Der blaue Reiter.* Herausgeber: Kandinsky, Franz Marc. München, R. Piper, 1912.

3. Paul Gauguin, Notes Eparses: Genèse d'un tableau. In *Paul Gauguin,* by Jean de Rotonchamp. Weimar, Graf von Kessler, 1906, pp. 218-20.

4. Painted in 1892. In the collection of A. Conger Goodyear, N. Y.

5. In the collection of Stephen C. Clark, New York.

6. *Further Letters of Vincent van Gogh to His Brother, 1886-1889.* Houghton Mifflin, 1929. Letter 534.

7. August Strindberg, *There Are Crimes and Crimes,* translated from the Swedish by Edwin Björkman. Scribner's, 1912.

8. T. S. Eliot, *Collected Poems,* "Preludes: III," Harcourt, Brace.

9. Ibid., "Portrait of a Lady."

10. Ibid., "The Love Song of J. Alfred Prufrock."

11. Andrei Belyi (Borís Nikolayevich Bugayev), *Masterstvo Gogolya.* Moscow, 1934.

12. Possibly that in the collection of Lord Kinnaird, Rossie Priory, Inchture.

13. This citation has been translated from Eisenstein's text.

14. Frédéric Portal, *Des couleurs symboliques dans l'antiquité, le Moyen-Age, et les temps modernes.* Paris, Treuttel et Wurtz, 1857. (Partly cited from Georg Friedrich Creuzer, *Réligions de l'Antiquité,* Vol. II, p. 87.)

15. Havelock Ellis, "The Psychology of Yellow." Popular Science Monthly, May, 1906.

16. Nikolai Yakovlevich Marr (1864-1934).

17. In an apocryphal letter published originally in Ogoniok (Moscow), May 16, 1926.

18. van Gogh, op. cit., letter 520.

19. Walt Whitman, *Leaves of Grass,* "To You."

20. Ibid., "Song of Myself."

21. Ibid., "Salut au Monde!"

22. Ibid., "Our Old Feuillage."

23. Walt Whitman, *Leaves of Grass*, "Song of the Redwood-Tree."
24. Ibid., "Sparkles from the Wheel."
25. Ibid., "Italian Music in Dakota."
26. Ibid., "When Lilacs Last in the Dooryard Bloom'd."
27. Ibid., op. cit.
28. Ibid., "The Wound-Dresser."
29. Ibid., "The Sleepers."
30. Portal, op. cit.
31. *Parisismen: Alphabetisch geordnete Sammlung der eigenartigsten Ausdrucksweisen des Pariser Argot von Prof. Dr. Césaire Villatte.* Berlin-Schöneberg, Langenscheidtsche Verlagsbuchhandlung, 1888.
32. Cited in Eric Partridge, *A Dictionary of Slang and Unconventional English.* London, Routledge, 1937.
33. John S. Farmer and W. E. Henley, *Slang and Its Analogues Past and Present*, Vol. VII. London, 1890.
34. Maurice H. Weseen, *A Dictionary of American Slang.* Crowell, 1934.
35. *Goethe's Theory of Colours*, translated from the German by Charles Lock Eastlake. London, John Murray, 1840.
36. Portal, op. cit., p. 212.
37. Denis Diderot, *Lettres à Sophie Volland.* Paris, Gallimard, 1930. Vol. 1. Lettre XLVII, 20 Octobre 1760.
38. James Frazer, *The Golden Bough, a Study in Magic and Religion*, Macmillan, 1934. Part I, "The Magic Art and the Evolution of Kings," pp. 15-16.
39. Maxim Gorky, "Paul Verlaine and the Decadents." *Samarskaya Gazeta* (Samara), Nos. 81, 85, 1896.
40. Ibid.
41. Havelock Ellis, "The Psychology of Red." Popular Science Monthly, August-September, 1900.
42. Max Nordau, *Degeneration.* Appleton, 1895. Book I: Fin de Siècle. (Cited from Alfred Binet, Recherches sur les Altérations de la Conscience chez les Hystériques. In Revue philosophique, Vol. XVII, 1889; and Ch. Féré, Sensation et Mouvement. In Revue philosophique, 1886, pp. 28-29.
43. *Poetry and Prose of William Blake.* Random House, 1939. Annotations to Sir Joshua Reynolds' Discourses, p. 770.
44. Filipp Andreyevich Malyavin. This painting is in the collection of the State Tretiakov Gallery, Moscow.
45. Goethe, op. cit.

SHOT VI

SHOT VII

SHOT VIII

SHOT IX

SHOT X

SHOT XI

SHOT XII

INDEX
Film Form and *The Film Sense*

INDEX

Film Form and The Film Sense

(FF indicates *Film Form;* FS indicates *The Film Sense*)

285